Authors
& Artists
for Young
Adults

ISSN 1040-5682

Authors & Artists for Young Adults

VOLUME 3

Agnes Garrett and Helga P. McCue,
Editors

 Gale Research Inc. • DETROIT • NEW YORK • FORT LAUDERDALE • LONDON

MAR '92

Managing Editor: Anne Commire

Editors: Agnes Garrett, Helga P. McCue

Assistant Editors: Dianne H. Anderson, Elisa Ann Ferraro,
Eunice L. Petrini, Linda Shedd

Sketchwriters: Catherine Coray, Catherine Courtney,
Johanna Cypis, Marguerite Feitlowitz, Mimi H. Hutson,
Deborah Klezmer, Dieter Miller, Beatrice Smedley,
Emily Squires, Karen Walker

Researcher: Catherine Ruello

Editorial Assistants: Marja Hiltunen, June Lee, Susan Pfanner

Production Manager: Mary Beth Trimper
External Production Assistant: Marilyn Jackman

Art Director: Arthur Chartow
Keyliner: C. J. Jonik

Production Supervisor: Laura Bryant
Internal Production Associate: Louise Gagné
Internal Production Assistant: Sharana Wier

Library of Congress Catalog Card Number
ISBN 0-8103-5052-1
ISSN 1040-5682

Printed in the United States of America

Contents

Introduction

"[Today's youth] is a generation whose grade-school years were informed and enlivened by Betsy Byars, who teaches the basic lesson to the next generation of book buyers: that a novel must entertain first before it can do anything else. But I don't get these readers until they hit puberty. They haven't even budded, and already the Blume is off. I don't get them till puberty, and it's the darkest moment of life. For while puberty is the death of childhood, it isn't the birth of reason.

"Puberty is the same gulag we all once did time in, robbed of the certainties of grade school and still years away from a driver's license. Puberty is waking up every morning wondering which sex you are, if any. Puberty is the practice of strict sexual segregation with all the girls on one side of an invisible line and all the boys on the other: big women, little men. Like a Shaker meeting but without the hope of eternal life. Puberty is no fun, and changing the name of the junior high to the middle school has fooled nobody. In America puberty is deciding at the age of twelve or so to divorce your own parents, charging irreconcilable differences. The children of the underclass hit the streets then and are thereafter out of reach of home and school and books. The children of the middle class recede to their rooms and lock themselves into elaborate sound systems, paid for by parents, that eliminate the possibility of a parental voice. They are free of us at twelve.

"I write for these people whose own parents haven't seen them for days. In our impotence we've reasoned that children must be given freedoms in order to learn how to handle them. But it doesn't work that way. The prematurely emancipated young transfer all their need for a dominating, problem-solving authority from weak adults at home and school to the peer group. The only government they recognize is the vengeful law-giving of each other.

"That's what I write: counterculture literature of individuality to a conformist readership. I write books for the knapsacks of young soldiers of both sexes going forth every school day hoping to survive the 'Chocolate War.' I write for the inmates of schools where you cannot win a letter sweater for literacy. You can win a letter sweater only for mindless conformity, for listening to language from the coach that would get the librarian into big trouble. I write for a generation of young people who don't have to drop by the library, even on the way to the Gifted Program. They don't have to drop by anywhere except, perhaps, the shopping mall."

—Richard Peck

"The time of adolescence is in itself a wonderful age to write about. It combines an idealism and honesty and a wily sophistication that no other time of life enjoys. The teenager has vitality and enjoys life although he sees the ugliness and absurdities as well as the joys.

"Adolescents are also engaged in some of the most important 'work' they will ever do. It is the time when one establishes one's identity and comes of age in a number of critical areas—social, political, cultural, sexual. Conflict prevails during these years with one's parents, teachers, peers and, most painfully, with oneself."

—Hila Colman

Authors and Artists for Young Adults is a new reference series designed to bridge the gap between Gale's *Something about the Author*, designed for children, and *Contemporary Authors*, intended for adults. This new series is aimed entirely at the needs and interests of the often overlooked young adults. We share the concerns of librarians who must send young readers to the adult reference shelves for which they may not be ready. *Authors and Artists for Young Adults* will give high school and junior high school students information about the life and work of their favorite creative artists—the people behind the books, movies, television programs, plays, lyrics, cartoon and animated features that they most enjoy. Although most of these will be present-day artists, the series is open to people of all time periods and all countries whose work has a special appeal to young adults today. Some of these artists may also be profiled in *Something about the Author* or *Contemporary Authors*, but their entries in *Authors and Artists for Young Adults* are completely updated and tailored to the information needs of the young adult user.

Entry Format

Authors and Artists for Young Adults will be published in two volumes each year. Each volume in the series will furnish in-depth coverage of about twenty authors and artists. The typical entry consists of:

—A personal section that includes date and place of birth, marriage, children, and education.

—A comprehensive bibliography or film-ography including publishers, producers, and years.

—Adaptations into other media forms.

—Works in progress.

—A distinctive sidelights section where secondary sources and exclusive interviews concentrate on an artist's craft, artistic intentions, career, world views, thematic discussions, and controversies.

—A "For More Information See" section arranged in chronological order to increase the scope of this reference work.

While the textual information in *Authors and Artists for Young Adults* is its primary reason for existing, entries are complemented by illustrations, photographs, movie stills, manuscript samples, dust jackets, book covers, and other relevant visual material.

A cumulative Author/Artist Index appears at the back of this volume.

Highlights of This Volume

A sampling of the variety of creative artists featured in this volume includes:

JUDY BLUME......Popular author of novels for and about young people, advises potential writers: "Don't let anyone discourage you or tell you that you don't have any talent because that can be a person who can't see beyond what's on his or her desk....Anyone who thinks he or she wants to write is usually already writing. Writing is a need that comes from within. You do it because you have to do it. I know one or two people who say they love writing, but for most of us, it's a love/hate relationship."

ROBERT CORMIER......Author of award-winning and often controversial books such as *The Chocolate War* and *I Am the Cheese,* admits that: "When *I Am the Cheese* was published, I never felt as though I'd written a young adult book. I write books with young people in them. I write with all the craft I can command....The barrier between children's books/young adult books/adult books is breaking down. Writers are rising above these labels."

GABRIEL GARCIA MARQUEZ......Latin American author who believes: "The style of my books is almost entirely that of my grandmother. Whenever she did not want to answer a question, she would invent fantasies so that I wouldn't be saddened by the truth of things. It was almost impossible for me to distinguish where reality left off and imagination took over; my head was full of images. The world of my childhood caused me to lose my fear of doing some things in literature, because anything is possible—just as it had been in my childhood."

CYNTHIA VOIGT......Winner of the 1983 Newbery Medal for *Dicey's Song,* who describes the event as: "A state of massive incoherence. I have not yet completely emerged from this state and suspect now I may never, but one of my first sensible thoughts during the time was 'I did not know good news could pack such a wallop.' "

ALICE WALKER......Author of the Pulitzer Prize-winning novel, *The Color Purple,* describes books as: "By-products of our lives. Deliver me from writers who say the way they live doesn't matter. I'm not sure a bad person can write a good book. If art doesn't make us better, then what on earth is it for?"

Forthcoming Volumes

Among the artists planned for future volumes are:

Douglas Adams	Paula Danziger	Barry Lopez
C. S. Adler	Jim Davis	Norma Fox Mazer
V. C. Andrews	Annie Dillard	Robin McKinley
Maya Angelou	Bob Dylan	Milton Meltzer
Jean Auel	Loren Eiseley	Walter Dean Myers
Avi	William Faulkner	Phyllis Naylor
Richard Bach	Russell Freedman	Joan Lowry Nixon
James Baldwin	Carlos Fuentes	Zibby O'Neal
Toni Cade Bambara	Bette Greene	Gene Roddenberry
Peter Beagle	Judith Guest	Ntozake Shange
Bianca Bradbury	Rosa Guy	Stephen Sondheim
Robin Brancato	Ann Head	Steven Spielberg
Sue Ellen Bridgers	Nat Hentoff	Mary Stolz
Edgar Rice Burroughs	Hermann Hesse	Mildred D. Taylor
Bruce Chatwin	Marjorie Holmes	Julian Thompson
Agatha Christie	John Hughes	J. R. R. Tolkien
Arthur C. Clarke	Victor Hugo	Garry Trudeau
Cameron Crowe	Bel Kaufman	Bill Watterson

The editors of *Authors and Artists for Young Adults* welcome any suggestions for additional biographees to be included in this series. Please write and give us your opinions and suggestions for making our series more helpful to you.

Acknowledgments

Grateful acknowledgment is made to the following
publishers, authors, and artists whose works appear in this volume.

ALADDIN BOOKS. Cover illustration by Ellen Thompson from *Portrait of Ivan* by Paula Fox. Cover illustration © 1987 by Ellen Thompson. Reprinted by permission of Aladdin Books, an imprint of Macmillan Publishing Company.

ATHENEUM. Jacket illustration from *From the Mixed-Up Files of Mrs. Basil E. Frankweiler* by E.L. Konigsburg. Copyright © 1967 by E.L. Konigsburg./ Jacket illustration from *Father's Arcane Daughter* by E.L. Konigsburg. Copyright © 1976 by E.L. Konigsburg./ Sidelight excerpts from *The Genesis of a Proud Taste for Scarlet and Miniver* by E.L. Konigsburg. Copyright © 1979 by E.L. Konigsburg./ Jacket illustration by Namiko Shefcik from *Izzy, Willy-Nilly* by Cynthia Voigt. Jacket illustration © 1986 by Namiko Shefcik. Jacket design and calligraphy © 1986 by Anita Karl./ Jacket illustration by Ronald Himler from *Sons from Afar* by Cynthia Voigt. Jacket © 1987 by Ronald Himler. All reprinted by permission of Atheneum Publishers, an imprint of Macmillan Publishing Company.

BALLANTINE BOOKS. Cover illustration from *Chronicle of a Death Foretold* by Gabriel Garcia Marquez. Translation © 1982 by Alfred A. Knopf, Inc. Reprinted by permission of Ballantine Books, a division of Random House, Inc.

BRADBURY PRESS. Jacket illustration by Paul Giovanopoulos from *Blow Live in the Sea* by Paula Fox. Copyright © 1970 by Paula Fox./ Jacket illustration by George Schmidt from *The Moonlight Man* by Paula Fox. Copyright © 1986 by Paula Fox./ Jacket illustration by Ray Cruz from *Deenie* by Judy Blume. Copyright © 1973 by Judy Blume./ Jacket illustration by Janet Halverson from *Forever...* by Judy Blume. Copyright © 1975 by Judy Blume. All reprinted by permission of Bradbury Press, an affiliate of Macmillan, Inc.

CARROLL & GRAF PUBLISHERS INC. Cover design and illustration by Tom KcKeveny from *The Drowned World* by J.G. Ballard. Copyright © 1962 by J.G. Ballard. Courtesy of Carroll & Graf Publishers Inc.

COLLIER BOOKS. Cover illustration by Kinuko Y. Craft from *Perelandra* by C.S. Lewis. Cover illustration © 1986 by Kinuko Y. Craft. Copyright © 1986 Macmillan Publishing Company, a division of Macmillan, Inc./ Cover illustration by Kinuko Y. Craft from *Out of the Silent Planet* by C.S. Lewis. Cover illustration © 1986 by Kinuko Y. Craft. Cover design by Lee Wade./ Cover illustration by Jerry Pinkney from *Throwing Shadows* by E.L. Konigsburg. Cover illustration © 1988 by Jerry Pinkney. All reprinted by permission of Collier Books, an imprint of Macmillan Publishing Company.

CONTINUUM. Sidelight excerpts from *Black Women Writers at Work* by Claudia Tate. Reprinted by permission of Continuum.

DELACORTE PRESS. Jacket illustration by Wendy Popp from *Fade* by Robert Cormier. Jacket illustration © 1988 by Wendy Popp. Reprinted by permission of Delacorte Press, a division of Bantam Doubleday Dell Publishing Group, Inc.

DELL PUBLISHING. Cover illustration from *Are You There God? It's Me, Margaret* by Judy Blume. Copyright © 1970 by Judy Blume./ Cover illustration from *A Day No Pigs Would Die* by Robert Newton Peck. Copyright © 1972 by Robert Newton Peck./ Cover illustration from *The Slave Dancer* by Paula Fox. Copyright © 1973 by Paula Fox./ Cover illustration from *A Proud Taste for Scarlet and Miniver* by E.L. Konigsburg. Copyright © 1973 by E.L. Konigsburg./ Cover illustration from *Soup for President* by Robert Newton Peck. Text © 1978 by Robert Newton Peck. Illustrations © 1978 by Alfred A. Knopf, Inc./ Cover illustration by Charles Robinson from *Soup's Drum* by Robert Newton Peck. Text © 1980 by Robert Newton Peck. Illustrations © 1980 by Alfred A. Knopf, Inc./ Cover illustration from *Tiger Eyes* by Judy Blume. Copyright © 1981 by Judy Blume./ Cover illustration by G. Watson from *I Am the Cheese* by Robert Cormier. Cover illustration © 1983 by G. Watson. All reprinted by permission of Dell Publishing, a division of Bantam Doubleday Dell Publishing Group, Inc.

DOUBLEDAY. Sidelight excerpts from *The Great Comic Book Heroes* by Jules Feiffer. Copyright © 1965 by Jules Feiffer./ Jacket illustration by Ben Stahl from *Last Sunday* by Robert Newton Peck. Copyright © 1977 by Robert Newton Peck./ Sidelight excerpts from *The Power of Myth* by Joseph Campbell and Bill Moyers. Copyright © 1988 by Apostrophe S Productions and Alfred van der Marck Editions, Inc. for itself and the Estate of Joseph Campbell. All reprinted by permission of Doubleday, a division of Bantam Doubleday Dell Publishing Group, Inc.

FABER & FABER. Sidelight excerpts from *John Boorman* by Michael Ciment. Reprinted by permission of Faber & Faber Ltd.

FARRAR, STRAUS & GIROUX. Jacket illustration by Robert Sabin from *A Place Apart* by Paula Fox. Copyright © 1980 by Paula

Fox./ Jacket illustration from *The Day of Creation* by J.G. Ballard. Copyright © 1988 by J.G. Ballard. Jacket design © 1988 by Wendell Minor. Both reprinted by permission of Farrar, Straus & Giroux, Inc

GROVE PRESS. Cover illustration from *Things Change* by David Mamet and Shel Silverstein. Cover design by Liadain Warwick Smith. Cover photograph by Stephen Vaughan. Copyright © 1988 by Wheatland Corporation. Used by permission of Grove Press.

HARCOURT BRACE JOVANOVICH. Sidelight excerpts from *Surprised by Joy: The Shape of My Life* by C.S. Lewis./ Sidelight excerpts from *Letters of C.S. Lewis*, edited by W.H. Lewis./ Sidelight excerpts from *In Search of Our Mothers' Gardens* by Alice Walker. Copyright © 1983 by Alice Walker./ Sidelight excerpts from *Living by the Word* by Alice Walker. Copyright © 1988 by Alice Walker. All reprinted by permission of Harcourt Brace Jovanovich, Inc.

HARPER & ROW. Illustration from *It Is the Poem Singing into Your Eyes: An Anthology of New Young Poets*, edited by Arnold Adoff. Copyright © 1971 by Arnold Adoff./ Sidelight excerpts from *A Prayer for Katerina Horovitzova* by Arnold Lustig. Copyright © 1973 by Arnold Lustig./ Jacket illustration from *The Poetry of Black America: Anthology of the 20th Century*, edited by Arnold Adoff./ Jacket illustration by Bernard Bonhomme from *Collected Stories* by Gabriel Garcia Marquez. Jacket illustration © Bernard Bonhomme. All reprinted by permission of Harper & Row, Publishers, Inc.

HOUGHTON MIFFLIN. Jacket illustration by Evaline Ness from *Island of the Blue Dolphins* by Scott O'Dell. Copyright © 1960 by Scott O'Dell./ Jacket illustration by Ted Lewin from *Sarah Bishop* by Scott O'Dell. Copyright © 1980 by Scott O'Dell./ Jacket illustration by Ruth Sanderson from *The Castle in the Sea* by Scott O'Dell. Jacket illustration © 1983 by Ruth Sanderson./ Jacket illustration by Margaret Bruno from *Alexandra* by Scott O'Dell. Jacket illustration © 1984 by Margaret Bruno./ Jacket illustration by Ted Lewin from *Streams to the River, to the Sea: A Novel of Sacagawea* by Scott O'Dell. Jacket illustration © 1986 by Ted Lewin. All reprinted by permission of Houghton Mifflin Company.

INDIANA UNIVERSITY PRESS. Sidelight excerpts from *From Hester Street to Hollywood* by Stephen J. Whitfield, edited by Sarah Blacher Cohen. Copyright © 1983 by Indiana University Press. Reprinted by permission of Indiana University Press.

ALFRED A. KNOPF. Sidelight excerpts from *Seven Voices: Seven Latin American Writers Talk to Rita Guibert* by Rita Guibert. Copyright © 1972 by Alfred A. Knopf, Inc., © 1976 by Rita Guibert. Reprinted by permission of the author./ Jacket illustration from *Love in the Time of Cholera* by Gabriel Garcia Marquez. Jacket photograph: *Poster Lady* by Edward J. Steichen. Copyright © 1988 by Alfred A. Knopf, Inc. Both reprinted by permission of Alfred A. Knopf, Inc.

J. B. LIPPINCOTT. Sidelight excerpts from *A Sounding of Storytellers*, edited by John Rowe Townsend. Copyright © 1979 by John Rowe Townsend. Reprinted by permission of Harper & Row, Publishers, Inc. In Canada by Penguin Books Ltd.

LITTLE, BROWN AND COMPANY. Jacket illustration by Chet Jezierski from *Fawn* by Robert Newton Peck. Copyright © 1975 by Robert Newton Peck./ Jacket illustration by Robert McGinnis from *Justice Lion* by Robert Newton Peck. Copyright © 1981 by Robert Newton Peck. Both reprinted by permission of Little, Brown and Company.

LIVERIGHT. Sidelight excerpts from *Interviews with Black Writers*, edited by John O'Brien. Copyright © 1973 by Liveright Publishing Corporation. Reprinted by permission of Liveright Publishing Corporation.

LONE EAGLE PUBLISHING. Sidelight excerpts from *5th Annual International Edition of Film Directors: A Complete Guide* by Michael Singer. Copyright © 1988 by Lone Eagle Publishing. Reprinted by permission of Lone Eagle Publishing.

LOTHROP, LEE & SHEPARD BOOKS. Jacket illustration by John Steptoe from *All the Colors of the Race* by Arnold Adoff. Illustrations © 1982 by John Steptoe. Reprinted by permission of Lothrop, Lee & Shepard Books, a division of William Morrow & Company, Inc.

OVERLOOK PRESS. Jacket illustration by Juan Suarez from *A Prayer for Katerina Horovitzova* by Arnost Lustig. Copyright © 1973 by Arnost Lustig. Reprinted by permission of The Overlook Press.

PADDINGTON PRESS. Sidelight excerpts from *Pied Pipers: Interviews with the Influential Creators of Children's Literature* by Justin Wintle and Emma Fisher. Reprinted by permission of Paddington Press and Peters Fraser & Dunlop Group Ltd.

PANTHEON BOOKS. Cover illustration, "Running Boy," by Robert Viclerey from *The Chocolate War* by Robert Cormier. Copyright © 1974 by Robert Cormier. Reprinted by permission of Pantheon Books, a division of Random House, Inc.

POCKET BOOKS. Cover illustration from *The Color Purple* by Alice Walker. Cover © 1983 by Simon & Schuster, Inc. Reprinted by permission of Pocket Books, a division of Simon & Schuster, Inc.

PRINCETON UNIVERSITY PRESS. Cover from *The Hero with a Thousand Faces*, Bollingen Series 17, by Joseph Campbell. Cover design by E. McKnight Kauffer. Copyright 1949, © renewed 1976 by Princeton University Press. Reprinted by permission of Princeton University Press.

UNGAR. Sidelight excerpts from *Dream Makers: Science Fiction and Fantasy Writers at Work* by Charles Platt. Copyright © 1987 by The Ungar Publishing Company. Reprinted by permission of the publisher.

UNIVERSAL PRESS SYNDICATE. Cartoon by Jules Feiffer from *Munro*. Copyright © 1959 by Jules Feiffer./ Cartoon by Jules

Feiffer from *Feiffer*. Copyright © 1987 by Jules Feiffer. All rights reserved. Both reprinted by permission of Universal Press Syndicate.

VIKING PENGUIN. Sidelight excerpts from *Writers at Work*, 6th Series, edited by George Plimpton. Copyright © 1984 by The Paris Review, Inc./ Sidelight excerpts from *Writing in Restaurants* by David Mamet. Copyright © 1986 by David Mamet. All rights reserved. Both reprinted by permission of Viking Penguin, a division of Penguin Books USA, Inc.

VINTAGE BOOKS. Cover illustration by Douglas Fraser from *The Story of A Shipwrecked Sailor* by Gabriel Garcia Marquez. Copyright © 1986 by Alfred A. Knopf, Inc. Reprinted by permission of Vintage Books, a division of Random House, Inc.

WALKER AND COMPANY. Sidelight excerpts from *Breakthrough: Women in Writing* by Diana Gleasner, amended by Judy Blume. Copyright © 1979 by Diana Gleasner. Reprinted by permission of Walker and Company.

FRANKLIN WATTS. Jacket illustration by Barbara Roman from *Lily and the Lost Boy* by Paula Fox. Jacket illustration © 1987 by Barbara Roman. Reprinted by permission of Franklin Watts, Inc.

Sidelight excerpts from "Conversation with John Boorman," by Linda Strawn, November/December 1972, in *Action*./ Sidelight excerpts from the Preface of *The Poetry of Black America*, by Arnold Adoff. Copyright © 1973 by Arnold Adoff./ Sidelight excerpts from "The Solace of a Playwright's Ideals," by Mark Zweigler, August 1976, in *After Dark*. Copyright © 1976 by Danad Publishing Inc. Reprinted by permission of David Mamet./ Sidelight excerpts from "I Lost It at the Movies," by David Mamet, June 1987, in *American Film*. Copyright © 1987 by *American Film*. Reprinted with permission of the publisher and the author./ Sidelight excerpts from "Can Great Books Make Good Movies? 7 Writers Just Say !" July/August 1987, in *American Film*. Copyright © 1987 by *American Film*./ Sidelight excerpts from "Making of a Classic," by Gabriel Garcia Marquez, July 1979, in *Atlas World Press Review*./ Cover illustration by Bascove from *Till We Have Faces: A Myth Retold* by C.S. Lewis. Cover illustration © 1979 by Bascove. Reproduced by permission of Bascove./ Sidelight excerpts from "Conversations," by Marian Christy, November 3, 1985, in *The Boston Globe*. Copyright © 1985 by Globe Newspaper Co. Reprinted by permission of the publisher./ Sidelight excerpts from "What Makes Bullet Run?" by Alice Digillo, July 14, 1985, in *Book World—The Washington Post*. Copyright © 1985 by *The Washington Post*./ Sidelight excerpts from "Fictions of Every Kind," by J.G. Ballard, February 1971, in *Books and Bookmen*. Copyright © 1971 by J.G. Ballard./ Sidelight excerpts from "Ballard at Home," by Douglas Reed, April 1971, in *Books and Bookmen*. Copyright © 1971 by Douglas Reed./ Sidelight excerpts from "An Interview with J.G. Ballard," in *J.G. Ballard: The First Twenty Years*, by James Goddard and D. Pringle. Copyright © 1976 by David Pringle. Reprinted by permission of J.G. Ballard and David Pringle. Bran's Head Books.

Sidelight excerpts from "Garry Marshall: Television's Man with the Midas Touch Turns to Film," by Tom Hinckley, August 1987, in *Cable Guide*. Reprinted by permission of the publisher./ Sidelight excerpts from " 'Empire of the Sun' Shines in Ballard's Eyes," by John H. Richardson, December 21, 1987, in *Chicago Tribune*. Copyright © 1987 by Chicago Tribune Company./ Sidelight excerpts from an article by C.S. Hannabus, Winter 1974-75, in *Children's Book Review*. Copyright © 1975 by Five Owls Press Ltd. All rights reserved. Reprinted by permission of the publisher./ Sidelight excerpts from "Man, Myth, and Magic," by Ray Comiskey, November 1985, in *Cinema Papers*./ Sidelight excerpts from "Arnold Adoff," in *More Books by More People*, edited by Lee Bennett Hopkins. Copyright © 1974 by Lee Bennett Hopkins. Reprinted by permission of Arnold Adoff. Citation Press./ Sidelight excerpts from "Memories of a Pro Bono Cartoonist," by Gary Groth, August 1988, in *The Comics Journal*. Reprinted by permission of the publisher./ Sidelight excerpts from taped interview produced by Random House/Miller, 1982, amended by Robert Cormier. Reprinted by permission of Robert Cormier./ Sidelight excerpts from "Lindsay Crouse," by Michael Segal, November 1987, in *Cosmopolitan*. Copyright © 1987 by The Hearst Corporation./ Sidelight excerpts from "Jules Feiffer," by Roy Newquist, 1964, in *Counterpoint*./ Sidelight excerpts from "Hunting the Buffalo," by Marilyn Stasio, March 19-April 1, 1977, in *Cue*. Copyright © 1977 by Cue Publications, Inc. Reprinted by permission of the author./ Sidelight excerpts from "Jogging with Mamet," by Robert Wahls, October 22, 1977, in *Daily News*, New York. Copyright © 1977 by New York News Inc. Reprinted with permission./ Sidelight excerpts from "Two on an Island," by Jan Cherubin, December 15, 1980, in *Daily News*, New York. Copyright © 1980 by New York News Inc. Reprinted with permission./ Sidelight excerpts from "Do We Underestimate Teenagers?" by Robert Cormier, Winter 1984-1985, in *Dell Catalog*. Reprinted by permission of Bantam Doubleday Dell Publishing Group, Inc./ Sidelight excerpts from *Judy Blume's Story* by Betsy Lee. Dillon Press./ Sidelight excerpts from "Happy Days Are 'Common' Now: TV/Film Champ Garry Marshall," by Gary Ballard, August 7-13, 1986, in *Drama-Logue*./ Sidelight excerpts from "Jules Feiffer, Cartoonist—Playwright—in Conversation with Christopher Durang," Winter 1987, in *The Dramatists Guild Quarterly*. Reprinted by permission of the publisher.

Sidelight excerpts from "A Visit with Scott O'Dell, Master Storyteller," by Allen Raymond, March 1984, in *Early Years*. Copyright © 1984 by Early Years, Inc. Reprinted with permission of the publisher, Norwalk, CT 06854./ Sidelight excerpts from "An Unexpected Pulitzer for Jules Feiffer," by David Astor, May 31, 1986, in *Editor and Publisher*./ Page of art by Jules Feiffer originally drawn for *The Spirit* by Will Eisner. Copyright © by Will Eisner. Reproduced by permission of Will Eisner./ Sidelight excerpts from "The Professor with a Thousand Faces," by Donald Newlove, September 1977, in *Esquire*. Copyright © 1977 by Esquire Associates. Reprinted by permission of the author./ Sidelight excerpts from "The Postman's Words," by Dan Yakir, March-April 1981, in *Film Comment*. Copyright © 1981 by the author. Reprinted by permission of the author./ Sidelight excerpts from "The Sorcerer," by Dan Yakir, May-June 1981 in *Film Comment*. Copyright © 1981 by the author. Reprinted by permission of the author./ Sidelight excerpts from "Mapping Out the Road to Camelot," by Tony Crawley, September 1987, in *Film Illustrated*./ Sidelight excerpts from "The Technology of Style," by James Verniere, June 1981, in *Filmmakers Monthly*./ Sidelight excerpts from "From Shanghai to Shepperton," by David Pringle, February 1982, in *Foundation*. Copyright © 1982 by the Science Fiction Foundation. Reprinted by permission of the author./ Jacket illustration by Michael Garland from *Tell Me If the Lovers Are*

Saturday Review Magazine./ Sidelight excerpts from "Growing Books at Wild Trees Press," by Pat Rose, v. 2, November-December 1986, in *Small Press*./ Sidelight excerpts from "Things I Wish I'd Known at 18," by J.G. Ballard, December 27, 1981, in *Sunday Express Magazine*. Reprinted by permission of the publisher./ Sidelight excerpts from "Breaking All the Rules—and Winning," by Rex Reed, February 15, 1976, in *Sunday News*./ Sidelight excerpts from "First Principles," by David Mamet, Summer 1981, in *Theater*. Copyright © 1981 by *Theater*, formerly *yale theatre*. Reprinted by permission of the publisher and the author./ Sidelight excerpts from "Trading in the American Dream," by David Savran, September 1987, in *American Theatre*. Reprinted in his *In Their Own Words: Contemporary American Playwrights*. Copyright © 1988 by David Savran. Used by permission of the publisher./ Sidelight excerpts from "J.G. Ballard Interviewed," by Hennesy Brendan, n. 39, Spring, 1971, in *The Transatlantic Review*./ Sidelight excerpts from "He Can Hiccough and Somebody Will Develop It Into a Series," by Dwight Whitney, May 19, 1979, in *TV Guide* Magazine. Copyright © 1979 by Triangle Publications, Inc./ Sidelight excerpts from *Presenting Robert Cormier* by Patricia Campbell. Copyright © 1985 by Twayne Publishers.

Sidelight excerpts from *The Fragrance of Guava* by Apuleyo Mendoza and Gabriel Garcia Marquez. Verso Editions./ Sidelight excerpts from "David Mamet, Remember That Name," July 5, 1976, in *The Village Voice*. Copyright © 1976 by The Village Voice, Inc. Reprinted by permission of David Mamet./ Sidelight excerpts from "David Mamet: Bulldog of the Middle Class," by Mary Cantwell, July, 1984, in *Vogue*. Copyright © 1984 by The Conde Nast Publications Inc. Courtesy of *Vogue*./ Sidelight excerpts from "Master Satirist at Work," by Holly Hill, May 7, 1976, in *Westchester Weekend*./ Sidelight excerpts from "All Work Is David Mamet's Play," by Jacques le Sourd, October 16, 1977, in *White Plains Reporter Dispatch*. Reprinted by permission of Gannett Westchester Rockland Newspapers./ Jacket of *In Search of Our Mothers' Gardens* by Alice Walker. Jacket design by Lem Rauk/Visible Ink. Jacket photograph by permission of AP/Wide World Photos./ Sidelight excerpts from "Time, Memory, and Inner Space," by J.G. Ballard, Spring 1963, in *The Woman Journalist*./ Sidelight excerpts from "J.G. Ballard: Slowly But Surely," by James Fallon, April 1, 1988, in *Women's Wear Daily*. Copyright © 1988 by Fairchild Publications./ Sidelight excerpts from *Fiction Is Folks* by Robert Newton Peck. Copyright © 1983 by Robert Newton Peck. Used by permission of Writer's Digest Books./ Sidelight excerpts from "Auschwitz-Birkenau," by Arnost Lustig, translated by Josef Lustig, Spring 1983, in *The Yale Review*. Copyright © 1983 by Yale University. Reprinted by permission of the editors./ Sidelight excerpts from "Garry Marshall: Having Fun and Happy Endings," an ABC Motion Pictures Press Department press release for "Young Doctors in Love," 1982.

Photo Credits

Arnold Adoff (with family): Jody Scotnicki; J.G. Ballard: copyright © by Fay Godwin; J.G. Ballard (in Shanghai and with his children): copyright © J.G. Ballard; Judy Blume: copyright © by George Cooper; Joseph Campbell (headshot and in office): Sarah Lawrence College; Robert Cormier: Findle Photography; Gabriel Garcia Marquez: copyright © 1988 by Helmut Newton; David Mamet: Brigitte Lacombe; Scott O'Dell: Jim Kalett; Cynthia Voigt: Walter Voigt; Alice Walker (in chair): L.A. Hyder; Alice Walker (headshot): copyright © by Sydney R. Goldstein.

Appreciation also to the Performing Arts Research Center of the New York Public Library at Lincoln Center for permission to reprint the theater stills from "Grown-Ups," "American Buffalo," and "Glengarry Glen Ross."

Authors & Artists for Young Adults

Arnold Adoff

B orn July 16, 1935, in New York, N.Y.; son of Aaron Jacob (a pharmacist) and Rebecca (Stein) Adoff; married Virginia Hamilton (a writer), March 19, 1960; children: Leigh Hamilton, Jaime Levi. *Education:* City College of New York (now City College of the City University of New York), B.A., 1956; Columbia University, further study, 1956-58; New School for Social Research, poetry workshops, 1965-67. *Politics:* "Committed to change, for full freedom for all Americans." *Religion:* "Freethinking Pragmatist." *Home:* 750 Union St., Yellow Springs, Ohio 45387. *Office:* Arnold Adoff Agency, P.O. Box 293, Yellow Springs, Ohio 45387.

■ Career

Poet, anthologist and writer. Board of Education, New York, N.Y., teacher in Harlem and upper west side of Manhattan, 1957-69; Arnold Adoff Agency, Yellow Springs, Ohio, literary agent, 1977—. Instructor in federal projects at New York University, Connecticut College, and other institutions; lecturer at colleges throughout the country; visiting professor, Queen's College, Flushing, N.Y., 1986-87; consultant in children's literature, poetry, and creative writing. Member of Planning

Commission, Yellow Springs; "general agitator" for full equality in education, jobs, and housing. *Military service:* New York National Guard.

■ Awards, Honors

I Am the Darker Brother was selected one of Child Study Association of America's Children's Books of the Year, 1968, *City in All Directions*, 1969, and *Sports Pages*, 1986; *It Is the Poem Singing into Your Eyes* was selected one of *School Library Journal*'s Best Children's Books, 1971, and *Black Is Brown Is Tan*, 1973; Notable Children's Trade Book in the Field of Social Studies from the Children's Book Council and the National Council for Social Studies, 1974, and one of International Reading Association and Children's Book Council's Children's Choices, 1985, both for *My Black Me*; Brooklyn Art Books for Children Citation from the Brooklyn Museum and the Brooklyn Public Library, 1975, for *MA nDA LA*; *It Is the Poem Singing into Your Eyes* was chosen one of New York Public Library's Books for the Teen Age, 1980, 1981, and 1982; Jane Addams Children's Book Award Special Recognition from the Jane Addams Peace Association, 1983, for *All the Colors of the Race*; Award for Excellence in Poetry for Children from the National Council of Teachers of English, 1988.

■ Writings

Poetry, Except As Noted:

Malcom X (biography; ALA Notable Book; illustrated by John Wilson), Crowell, 1970.

MA nDA LA (picture book; ALA Notable Book; illustrated by Emily Arnold McCully), Harper, 1971.

Black Is Brown Is Tan (illustrated by E. A. McCully), Harper, 1973.

Make a Circle Keep Us In: Poems for a Good Day (illustrated by Ronald Himler), Delacorte, 1975.

Big Sister Tells Me That I'm Black (illustrated by Lorenzo Lynch), Holt, 1976.

Tornado! Poems (illustrated by R. Himler), Delacorte, 1977.

Under the Early Morning Trees: Poems (illustrated by R. Himler), Dutton, 1978.

Where Wild Willie (illustrated by E. A. McCully), Harper, 1978.

Eats: Poems (illustrated by Susan Russo), Lothrop, 1979.

I Am the Running Girl (illustrated by R. Himler), Harper, 1979.

Friend Dog (illustrated by Troy Howell), Lippincott, 1980.

OUTside/INside Poems (illustrated by John Steptoe), Lothrop, 1981.

Today We Are Brother and Sister (illustrated by Glo Coalson), Lothrop, 1981.

Birds: Poems (illustrated by T. Howell), Lippincott, 1982.

All the Colors of the Race: Poems (ALA Notable Book; illustrated by J. Steptoe), Lothrop, 1982.

The Cabbages Are Chasing the Rabbits (illustrated by Janet Stevens), Harcourt, 1985.

Sports Pages (illustrated by Steve Kuzma), Lippincott, 1986.

Greens (illustrated by Betsy Lewin), Morrow, 1988.

Chocolate Dreams, Lothrop, 1988.

Flamboyan, Harcourt, 1988.

Editor; Anthologies For Young Adults And Adults, Except As Noted:

I Am the Darker Brother: An Anthology of Modern Poems by Negro Americans (ALA Notable Book; illustrated by Benny Andrews), Macmillan, 1968.

Black on Black: Commentaries by Negro Americans, Macmillan, 1968.

City in All Directions: An Anthology of Modern Poems (illustrated by Donald Carrick), Macmillan, 1969.

Black Out Loud: An Anthology of Modern Poems by Black Americans (juvenile; ALA Notable Book; illustrated by Alvin Hollingsworth), Macmillan, 1970.

Brothers and Sisters: Modern Stories by Black Americans, Macmillan, 1970.

It Is the Poem Singing into Your Eyes: An Anthology of New Young Poets, Harper, 1971.

The Poetry of Black America: An Anthology of the Twentieth Century (ALA Notable Book), Harper, 1973.

My Black Me: A Beginning Book of Black Poetry (juvenile; ALA Notable Book), Dutton, 1974.

Celebrations: A New Anthology of Black American Poetry (ALA Notable Book), Follett, 1977.

Contributor of articles and reviews to periodicals.

■ **Work In Progress**

Poetry, picture books, anthology of women's poetry, anthology of American Indian poetry. A series of autobiographical novels. "Most of the material has to do with my parents and grandparents coming to this country from Russia and their life in the South Bronx. Much of my old neighborhood—Kelly Street, Fox Street—was utterly destroyed in the 1970s. All of the tales are told from the viewpoint of a thirteen-year-old male. The stories owe a lot to folk literature where truth and exaggeration blend into one; where fact and fancy tend to blur. This is the first time I've attempted to write extended prose fiction. For years the novel form terrified me, because I have worked in the relatively short forms of poetry."

■ **Sidelights**

Born July 16, 1935 in New York City, the son of an immigrant father who left his native border town of Russia and Poland to settle in the South Bronx, a rich heritage was imprinted on the young Adoff. "My father told marvellous stories of *shtetl* life and his early years in lower Manhattan. But in our home, as in so many others, the emphasis was on being American with a keen sense of Jewish, even though there was very little religious orientation. There was a tradition of liberal, free-thinking females in the family. My mother was involved in Zionist and civil rights causes. I recall when a black Baptist congregation reclaimed a derelict church in our neighborhood, my mother playing her violin, welcoming the new congregation.

"From an early age, women have played an extraordinarily important part in my life. I was raised by women who were extremely vital not only in the home but outside as well. My mother was passionately active on behalf of the Israeli Pioneer Women, a group aligned with the Labor

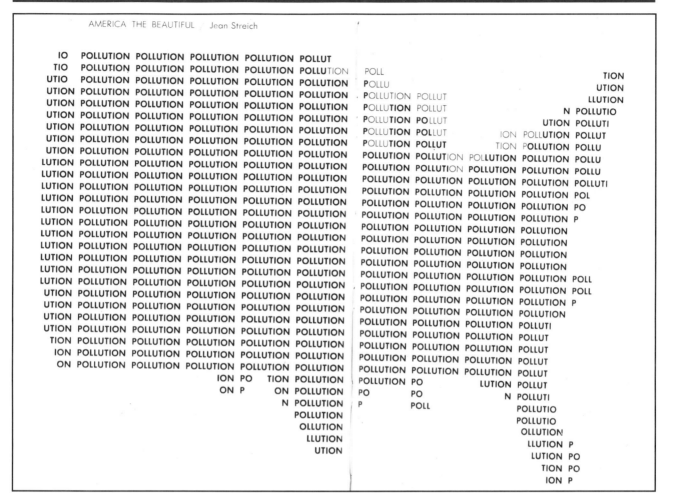

Illustration from *It Is the Poem Singing into Your Eyes: An Anthology of New Young Poets*, edited by Arnold Adoff.

Party whose main function it was to raise funds for hospitals, ambulances and various good works in Israel. My maternal grandmother would never allow me to join the Boy Scouts, because they wore uniforms and carried knives—for her, a sure sign of creeping fascism. These were women who brought a great deal of the outside world into our home, often in subtle ways. Their cooking was one example. Recipes in our house originated from Russia, Poland, Germany, Hungary, and Roumania. As I grew older, I came to recognize which dishes came from where. A small thing, perhaps, but nonetheless a way of maintaining traditions, keeping the heritage alive, and of being conscious of a huge world beyond our windows.

"My family was vocal. Everyone talked at once, read a great deal, and held to their opinions with great passion. Discussions were volatile, emotional, intellectual—all those energies rolled into one. In order to hold status within the family, you had to speak loudly and articulately on such burning topics as economics, socialism, the Soviet Union,

and how to be assimilated into the larger society without losing one's Jewishness. There was always a sense of temporariness in being a Jew in America (in being a Jew anywhere, for that matter). I suppose that on some level we were waiting for the next pogrom to turn the corner of 172nd Street and Boston Road. The house was always full of newspapers and magazines— *PM* (a socialist paper), the *Forward* (in which Isaac Singer originally published so much of his work), the *Star*, the *New Yorker*. My grandmother, however, drew the line at the funnies, which were strictly *verboten*. Too low-brow. So adamant was she about that that she refused to buy the Sunday editions of the newspapers.

"My father's pharmacy, a focal point in our neighborhood life, was a block away from where we lived. He was there from early in the morning until quite late in the evening. As a young child I liked to play behind the counter, dipping crepe paper in water to create colored waters which I would then mix, pretending they were pharmacist's chemicals.

I also counted pills, compounded salves and delivered prescriptions, becoming very familiar with the musty odor in the apartments of old people who had been sick and shut in for a long time. In lots of ways, the pharmacy was a bellwether. One window display I'll never forget went up during World War II: ostensibly for a particular roach spray, it portrayed Hitler, Stalin, and Mussolini as roaches. The pharmacy was also a locus for collections for the war—cardboard (which the store had in great quantities) was particularly valuable. I was the undisputed 'cardboard king' of the neighborhood war effort.

"Ours was a mixed working class neighborhood—Polish, Irish, Italian, Jewish, and German—of garment people, shop people, and union people. We children played together in the streets and on the stoops during kite-flying season, stick-ball season, marble season. I suspect the fellows who sold toys to the local candy store made up the seasons, depending on what they could get from the wholesalers. My brother and I were never allowed to own bonafide sports equipment. Our family was not atypical in this. Parents expected their sons to grow up to become doctors, lawyers, accountants. There were strict quotas in medical and law schools in those days, so Jews had to do exceedingly well just to have a shot at admission. The dirtiest words in my family were 'truck driver,' even before the teamsters. If you didn't go to college and do well, then you would go to hell, not to be eternally consumed by flames, but to lead the unending life as a truck driver.

"From the age of ten or so, I started attending a neighborhood Zionist school, where we studied the Old Testament and, of course, Zionism as well as other aspects of Jewish history and culture. I went there after school, and when I was older, in the evenings. I also took courses at the Jewish Teacher's Seminary and People's University, another Zionist educational institution. These schools were important to me not only because I was intensely interested in things Jewish, but because, unlike my high school, there were girls. I realized early on that girls generally were much more mature than boys their age. I gravitated toward girls with literary and artistic interests and they became my closest friends.

"I went to Stuyvesant High School on Fourteenth Street in Manhattan with the intention of becoming a doctor. I soon discovered that I was a wash-out at organic chemistry and similar subjects, and had to rethink my career plans, such as they were. I felt like a fish out of water at that school because I was

not a scientist in the depths of my soul. Perhaps the best thing about Stuyvesant was that it was relatively far from home. I took the Third Avenue El down from the Bronx and then the subway. This was during the late forties and early fifties when the city was safe and no thought was given to danger. My happiest memories are of Stuyvesant Center on Fridays, 'St. Paramount's Day,' when we cut school to spend the afternoon at the movies.

"Our house was filled with music. My mother played the violin, my aunt sang, the radio played opera, gospel, and jazz. I began to see our culture as segregated. What was called 'American culture' most often did not include black or Latino culture. I started sneaking into jazz clubs when I was sixteen, beginning at Birdland, where Sarah Vaughan, Dizzie Gillespie and Tito Puente often played, to the Village Vanguard, Jimmy Ryan's and Eddie Condon's. I remember seeing Mingus, Max Roach, Bud Powell, Lester Young and Charlie Parker sharing the same tiny stage playing at each other's throats. Enough genius electricity to burn Birdland down. There were places that featured Dixieland where the midnight ritual was everyone dancing to 'When the Saints Come Marching In.' Later I would go to the Apollo and the Cotton Club, both in Harlem. By the time I graduated high school, jazz was the only music I listened to. It pushed out the boundaries of my world.

"I was still at odds about what I wanted to do and what I should do: become a poet or a pharmacist like my father. I continued to write poetry, and enrolled in the Columbia University School of Pharmacy. I became so unhappy with my choice, however, that I ran away from home in the most literary sense imaginable, leaving no note, but my copy of Thomas Wolfe's *You Can't Go Home Again* opened to a salient passage. Instead of going to school that day, I packed a bag, went to the bus station and bought a ticket for Chicago, the only other city that existed for New Yorkers. I had in mind to get a job, become an adult, write poetry. I got a room in a sleazy hotel, went to a bar for a Singapore Sling and bought a pair of chinos. Then I called my parents (nice Jewish boy that I was, I didn't want to worry them). 'Study anything you want, but **COME HOME!**' I went home on the next train, and enrolled at City College.

"They didn't have creative writing programs in those days, and I was still intensely interested in politics, so I majored in history. I minored in literature, but was loathe to major in it lest I end up a flunky poet/English teacher. My plan was to become a history professor and write poetry. City

College was truly an amazing place during the 1950s. One of my teachers was Richard Myers, who argued Brown vs. Topeka Board of Education [the landmark school desegregation case]. I learned tremendous amounts of Constitutional law. I was passionate about my studies in history. I also wrote for the college newspaper and literary magazine. Writers important to me at that time were e.e. cummings, Gertrude Stein, and Langston Hughes whose work led me to other black poets and writers. Of course Joyce loomed large, as did Dylan Thomas. We loved Bernard Shaw for his politics and vegetarianism. We would sit for hours in the college cafeteria arguing about poets and poetry.

"A seminal event for me in college was the opportunity to meet Charles Mingus, who had been invited to lecture by the jazz club, of which I was president. Without a doubt, he was the most impressive person I had ever met. From then on, I went to see him wherever he played, and we got to know each other. In time, he would become my spiritual father.

"As always, I was politically active. It is a myth that the fifties was a decade during which nothing much happened. It was far from a quiet time. A number of us were arrested for fighting to protect civil liberties on campus. The Students for Democratic Action picketed in Baltimore to protest the fact that blacks were not allowed to eat at the same lunch counters as whites. There were FBI agents on campus.

"I applied to Columbia's political science department for graduate work. I was totally committed at the time, but the counselor who interviewed me said, 'This isn't your field. You won't graduate from here and go on to be a professor. You'll become a writer.' 'No,' I insisted. 'I want to go here. Really, really.' My grades were excellent, my parents could afford the tuition, he relented. But he turned out to be right, and I've often wondered at his prescience. I did all the required coursework for a Ph.D. in American history, but left unfinished my dissertation on the Federal Emergency Relief Administration and the New Deal, 1932-33. Again, the teachers I had were phenomenal—Richard Hoffstedter, my academic advisor, won a Pulitzer Prize while I was there; Henry Steele Commager was my thesis advisor.

"In grad school I had a job teaching seventh-grade social studies at a *yeshiva* in the Brownsville section of Brooklyn. One hundred thirty-five dollars every two weeks, and we had to cash the checks in Brooklyn. If I took my check up to the Bronx to cash it at my father's drugstore, by the time it went through the banks, it would bounce. This was a very poor *yeshiva*. However, it was quite an interesting place as many of the students were from as far away as South America. The job also gave me confidence knowing I could stay alive outside grad school. This was important, because after two years I wanted to leave. The desire to live independently and focus on my writing had become overpowering.

"I moved to the Village, rented an apartment across from New York University, painted three of its four walls chocolate brown and began to live. I supported myself with substitute teaching and spent the rest of my time writing and going to jazz clubs. I also became Mingus' manager. He taught me much about living. I have a trunk full of notes from this period—things Mingus said and did, and running chronicles of the Village club scene. I haven't opened it since the fifties, but plan to use much of the material in the second book in my new series of autobiographical novels.

"I met Virginia Hamilton through Mingus in 1958. She, too, was living in the East Village working on a novel. I had heard about this brilliant young writer from Ohio, but nothing I had been told quite prepared me for the rarity of the woman. She was a

Jacket painting for the 1973 collection edited by Adoff.

ninety-eight-pound, fresh-faced Ohio farm girl, wore an extremely unusual boyish black-and-white plaid coat and boots and had marvellous curly hair, which she cut herself. She embodied all my ideals of an independent woman: she could think, she was a writer, she was an artist. Mingus had a crush on Virginia as well, but while he was involved playing his long sets, I spent time talking with her. One night we left a club with Mingus and as we pulled up to her door, I asked for her phone number. She whispered it in my ear. I didn't say another word to anyone until I got home, so intent was I on keeping it in my memory. As soon as I got in, I called her (this must have been four in the morning), and what does a poet do when he's trying to impress the woman of his dreams? Well, he reads her his poetry, which I did, not realizing that Virginia had no heat in her apartment and was freezing to death while I declaimed. The next day I went over to her place, and we weren't separated again until 1963 when she went to the hospital to have our first child. We were married in 1960.

"I was staying up all night in the clubs, sleeping mornings and teaching public school in the afternoons, which wasn't leaving me enough time for writing. So I cut back on the music scene and focused on my poetry. The Village was a vibrant community of painters, writers, musicians who would meet in the coffeehouses and talk art. As a poet I have been more influenced by musicians and painters than by other writers. People who see my very early work, in which I used no capital letters, say, 'Oh, yes, you were reading cummings.' But I didn't read cummings until later. My reasons then for not using capital letters had to do with certain surrealist paintings I saw at the Museum of Modern Art. Man Ray was an important influence, as was Picasso, the Russian Constructivists and other painters and sculptors influenced by technology and things industrial. I was very excited by collaborations between visual artists and writers, particularly by their *livres d'art* published in Europe.

"Shortly after Virginia and I were married, we went to Paris for one month and then to Spain for six. We rented a little house near Torremolinos, and settled in with our two green Olivettis, she working on an adult novel, I on my poetry. In 1965, we again went to Argeles-sur-Mer, a tiny village on the Mediterranean coast of France, near Spain for six months of uninterrupted writing. This time we took our two-year-old daughter, Leigh, eleven suitcases, a trunk, and a teddy bear tied to a stroller. The French had never seen a child carried in a gerry-pack and because I carried Leigh around

on my back most of the time, or pushed her in the stroller, they assumed she was congenitally unable to walk. We took a short break and went to Paris, during which time our daughter took her first steps. We later learned that when we returned to Argeles-sur-Mer, people thought a miracle had been worked for Leigh at Lourdes.

"One day I brought home a magazine with the famous photograph of the black man throwing a firebomb in Watts. That forced us to think seriously about whether we wished to remain in Europe. Virginia is black, our children brown—we felt somehow that it would be wrong to stay. Besides, it all seemed very exciting and we didn't want to be removed from the action. So we returned to New York, where we threw ourselves into our work and as much political work as we could handle.

"I resumed collecting black literature, which I had begun in the late 1950s and early 1960s teaching in Harlem and on Manhattan's Upper West Side. I would dig up old magazines like *Dial* and look for specifically black periodicals like *Opportunity, Urban League, Negro Digest, Black Digest, Black World*, most of which no longer exist. I'd haunt bookshops all over town. One of my favorites was University Books on Fourteenth Street on the ninth floor of an old building. You'd get out of the old freight elevator and there you would be in the center of this wonderful world of things African."[1]

"As a teacher I had students who wanted life in those dusty classrooms. They wanted pictures of themselves inside themselves. I began to bring some in. I was the dealer. The pusher of poems and stories. Plays and paintings. Jazz and blues. And my students began to push on me. To deal their sounds and write their poems. And I was made to become serious about myself. To get my head together and attempt to go beyond the classrooms and students and schools. To go beyond the racist textbooks and anthologies that were on the shelves and in the bookstores."[2]

"One day I asked a friend, who was an editor at Macmillan, to make some copies for one of my classes. While standing at the machine, she read the poems and was overwhelmed by their quality and importance. She 'smelled' a book, in other words, and arranged for me to meet with the editor-in-chief of the house. The time was right. People in publishing were beginning to recognize that our national bibliography was not sufficiently representative of black writers and that the balance had to be addressed. There was a good deal of money around then for such projects as anthologies of black poetry. My first book, which was published in 1968, was *I Am the Darker Brother: An Anthology of Modern Poems by Negro Americans.*

"My history training served me well with the anthologies. My research skills were well honed, and I had a natural historical perspective, which is very helpful when you're working with a lot of material from different periods. Doing an anthology is a bit like solving a mystery: instead of being 'hot on the trail' of criminals, one is in 'hot pursuit' of clues to literary movements and submovements. I went to extraordinary efforts to track down poets whose work had appeared in little magazines thirty or more years ago. Sometimes, poets were pleased to be 'rediscovered,' but sometimes they preferred to be left alone, allowed to go out of print, saying that their poetry 'belonged to a different time, a different life.' It's an interesting phenomenon, poets who disappear—an unsettling phenomenon.

"I saw *I Am the Darker Brother* as the end of my anthologizing, but it was just the beginning. With every anthology, I uncovered more and more material. Each pointed to the need for yet another. And my own passion for the task intensified. *The Poetry of Black America* is the largest anthology of black verse ever published in the United States. It contains six hundred poems, although my manuscript consisted of three thousand poems that richly deserved to be included. The final choices were among the most agonizing selections I have ever had to make."[1]

"I want my anthologies of Black American writing to make Black kids strong in their knowledge of themselves and their great literary heritage—give them facts and people and power. I also want these Black books of mine to give knowledge to White kids around the country, so that mutual respect and understanding will come from mutual learning. We *can* go beyond the murders and muddles of the present.

"Children have to understand that the oversimplifications they get in classrooms, along with the token non-White artists represented, are not the true American literature. Melvin Tolson stands with Robert Frost as does Robert Hayden with Robert Lowell. The great force and numbers of the current, most exciting generation of Black writers in the history of this country is overwhelming to the White educator, textbook writer, and guardian-of-the-culture who wish to preserve the mainstream culture in its basic White dress. But for those who want the truth, for themselves and for their students, using an anthology is the first step

to discovery. The anthology then leads to individual works of the writers."[3]

Adoff does not consider himself a spokesperson for the black community. "Blacks and other so-called minorities have too many outside spokespersons. They're quite capable of speaking on their own behalf. I never want to be caught in that trap, and have stayed away from reviewing books by black authors or writing critical essays on literary works by blacks. I have no intention of encroaching on the terrain of black intellectuals and black writers.

"The negative aspect of doing so many anthologies was that people came to think of me primarily as an anthologizer, which made it difficult to get my first books of poetry published and reviewed. The publishing media, it seems, has trouble with people who wear more than one hat. I, however, have always thought of myself as a poet first.

"Shortly after we returned from France in 1965 I enrolled in the New School to study poetry with Jose Garcia Villa, an absolutely brilliant Philippine-American poet. Jose became my second spiritual father, and I studied with him for several crucial years. He talked about creating a poetry that was as

Dust jacket from Adoff's 1982 book.

pure as music. In one of his books, a comma separates every word—his so-called 'experiments.' His extremism based on an exhaustive knowledge of the art and craft of poetry set him apart.

"A poem must have form and physical shape which should serve to promote its message. I use the image of invisible rubber bands pulling the reader's eye from the last letter of the last word in the first line down to the first letter of the first word in the last line. The eye should be able to travel freely, and not get hung up on any clanking chains holding the work together. The music of language greatly affects meaning—most obvious where a given line is broken. I hate to see poetry reprinted in newspapers or magazines that adhere to a strict prose format and indicate line breaks with slashes. A poem printed like prose automatically loses its intrinsic meaning. Ideally, each poem should be read three times: for meaning, for rhythm, for technical tricks. My poems demand active participation.

"My first book, *MA nDA LA*, is a poem about the music of the 'ah' vowel sound. Logically, the poem makes no sense and is not supposed to. I sent it to my editor at Macmillan, who sent it back because she didn't understand it. I then sent it to editor Ursula Nordstrom, who also didn't understand it but thought that 'it sings, and we love it, and we're going to try to find an illustrator.' They found the ideal artist in Emily McCully. She gave the poem a racial, geographic and social context, none of which is in the poem."[1]

Adoff's second book of original poetry, *Black Is Brown Is Tan*, was one of the first children's books published in this country to deal directly with growing up in an interracial family. "Of course I was thinking of my children. The book is for them, and, really, for all the beautiful interracial kids in the world. Gentle though it may be, it was the target of a citizens vigilante group in a suburb of New Haven, Connecticut. Too embarrassed to admit racist undertones, they argued against the book because I used no capitalization. Happily, this group did not prevail. Other books of mine have been similarly attacked, but have always been ultimately saved from censorship."[1]

His original collections consist of books of poems on a particular subject, like *Eats, Tornado! OUTside/INside Poems* or *Birds*, and books of poems from the viewpoint of a particular character, like *I Am the Running Girl* or *Sports Pages*. "*Sports Pages* I consider a breakthrough. Not only did I manage to work in a longer form of a combination of poetic

prose and poetry, but I was able to deal with some autobiographical material using individual voice in the midst of organized activity.

"Individual poems start out as a teasing rhythm or an elusive hint of melody in my ear. From these initial fragments is born the language of my poems. It can be a slow, laborious, and mysterious process. It is not unusual for them to go through seventy-five drafts. I tell my students that I have a 'learner's permit' in poetry (I've been writing poetry for over forty years). I still question, still feel unsure. This is, afterall, part of being a poet. With each attempt he sees the world for the first time. Too, the creative process plays on dualities: normal/abnormal, sane/insane, happy/sad, vulnerable/guarded. The tension between these polar opposites can tear you apart.

"A duality I consciously play within my work is the 'mundane' and the 'fantastical.' A lot of my poems have to do with normal, everyday things, like eating a Hostess Twinkie every day of your life. What counts is not eating the Twinkie, but the perspective of the act. I happen to believe that eating a Hostess Twinkie can be a fantastical experience. Anything can be a fantastical and even mystical experience. It all depends on the way you look at it. Children understand this concept very well.

"I began writing for kids because I wanted to effect a change in American society. I continue in that spirit. By the time we reach adulthood, we are closed and set in our attitudes. The chances of a poet reaching us are very slim. But I can open a child's imagination, develop his appetite for poetry, and most importantly, show him that poetry is a natural part of everyday life. We all need someone to point out that the emperor is wearing no clothes. That is the poet's job.

"I know, too, that I write for children because the child in me is still very much alive. A book that will forever remain dear to my heart is *It Is the Poem Singing into Your Eyes*, an anthology of poems by young people. I was able to convince a publisher to accept mail from young poets from all over the country, which normally they are most hesitant to do. I sent flyers to schools, put notices in the *New York Times Book Review* and similar publications, and, lo and behold, we got over six thousand submissions. The tragedy—and I do consider it a tragedy—is that I was allowed to publish only one hundred poems. There were many, many, many poems that were absolutely superb. Most of the poems in the book were by sixteen- and seventeen-

Arnold Adoff and Virginia Hamilton with their children.

year-olds, and some by ten-year-olds. One of the poets, August Wilson, is now a Pulitzer Prize-winning playwright. The title of the volume was suggested by one of my young correspondents. I loved her statement—a poem truly does sing into your eyes and then on into your mind and soul."[1]

Adoff lives with Virginia Hamilton and their children in Yellow Springs, Ohio. "Virginia teases me that I 'kidnapped' her twice to Europe; the third time she 'kidnapped me' to her home town where most of her family still lives. We bought some land behind her parents' farm, built a house and settled in. Sometimes I marvel to find myself living here after so many years as an inveterate New Yorker. I liked the idea that our kids could walk across the fields to their grandmother's house for homemade cookies. Antioch College in Yellow Springs creates a lot of literary and artistic activity here. For that matter, a wife who is a brilliant novelist and two kids who are talented musicians, create a lot of scintillating activity within my own walls.

"During the academic year, we keep an apartment in New York City. For the last couple of years, Virginia and I have been distinguished visiting professors at Queens College. We team-teach, using only our own books. Most of our students are professional teachers who are living in the world of children, which makes the process stimulating and immediate for all of us. They can apply something we taught in class the day before. The department has a special relationship with the Louis Armstrong School in Queens, a magnet for the arts. Each year Queens College sponsors a conference on children's literature, attracting the best and brightest authors in the field."[1]

A legendary teacher, Adoff has written extensively on his experiences and methods. "If you really want to write," he advises, "you must read, read, read. Steep yourself in the field of children's literature, if that is what you want, or if you want to be a novelist, read many novels. Set aside some daily time for writing. Assign yourself long- and short-term writing and reading projects. Discipline yourself. I recognize the worth of writing workshops, although writing is a solitary activity. For one thing, it's nice to be in the company of other writers, to deal with deadlines, and to subject your work to criticism. However, avoid, like the plague, any writing teacher who emphasizes the importance of 'self-expression.' Self-expression is not positive. A diary is for self-expression and similar forms of spilling guts. A poem is a work of art. And any poet, be it a ten-year-old kid or a poet with forty years of practice, should have in mind to make a work of art."[1]

Footnote Sources:

[1] Based on an interview by Marguerite Feitlowitz for *Authors and Artists for Young Adults.*
[2] Arnold Adoff, "Preface," *The Poetry of Black America,* Harper, 1973.
[3] Lee Bennett Hopkins, editor, "Arnold Adoff," *More Books by More People,* Citation, 1974.

■ For More Information See

Horn Book, April, 1970, June, 1970, February, 1972, December, 1972, August, 1982 (p. 420).
Kirkus Review, April 15, 1970.
Publishers Weekly, July 13, 1970 (p. 86ff), August 26, 1988 (p. 88).
Bulletin of the Center for Children's Books, September, 1970.
New York Times Book Review, September 6, 1970, January 23, 1972.

Martha E. Ward and Dorothy A. Marquardt, *Authors of Books for Young People,* second edition, Scarecrow, 1971.
Top of the News, January, 1972 (p. 152ff), winter, 1981 (p. 192ff).
Judith Wagner, "More Vivid Than Daylight," *Cincinnati Enquirer,* January 5, 1975.
Antioch Review, fall, 1975.
Authors in the News, Volume 1, Gale, 1976.
Doris de Montreville and Elizabeth D. Crawford, editors, *Fourth Book of Junior Authors and Illustrators,* H. W. Wilson, 1978.
Washington Post Book World, November 11, 1979.
Children's Literature in Education, Volume 11, number 3, 1980.
Arnold Adoff, *All the Colors of the Race,* Lothrop, 1982.
School Library Journal, March, 1982, May, 1986 (p. 86), June/July, 1988 (p. 107).
Interracial Books for Children Bulletin, number 1, 1983, number 6, 1984.
Language Arts, April, 1983, March, 1985 (p. 235ff).
D. L. Kirkpatrick, editor, *Twentieth-Century Children's Writers,* St. Martin's, 1983.
Children's Literature Review, Volume VII, Gale, 1984.
Lion and the Unicorn, Volume 10, 1986 (p. 9ff).

J. G. Ballard

The Drowned World, Berkley, 1962.
The Burning World, Berkley, 1964 (revised
edition published in England as *The Drought*,
J. Cape, 1965).
The Drowned World [and] *The Wind from
Nowhere*, Doubleday, 1965.
The Crystal World, Farrar, Straus, 1966.
Crash, Farrar, Straus, 1973.
Concrete Island, Farrar, Straus, 1974.
High-Rise, J. Cape, 1975, Holt, 1977.
The Unlimited Dream Company, Holt, 1979.
Hello America, J. Cape, 1981, Carroll & Graf,
1988.
Empire of the Sun, Simon & Schuster, 1984.
The Day of Creation, Gollancz, 1987, Farrar,
Straus, 1988.
Running Wild, Hutchinson, 1988, Farrar,
Straus, 1989.

Story Collections:

The Voices of Time and Other Stories, Berkley,
1962.
Billenium and Other Stories, Berkley, 1962.
The Four-Dimensional Nightmare, Gollancz,
1963, revised edition, 1974.
Passport to Eternity and Other Stories, Berkley,
1963.
The Terminal Beach, Gollancz, 1964, revised
edition, Berkley, 1964.
The Impossible Man and Other Stories, Berkley,
1966.
The Disaster Area, J. Cape, 1967.
*By Day Fantastic Birds Flew through the
Petrified Forests*, Esographics for Firebird
Visions, 1967.

Born James Graham Ballard, November 15,
1930, in Shanghai, China; son of James (a
businessman) and Edna (Johnstone) Ballard;
married Helen Mary Matthews, 1953 (died, 1964);
children: James, Fay, Beatrice. *Education:* Attended King's College, Cambridge University, 1949-1951. *Home:* 36 Charlton Rd., Shepperton, Middlesex, England. *Agent:* Margaret Hanbury, 27
Walcot Sq., London S.E. 11, England.

■ Career

Writer. Trustee, Institute for Research in Art and
Technology. *Military service:* Royal Air Force,
1954-55; became pilot.

■ Awards, Honors

Guardian Fiction Prize, Booker Prize nomination,
and James Tait Black Memorial Prize from the
University of Edinburgh, all 1984, all for *Empire of
the Sun*.

■ Writings

Novels:

The Wind from Nowhere, Berkley, 1962.

The Day of Forever, Panther Books, 1967, revised edition, 1971.

The Overloaded Man, Panther Books, 1967.

The Atrocity Exhibition, J. Cape, 1970, published as *Love and Napalm: Export U.S.A.,* Grove, 1972.

Vermilion Sands, Berkley, 1971.

Chronopolis and Other Stories, Putnam, 1971.

Low-Flying Aircraft and Other Stories, J. Cape, 1976.

The Best of J. G. Ballard, Futura, 1977, revised edition published as *The Best Short Stories of J. G. Ballard,* Holt, 1978.

The Venus Hunters, Granada, 1980.

Myths of the Near Future, J. Cape, 1982.

Memories of the Space Age, Arkham, 1988.

Other:

(Editor with others) *Best Science Fiction from "New Worlds,"* Medallion, 1968.

(Contributor) *The Inner Landscape,* Allison & Busby, 1969.

(Author of introduction) *Salvador Dali,* Ballantine, 1974.

(Author of introduction) Brian Ash, editor, *The Visual Encyclopaedia of Science Fiction,* Pan Books, 1977.

(Contributor) V. Vale and Andre Juno, editors, *Re/Search: J. G. Ballard,* Re/Search Media, 1984.

Also author of *Rolling All the Time.* Contributor to periodicals, including *New Worlds, Magazine of Fantasy and Science Fiction, Amazing, Fantastic, Ambit, Guardian, Transatlantic Review, Triquarterly, Playboy, Encounter,* and *Evergreen Review.* Prose editor, *Ambit,* 1964—.

■ Adaptations

"The Unlimited Dream Company," Royal College of Art School of Film and Television, 1983.

"Empire of the Sun" (motion picture), starring Christian Bale and John Malkovich, directed by Steven Spielberg, Warner Bros., 1987, (cassette), G. K. Hall.

"The Drowned World" (cassette), G. K. Hall, 1987.

■ Work In Progress

A novella.

■ Sidelights

November 15, 1930. Born in Shanghai, China to James and Edna (Johnstone) Ballard. "Shanghai was a huge, wide open city full of political gangsters, criminals of every conceivable kind, a melting pot for refugees from Europe, and White Russians, refugees from the Russian Revolution—it was a city with absolutely no restraints on anything. Gambling, racketeering, prostitution, and everything that comes from the collisions between the very rich—there were thousands of millionaires—and the very poor—no one was ever poorer than the Shanghai proletariat. On top of that, superimpose World War II...."[1]

"My father was a chemist originally. He joined a big Manchester firm of textile manufacturers—this was before I was born—and he moved into the management field. They had a subsidiary in Shanghai of which he was the chairman and managing director throughout the 1930s and into the '40s."[2]

"I was brought up largely by servants and my memories of childhood are of wandering around the Chinese areas of the city on my own or of being driven out by the Russian chauffeur to visit the abandoned battlefields a few miles away in the countryside."[3]

"...War in all its forms was institutionalized in Shanghai, after the Sino-Japanese War began in 1937....I remember seeing a lot of troops, and going out frequently to the battlefields around Shanghai where I saw dead soldiers lying around, dead horses in the canals and all that sort of thing."[2]

"...I remember when the Japanese entered China after Pearl Harbour, in December 1941. I was going to do the scripture exam at the end-of-term examinations at the school I went to. Pearl Harbour had just taken place, the previous night I suppose, and I heard *tanks* coming down the street. I looked out the window and there were Japanese tanks trundling around. It doesn't sound like very much, but if tanks suddenly rolled down [the] street you'd have a surprise: Russian tanks say. The Japanese took over the place, and they segmented Shanghai into various districts with barbed wire, so you couldn't move from Zone A to Zone B except at certain times. They'd block off everything for security reasons, and on certain days the only way of going to school was to go to the house of some friends of my parents who lived on one of these border zones, between I think the French Concession and the International Settlement. There was an abandoned night club, a gambling casino called the Del Monte...a huge building in big grounds. We'd climb over the fence and go through, and go up the main driveway on the other side of the border-zone, and go to school. This abandoned casino, a huge multi-storied building, was decorated in full-blown Casino Versailles style, with figures holding up great prosceniums over bars and huge roulette tables. Everything was junked. I remember a roulette table on its side and the whole roulette wheel section had come out, exposing the machinery inside. There was all this junk lying around, chips and all sorts of stuff, as if in some sort of tableau, arranged...by a demolition squad. It was very strange...."[4]

"I was sent to the Cathedral School in Shanghai before the war. A very authoritarian English clergyman was the headmaster there, and he used to set lines. It's the most time-wasting enterprise one could imagine, but he would say '500 lines. Carruthers! 600 lines. Ballard!' for some small infringement. Five hundred lines was about 30 pages of a school exercise book. You were supposed to copy out school texts, and I remember starting to copy from a novel about the Spanish Armada....

"I suddenly realized—I was only about nine or ten—that it was easier, and it would save a lot of effort, if I just made it up, which I did. So from then on I would make up my own narratives. I think the authoritarian clergyman must have

J. G. Ballard in Shanghai, 1936.

scanned my lines because he reprimanded me by saying: 'Ballard, next time you pick a book to copy your lines from don't pick some trashy novel like this!' He didn't realize I'd written it myself....

"I remember the very first little book I produced. Of course it was never printed, but it was my first effort at a book. It was about how to play Contract Bridge. I learned to play the game at an early age, because Bridge-playing was all the rage. I must only have been about eleven....My mother used to hold Bridge parties, almost every afternoon it seemed. To a child the bids conjure up a whole world of mystery because they don't seem to be related to anything. 'One heart, two hearts, three diamonds, three no trumps, double, redouble—what the hell does all this mean?' I thought, I used to pace around upstairs listening to these bids, trying to extract some sort of logical meaning. I finally persuaded my mother to explain how Contract Bridge was played. I was so impressed by the discovery of what bidding meant—deciphering these cryptic and mysterious calls, particularly when I discovered they relate to the whole world of conventions so that they are a code within a code—that I wrote a book. I think I filled a school exercise book on the basic rules of Contract Bridge and what the main conventions were—I even had a section on 'Psychic Bidding,' which was pretty good for an 11-year-old! It was quite an effort of exposition...."[2]

At the age of twelve, Ballard and his parents and sister were among a group of 2,000 who were interned in a Japanese prison camp, about ten miles from Shanghai. "The Japanese didn't intern everybody simultaneously. It was staged, and I think it took six months or so before we were interned. We had very hot summers and cold winters in Shanghai, and I remember wearing light clothes when we arrived in the camp. Pearl Harbour was in December 1941, so it must have been the following summer. To me, the period of internment wasn't a huge surprise as my life had changed continuously. From a huge house with nine servants, a chauffeur-driven Packard and all the rest of it, I was suddenly living in a small room with my parents and sister. Although that may seem an enormous jump, in fact it was all part of a huge continuum of disorder....

"I have—I won't say *happy*—not unpleasant memories of the camp. I was young, and if you put 400 or 500 children together they have a good time whatever the circumstances. I can remember the acute shortage of food in the last year, and a general breakdown of facilities. Drinking water

was no longer brought in by road tanker to the camp for the last year or more, once the tide turned against the Japanese. I remember a lot of the casual brutality and beatings-up that went on— but at the same time we children were playing a hundred and one games all the time! There was a great deal of illness, and about three-quarters of the people in the camp caught malaria, though not my family, thank God. My sister, who is seven years younger than me, nearly died of some kind of dysentery. I know my parents always had very much harsher memories of the camp than I did, because of course they knew the reality of the circumstances. Parents often starved themselves to feed their children. But I think it's true that the Japanese do like children and are very kindly towards them. The guards didn't abuse the children at all.

"I saw it all from a child's eye, and didn't notice the danger. Right next to the camp was a large Japanese military airfield (I think it's now Shanghai International Airport). This was under constant attack in the last year or so from American bombers and low-flying fighters. The perimeter fence of the camp was in effect the perimeter of the airbase. We looked right out over the airfield. Although we had a curfew imposed by the Japanese during the air attacks, they became so frequent—almost continuous towards the closing stages—that we were often out in the open with anti-aircraft shells bursting over our heads. I daresay my parents were driven frantic by all this, but children don't remember. It wasn't like a dream, because dreams often *are* unpleasant and full of anxiety. I had no sense of anxiety. I don't remember any fear, but I look back now and I think 'My God, why didn't I turn and run!' I was totally involved but at the same time saved by the magic of childhood."[2]

"I came to puberty in the camps, so I avoided the strangled attitudes to sex you get in most English public schools. Girls were everywhere, and there was far less privacy than there is in ordinary life. Actually, I think it was the best possible upbringing in that respect."[5]

"...I went on writing little short stories and pieces...just adventure stories and thrillers, my own variants on whatever I happened to be reading."[2]

"The whole landscape out there had a tremendously powerful influence on me, as did the whole war experience. All the abandoned cities and towns and beach resorts that I keep returning to in my fiction were there in that huge landscape, the area just around our camp. . . ."[4]

Following the war, Ballard continued on to England and began the adjustment to an entirely different way of life. "My father stayed in China, and I came over with my mother and sister. We had friends who lived down in the West Country, near Plymouth, and my mother rented a house there for a couple of years. . . .

"England seemed a very strange country. Both the physical landscape and the social and psychological landscapes seemed fit subjects for analysis—extremely constrained and rigid and repressed compared with the sort of background I had. To come from Shanghai, and from the war itself where everything had been shaken to its foundations, to come to England and find this narrow-minded puritanical world—this was the most repressed society I'd ever known!"[2]

Jacket from the novel based on Ballard's boyhood experiences in Shanghai.

"I went to the Leys School in Cambridge for a couple of years in the late 1940s. I disliked it intensely, but I'd been through so many strange experiences before and during the war that it was just another strange experience that I coped with. I wasn't unhappy there, actually. I had a great deal more experience of life in general than almost all the boys that I met there. Although they'd lived in Britain during the war, they'd had very sheltered lives (the school had been evacuated to Scotland). I didn't have anything very much in common. The big saving for me was that the Leys School was in Cambridge itself. I'd sneak off to the Arts Cinema to see all the French films of the '40s. I'd go to the Cambridge Film Society and soak myself in 'The Cabinet of Dr Galigari' and all those experimental films of the '20s. And there were always art exhibitions of various kinds on in Cambridge. Also, I had two or three friends among the boys in the class above mine who went up to Cambridge University to read medicine, and through them I had an early entry into Cambridge undergraduate life. I used to visit the colleges. If I'd gone to a school out in a remote corner of Dorset or somewhere it would have been a bit of a strain, but being in Cambridge it was like being a member of a junior college there, which was a big help to me."[2]

Having developed an interest in psychology, Ballard went on to study medicine at King's College, Cambridge University. ". . .My chief reason for reading medicine when I went up to King's College was that I wanted to become a psychiatrist—a sort of adolescent dream, but I was quite serious about it. . . .

"I. . .began to devour every library I could lay my hands on when I was 16 or 17. I read a good number of Freud's major works then, plus a lot of other works on psychoanalysis and psychiatry. Jung, of course, who was really a great imaginative novelist (in a sense, Freud is too!). But while I was still at school I was reading not just psychoanalytic texts but all the leading writers of the day—Kafka of course, and Hemingway—the strange sort of goulash of writers and poets that you read when you're that age.

"I was already writing experimental fiction, what might be classed as avant-garde fiction. I'd been writing bits of fiction ever since I was quite a small child. I wanted to become a writer, there's no question about that, but I didn't see writing and a medical career as mutually exclusive. I wanted to study psychiatry professionally, and first of course I had to gain a medical degree—which was five years ahead, then two years doing the Diploma of

Psychological Medicine: seven years in all. That seemed a lifetime away, and I took for granted that I would write my own fiction throughout this period. I didn't see myself as a professional writer; it didn't occur to me that I could become one just by *decision*. I was writing a lot of fiction—I don't say it was particularly naive—but it was very experimental and heavily influenced by all the psychoanalysis I'd read, by all the Kafka and so on....''[2]

After winning a short story contest at Cambridge, Ballard decided to give up medicine and dedicate himself to writing. ''My father said, with a chemist's logic, 'Well, if you want to be a writer you should study English.' So I went to London University, read English, and they turfed me out at the end of the year, deciding I hadn't got what it took to be a student of English Literature. I was then about 22. I went to work for an advertising agency called Digby Wills Ltd., where I wrote copy—for lemon juice, among other things. I was there for three or four months. Then I worked as an encyclopaedia salesman. That was fascinating, one of the most interesting periods in my life. It lasted about six months, I think. Simply going into so many people's homes, I was conducting my own Gallup survey of English life. An encyclopaedia salesman has to start at number one—knock, knock—and then go on to number two. You must knock on every door and try to get in. You have to overcome the feeling that because the lace curtains look a little intimidating you won't knock here— you must go in. And it's quite extraordinary, the variety of human lives....It was fascinating.''[2]

In 1954 Ballard joined the Royal Air Force and was sent to Canada to train as a pilot. ''I thought I'd like to try flying, to see what it was like. I thought I'd like to try service life, because it was at least sort of forward-looking and that helped....I was in a bit of a dead-end. I hadn't started reading SF [science fiction]. I wanted to be a writer. I was writing short stories, planning a novel like any novice, but I wasn't organised. It struck me—I was very interested in aviation—that it might be worth going into the service for a couple of years—one of those short service commissions they had then. You could go in for a very short space of time, just to see what it was like. But in fact it wasn't anything. It was completely unlike anything I imagined. I didn't like service life at all. Also, I spent my entire period in Canada, out in the back of beyond....

''There was nothing to do, nothing to read on the newsstands. There were no national papers, just local papers. These were packed with stuff about curling contests and ice-hockey. They relegated international news to about two columns on the back page. The papers were packed with ads for local garages and so forth—you know, this was Moosejaw, Saskatchewan. *Time* magazine was regarded as wildly highbrow. The only intelligent reading-matter was science fiction! This was in '54. I suddenly devoured it. This was the heyday of these magazines, there were dozens of them, or seemed to be....

''I started reading it all then, and I started writing it very soon after I started reading it, and *then* I stopped reading it.

''The moment I got myself organised I wanted to get out of the RAF and get back to London, and start churning the stuff out. So I resigned my commission and came back to England.''[4]

When he returned to London, he married Helen Mary Mathews. ''I got married in '53, I suppose. Time went by very rapidly, with the baby around....I worked in a couple of libraries for about six months—Richmond Borough Library, or Sheen Public Libraries, I can't really remember. But I spent a lot of time writing, and of course I had a young wife and child....The period of great financial stringency was after I got married that *was* the difficult period.''[2]

By the late fifties the Ballards had three children, James, Fay, and Beatrice. Struggling to make ends meet, Ballard sent a short story to Ted Carnell, editor of *New Worlds Magazine,* who was instrumental in helping to launch Ballard's career. ''I remember submitting stories to Carnell's magazines only out of desperation. And of course he bought the very first one. I think 'Prima Belladonna' was the first I wrote, although it may not have been the first I submitted. Whatever the case, it and 'Escapement' went to him within weeks if not days....

''He wrote to me saying 'Extraordinary story, with fascinating ideas—I'm going to publish it and will pay you 2 pounds a thousand....' I was amazed. I was 25...and it was an extraordinary event. To have your first published work in a commercial magazine....I was overjoyed. I sent him the next story, which I'm almost certain was 'Escapement,' and he took that and I was well away. I never thought about submitting stories anywhere else for years, simply because Ted Carnell was sitting there. He never rejected a single story, ever. He must have taken 30 or 40 from me. In one or two cases he suggested alterations, that certain sections could be expanded, and I think I always took up his suggestions, expanded a particular scene or made something slightly clearer. But he never really wanted any rewriting. The only things he sometimes changed were the titles, but not too often. . . .

"In 1957 Ted said 'I can get you a job on one of the journals upstairs.' In fact it was round the corner at McLarren's offices, where all these technical and trade journals were published. I jumped at it. I worked there for six months, and then somehow I heard that there was a vacancy as assistant editor on *Chemistry and Industry,* at a much better salary, and I went there. That was a very good choice—apart from anything else, because of all the scientific journals which came into the offices and I devoured. And the hours were pretty lax. I was even able to do a bit of writing in the office, which was a big help. *Chemistry and Industry* was published by the Society of Chemical Industry, in Belgrave Square. I was there for three or four years

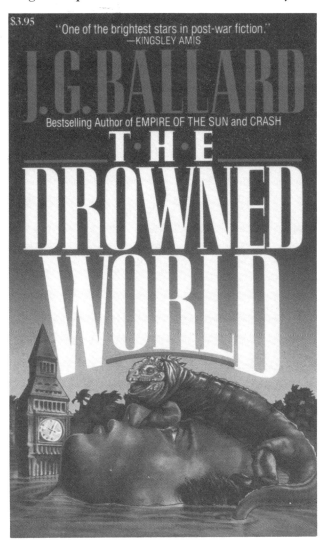

Paperback cover for Ballard's second novel.

J.G. BALLARD

AUTHOR OF EMPIRE OF THE SUN

THE DAY OF CREATION

A NOVEL

Jacket from the 1988 hardcover.

as assistant editor. I did practically everything. The editor was a chemist but he was not a journalist and he knew nothing about magazine production. This was a weekly journal, of about 50 pages, including a mass of formulas and tabular material. It was quite an enterprise, and I enjoyed it. . . ."[2]

1960. Moved from London to Shepperton. ". . .I was thirty or thereabouts, and I realized I was getting nowhere. We'd come to live here, out of necessity. We were driven out of London   once you had small children you were anathema. . . ."[4]

Once settled in Shepperton, Ballard wrote his first published novel, *The Wind from Nowhere.* ". . .I had this very long railway journey up to Central London to my office every day. There I was coming home with these small children running around, and I was absolutely exhausted. My wife had had all these babies and she was tired. I knew the one thing I had to do was make a complete break and become a full-time writer. I knew I'd never write a novel—a serious novel—while I was not getting home till 8 o'clock in the evening. I was just too tired. But I had this fortnight's holiday coming up, and my wife as a joke said—we hadn't enough money to go away—'why don't you write a novel in a fortnight? So I thought: Good. That's sensible talking.' I'd already got, through Carnell, certain contacts with the American paperback people and I had a feeling that if I wrote a novel I would sell it, even if I wasn't going to get very much money. In those days 300 could keep you going for a long time. So I said: 'I'll write a novel in ten days, six thousand words a day, during this holiday,' and I thought: 'What shall I do?' So I had this idea about a whirlwind. I was tempted to approach it seriously. I mean, it could have been done on a completely serious level. . .and I nearly did it that way. I don't know whether it would have been any better, because the wind thing isn't that interesting. So I thought I'd use all the cliches there are, the standard narrative conventions, and I sat down at the typewriter and I wrote the book. Six thousand words a day, which is quite a lot. I kept it up, and when I went back to the office I had the manuscript of a novel, which Carnell sold. He was then acting as my agent. I think I got 300—*then*, though of course it's gone on and on. But that was enough and immediately I sat down and started writing *The Drowned World*. I wrote it in a short version first, and then expanded that to a novel."[4]

Set in London in the twenty-first century, *The Drowned World* takes place in a time when fluctuations in solar radiation caused the melting of the earth's ice-caps and the rising of the seas. "Certainly my own earliest memories are of Shanghai during the annual long summer of floods, when the streets of the city were two or three feet deep in a brown silt-laden water, and where the surrounding countryside, in the center of the flood-table of the Yangtze, was an almost continuous mirror of drowned paddy fields and irrigation canals stirring sluggishly in the hot sunlight. On reflection it seems to me that the image of an immense half-submerged city overgrown by tropical vegetation, which forms the centerpiece of *The Drowned World*, is in some way a fusion of my childhood memories of Shanghai and those of my last 10 years in London."[6]

Ballard described *The Drowned World* and his next two novels, *The Drought* and *The Crystal World*, as tales of psychological fulfillment. "All three novels are nominally set in the future, but they're not predictions. They could have been set in the past or the present. The message they contain isn't dependent on the time setting as such. What was valid yesterday is valid today, and will be valid tomorrow. My psychological landscapes are the sort that might be perceived by people during major mental crises—not literally of course, but they represent similar disturbed states of mind."[7]

The Crystal World, the story of a leprosy doctor who arrives in West Africa, began as a short story entitled "The Illuminated Man." The story was then expanded to a serial and later became the novel. The strength of the novel lies more in its visual imagery than in its plot. The powerful descriptions are often termed hallucinatory. ". . .A lot of people who knew I had taken acid thought I had written the book on the basis of that. I wrote the book in '64, I think, but I didn't take LSD until 1967 or '68. The curious thing is that the book does convincingly, in my experience, describe what an LSD vision is like; particularly the effects of light and time. And it made me feel that in fact the imagination can reach those visions that LSD elicits—you can systematically assemble into the critical imagination those visions that LSD elicits biochemically. You can reach the base of the brain, as it were; the unaided imagination is equal to any task put upon it. One doesn't need the stimulus of powerful drugs to trick the imagination, if you persist enough. . . ."[8]

Often referring to himself as an "imaginative writer," Ballard places great stock in both his own and his reader's imagination. He sees science fiction as an appropriate link to the imagination, and has rejected traditional modes of the genre to make room for a science fiction of the present day. "I think science fiction should turn its back on space, on inter-stellar travel, extraterrestrial life forms, galactic wars and the overlap of these ideas that spreads across the margins of nine-tenths of magazine sf. . . .

"I've often wondered why sf shows so little of the experimental enthusiasm which has characterized painting, music and the cinema during the last four or five decades, particularly as these have become whole-heartedly speculative, more and more concerned with the creation of new states of mind, new levels of awareness, constructing fresh symbols and languages where the old cease to be valid. Similarly, I think science fiction must jettison its present narrative forms and plots. Most of these are far too explicit to express any subtle interplay of character and theme. Devices such as time travel and telepathy, for example, save the writer the trouble of describing the inter-relationships of time and space indirectly. And by a curious paradox they prevent him from using his imagination at all. . . .

Ballard with his children: Bea, Fay and Jimmy in 1964.

"The biggest developments of the immediate future will take place, not on the Moon or Mars, but on Earth, and it is *inner* space, not outer, that needs to be explored."[9]

"The subject matter of SF is the subject matter of everyday life; the gleam on refrigerator cabinets, the contours of a wife's or husband's thighs passing the newsreel images on a color TV set, the conjunction of musculature and chromium artifact within an automobile interior, the unique postures of passengers on an airport escalator—all in all, close to the world of the Pop painters and sculptors, Paolozzi, Hamilton, Warhol, Wesselmann, Ruscha, among others. The great advantage of SF is that it can add one unique ingredient to this hot mix—words."[10]

1964. Mary Ballard died of pneumonia. "I was a single parent as well as a full-time author. If I had not been a full-time writer I couldn't have brought up my children. Somebody else would have had to do it for me, at least during the daylight hours. Conversely, if I'd had to go out to work I couldn't conceivably have written. If I had not been here with the children all day long I would not have been able to write....I drove them to and from school. I did everything. We had an integrated, rich, family life blazing away twenty-four hours a day!"[2]

"I think Orwell, at one phase in his life, looked after his son by himself—admittedly, only for something like a year or two—I was able to. It wasn't as difficult actually, as it may seem. I was tremendously involved with my children and they were a great source of strength. I genuinely like children—I like being with children, other people's as well as my own. As for finding the time to write: they went to school. Even when they were here I was able to work with three children playing in the next room. That never bothered me. I drank a great deal of alcohol, to be honest. I used to have my first large whisky at nine in the morning....That helped."[9]

Ballard's later novels marked significant departure from his earlier, less violent stories. Works like *The Atrocity Exhibition* (1970) conduct an exploration of violence in relation to technology and modern society. "*Atrocity Exhibition* is set in the present. Its landscape is compounded of an enormous number of fictions, the fragments of the dream machine that produces our life-style right now. I mean fictions like TV, radio, politics, the press, and advertising, that are all expressions of people's imaginative aims. Life is an enormous novel.

"My book deals with the irrational violence of modern society, the side of our culture that could be described as an atrocity exhibition. We're all spectators (often bored ones) at tragedies like Vietnam. Real violence, frequently live, as it occurs, becomes part of a huge entertainments industry. The Romans used to gather round arenas to have orgasms over vaudeville shows of real murder and rape. We laugh dismissively at the fairly common SF plot of a future in which the public enjoys similar amusements, only via their TV sets. Yet what is a lot of today's live and recorded news and documentary material if not a variation on just this theme?

"*Atrocity Exhibition* portrays a doctor who's had a mental break-down. He has been shocked and numbed....To make sense of the modern world he wants to immerse himself in its most destructive elements. He creates a series of psycho-dramas that produce grim paradoxes. They suggest things like the possibility of Vietnam having some good effects, or of car crashes serving a useful purpose within the societal organism, or of a purgative aspect to the assassination of public figures, just as there used to be in ancient ritual murders, and always has been in the death of charismatic figures like Christ."[7]

"...I see [*The Atrocity Exhibition*] as a metaphor for life in the 1970s. It says everything about depraved public tastes being created by the overlay of public violence and private fantasy. Just as sex is the key to the Freudian world, so violence is the key to the external world of fantasy that we inhabit. There's this clash between what we all believe to be true, such as that violence is bad in all its forms, and the actual truth, which is that violence may well serve beneficial roles—much as we might deplore it."[11]

1973. *Crash*, the story of a man perversely obsessed with automobile accidents was published. "When I set out to write *Crash* I wanted to write a book in which there was nowhere to hide. I wanted the reader, once I'd got him inside the book, never to lose sight of the subject-matter. It would have been very easy to write a conventional book about car-crashes, in which it was quite clear that the author was on the side of sanity, justice, and against injuring small children, deaths on the road, bad driving, etc. What could be easier. I chose to completely accept the demands of the subject-matter, which was to provoke the reader by saying that these car-crashes are good for you, you thoroughly enjoy them, they make your sex-life richer, they represent part of the marriage between sex, the human organism and technology. I say all these things in order to provoke the reader and also to test him. There may be truth in some of these sentiments, disagreeable though they are to consider. Nobody likes that: they'll think 'God, the man's mad'—but any other way of writing that book would have been a cop-out I think."[9]

In an attempt to further bridge the distance between fiction and reality, Ballard named the protagonist of *Crash* after himself. "...That was part of the whole business of being absolutely as honest as I could. I wanted a first-person narrator to stand between Vaughan [the anti-hero] and the reader—the honest thing to do was to give him my own name. Although the superficial landscapes of the book's 'Ballard' and my life are different, there are many correspondences. Also, I wanted to anchor the book more in reality; I had a named film-star, who never speaks, of course. The constant striving of the writer over the last few years has been to lower the threshold of fiction in what he writes, to reduce the amount of fiction. One's seen this in the theatre over the last fifteen years, and in the visual arts it started a long, long time ago. The move is to reduce the fictional elements in whatever one is doing and get it to overlap reality as much as possible, rather than keep it separate from reality and ordinary experience."[4]

Believing that contemporary culture continues to fuse fiction with reality, Ballard has relied on his own personal obsessions in hopes of reaching relevant truths. "I couldn't take an objective view—I don't think one *can* be objective about the modern landscape. Since, say, 1945, where the specters of mass psychosis stride across the communications landscape (the specters of the atom bomb, of the Nazi death camps, of the misuse of science, and so forth) I think that one no longer can be objective. One can no longer *pretend* to an objective view of the world, one *must* be subjective. One's entering into a paradoxical realm where the psychopath is the only person who can imagine—who is capable of imagining—*sanity*, of conceiving what sanity is....I think one needs to take a wholly subjective viewpoint, and press one's obsessions almost to the point of madness, if not *to* the point of madness.

"I deliberately exploit my own obsessions. In fact, as a writer all I do is to follow my own obsessions, whatever they may be—car crashes or the media landscape or Ronald Reagan or what have you. I deliberately use my obsessions because I can *trust* my obsessions, or rather, I can *rely* on them— they're strong enough to provide the main imaginative impetus."[11]

In his science fiction, often considered to be a visionary exploration of the future of man, television and the media are implicit in Ballard's predictions. "What I hope the computer and TV revolution will bring about is a scientific information channel where you can just press a button and....I want a much higher throughput of information in my life than I can get my hands on—I want to know everything about *everything!*...I want to know *exact details, hard information* about *everything.* I want to know what Charles Manson has for breakfast—*everything!* It's very difficult to get this information....

"The paradox is, we've got this enormous communications flow—satellite communications, cable TV systems, video and all the rest of it, and yet less and less of it is actually being *transmitted.* All you're getting is the umpteenth return of 'The Omen' or 'Jaws.' I'd rather watch a really *hard* documentary about sharks, lasting two hours, then watch 'Jaws.' It'd be much more interesting. With no holds barred—not the sort of documentary prepared for a convention of marine biologists. It's *that* that one wants to get hold of, but—access is a problem...."[8]

Ballard has a well-regulated writing schedule. "Two hours in the late morning, two in the early afternoon, followed by a walk along the river to think over the next day. Then at six, scotch and soda, and oblivion.

"Every day, five days a week. Longhand now, it's less tiring than a typewriter....I do a first draft in longhand, then do a very careful longhand revision of the text, then type out the final manuscript. I used to type first and revise in longhand, but I find that modern fiber-tip pens are less effort than a typewriter. Perhaps I ought to try a seventeenth-century quill. I rewrite a great deal, so the word processor sounds like my dream. My neighbor is a BBC videotape editor and he offered to lend me his, but apart from the eye-aching glimmer, I found that the editing functions are terribly laborious. I'm told that already one can see the difference between fiction composed on the word processor and that on the typewriter. The word processor lends itself to a text that has great polish and clarity on a sentence-by-sentence and paragraph level, but has haywire overall chapter-by-chapter construction, because it's almost impossible to rifle through and do a quick scan of, say, twenty pages. Or so they say."[12]

"This chap next door has only got 35,000 characters (about 7,000 words) on his computer, which creates problems. He was pounding his desk, saying, 'I need *more memory!*' So terribly funny—I thought, 'What's going on here? This world is mad!'"[6]

"I set myself a target, about a thousand words a day—unless I just stare out of the window, which I do a lot of anyway. I generally work from a synopsis, about a page when I'm writing a short story, longer for a novel. Unless for me the thing works as a story, unless it works on the anecdotal level, unless I feel it holds the attention of the reader, I don't bother with it. It's got to work on that level, as a pure piece of story-telling. If it does I begin writing. I spend a tremendous amount of time, I won't say doing research, but just soaking myself in the mental landscapes, particularly of a novel. Most of the time I'm thinking about what I'm writing, or hope to write. Particularly with *Crash* and *The Atrocity Exhibition.* I was carrying these for something like six or seven years. I was totally immersed mentally in this very overcharged world. It was an exciting time, but very tiring."[4]

"...I generally begin a book with a large sheaf of notes, covering everything from the main themes to the details of the setting, the principal characters, et cetera, all of which I've daily speculated upon in the months before I begin....I've never had a creative block, touch wood. I've never had any problems stimulating my imagination. Rather the opposite. At times, I need to damp it down.

"I've never aborted or abandoned anything, perhaps because everything I've written has been well-prepared in my mind. I write the complete first draft before returning to the beginning, though of course I'm working from a fairly detailed synopsis, so I'm sure of my overall structure. I then do a fair amount of cutting of superfluous phrases, occasionally of paragraphs of pages....

"Writing a novel is one of those modern rites of passage, I think, that lead us from an innocent world of contentment, drunkenness, and good humor, to a state of chronic edginess and the perpetual scanning of bank statements. By the eighteenth book, one has a sense of having bricked oneself into a niche, a roosting place for other people's pigeons. I wouldn't recommend it.

"A lifetime's experience urges me to utter a warning cry: do anything else, take someone's golden retriever for a walk, run away with a saxophone player. Perhaps what's wrong with being a writer is that one can't even say 'good luck'—luck plays no part in the writing of a novel. No happy accidents as with the paint pot or chisel.

I don't think you can say anything, really. I've always wanted to juggle and ride a unicycle, but I dare say if I ever asked the advice of an acrobat he would say, 'All you do is get on and start pedaling....'"[12]

The book which finally launched him to star status in the United States was *Empire of the Sun,* a semi-autobiographical story about his childhood in the Shanghai prison camp. Adding to the success of the novel was the film version directed by Steven Spielberg. "In order to write the book I knew I would have to re-expose my adolescent self to all those dangers. While children are adolescent, they need to be protected."[13]

"I waited 40 years (to write *Empire of the Sun*). Maybe I needed to wait that long; it took me 20 years to forget, and 20 years to remember it all again."[14]

"The background and settings are as accurate as memory permits. Only the foreground events are invented."[13]

"This wasn't a subject for fantasy. It was too extraordinary and bizarre. I didn't need to fantasticate it further.

"...I set up to debunk an awful lot of cliches that spring up about human behavior in a war. Most people don't behave heroically. The opportunities for heroism don't exist.

"Take 2,000 people from Los Angeles and starve them for three years, and how would you expect them to behave? A few do heroic things: there are a few malingerers, but most people sink into a torpor."[14]

Ballard was pleased with the film and with his cameo appearance as John Bull.

1987. *The Day of Creation* was published. Set in Central Africa, it is the story of Dr. Mallory who travels to a small town to run a clinic, only to find that guerilla and paramilitary activity have left him without patients. Dr. Mallory sets out to bring water to the region to make the area bloom again. "In many ways one could almost say my new book is the story of the young Jim in *Empire* and what happens to him when he grows up."[15]

Ballard has remained in Shepperton for almost thirty years. With his children grown and away from home, he chooses to spend much of his time alone. "...I look at myself here, living in a small suburban house with a rusting car outside and a television set that doesn't work—the only thing that works here is the corkscrew—and I feel it

Christian Bale starred in the 1987 Warner Bros.' film, "Empire of the Sun."

must be a joke. What am I doing here? I must be a character in a Pinter play, or in a sitcom that has got out of the control of its scriptwriters.

"If my 18-year-old self came here he would take one look, do a fast U-turn, and disappear in a cloud of dust. He'd be appalled. But does that mean I regret my life? No. I think since 18 I've had a very interesting and, on the whole, happy life. And yet I would change it all. Apart from my three children, the happy years of my marriage, and some of the books I've written, I would change everything.

"I wish I'd done so many more things than I have done. I wish I'd flown a man-powered aircraft across the Atlantic, or assassinated a tyrant. I wish I'd had more children. I wish I'd had more dogs, I particularly wish I'd had more wives. Wives are an excellent thing and one should have as many of them as possible. That is certainly one piece of advice I would give to any 18-year-old: get married on leaving school and remain married at all times, whatever happens. If a marriage comes to an end, remarry as quickly as possible. Married people are much happier, there's been endless scientific research to confirm that. I had 10 very happy years until my wife's tragic death and I think I made her

happy, too. The only reason I haven't married again is that no one has accepted my proposals.

"What's so sad about most people's lives, my own included, is that they accept the roles that are given to them: they become a stockbroker or a secretary or a science fiction writer and just carry on with it, rather like a minor actor in 'Crossroads.' I think I might have had a much more interesting life if I'd never been a writer. I put too much of myself into my writing, but there we are."[5]

Footnote Sources:

[1] Charles Platt, *Dream Makers: Science Fiction and Fantasy Writers at Work*, Ungar, 1987.
[2] David Pringle, "From Shanghai to Shepperton," *Foundation*, February, 1982.
[3] John Wakeman, editor, *World Authors 1950-1970*, H. W. Wilson, 1975.
[4] James Goddard and D. Pringle, "An Interview with J. G. Ballard," *J. G. Ballard: The First Twenty Years*, Bran's Head Books, 1976.
[5] J. G. Ballard, "Things I Wish I'd Known at Eighteen," *Sunday Express*, December 27, 1981.
[6] J. G. Ballard, "Time, Memory, and Inner Space," *Woman Journalist*, spring, 1963.
[7] Douglas Reed, "Ballard at Home," *Books and Bookmen*, April, 1971.

[8] Andrea Juno and V. Vale, "Interview with JGB,"*Re/Search,* number 8/9, 1984.

[9] D. Pringle, *J. G. Ballard: A Primary and Secondary Bibliography,* G. K. Hall, 1984.

[10] J. G. Ballard, "Fictions of Every Kind," *Books and Bookmen,* February, 1971.

[11] Brendan Hennesy, "J. G. Ballard," *Transatlantic Review,* spring, 1971.

[12] Thomas Frick, "The Art of Fiction LXXXV: J. G. Ballard," *Paris Review,* winter, 1984.

[13] David Lehman and Donna Foote, "Prisoner in Shanghai," *Newsweek,* January 28, 1985.

[14] John H. Richardson, "'Empire of the Sun' Shines in Ballard's Eyes," *Chicago Tribune,* December 21, 1987.

[15] James Fallon, "J. G. Ballard: Slowly But Surely," *Women's Wear Daily,* April 1, 1988.

■ For More Information See

Periodicals:

New Worlds, November, 1959, May, 1962 (p. 117ff), July, 1966, October, 1966.

Library Journal, July, 1970.

Books and Bookmen, July, 1970 (p. 6ff), March, 1976 (p. 59ff), July, 1976 (p. 74ff), March, 1977 (p. 59ff), September, 1984 (p. 12ff).

Times Literary Supplement, July 9, 1970 (p. 741), November 30, 1973 (p. 1466), April 26, 1974, December 5, 1975, January 14, 1977 (p. 26), November 30, 1979, June 12, 1981, September 24, 1982 (p. 1031), September 14, 1984.

Penthouse, September, 1970, April, 1979.

Studio International, October, 1971 (p. 136ff).

New Yorker, July 29, 1972 (p. 33ff).

Evergreen Review, spring, 1973 (p. 137ff).

Writer, June, 1973.

Foundation, July, 1973 (p. 48ff), November, 1975.

Algol, November, 1973 (p. 36ff).

Magazine Litteraire, April, 1974.

New Statesman, May 10, 1974 (p. 669), November 15, 1975, December 3, 1976 (p. 812ff), September 17, 1982 (p. 21).

Listener, December 11, 1975.

Science-Fiction Studies, July, 1976 (p. 150ff), November, 1985 (p. 297ff).

Magazine of Fantasy and Science Fiction, September, 1976.

New York Times, May 11, 1977, October 13, 1984.

Search and Destroy, number 10, 1978.

Washington Post Book World, November 25, 1979, October 28, 1984.

Thrust: Science Fiction in Review, winter, 1980.

Vector, January, 1980.

Heavy Metal, April, 1982 (p. 38ff).

Essays in Literature, fall, 1983 (p. 209ff).

Times (London), September 20, 1984.

American Film, October, 1987 (p. 57ff).

Rolling Stone, November 19, 1987 (p. 76ff).

Daily News, December 6, 1987 (p. 3).

San Francisco Chronicle, December 11, 1987 (p. E-3), December 25, 1987 (p. E-13).

Publishers Weekly, March 11, 1988 (p. 82ff).

Current Biography, May, 1988 (p. 10ff).

Books:

Langdon James, editor, *The New Science Fiction,* Hutchinson, 1969.

Robert Silverberg, editor, *The Mirror of Infinity,* Harper, 1970.

Lois Ross and Stephen Ross, *The Shattered Ring: Science Fiction and the Quest for Meaning,* John Knox Press, 1970.

J. G. Ballard, *Crash,* J. Cape, 1970, Farrar, Straus, 1973.

J. G. Ballard, *The Atrocity Exhibition,* J. Cape, 1970, published as *Love and Napalm: Export U.S.A.,* Grove Press, 1972.

Thomas D. Clareson, editor, *SF: The Other Side of Realism—Essays on Modern Fantasy and Science Fiction,* Bowling Green University Popular Press, 1971.

Brian Aldiss and Harry Harrison, editors, *SF Horizons,* two volumes, Arno Press, 1975.

Contemporary Literary Criticism, Gale, Volume III, 1975, Volume VI, 1976, Volume XIV, 1980, Volume XXXVI, 1986.

Contemporary Fiction in America and England, 1950-1970, Gale, 1976.

T. D. Clareson, editor, *Voices for the Future: Essays on Major Science Fiction Writers,* Bowling Green University, Volume I, 1976, Volume II, 1979.

R. Silverberg, editor, *Galactic Dreamers: Science Fiction as Visionary Literature,* Random House, 1977.

D. Pringle, *Earth Is the Alien Planet: J. G. Ballard's Four-Dimensional Nightmare,* Borgo Press, 1979.

T. D. Clareson, editor, *Voices for the Future: Essays on Major Science Fiction Writers,* Volume II, Bowling Green University Popular Press, 1979.

Keith Neilson, editor, *Survey of Science Fiction Literature,* Salem Press, 1979.

Charles Platt, *Dream Makers: The Uncommon People Who Write Science Fiction,* Berkley Publishing, 1980.

Mark Rose, *Alien Encounters: Anatomy of Science Fiction,* Harvard University Press, 1981.

Alan Burns and Charles Sugnet, editors, *The Imagination on Trial: British and American Writers Discuss Their Working Methods,* Allison & Busby, 1981.

Dictionary of Literary Biography, Volume XIV: *British Novelists since 1960,* Gale, 1983.

Colin Greenland, *The Entropy Exhibition: Michael Moorcock and the British 'New Wave' in Science Fiction,* Routledge & Kegan Paul, 1983.

Contemporary Authors New Revision Series, Volume 15, Gale, 1985.

Peter Brigg, *J. G. Ballard,* Starmont House, 1985.

D. Pringle, *Science Fiction: The 100 Best Novels,* Carroll & Graf, 1985.

Short Story Criticism, Volume 1, Gale, 1988.

Judy Blume

B orn February 12, 1938, in Elizabeth, N.J.; daughter of Rudolph (a dentist) and Esther (Rosenfeld) Sussman; married John M. Blume (an attorney), August 15, 1959 (divorced, 1975); married Thomas Kitchens (a physicist), 1976 (divorced, 1979); married George Cooper (a law professor and writer), June 6, 1987; children: (first marriage) Randy Lee (daughter), Lawrence Andrew; stepchildren: Amanda. *Education:* New York University, B.A., 1960. *Religion:* Jewish. *Residence:* New York, N.Y. *Agent:* Harold Ober Associates, Inc., 40 East 49th St., New York, N.Y. 10017.

■ Career

Writer of juvenile and adult fiction. Founder of Kids Fund, 1981. *Member:* Society of Children's Book Writers (board member), Authors Guild (board member), PEN, National Coalition Against Censorship (board member), Planned Parenthood Advocates (board member).

■ Awards, Honors

Are You There God? It's Me, Margaret was selected one of *New York Times* Outstanding Books of the Year, 1970, and *Blubber,* 1974; Golden Archer Award from the Department of Library Science, University of Wisconsin-Oshkosh, 1974, for *Are You There God? It's Me, Margaret.*

Nene Award from the Hawaii Association of School Librarians and the Hawaii Library Association, 1975, for *Are You There God? It's Me, Margaret,* and 1982, for *Superfudge;* Charlie May Simon Children's Book Award from the Arkansas Elementary School Council, and Sequoyah Children's Book Award from the Oklahoma Library Association, both 1975, Massachusetts Children's Book Award from the Education Department of Salem (Mass.) State College, 1977 and 1983, and Rhode Island Library Association Award, 1978, all for *Tales of a Fourth Grade Nothing;* Pacific Northwest Young Reader's Choice Award from the Pacific Northwest Library Association, 1975, for *Tales of a Fourth Grade Nothing,* 1977, for *Blubber,* and 1983, for *Superfudge;* Young Hoosier Award from the Association for Indiana Media Educators, 1976, for *Are You There God? It's Me, Margaret,* and 1983, for *Superfudge.*

Arizona Young Readers Award from the Arizona State University and the University of Arizona-Tempe, 1977, for *Tales of a Fourth Grade Nothing,* and 1983, for *Superfudge;* Georgia Childrens Book Award from the College of Education of the University of Georgia, 1977, for *Tales of a Fourth Grade Nothing,* and 1983, for *Superfudge;* South Carolina Children's Book Award from the South Carolina Association of School Librarians, 1977, for *Tales of a Fourth Grade Nothing,* and 1978, for *Otherwise Known as Sheila the Great;* Children's

Choice Election Award from the Harris County (Tex.) Public Library, third place, 1978, first place, 1979-1987; North Dakota Children's Choice from the Children's Round Table of the North Dakota Library Association, 1979, for *Are You There God? It's Me, Margaret*, 1980, for *Tales of a Fourth Grade Nothing*, 1982, for *Superfudge*, and 1983, for *Blubber*.

West Australian Young Readers' Book Award from the Library Association of Australia, 1980, for *Tales of a Fourth Grade Nothing*, and 1982, for *Superfudge*; Texas Bluebonnet List, 1980, Children's Choice from the International Reading Association and the Children's Book Council, 1981, Colorado Children's Book Award from the University of Colorado, Texas Bluebonnet Award from the Texas Association of School Librarians and the Children's Round Table, Tennessee Children's Choice Book Award from the Tennessee Library Association, and Utah Children's Book Award from the Children's Literature Association of Utah, all 1982, Garden State Children's Book Award from the New Jersey Library Association, and Golden Sower Award from the Nebraska Library Association, both 1983, Land of Enchantment Book Award from the New Mexico Library Association and the New Mexico State International Reading Association, 1984, and Sunshine State Young Reader's Award from the Florida Association for Media in Education, 1985, all for *Superfudge*; Michigan Young Reader's Award from the Michigan Council of Teachers, 1980, for *Freckle Juice*, and 1981, for *Superfudge*; Great Stone Face Award from the New Hampshire Library Association, 1980, for *Are You There God? It's Me, Margaret*, 1981, for *Tales of a Fourth Grade Nothing*, and 1981, 1983, 1985, for *Superfudge*.

United States Army in Europe Kinderbuch Award, 1981, for *Tales of a Fourth Grade Nothing*, and 1982, for *Superfudge*; Today's Woman Award from Council of Cerebral Palsy Auxiliary, Nassau County, 1981; CRABery Award, 1981, for *Superfudge*, and 1982, for *Tiger Eyes*; *School Library Journal's* Best Books for Young Adults, 1981, selected one of New York Public Library's Books for the Teen Age, 1982, Dorothy Canfield Fisher Children's Book Award from the Vermont Department of Libraries and the Vermont Congress of Parents and Teachers, and finalist, American Book Award from the Association of American Publishers, both 1983, and Blue Spruce Colorado Young Adult Book Award from the Colorado Library Association, 1985, all for *Tiger Eyes*.

Outstanding Mother Award, 1982; Buckeye Children's Book Award from the State Library of Ohio, 1982, for *Superfudge*, and 1983, for *Tiger Eyes*; Sue Hefly Book Award from the Louisiana Association of School Libraries, 1982, for *Superfudge*, and Honor Book, 1982, for *Starring Sally J. Freedman as Herself*; Eleanor Roosevelt Humanitarian Award, 1983; Iowa Children's Choice Award from the Iowa Educational Media Association, 1983, for *Superfudge*, and 1985, for *Tiger Eyes*; Young Reader Medal from the California Reading Association, 1983, for *Superfudge*, and *Tiger Eyes*; Jeremiah Ludington Memorial Award from the Educational Paperback Association, 1983, for "a significant contribution to children's and paperback books"; Milner Award from the Friends of the Atlanta Public Library, 1983, for children's favorite living author; *The Pain and the Great One* was selected one of Child Study Association of America's Children's Books of the Year, 1985, *Then Again, Maybe I Won't*, *Superfudge*, and *It's Not the End of the World*, 1987; *Letters to Judy* was selected one of American Library Association's Best Books for Young Audlts, 1986; Children's Choice Award from the Mesa Public Library (Ariz.), 1987, for *Superfudge*.

■ Writings

The One in the Middle Is the Green Kangaroo (illustrated by Lois Axeman), Reilly & Lee, 1969, new edition (illustrated by Amy Aitken), Bradbury, 1981.
Iggie's House, Bradbury, 1970.
Are You There God? It's Me, Margaret (ALA Notable Book), Bradbury, 1970.
Then Again, Maybe I Won't, Bradbury, 1971.
Freckle Juice (illustrated by Sonia O. Lisker), Four Winds, 1971.
Tales of a Fourth Grade Nothing (illustrated by Roy Doty), Dutton, 1972.
It's Not the End of the World, Bradbury, 1972.
Otherwise Known as Sheila the Great, Dutton, 1972.
Deenie, Bradbury, 1973.
Blubber, Bradbury, 1974.
Forever..., Bradbury, 1975.
Starring Sally J. Freedman as Herself, Bradbury, 1977.
Superfudge (sequel to *Tales of a Fourth Grade Nothing*), Dutton, 1980.
The Judy Blume Diary: The Place to Put Your Own Feelings, Dell, 1981.
Tiger Eyes, Bradbury, 1981.

The Pain and the Great One (illustrated by Irene Trivas), Bradbury, 1984.
Letters to Judy: What Your Kids Wish They Could Tell You, Putnam, 1986.
(Contributor) *Once Upon a Time...*, Putnam, 1986.
Just as Long as We're Together, Orchard Books, 1987.
The Judy Blume Memory Book, Dell, 1988.

Adult:

Wifey, Putnam, 1978.
Smart Women, Putnam, 1984.

Blume's books have been translated into fourteen languages, including German, Scandinavian, French, Dutch, Hebrew, Spanish, and Japanese. Contributor to *Free to Be...You and Me*, for the *Ms.* Foundation, 1974.

■ Adaptations

Films:

"Forever," CBS-TV, February 6, 1978.
"Otherwise Known as Sheila the Great" (25-minute color 16mm film or videocassette), written by Judy Blume, directed by son, Lawrence Blume, produced by J. Blume and L. Blume, Barr Films, January, 1989.

Cassettes:

"Wifey," Audio Book, 1979.
"Freckle Juice" (includes teacher's guide), Listening Library, 1982.
"Blubber" (includes teacher's guide), Listening Library, 1983.
"The One in the Middle Is the Green Kangaroo" (includes teacher's guide), Listening Library, 1983.
"Deenie" (includes teacher's guide), Listening Library, 1983.
"Are You There, God? It's Me, Margaret," Listening Library, 1985.
"It's Not the End of the World," Listening Library, 1985.
"The Pain and the Great One," Listening Library, 1985.
"Iggie's House," G. K. Hall, 1986.

Filmstrip With Cassette And Teacher's Guide:

"Blubber," Pied Piper, 1984.
"Freckle Juice," Pied Piper, 1984.
"Superfudge," Pied Piper, 1984.

Paperback cover for Blume's multi-award-winning novel.

■ Work In Progress

"A novel about Rachel Robinson, a character from *Just as Long as We're Together*."

■ Sidelights

Blume was born on February 12, 1938 in Elizabeth, New Jersey. An imaginative child, she grew up in a large brick house filled with books on Shelley Avenue, amusing herself by reading or listening to favorite radio programs with her older brother, David.

As one of the most popular authors of novels for and about young people, Blume believes that her ability to recall memories of her own youth is a key to her popularity. "My mother was shy and quiet and very well organized. She loved to read. When I came home from school in the afternoon she was

Jacket illustration by Ray Cruz.

always there, waiting, curled up in her favorite chair, reading a book. My father was outgoing, fun, vital, vibrant. I was very close to him. He was a dentist but spent as much time as he could in his basement shop, working with his hands. He built me a beautiful desk and was proud of the fact that there wasn't one nail in it. When I was small he would sit me up on the workbench, with a hammer and nails so that I would feel I was included, and sharing something special with him. My brother was four years older than me and very clever, very mechanically inclined. He built radios and other electronic equipment. He spent even more time than my father in the workshop. He was very shy and quiet, like my mother. I was an entertainer, more like my father.

"And yet, like most children, I sometimes felt alone. We didn't talk about problems in our family. We kept our feelings to ourselves. My father said that we could talk about anything, but somehow, we didn't. I hated family secrets.

"I had a lot of questions but I was afraid to ask them. I was curious about sex but no one gave me any information. My father gave me a brief, but totally confusing explanation about menstruation when I was nine, and then, at ten, tried to tell me where babies came from. Again, the explanation was confusing. Besides, I already knew, more or less.

"My friends at school had told me, but much of the information I picked up that way was incorrect. One of my friends had a book. Her parents had given it to her. She and I would read it again and again. But it wasn't as straightforward as we would have liked.

"I was a somewhat fearful child. Perhaps imaginative children always are. I was afraid of the dark, afraid of strange noises, afraid of dogs, afraid of my brother when he walked into my bedroom with a sheet over his head, calling 'Oooooooohhhhh....' and thunderstorms terrified me. They still do, although I am working on overcoming that fear.

"I liked radio shows, movies, and going to the children's room at the public library.... I would sit on the floor with the books, sniffing them. My favorite was *Madeline*. When I was older I liked the Betsy-Tacy books by Maud Hart Lovelace, and the Oz books, and Nancy Drew mysteries. But I didn't find real satisfaction in reading until I was older. Because there weren't any books with characters who felt the way I felt, who acted the way I did, with whom I could identify. I think I write the kinds of books I would have liked to read when I was young.

"I loved to dance. I took dancing lessons from the age of three. I still love to dance and, in the last few years, took tap dancing lessons every day."[1]

Blume was an "A" student throughout school. During summer vacations, she attended a girls' camp in Connecticut, Camp Kenwood. "I was a good girl, had to do well, please everyone. That was my role in life. Perhaps it was because my brother was a rebel. He kicked his kindergarten teacher in the stomach.

"Yet I had many anxieties which I don't think I was even aware of then. I worried a lot and I suffered from eczema and other allergic problems."[1]

Blume attended Battin High School (an all girls' public high school), where she sang in the chorus, studied modern dance, and worked on the school newspaper. "There was no such thing as sexism at our school. We ran the show. The paper, the yearbook, the clubs, the politics."[2]

Hardcover jacket from Blume's 1975 novel.

Blume with Leah Foster (the girl who portrays Sheila), between takes on the set of "Otherwise Known as Sheila the Great."

Graduating with high honors, Blume chose Boston University, but after losing her first year to illness, transferred to New York University. "That was the beginning of my troubles with illness. I had mononucleosis then and for the next ten years a variety of other illnesses.

"Now I'm convinced that many of my problems were caused by emotions. It bothers me that no doctor was ever wise enough to suggest that maybe some therapy or counselling was needed."[3]

In her sophomore year, she met and fell in love with John Blume, a young lawyer. They were married the following year, on August 15, 1959. "My father always encouraged me to get out there and catch the moon. But after a few years of marriage I began to think, *Well, kid, this is where it's at for you. He does whatever he wants, and you stay home and make sure everything runs smoothly.* As a young child, I had missed the traditional female brainwashing. Maybe that's why I was so resentful later on....As a young woman my mother prepared me for marriage and motherhood, but it wasn't enough. I needed something of my own. Perhaps it would have been different if I had

chosen a marriage partner who encouraged me to have a career."[3]

By the time Blume graduated from New York University she was expecting her first child. Her daughter, Randy Lee, was born in 1961, and two years later her son, Larry. She also began to write. "Then I received a brochure from New York University. It came from the School of Continuing Education and one of the courses offered was *Writing for Children and Teens.* I thought that must be an omen, so I registered for the course. I didn't believe (and I still don't) that anyone can teach you to write, but I needed professional encouragement and advice."[4] "One day a week I'd leave the kids at home and take a train into New York. I had supper alone at a restaurant and then I went to my class. It was the first time in my life I ever really felt independent."[5]

"What I did was write like crazy so I had something to turn in every week. My teacher was supportive and gave me the encouragement I needed. She would write me little notes telling me I would be published one day. Class time was divided between lectures on writing and the professional world of the writer. We learned how to prepare a manuscript for submission, how to write a covering letter, how to market our own work and whether or not it was essential to have an agent. Occasionally we had guest lecturers—editors, writers, agents. I began to feel like a professional writer. During this time I wrote several short stories and a version of what would become *The One in the Middle Is the Green Kangaroo*. When the course ended after one semester, I took it again. I didn't want to lose that professional contact."[4]

"It occurred to me that what I really loved most was to read novels. I thought it would be fun to try to write the kinds of books I wished I'd had to read when I was young. Books about real life. So I decided to try it."[6]

"During the second semester I wrote and handed in one chapter a week, as if it were homework. These chapters became a first draft of my first novel, *Iggie's House*. At the same time, after two and a half years of rejection slips, I sold a few stories to magazines: 'The Flying Munchgins' and 'The Ooh-Ooh-Aah-Aah Bird.' Toward the end of the semester a version of 'Iggie's House' was accepted for serialization by *Trailblazer* magazine. And then, in late spring, *The One in the Middle Is the Green Kangaroo* was accepted for publication as a picture book by Reilly & Lee. I was overjoyed, hysterical, unbelieving! I felt like such a celebrity."

"I subscribed to various writer's magazines and in one of them I read about a new publishing company—Bradbury Press— who were looking for realistic middle grade fiction. I sent them the manuscript of *Iggie's House*. They were interested enough to meet with me. I spent hours with Dick Jackson, the editor of Bradbury. He could not offer to publish *Iggie's House* as it was, but if I was willing to rewrite....I went home and began immediately. I wrote and rewrote for a month. Finally, when I had done all I thought I could do, I sent the manuscript back to them. Several weeks later they called with the great news that they were accepting the book for publication."

About these first two books she admitted: "They aren't very good but I learned something from them. The most important lesson is that until you pull it out of your own heart it doesn't really work. Actually, I'm glad I didn't have instant success. I think it was healthy for me—made me define my ideas."[3]

Iggie's House, was about a black family who moved into a white neighborhood. It addressed the issue of racial prejudice but was criticized by some for being too simplistic. "One review was very painful. If I hadn't already finished another book I don't know if I could have gone on." The book was *Are You There God? It's Me, Margaret*, written from her own experiences as a twelve-year-old. "In *Margaret* I just let go and wrote what I wanted to write and told the truth about what I'd felt."[2]

This novel had two themes: Margaret Simon's preoccupation with puberty and her search for a religious identity. Blume was praised for her accurate rendering of teenage dialogue and her humorous treatment of a universal female concern, although several critics considered her description of Margaret's bodily changes overly graphic. In a 1971 *Publishers Weekly* review, Lavinia Russ praised Blume: "With sensitivity and humor, Judy Blume has captured the joys, fears and uncertainty that surround a young girl approaching adolescence. Margaret Simon, almost 12, frequently chats with God, relaying all her problems concerning puberty and religion (she is the only child of non-religious, mixed-marriage parents). Margaret's story is any young girl's story, but when Judy Blume writes it there is an exception—it is directed toward each reader individually."

Despite controversy, *Are You There God? It's Me, Margaret* was named one of the Outstanding Children's Books of 1970 by the *New York Times*.

Asked why she usually writes about middle-class America, Blume replied: "Because that's what I know best. That's how I was raised and that's how I live, and I think we write best about the things we really do know about. I set most of my [early] books in suburban New Jersey because that is where I grew up. And I think that when it's very real to you it's very real to your readers. I need to get to know a place before I can set a book there. I need to be able to see it in my mind as I write, just as I must *hear*, the characters talking when I write dialogue. *Margaret* came right out of my own sixth-grade life, except for the family situation. Her feelings, her actions, her friends, her concerns—they were all the things we were interested in in sixth grade. I never wrote it thinking it would be widely accepted as the way kids think today, but apparently they do."[4]

"I think that a lot of adults in our society are uncomfortable with their own sexuality, and therefore their children's sexuality is a threat to them. That's not true of everyone of course. I have had some very negative responses from adults, but I've also had some very positive ones. The negative

From the movie "Otherwise Known as Sheila the Great." Script by Judy Blume, directed by Lawrence Blume, 1989.

responses don't usually come to me directly, but through a librarian or some other intermediary who tells me about some parent who comes in carrying a book of mine demanding that it be removed....

"[My editor and I] talk a lot over each book. When I finish a manuscript I send it in to [him] and he reads it, and hopefully he'll like it and want to publish it. One time many years ago when I was just starting out he really didn't like the book and asked me not to publish it. It's in the bottom of the closet now. I'm glad it's there. Anyway, after he's read the manuscript I go to his office or he comes to my house and we sit together all day and talk about it. First we talk about general ideas—the plot and the characters. I take notes furiously. Then we go over the book page by page, scribbling all over it. After that I take it home with me and work on it for several weeks at least. I usually wind up rewriting at least half. In *Are You There God? It's Me, Margaret* I think there were seventy-five pages that I totally rewrote. But a book grows. I love the rewriting—that's the best part of it. The hardest part is the first draft—that's torture, and always takes the longest. And when it's done I think I'll never be able to do it again, I'll never get another idea. The second draft is lots of fun, because it's all there, and all I have to do is get it right."[4]

Besides writing from personal experiences, many of Blume's ideas for her stories came from her own family and friends. Her book *Blubber* was based on an experience that daughter Randy related. She told Blume how her classmates teased a fat girl in her fifth grade until one day, when the teacher left the room, they locked the girl in a closet. "...The one thing I wanted desperately to do in *Blubber*, which is about fifth graders, was to let them use the language they really use. I think kids reach their peak of nastiness in fifth grade: they can be very cruel to each other. Up until that point I hadn't really tackled language as kids use it."[4]

Deenie, which was published in 1973, dealt with a thirteen-year-old who must cope with curvature of the spine. "I usually start with the character and a basic situation in mind. Everything else is a surprise to me. That's the fun of writing a novel. To find out what's going to happen. In the case of Deenie I'd met a fourteen-year-old with scoliosis. She and several other girls also being treated for scoliosis were very open about their feelings and experiences. Writing *Deenie* required research, for the first time. It was important to be medically accurate. (Since I wrote the book there are more options available for treating scoliosis.) So I went to the hospital and watched teens being molded and fitted for body-braces, because I wasn't able to visualize it on my own. My favorite scene in the book is the scene in the plaster-room. All of the dialogue in that scene is real. I sat in there with a pencil and a notebook (with the doctor's and the patient's permission) and wrote down everything that was said. The children were very frightened and said almost nothing. So I had to become Deenie, I had to try to put myself in her place and imagine what I might be thinking and feeling."[4]

Because *Deenie* discusses openly such controversial subjects as masturbation, the book was banned from elementary schools by the Gwinnett County (Georgia) Board of Education. But Blume says, "Kids have a right to read about themselves. They've been denied that right for a long time."[2]

"I think I write about sexuality because when I was young, that's what I most wanted to know about. I identify very strongly with kids. Twelve- and thirteen-year-olds feel things very intensely. They need to know about what they are feeling, and more than anything else, they want reassurance that their feelings are normal. Besides, sex is very interesting."[3]

The volume of Blume's fan mail seems to reinforce the fact that she is held in high regard by her readers. Hundreds of letters arrive each week not only praising her books but also asking her for advice or information.

Some adults take exception to her tendency to avoid resolving her fictional dilemmas, but the majority of critics believe that is to her credit. One such critic, Robert Lipsyte, wrote in *The Nation*: "Blume explores the feelings of children in a nonjudgmental way. The immediate resolution of a problem is never as important as what the protagonist. . .will learn about herself by confronting her life. The young reader gains from the emotional adventure story both by observing another youngster in a realistic situation and by finding a reference from which to start a discussion with a friend or parent or teacher. For many children, talking about a Blume story is a way to expose their own fears about menstruation or masturbation or death."

What seems more disturbing to some parents is Blume's treatment of mature issues and her use of frank language. "Menstruation, wet dreams, masturbation, all the things that are whispered about in real school halls are written about" in her books, maintained interviewer Sandy Rovner in the *Washington Post*. In a review of *Are You There God? It's Me, Margaret,* a critic for *Kirkus Reviews* wrote that "there's danger in the preoccupation with the physical signs of puberty, [for] the effect is to confirm common anxieties instead of allaying them." And writing in *Book Window* George W. Arthur remarked that while *Are You There God? It's Me, Margaret* is basically "very funny," he felt "there are features of the book which are overstressed and detract from the author's easy handling of most of the topics she covers."

Other adults defend Blume's choice of subject matter. For example, Natalie Babbitt asserted in the *New York Times Book Review*: "Some parents and librarians have come down hard on Judy Blume for the occasional vulgarities in her stories. Blume's vulgarities, however, exist in real life and are presented in her books with honesty and full acceptance." Remarked Julia Whedon in the *New York Times Book Review*: "Kids read her books with a blushing curiosity once reserved for certain words in the dictionary, parts of the Bible and naughty passages in Hemingway. They know they will find some frank discussion of prurient matters like breasts and menstruation. Some of her readers may also have read [Erica Jong's] *Fear of Flying,* yet they reread *Are You There God? It's Me, Margaret.*"

And then came *Forever,* which was one of the most heavily censored and hotly debated books to come along in 1975. It also was labelled an adult book for lack of a better category. "There was no category called Young Adult when I wrote that book. If I wrote it today, and if it were published, it would be published as a young adult novel, but it certainly was not an adult book. I intended it for readers, like my daughter, who was fourteen at the time I wrote it, but my publisher (a children's book publisher), didn't know what to do with it. So I think they put the adult label on to protect themselves, but they never checked with me first.

"I have always said, and I still say that I don't know what a young adult novel is. If you don't fit neatly into a category yourself and if you like to write up

Cover from the paperbound edition of Blume's multi-award-winning novel.

or down for every age group, somehow book stores don't know what to do with you. If a bookstore has a young adult section, *Tiger Eyes* should be there; if you've got a lot of Norma Klein books there, then *Forever* is there. As far as I can see, young adult books means there is a teenage protagonist but these books are read mainly by eleven and twelve-year-olds. I don't like labels and I don't like categories. I write for readers of all ages."[7]

In 1975 Blume's sixteen-year marriage ended. "To the outside world it seemed to be a nice marriage, but inside I was dying. When a marriage is about to dissolve the children want to know why and they have a right to know. They're thinking, 'How is this going to mess up my life?' 'What's going to happen to me!'"[3]

A year later, Blume married physicist Thomas Kitchens and moved to Santa Fe. Although her second marriage ended in divorce, she believes strongly in marriage. "But the partners have to be right for each other. That means not jumping in and hoping for the best. You can't hope that the

other person will turn out to be what you want. Loving means liking and respecting and caring—taking the time and trouble to learn about the other person. I am a loving person, and I love hard. When you do love that intensely, you open yourself up to be hurt, but it's worth it. You can't be afraid to make mistakes. You can't spend your life saying, 'What if.'"[2]

In 1977, Blume wrote *Starring Sally J. Freedman as Herself,* largely an autobiographical novel. "...[It's] primarily a warm and funny and loving family story. I laughed and I cried while writing it. But some of the reviews made me come close to throwing away my typewriter.

"My treatment of the Holocaust is absolutely accurate from the point of view of the child I was in the 1940s. At that time, we didn't really *know* anything. We hadn't seen the pictures, we couldn't even imagine the realities. So that kind of fantasy about the war is what went on in a lot of kids' heads, especially those who were Jewish and who heard their families talking about things they really didn't understand."[6]

"...*Starring Sally J. Freedman as Herself* [was] a very important book to me. I thought it was my best effort and that I had done something I hadn't done before."[3]

Wifey, her first adult novel, was published in 1978. "I wrote *Wifey* because I felt a great need for change. And to share another part of myself."[8]

"I will continue to write for both young people and adults. I need to explore experiences and feelings of all ages in my work."

"I'm very proud of *Wifey.* It was difficult, but it's something I very much wanted to do.

"I think I've written about the kind of person I was raised to be and could have remained if I had not met up with the good fortune of finding creative work."[3]

"There's been an awful lot made of the explicit sex in *Wifey,* and I find that peculiar. I see my book as being very realistic, and as ludicrous as many of Sandy's thoughts are, people have ludicrous thoughts, and I think we should write about it more—so that people who have these thoughts and fantasies can read it and say, 'ah-h-h-h, I'm not the only one. I'm so glad.'"[8]

Six years later, Blume wrote *Smart Women.* "I think *Wifey* is a funnier book, but I think I've created my best young characters in *Smart Women.* Although I don't seem to be able to write well about being in love; the kind of romantic sex that is sweet and loving. When I was about to begin it, I told my kids that I was going to write about teenagers who are real and are not necessarily terrific, but then, of course, I couldn't really do it because I did tend to identify with my characters. This book is for young adults as well as for adults.''[7]

In 1981 Blume departed from the world of early adolescence in favor of examining the effects of loss and senseless violence in *Tiger Eyes*. Some critics considered this novel her most accomplished work. Jean Fritz, in a 1981 *New York Times* book review, called it ''...A masterly novel, not to be dismissed as simply another treatment of death and violence. The reader empathizes not only with the heroine but with all the other characters. Each has his own story, and each lights up some aspect of the American scene. Take Uncle Walter, for instance, who spends his days making atom bombs yet misses the irony in his overprotection of Davey; he's so sensitive to danger that he won't let her take Driver's Ed. Surely *Tiger Eyes* belongs at the top of Judy Blume's list.''

''I used to think inspiration came from within—from the child I was. I felt I could write books like *Blubber* and *Tales of a Fourth Grade Nothing* because I could project myself back and *be* nine or ten years old. I could remember the smells, how things felt, what I thought. I think now that an awful lot of my inspiration came from living with kids....''[8]

''I feel...that I am finally grown up. Not completely, of course, because we never stop growing and changing. But for the first time I feel in control of my own life. And that is a very good feeling.''

''I look at my son and daughter who are in their twenties, and am grateful for all we can share. I'm so glad I had them when I did.''[3]

Blume felt so strongly about the lack of communication between young people and their parents (''from their letters telling me'') that she established the Kids Fund in 1981. Financed with royalties from her *The Judy Blume Diary: The Place to Put Your Own Feelings*, *Letters to Judy: What Your Kids Wish They Could Tell You*, and *The Judy Blume Memory Book*, as well as other projects, the fund contributes approximately $40,000 a year to various non-profit organizations set up to help young people.

About her book, *Letters to Judy*, a collection of letters from her readers (tied together with autobiographical anecdotes), Blume commented: ''...It's

been an emotional and draining kind of writing, unlike anything I've ever done.

''I get thousands of letters every year. For the most part these kids all have quite similar things to say: they feel alone in the world, they don't feel they can talk to anyone—particularly their parents—and they wish their parents would listen more carefully to them when they do talk. They don't seem to have anyone they can open up to, so they write to me, and I think this is therapeutic for them.''[8]

''I organized the letters into categories by subject matter. They reminded me of my own childhood, and my life as a parent. A lot of things I hadn't thought about for years rose to the surface. One thing that has become very clear to me, and I've told this to my kids, and to my mother, is that it's all so circular. You vow when you are a kid that you'll never behave the way your parents do and then you have your own children and they vow they will be very different from you when they become parents. It's a circular affair.

''I felt a moral obligation not to profit from the sale of this book so all my royalties were donated to the Kids Fund to support programs that deal with the issues the kids most often write about.

''This book has been such an emotional project that I need to write something more lighthearted now. I need to laugh and to help my readers laugh, although I never know what will happen when I sit down to begin again.''[9]

Blume lives in New York City now, following seven years in New Mexico. ''Randy and Larry graduated from college and went out into the world. Randy is a pilot for a commercial airline company and Larry is a filmmaker. Amanda, my stepdaughter, is a college student. I discovered that even without children in the house I can *still* write books from a young person's point of view. Of course the thousands of letters from my young readers keep me in touch with their concerns but the child within is still very close to the surface.

''My husband is writing full time now so my life as a writer isn't as lonely as it once was. In fact my life is so exciting these days that finding the time to sit down and start a new book gets more and more difficult. For six months my son and I collaborated on a movie. It was my first and his third film. We decided to do an adaptation of my book *Otherwise Known as Sheila the Great*. I wrote the script, Larry directed and we produced together. It was a *real experience* for me. I haven't decided yet if I will do it again but I'm very proud of our effort. I loved seeing Sheila come to life on the screen. Now I am determined to get back to book writing. A novel about Rachel Robinson, a character from *Just as Long as We're Together* is my next project and after that...well, I do have an idea for another adult novel but...."

"I get many letters from young people who write or think they want to write. Anybody who thinks he or she wants to write is usually already writing. Writing is a need that comes from within. You do it because you have to do it. I know one or two people who say they love writing, but for most of us, it's a love/hate relationship.

"I tell young people who want to write, don't let anyone discourage you or tell you that you don't have any talent because that can be a person who can't see beyond what's on his or her desk."[7]

When young writers ask Blume for constructive criticism, she doesn't comment. "Even if I read it, I don't make comments because I'm not a writing teacher and I'm not an editor. You just have to set up some rules for yourself. I am just not able to do that."[7]

Footnote Sources:

1 Judy Blume, *Parents*, May, 1979. Amended by Judy Blume.
2 Betsy Lee, *Judy Blume's Story*, Dillon Press, 1981.
3 Diana Gleasner, *Breakthrough: Women in Writing*, Walker, 1980. Amended by Judy Blume.
4 Justin Wintle and Emma Fisher, *The Pied Pipers*, Paddington Press, 1975. Amended by Judy Blume.
5 Joyce Maynard, "Coming of Age with Judy Blume," *New York Times Magazine*, December 3, 1978. Amended by Judy Blume.
6 Sybil Steinberg, "Judy Blume," *Publishers Weekly*, April 17, 1978. Amended by Judy Blume.
7 Based on an interview by Marguerite Feitlowitz for *Authors and Artists of Books for Young Adults.*
8 Kathleen Hinton-Braaten, "Writing for Kids without Kidding Around," *Christian Science Monitor*, May 14, 1979. Amended by Judy Blume.
9 *Publishers Weekly*, January 3, 1986. Amended by Judy Blume.

■ For More Information See

Library Journal, December 15, 1969, January 16, 1970.
School Library Journal, December, 1970 (p. 42), May, 1974 (p. 53), November, 1974 (p. 54), May, 1977 (p. 59), January, 1981, January, 1985 (p. 7), March, 1986 (p. 93), November, 1986 (p. 30).
Publishers Weekly, January 11, 1971 (p. 62), October 8, 1973 (p. 97).
Booklist, January 15, 1971 (p. 418), July 1, 1972 (p. 941), January 1, 1975 (p. 459).
Boston Globe, January 30, 1971.
Bulletin of the Center for Children's Books, February, 1971 (p. 87), July/August, 1972 (p. 166), April, 1974 (p. 123), May, 1975 (p. 142), March, 1976 (p. 106).
English Journal, September, 1972 (p. 936), March, 1976 (p.90).
Jacqueline Weiss, "Judy Blume" (videocassette), Profiles in Literature, Temple University, 1973.
Psychology Today, September, 1974 (p. 134).
Elementary English, September, 1974.
Children's Literature Review, Volume II, Gale, 1976.
Times Literary Supplement, October 1, 1976 (p. 1238), April 7, 1978 (p. 383), November 23, 1979.
New Statesman, November 5, 1976 (p. 644), November 14, 1980.
Junior Bookshelf, February, 1977 (p. 49).
Washington Post Book World, August 14, 1977 (p. F4), October 8, 1978, November 9, 1980, September 13, 1981 (p. 9), February 12, 1984.
Doris de Montreville and Elizabeth D. Crawford, editors, *Fourth Book of Junior Authors*, H. W. Wilson, 1978.

Despite controversy and censorship by several school boards, Blume's books continue in popularity.

Top of the News, spring, 1978.
Book Window, summer, 1978 (p. 22).
Chicago Tribune, September 24, 1978.
Lion and the Unicorn, fall, 1978 (p 72).
People Weekly, October 16, 1978 (p. 47), August 16, 1982, March 19, 1984.
D. L. Kirkpatrick, *Twentieth-Century Children's Writers,* St. Martin's, 1978, 2nd edition, 1983.
Writer's Digest, February, 1979, January 1, 1980 (p. 18).
Detroit News Magazine, February 4, 1979.
Contemporary Literary Criticism, Gale, Volume XII, 1980, Volume XXX, 1984.
Commentary, March, 1980 (p. 65).
Commonweal, July 4, 1980.
Los Angeles Times Book Review, October 5, 1980.
Washington Post, November 3, 1981.
Nation, November 21, 1981 (p. 551).
Newsweek, December 7, 1981.
New York Times Magazine, August 23, 1982.

Time, August 23, 1982.
Teen, October, 1982.
New York Times, October 3, 1982.
New Yorker, December 5, 1983 (p. 191).
Detroit Free Press, February 26, 1984.
Book and Author, March/April, 1984.
"A Split Decision: Judy Blume in Peoria," *Newsletter on Intellectual Freedom,* March, 1985.
Alleen Pace Nilsen and Kenneth Donelson, *Literature for Today's Young Adults,* 2nd edition, Scott, Foresman, 1985.
Daniel Paisner, "Dear Judy: My Mother Doesn't Understand Me...," *Daily News,* May 13, 1986.
"A Conversation with Judy Blume," *Woman's Day,* June 28, 1988.
Children's Literature in Education, Volume 19, number 4, 1988.

Collections:

Kerlan Collection at the University of Minnesota.

John Boorman

Born January 18, 1933, in Shepperton, England; son of George and Ivy (Chapman) Boorman; married Christel Kruse, 1957; children: Telsche, Katrine, Daisy, Charley. *Education:* Attended Salesian College. *Home:* The Glebe, Annamoe, Wicklow, Ireland. *Agent:* Edgar Gross, International Business Management, 1801 Century Park East, Suite 1132, Los Angeles, Calif. 90067.

■ Career

Director, producer, and screenwriter. British Broadcasting Corp. (BBC) Radio, London, England, broadcaster and film critic, 1950-54; Independent Television News (ITN), London, film editor, 1955-58; Southern Television, Southampton, England, director and producer of documentary films, 1958-60; BBC Television West, Bristol, England, head of documentaries, 1960-64; independent film producer, director, and screenwriter, 1965—. Operated dry cleaning business as a youth; director of television documentaries, including "Citizen '63" (series), BBC-TV, 1963; "The Newcomers" (six-part series), BBC-TV, 1964. Chairman of National Film Studios of Ireland, 1975-85; governor, British Film Institute, 1985—; founder, *Day by Day* (television maga-

zine). *Military service:* British Army, 1951-53, served in National Service; became sergeant.

■ Awards, Honors

Voted best director at Cannes Film Festival, 1970, for "Leo the Last"; Chevalier de l'Ordre des Arts et Letters, 1985; Award for Best Director, and Award for Best Screenplay, both from the New York Film Critics Circle, both 1987, and Academy Award Nomination for Best Director, 1988, all for "Hope and Glory."

■ Writings

(With Bill Stair) *The Legend of Zardoz* (novelization of Boorman's screenplay "Zardoz"), New American Library, 1974.
The Emerald Forest Diary, Farrar, Straus, 1985.

Screenplays:

(With Alex Jacobs; also director) "Point Blank," Metro-Goldwyn-Mayer, 1967.
(Also director) "Leo the Last," United Artists, 1969.
(Also director and producer) "Zardoz," Twentieth Century-Fox, 1973.
(With Rospo Pallenberg; also director and producer) "Excalibur," Orion, 1981.
(Also director and producer) "The Emerald Forest," Embassy Films, 1985.
(Also director and producer) *Hope and Glory*, Columbia, 1987, Faber, 1987.

Director of Motion Pictures:

"Catch Us If You Can," Bruton Film
    Productions, 1965 (released in the United
    States as "Having a Wild Weekend," Warner
    Bros., 1965).
"Hell in the Pacific," Selmur Pictures, 1968.
(Also producer) "Deliverance," Warner Bros.,
    1972.
(Also co-producer) "Exorcist II: The Heretic,"
    Warner Bros., 1976.

Producer:

(With Claude Nedjar) "Dream On," Columbia,
    1984.

Free-lance film critic for newspapers and magazines, including *Manchester Guardian,* 1950-54.

■ Adaptations

"Excalibur," CBS-TV, July 16, 1985.

■ Sidelights

Regarded as one of Britain's most imaginative and
technically brilliant film directors, John Boorman
works in such diverse genres as supernatural
horror, social comedy, science fiction, action-ad-
venture, and the thriller. Often his films examine
the interplay of social myth and individual instinct.
"My films are nearly always involved with an
individual contending with society in some way.
Society seems to be a hostile thing. And also
there's the relationship between the individual and
nature, natural forces. For me, the world, the
planet, is a very dangerous place to be. We're
lulled into a sense of security by our daily lives, but
we are hurtling through space at a tremendous
speed on a very unstable piece of ground."[1]

January 18, 1933. "I was born at No. 50 Rosehill
Avenue, Carshalton [England], a monotonous street
of those semidetached suburban houses of which
four million were built between the wars."[2]

"I grew up surrounded by women and I'm glad I
did. The exclusive company of men, in school and
the army, always struck me as quite terrifying. I
think the way in which women have moderated,
even changed, my outlook on things is exactly what
I need.

"I was never too close to my father, though we
were both mad about sport. But I was always a
disappointment to him as he believed I ought to
have played cricket or football for England. Nothing I've accomplished since ever compensated for

the fact that I didn't turn out to be a sports
champion."[3]

One of Boorman's first memories was of the war: "I
was nearly evacuated from England when hostili-
ties broke out. There was a plan to send children to
Canada and Australia, and my mother had an aunt
in Australia. My sister and I were supposed to
leave, except that we got no further than the
railway station. There were thousands of weeping
children there. My mother simply couldn't bear the
thought and led us both back home."[3]

1940. The Battle of Britain made a lasting impression on seven-year-old Boorman. "For a child it
was a wonderful experience. I'd stand in the
garden of our house watching Messerschmitts and
Spitfires battling it out in the sky. Our school was
bombed over and over again and, half-way through
a lesson, we'd have to scurry to the shelters. We sat
on two rows of wooden benches inside a bunker
and we'd recite the multiplication tables from
inside our gas masks. At night my friends and I
would go looting through the bombed houses—
what treasures we unearthed!"[3]

"After an air raid people would feel an exhilaration
about being alive, having survived it. There was a
determination to live life to the full. This led to a
lot of reckless behavior, but there was a comradeship that was very strong, a sense of having
charmed lives. You could aim bombs at us but you
couldn't hit us! And there was a very personal
aspect for me, as well. When our house burned
down...it gave me a sense that possessions and
material things were very doubtful and temporary.
I had an aversion, after that, to owning things."[4]

Boorman's formal education ended at age sixteen.
At eighteen he was writing about the cinema—
reviews and interviews—for the BBC radio, thus
fulfilling one of his earliest ambitions: "[to] work in
the cinema. Having grown up in Shepperton, I
would often visit the studios, which were quite
close to our home. I remember saying to myself, as
I watched a scene being shot, 'What a good idea to
reorganize the world!' "[3]

1956. Worked as a trainee in a cutting room under
a film editor named Brian Lewis. "He really taught
me everything I know though he almost despaired
of me, since I wasn't very gifted to start with.

"I would write every day, but I stopped shortly
after entering television, as I felt that they were
two antithetical occupations, two diametrically
opposed ways of thinking."[3]

Sebastian Rice-Edwards starred in the 1987 movie "Hope and Glory" which Boorman wrote and directed.

While working as a film editor for ITN (Independent Television News), Boorman married Christel Kruse.

1958. Produced, edited and occasionally directed a weekly current events program called "Southern Affairs," then moved to another series entitled "Day by Day." "I knew what I wanted—in particular, I was eager to get away from a purely journalistic approach. I was a director of documentaries and knew how to get out into the street and see the world. I'd choose colleagues who had a personal vision of things....It was very exciting, very stimulating; we portrayed reality such as it appeared to the group of young people that we were."[3]

1959. Daughter Telsche was born. A year later Katrine.

1963. Initiated a series called "Citizen 63". "I was trying to extend the boundaries of documentary by dramatizing the material as much as possible in order to come up with some deeper truths about the country and its inhabitants."[3]

"People talked about [the documentaries] being the first *cinema-verite* films made in England. They weren't. They were rather stylised and carefully made programmes in which people consciously played themselves."[5]

"There were aspects of my subjects' personalities that I found awkward to deal with in documentary terms. And I realized that it could be dangerous for them to suffer this kind of exposure. You have the choice between a general, and therefore superficial, approach or a more personal and truthful point of view—but, in the latter case, you usually end up by hurting someone."[3]

1964. Boorman made a film entitled "The Quarry" about a sculptor for an arts series. "I was impatient to tackle a fictional subject and probably overloaded 'The Quarry' with too many themes and ideas.

"I was trying to interpret the Arthurian legend in order to understand the spell it had cast over me.

And it was Jung, whom I was reading at the time, who enabled me to comprehend the power and importance of myth. I'd been watching the world change around me and trying to interpret it, and Jung helped me see things more clearly."[3]

1965. Directed first feature film, "Catch Us If You Can." "It was a chance to make a film. I'd gained a reputation in TV, and so the producer David Deutsch asked me to do it. I'd been working on a film script anyway, about the legend of the Grail. But this wasn't to be it. Nobody will ever let you make your first film, you know. Deutsch had the money because it was going to be a film with a pop group, the Dave Clark Five, in it—that's what was wanted."[6]

"We locked ourselves in a room and did it in three weeks. [Peter Nichols, the screenwriter] made a wonderful dedication on the screenplay: 'To Valium, without which this script would not have been written.'

"'Catch Us If You Can' was a journey through England that involved a series of encounters with aspects of the society that the protagonists—the man and the woman—were trying to escape: The phony advertising world."[7]

"The film's narrative is that of a journey. But making a film is in itself a journey, an exploration. I never know where it's going to take me; and if I did know, I couldn't bear the idea of all the effort in store for me. What motivates me is the process of discovery. When I begin shooting, I don't really know what my theme will be. Once the film is completed, I look back on it all, everything that's happened to me becomes clearer, and it's then that I understand the true meaning of what I've achieved.

"I think that what I really hoped to convey was my conflict with English society and the class system I'd encountered at the BBC. On the one hand, I'm tremendously fond of many aspects of my native country; on the other hand, I feel as though I'm almost a foreigner in it."[3]

1966. Completed one last documentary on D.W. Griffith entitled "The Great Director." "Griffith conceived film to be the universal language promised in the Bible and a harbinger of the Millennium. It must, after all, have seemed a new, universal language. For me, Griffith was the very source of the cinema."[3]

Twins, Daisy and Charley, were born.

1967. Directed "Point Blank," his first film for an American company. Starring Lee Marvin, it "was about a fractured man who was broken and distorted by what had happened to him. It was done in the form of a gangster picture, but you could say it was really about a nervous breakdown, and the way a man in that state sees the world and the people around him. What's terrific about doing a genre picture is that those things can be externalized and dramatized."[8]

Many of the exotic Los Angeles locations in "Point Blank" were found "by getting lost when I first went there. I stumbled into them. I think it's rather important to lose one's way."[9]

"The system — Metro-Goldwyn-Mayer — intervened and said: 'Tell us what you want and we'll find it for you. If you want a house, we have a department for that sort of thing and it'll find it for you. A photographer will take photographs of ten different houses and you can choose the one you want.' That was of no use to me at all, since I couldn't know what I was looking for until I saw and recognized it, and I certainly couldn't describe it in advance. That's why they seldom use their own natural environment.

"The shoot was both difficult and exhilarating, since we were inventing new ideas all the time. For instance, I wasn't happy with the Carroll O'Connor scene in the luxury house, as it was in the script. I discussed the problem with Carroll, who's a very inventive actor, and we conceived the scene where he turns to Marvin and tells him that he's a crook and that he can't pay him....When MGM executives viewed the rushes, they were furious, as that scene hadn't been in the script. The next day in the afternoon, my assistant, Al Jennings, came looking for me on the set: the studio wanted us to stop filming, they thought I'd gone crazy and wanted me to see a psychiatrist!

"I'd decided to make each scene monochromatic. One day, the head of the art department called a meeting to let it be known that he declined all responsibility for the film. He announced: 'There's one scene in a green office with green furniture and seven men wearing green suits, green ties and green shoes. I haven't seen anything like it since "The Wizard of Oz." The film will be unreleasable and we're going to make fools of ourselves.' I was amazed he did not understand how film emulsion reacts to tones of the same colour, or the relation between reality and the cinema."[3]

"I was very arrogant at the time, not the humble man you see in front of you today. I was familiar

Lee Marvin starred in the 1968 Boorman-directed film "Hell in the Pacific."

with the theories of the New Wave and the French writing on the cinema. I felt as Godard said, that you could use the audience's familiarity with this kind of story to *not* show certain scenes. It was enough to give them an image and their knowledge would trigger the rest. That's what I set out to do. I wanted to make very bold, very stark, powerful compositions—to express coldness."[7]

"Film is a living language and it is constantly changing, its grammar constantly altering. It's very strange, for instance, that when I made 'Point Blank' a lot of audiences found it incomprehensible. Then, two years later, it was revived and nobody even asked questions. Nobody. The techniques had been absorbed in that time; audiences are able to absorb techniques very quickly. One problem is that the language of film moves at a frightening rate and audiences can catch up and you can find yourself lagging behind. They're ahead of you, particularly children; they've been watching television and can tell you exactly what is going to happen next."[10]

1968. Boorman directed "Hell in the Pacific," starring Lee Marvin and Toshiro Mifune. It was about two men, an American and a Japanese, stranded together on a tiny island during World War II. "The racial aspect...interested me—the relationship between a Japanese and an American, both of them from a military background but separated by so many factors.

"We found this island of Palau, which looks both inhospitable and strangely beautiful—the coconut palms had been destroyed by disease, the rocks had been eroded and the jungle is overgrown and descends right to the beach. The shoot was very difficult because we were miles from anywhere. An ancient DC4 would land every two weeks, which meant that I couldn't fire anyone as we'd have had him on our hands for a fortnight!

"I wanted to go much further in the scenes where they (Marvin and Mifune) retrogress, where they begin to behave like animals, but I couldn't persuade Mifune to do it. He believed he was defending the honour of Japan. Just as Marvin wanted to

1 Ned Beatty, Herbert 'Cowboy' Coward, Burt Reynolds and Jon Voight (*Deliverance*).
2 Jon Voight (*Deliverance*).
3 Burt Reynolds, Billy McKinney and Ned Beatty (*Deliverance*).

Burt Reynolds, Billy McKinney, Ronny Cox, Jon Voight and Ned Beatty (*Deliverance*).

From *John Boorman* by Michel Ciment.

relive his personal experience, so Mifune wanted to relive the war—with Japan on the winning side. He refused to do anything that might have been considered uncouth; he was determined to retain his honour. In a way, he was right: in that kind of situation, the Japanese are probably far more resourceful and far less likely to go to pieces. That apart, like all Japanese, he has a highly developed sense of honour and no sense of honesty.

"What I was able to achieve was very limited; and the film became simpler and simpler to the point where, by the end, I began to wonder if it really existed—in particular because I had shot the whole film with an Ariflex camera and without sound. When I edited it, I found myself with two hours of silent cinema, two hours of foliage!

"People of different cultures and races can only live together, can only coexist if they have a common objective. In this case, for example, building a raft. Once the job is finished, there's no further contact. It's pointless to say 'people ought to try and get on with each other or they ought to understand the need for mutual respect.' What they need is a shared objective."[3]

1970. Boorman won the Directors Award at the Cannes Film Festival for "Leo the Last." *Time* magazine called the screenplay "a combination of Harold Pinter and introductory civics."[11] The London *Observer* called it "witty, surreal, inexplicit and surely the Best British Film since the War."[11]

"It was the first time I had the opportunity of working without outside interference. United Artists left me completely free and I was very relaxed. I was able to experiment, to go my own way, to reject all kinds of limitations, to blend allegory with social comment and psychological study, and see whether I could switch from one to the other and still follow a narrative line."[3]

"It was about a man who was very sophisticated, over-bred, cut off from his feelings, inhibited; and he's looking out into the black world of the street, at people who had come from Africa and were vibrant with life. He's looking out into a past of vitality and vigour, and he becomes intrigued with it. But, because of his inhibitions and breeding, he can't make any contact with it. He even says so, where he says 'I love mankind, but only from a distance. The closer I get, the further away I feel'"[8]

"So much of the talk we hear about the brotherhood of man is really pretty empty. In 'Leo the Last' I was making the point that people get very worried about a war in Vietnam or somewhere while the old lady next door is dying of starvation."[6]

"The cinema would appear to be going in two directions: in the one case, *cinema-verite*; in the other, abstraction or allegory. Both are valid, but I'm more attracted to the latter."[3]

"At that stage, I was exploring other cinematic possibilities. The sound track was a stylized collage of voices and music and quotations, and this again reflected the mind of the man, Leo, played by Marcello Mastroianni. Except in one or two countries like France it was a total failure, which dissapointed me at the time. But, looking back at it, I could see it was too difficult, really."[8]

"In many respects, I find it the most interesting of all my films, even if it's not perhaps completely successful. I like the way it juggles several balls in the air without dropping any of them, and also the idea of variations on a theme with different interlocking and mutually influential elements."[3]

"Leo the Last" was edited in Ireland, which began Boorman's abiding love for that country. "It got to something inside me, it seemed to correspond to my own inner landscape. Ireland escaped the Industrial Revolution, it has a medieval side to it, the countryside hasn't been spoiled and pillaged as it has elsewhere. We were looking for a holiday cottage. One Saturday, my wife visited a former presbytery in the Wicklow area, which was to be auctioned off the following Monday. We went to the auction out of curiosity and returned from it owners of the house. For me, it's become a sanctuary from the ravages of the film industry; and, when I'm not filming that's where I'm to be found. Ireland is, in fact, an extremely dangerous drug. It's hard to live without it."[3]

1972. Boorman directed "Deliverance," based on the novel by James Dickey, starring Burt Reynolds, John Voight and Ned Beatty. "The big trauma that America's going through at the moment, as big as anything that happened there, is the realization that America is finite, that it's resources are limited. It's like being told that God is dead. And this is also what 'Deliverance' is about. There's this wild river which is going to be damned and going to disappear, all in order to provide more air conditioners and sprinklers on the lawns of Suburbia. It's not something that the critics have touched on much, but in talking to people it seems to have hit them hard."[11]

Charley Boorman (center) starred in the 1985 Embassy Films' release "The Emerald Forest."

"I think that urban life, that the separation it represents from natural forces—such as various ways of exercising the body and dealing with certain failures—is finally very dangerous and destructive.

"Now I don't know what the answer is, but that is what 'Deliverance' is about. This man is an easygoing sort of guy with a nice wife and kids and job and he is drawn into this adventure where he must respond to an awful situation and forces arise in him that he didn't even know existed. And he learns when he responds that he actually, in a sense, enjoys it and that the man, the role he has been playing with pleasure all his life, has been some kind of fraud because it wasn't really the whole man at all, only part of him.

"What do you say about that? I mean, I hate violence. I'm for civilized, controlled behavior; however, human beings aren't really like that.

"We look upon (nature) as a kind of painting or a documentary film, as a beautiful thing to observe and to take some kind of pleasure in, and it's not that at all. It's partly that but it really has to do with animals eating each other and preying upon one another and that's the marvelous paradox."[10]

"This film is like a nightmare. Like a bad dream and that's good....Adults...love to be scared because it helps ease the pain of what might happen to you. Now if stories didn't exist and you didn't know in advance the possibilities of other things, you would die of shock at the first encounter with any kind of unpleasantness. They are a kind of preparation for whatever might happen. So are dreams and nightmares."[10]

The film was praised for its stunning beauty and seamless melding of allegory and adventure story. "Style has to do with the total environment of a film. I try to discover the landscape of the film. Every movie is a world, and you must try to make that world consistent.

"For 'Deliverance' I had to find a river that would externalize the story. Finally, when I found it, the color was wrong. It was too benign; I wanted something nightmarish. Then I remembered the early experiments with desaturation that John Huston did. So I went to Technicolor and asked them if we could reduce the color level. We devised a whole system to achieve it and afterwards I desaturated the whole film in the laboratory. It took three months to get that look."[12]

1973. The success of "Deliverance" helped Boorman get financing for his ambitious science-fiction epic, "Zardoz," starring Sean Connery. "I always seem to be attacking the same theme from a different perspective. Because in 'Zardoz' you have this notion, again, of the primitive and the over-civilized coming into conflict, and the sense that, once that process of over-breeding and over-development takes place, some kind of juice is lost."[8]

"What I have postulated in 'Zardoz' is that the Machine has stopped, but by the time it stopped non-machine technology was able to take over permitting an elite to survive, the Vortex community. The Vortex is really like a spaceship, self-sustaining, self-regenerating, independent of the cruder machines on which we now depend but, of course, it is by definition sterile."[13]

"The film is about today, about contemporary society, and all the characters, the Brutals, the Exterminators, the Eternals, the Renegades and the Apathetics, are aspects of the human condition—they're all tendencies that we have in each of us, taken to extreme forms."[14]

"Before shooting started, I was very much struck by a newspaper article I read. It dealt with an experiment conducted on a colony of mice. Living in ideal conditions, they began to behave like the inhabitants of the Vortex such as I had imagined them. Some of them became apathetic; the females began to dominate the males who stopped working and played all day long. Others became agressive—genuine Renegades. And they ceased to reproduce. The article helped me in my discussions with the cast of the film, who were very concerned about their roles, about the sexuality of the characters—for it wasn't an easy film for the actors.

"For this film, which is more dreamlike than the others, I felt curiously freer in my use of colors, much more at ease in its fantastic universe....I felt liberated, I could let my imagination roam freely, whereas in those films of mine which take place in perfectly familiar settings, I have to simplify, I have to eliminate the kind of inessential detail that gets in the way."[3]

"For Zed's struggle with the crystal we built a mirror-maze, about seventy feet across, with mirrors everywhere set at angles to each other; and the interesting thing is that everybody who worked inside it found it unbearable after a while. We all went mad.

"I wanted a diffused, rather gentle light....so we actually used smoke throughout the film....I think the effect for an audience is to make it misty and

Daily Variety ad, March 24, 1988.

mysterious, a dream-like world you can't quite get hold of.''[14]

''If there is a moral in all this it's one for the futurologists themselves. Too often, it seems to me, they ignore the power of evolution itself to upset the equation. Some new mutation, something we encounter on the way, some unimagined factor can change the course ahead. Science and logic are not infallibles. Paradox has a poetry of its own. For example, my Vortex people have forgotten what death is like and, as a result, life has lost its vital savor. It is a psalm to paradox, a knee bent to the cruel majesty of nature.''[13]

1976. Directed ''The Heretic,'' a sequel to ''The Exorcist'' starring Richard Burton and Linda Blair. ''It's a fascinating story dealing with spiritual evolution and the need for God....I intend to investigate the characters and ideas more thoroughly and make the story more terrifying and profound. Some people felt that the first 'Exorcist' was destructive. I think of this one as a healing movie.''[15]

''We devoted a lot of thought and work to the film's visuals....Not only did we want the African forms and the New York settings to resemble each other, we also tried to evoke the theme of the locusts in other visual elements: in aeroplanes, for example, or the clinic, which is shaped like a hive with cells and glass partitions, further isolating characters who are already rather solitary creatures capable of communicating only with the synchronizer. In addition, the theme of the mirror finds its correlative in the skyscraper which reflects Louise Fletcher and Kitty Winn, fragmenting their personalities and their universe....What was important...was to 'elevate' reality, to give it another dimension in order to create a sort of correspondence.''[3]

Unfortunately, however, ''I made the fundamental error of making a film which didn't give audiences what they expected to get. They were looking for blood—and there wasn't any. So they demanded mine instead. They came into the arena and there was the Christian but no lions. The results were disastrous.''[7]

''I almost gave up, because having made 'Zardoz,' which was also a resounding failure in the States, I felt I didn't really know anymore how to connect with the audience. I didn't want to make the stuff the studios wanted to make—straightforward kinds of movies—and was ready to do something else. I was considering—not giving up filmmaking because that's what I've done all my life—but perhaps abandoning the attempt to connect with a mass audience and make smaller films."[7]

1981. Directed "Excalibur," which was a commercial success, attracting favorable reviews as well. "Fantasy was so much a part of my life. We had illustrated children's stories, and there was one about King Arthur that changed me forever. I still remember the thrill of this hand holding a sword in the lake. And armor: while we were making 'Excalibur,' I climbed into a suit of armor and felt—for the first time in my life—totally safe."[16]

"At the age of eighteen, I was very influenced by Powys, by those immense novels of his which are whole continents in themselves: you can get lost in them and can only read them when you're young and have the time! I was struck, at that period of my life, by the power of the Arthurian resonances, which I rediscovered in Eliot's *The Waste Land* and numerous other works. It was as though with almost everything I read, I'd find myself confronted with the Grail cycle."[3]

"I've used the iconography and also the structures—the 'quest' structures particularly—in the various films I've done. The whole legend kept impinging on me."[17]

With writer Rospo Pallenberg, Boorman adapted the stories of Arthur based on Thomas Mallory's *Le Morte d'Arthur*. "[It was] the first time anyone's dealt with the entire sweep of the King Arthur legend from his conception to his death. Such a project has been a personal obsession of mine for some time."[18]

"One of its main themes is the relationship between the old magic—the old religion—and the coming of Christianity. For me, the most important aspect of the story is the loss of magic to mankind. At one time, man had a magical relationship with the universe, a oneness with nature. We all feel the loss of that, and a yearning to regain what was lost. That's what the legend is about—the loss of nature, and the attempt to find it again through the Grail."[19]

"For a century now, we've been rushing headlong into the future; we've made a cult out of progress and we've forgotten our former selves, our former patterns of behaviour, whose origins can be traced to the Middle Ages. We no longer have any roots; and today, in particular, when we contemplate the possible destruction of our planet, there's a thirst, a nostalgia for the past, a desperate need to understand it. We are attracted to the legend of the Grail because it speaks to us of a period when nature was unsullied and man in harmony with it."[3]

"If there was ever an Arthur, he's cited in about the sixth century. But the date is the least important thing really. I think of the story, the history, as a myth. The film has to do with *mythical* truth; it has to do with man taking over the world on his own terms for the first time. So the first trap to avoid is to start worrying about when or whether Arthur existed."[19]

"The most significant thing about the Middle Ages—the Dark Ages, perhaps—is that it was an untamed world and man had a minor role in relation to the animal kingdom. It was the mystery of the forest. I tried to sketch this mystery by choosing locations that would suggest a pristine world, a world that hasn't been used up."[7]

The film was shot on location in Ireland, not far from where Boorman and his family lived. "There is a primal quality to this country, the landscape has a wildness. The light is almost magical though it does change a lot, which doesn't help. It is said you can have all four seasons in one day, and I've known it to happen more than once...."[20]

Shooting "Excalibur" was agony for Boorman. "First of all, I was fighting to hold the budget down. I had that nagging at me the whole time. We were falling behind schedule and trying to catch up....pushing people! Secondly, it was the worst summer for a hundred years, and you know how bad the summers are in Ireland, anyway, let alone that. We worked in mud and rain *the whole time!* Then the armour...and the horses...and the special effects. They were just the end.

"We got someone to catch the crows, we built them a cage with foliage in it, we kept them hungry, and then we put in the sheep's eye. And it took *three months!* It took us two months to get the crows trained. Then we had a big gale, the whole cage collapsed, they flew away and we had to start again. Eventually we got the scene, but some people don't like it very much.

"We made 250 suits in metal which I think is more armour than has been made since the Crusades."[5]

"We tried to transform the landscape, to make it magical. This time I didn't want to do it in a laboratory after the film was shot. So we did it by actually lighting exteriors. Now it's common to use light outside to bring up the faces or when the

The wedding of King Arthur and Guenevere in the movie "Excalibur." Starring Nigel Terry and Cherie Lunghi, it was released in 1981.

shadows are too deep. But what we did was to shoot outside and to use light as we would inside. For example, we used green light on green, which is a very painterly thing, to give a luminosity, an otherworldly look.

"I'm extremely aware of the relation between space and the tensions you can create by manipulating the actors and the camera. I never use a close-up unless it has been earned. To throw a character at the audience in close-up is intimidating and rude. An intimacy between character and audience has to be discovered first."[12]

"When you direct a film in which there's an abundance of elements—different sets and costumes, extras, horses, wigs, armour—it takes a considerable time to assemble and control them. Even if you have twenty weeks of shooting instead of the six or seven for a modestly budgeted film, ninety percent of your time is spent preparing shots, not directing the actors on camera. As a result, you have in fact far less time to shoot intimate scenes than in an inexpensive film, where the director is better able to focus his attention on that essential aspect of his work. That's why, in so many epics, the performances are often stiff, whereas the rest may be brilliantly filmed. The fact is, quite simply, that the director hasn't had time to concentrate on them. When you film a scene as simple as the one in the convent between Arthur and Guenevere, there are 150 crew members waiting for you to finish, which represents an enormous pressure on both your work and the actors. Everyone is conscious of how much time is passing and how much each minute is costing."[3]

"It is, I think, extremely lonely making films. Although, against that, I'd have to say that one of the pleasures is the kind of intense relationship you enter into with your collaborators, actors and principal technicians. . . .The whole process of film-making is, in many ways, a very satisfactory way of life—except for the director!

"I think what Merlin does in relationship to the story is very much like the relationship of a film director to a film, because he is trying to make magic. . .and he is also trying to. . .control events. Sometimes with sleight of hand, he invents characters which he develops. He casts them and they suddenly get away from him and do things that he didn't expect, which also happens to Merlin. I think any film-maker can identify with Merlin very well."[5]

Boorman has often used his family in his films. In "Excalibur," twenty-three-year-old Katrine played Igrayne, mother of Arthur. Daughter Telsche was production assistant. His wife, Christel, often helped with costumes, and he cast his thirteen-year-old son, Charley, as Arthur's bastard son, Mordred. "I needed a boy who was beautiful and evil and he was happy enough to buy himself a bicycle out of my insinuating my blood into the royal line!"[5]

1985. Boorman finished "The Emerald Forest," which was shot mainly on location deep in the rain forest of Brazil. "Undisturbed for one hundred million years, rampant, spiteful, tangled, a place of barbed thorns, spiked leaves, resins that burn, poisonous fruits, grasses that reach out to clutch you, huge ants that sting like snakes, caterpillars whose hair raises welts on your skin, tarantulas a foot across wearing 'mink coats'. (Rain) is not like any rain we know. When it comes, it is so dense there is no air to breathe. You inhale vapor. You are drowning in your own element.

"The rain forest is threatened by the construction of a huge dam, which will flood vast areas and stop the flow of the river. It forces two tribes away from their home, and brings tragedy to the white dam-builder and his son. What happens shows the difference between living in harmony with nature and exploiting it."[21]

"What appealed to me in the first place was that it's such a moving human story of a father looking for his son. It takes urban man into a relationship with nature that is primeval because the rain forest puts you back at the beginning of things."[22]

"I've come to feel—and this is what the film is saying really—that we have to find a better way to relate to the other species of animals and plants that we share the planet with. And I don't think it's just a matter of saying we've got to stop the invading concrete. It's more fundamental than that—it's a matter of respect. We've got to cease being so predatory and destructive, we've got to treat the other species as equals."[23]

While still in negotiation, Boorman pressed ahead with the film. One of his plans was to spend some time with a primitive tribe called the Xingu in the heart of the Brazilian rain forest. "I've always dealt with the loss of grace in my movies. These people live in a state of grace. In a magical harmony with their environment. It was a powerful thing to witness."[22]

"It was like stepping into a time machine and going back into the history of the human race and discovering what life was like at that stage in human development. They all live completely naked, men and women. They spend their lives trying to reach the spirits of the forest and the animals around them, and to coming into harmonious contact with them."[24]

When the filming was done, Boorman returned to England to edit "Emerald Forest." "Because of the way I make films—looping all the dialogue, building a soundtrack—the total effect is not apparent until all the tracks have been mixed and dubbed. This process. . .takes five weeks. Each of the fourteen reels of the film will have some fifty tracks—dialogue, effects, music—which will be mixed down to a six-track magnetic stereo, then to a four-track optical stereo and finally to a mono-optical track, for the various projection systems on which it must play."[25]

1987. Boorman's latest film "Hope and Glory" was released. "I started with this idea that at the age of seven you start to become conscious, you find yourself living in this family. It's like coming in halfway through a movie—all this stuff has been going on, there's all this history, you're trying to catch up with the story. Only during the course of the film does he gradually understand the family that he's a member of."[16]

"The movie is very much the story of my experiences—the story of the war from a child's point of view. To a six-year-old, they were very exciting times, terrific times; everything was turned upside down; fathers were away, there was very little supervision; bomb sites were our playgrounds and there was a wonderful ruined house that was our hideaway."[26]

"Interestingly enough, a lot of young people were shocked that one could suggest that war could have enormous levity and fun, because they're brainwashed to the idea that war is continuous horror. But people who were there said: 'That's how it was.'"[27]

"The film was inspired by my admiration, affection and indeed awe for my mother and her three sisters.

"My mother found herself still trapped in that suburban street, exiled from her beloved Thames and married to a man she was deeply fond of, but did not love. The friendly bombs fell and she gathered up her children and fled to Shepperton. I became immersed in the enchanted river world of my mother's childhood. I swam and fished and became skillful in handling all manner of boats, skiffs, punts, and canoes. My whole life was the river, in it, on it, by it, of it.

"That river has flowed in my mind and memory all my life, a comfort, an inspiration, and a consolation. The greatest satisfaction of this enterprise was to catch something of it on film."[2]

"I gave. . .[my family] the script to read. I wouldn't have made it had they disapproved. My older sister, who was the model for Dawn, collapsed and took to her bed for three days. All the things she'd been up to as a teen-ager that she'd thought she'd got away with had actually been observed by a small boy. Once she got over it, she was delighted with the whole thing."[27]

". . .We had a wondrous atmosphere, with the children working on it, my own kids, and with my mother and her sisters and my sisters coming all the time to visit and advise. We were in a state of grace, which you need to be in to make a movie."[17]

"What drove me to filmmaking is the opportunity to exercise control over events having been brought up in an atmosphere of total chaos."[28]

"I used to feel guilty about filmmaking. All the carpenters and the plasterers could be building people houses. Doing something useful. Now I'm resolved in that respect. Movies are terribly wasteful, but now I feel that that's the only thing to do with materials in our society. Take them all and turn them into light and shadow and dreams."[12]

What's in the future for John Boorman? "I've perhaps exhausted my interest in big epic storytelling and am moving toward simpler human stories. In the past I've hidden behind the epic canvas. You can lose yourself among those thousands of extras more easily than with a couple of characters in a room. Now. . .I think it's a matter of opening my heart."[4]

Footnote Sources:

[1] David Sterritt, "Ideas Should Burst 'Like Fireworks' from the Screen," *Christian Science Monitor*, March 8, 1974.

[2] John Boorman, "Behind the Scenes: War Games," *American Film*, October, 1987.

[3] Michel Ciment, *John Boorman*, Faber, 1985.

[4] David Sterritt, "'Hope and Glory': A Director's Memoir," *Christian Science Monitor*, October 16, 1987.

[5] Tony Crawley, "Mapping Out the Road to Camelot," *Film Illustrated*, September, 1987.

[6] Gordon Gow, "Playboy in a Monastery," *Films and Filming*, February, 1972.

[7] Dan Yakir, "The Sorcerer," *Film Comment*, May-June, 1981.

[8] Ray Comiskey, "Man, Myth, and Magic," *Cinema Papers*, November, 1985.

[9] David Elliott, "Boorman's 'The Emerald Forest' Represents Realization of a Vision," *New York Tribune*, July 8, 1985.

[10] Linda Strawn, "Conversation with John Boorman," *Action*, November-December, 1972.

[11] "'Zardoz' Biography," Press Release, Twentieth Century-Fox, n.d.

[12] James Verniere, "The Technology of Style," *Filmmakers Monthly*, June, 1981.

[13] "Final Production Notes/'Zardoz,'" Press Release, n.d.

[14] Phillip Strick, "Zardoz and John Boorman," *Sight and Sound*, spring, 1974.

[15] Omar Hendrix, "What Will 'Jaws' and 'Exorcist' Do for an Encore?" *New York Times*, June 27, 1976.

[16] David Edelstein, "The Once and Future King," *Village Voice*, October 27, 1987.

[17] Harlan Kennedy, "The World of King Arthur According to John Boorman," *American Film*, March, 1981.

[18] Stephen M. Silverman, "Boorman's View of King Arthur," *New York Post*, April 4, 1981.

[19] Bob Martin, "Excalibur," *Fangoria*, February, 1981.

[20] Michael Owen, "Here Come the Swords and Sorcerers," *New York Times*, February 22, 1981.

[21] "John Boorman: Touching the Past in 'The Emerald Forest'," Press Release, n.d.

[22] Desmond Ryan, "A Director Learns Grace in the Jungle," *Philadelphia Inquirer*, July 7, 1985.

[23] Graham Fuller, "Jungle John," *Stills*, November, 1985.

[24] Ken Ferguson, "Paradise Lost," *Photoplay*, January, 1986.

[25] J. Boorman, *The Emerald Forest Diary*, Farrar, Straus, 1985.

[26] Marilyn Beck, "War Isn't Hell to a Six-Year-Old," *Daily News*, May 27, 1987.

[27] "War Is Fun—Onscreen," *New York Times*, October 23, 1987.

[28] "Families Preoccupy Boorman," *Variety*, February 24, 1988.

■ **For More Information See**

Films and Filming, March 1968 (p. 25).
Sight and Sound, winter, 1969/70 (p. 20ff), autumn, 1985 (p. 292ff).
New York Times, August 20, 1972, (p. 9), February 25, 1974 (p. 19), June 30, 1985 (p. 15), February 13, 1988.

Variety, June 13, 1973, June 29, 1977 (p. 6), July 22, 1987 (p. 36), January 15, 1988 (p. 6).

Times (London), March 3, 1974 (p. 44).

Daily News (New York), August 25, 1976, (p. 26), July 4, 1977, (p. 12), April 5, 1981, (p. 1), July 6, 1985 (p. 11).

Pauline Kael, *Reeling,* Little, Brown, 1976.

Monthly Film Bulletin, October, 1977.

Village Voice, April 29-May 5, 1981 (p. 54).

Film Comment, May-June, 1981, November-December, 1985 (p. 47ff).

"'Excalibur,'" *Cinefantastique,* summer, 1981.

Starlog, March, 1982 (p. 19ff).

Washington Post, July 3, 1985.

New York Post, July 6, 1985 (p. 10).

"John Boorman Bet His Career on His Son, Charley—and Won," *People Weekly,* August 19, 1985.

"John Boorman in Conversation with Philip French" (videocassette), ICA Video, n.d.

American Film, October, 1986 (p. 53ff).

Joseph Campbell

Folklore Society, American Oriental Society, American Society for Study of Religion (vice-president, 1969-72; president, 1972-75), American Academy of Psychotherapists (honorary member), Century Club, New York Athletic Club.

■ Awards, Honors

Proudfit fellow, 1927-28, 1928-29; National Institute of Arts and Letters Award for his contributions to creative literature, 1949, for *The Hero with a Thousand Faces;* Grants-in-aid for editing Zimmer volumes, 1946-55; Distinguished Scholar Award from Hofstra University, 1973; D.H.L., Pratt Institute, 1976; Frederic G. Melcher Award from the Unitarian Universalist Association for contribution to religious liberalism, 1976, for *The Mythic Image;* Medal of Honor for Literature from the National Arts Club, 1985.

■ Writings

(With Henry Morton Robinson) *A Skeleton Key to "Finnegans Wake,"* Harcourt, 1944, reissued, Penguin, 1977.

The Hero with a Thousand Faces, Pantheon, 1949, revised edition, Princeton University Press, 1980.

The Masks of God, Viking, Volume I: *Primitive Mythology,* 1959, Volume II: *Oriental Mythology,* 1962, Volume III: *Occidental Mythology,* 1964, Volume IV: *Creative Mythology,* 1968.

Born March 26, 1904, in New York, N.Y.; died October 30 (one source says October 31), 1987, in Honolulu, Hawaii; son of Charles William (an importer and wholesaler) and Josephine (Lynch) Campbell; married Jean Erdman (a dancer and choreographer), 1938. *Education:* Attended Dartmouth College, 1921-22; Columbia University, A.B., 1925, M.A., 1927, additional graduate study, 1927-29; graduate study at University of Paris, 1927-28, and University of Munich, 1928-29. *Residence:* Hawaii. *Agent:* Timothy Seldes, 522 Fifth Ave., New York, N.Y. 10017.

■ Career

Author, editor, mythologist. Canterbury School, New Milford, Conn., teacher, 1932-33; Sarah Lawrence College, Bronxville, N.Y., member of literature department faculty, 1934-72. Lecturer, Foreign Service Institute, U.S. Department of State, 1956-73; trustee, Bollingen Foundation, 1960-69; president, Creative Film Foundation, New York, N.Y., 1953-63; member of board of directors, Society for the Arts, Religion and Contemporary Culture, beginning 1967; president of board of directors, Theater of the Open Eye, New York City, beginning 1973. *Member:* American

The Flight of the Wild Gander: Explorations in the Mythological Dimension (essays), Viking, 1969.

Myths to Live By, Viking, 1972.

The Mythic Image, Princeton University Press, 1974.

(With Richard Roberts) *Tarot Revelations,* Alchemy Books, 1980.

The Historical Atlas of World Mythology, Harper, Volume 1: *The Way of the Animal Powers,* 1983, Volume 2: *The Way of the Seeded Earth,* 1988.

The Inner Reaches of Outer Space: Metaphor as Myth and as Religion, Harper, 1985.

(With Bill Moyers) *The Power of Myth,* Doubleday, 1988.

Joseph Campbell (in Conversation with Michael Toms), *An Open Life,* Larson Publications, 1988.

Renewal Myths and Rites of the Primitive Hunters and Planters, Spring Publications, 1989.

Editor:

Heinrich Robert Zimmer, *Myths and Symbols in Indian Art and Civilization,* Pantheon, 1946, reissued, Princeton University Press, 1971.

H. R. Zimmer, *The King and the Corpse: Tales of the Soul's Conquest of Evil,* Pantheon, 1948, reissued, Princeton University Press, 1971.

H. R. Zimmer, *Philosophies of India,* Pantheon, 1951, reissued, Princeton University Press, 1969.

The Portable Arabian Nights, Viking, 1952.

H. R. Zimmer, *The Art of Indian Asia,* Pantheon, 1955, second edition (two volumes), Princeton University Press, 1960.

Myths, Dreams, and Religion, Dutton, 1970.

The Portable Jung, Viking, 1972.

(And author of introduction) Rato K. Losang, *My Life and Lives: The Story of a Tibetan Incarnation,* Dutton, 1977.

General editor of "Papers from the Eranos Yearbooks" series, including *Spirit and Nature,* 1954, *The Mysteries,* 1955, *Man and Time,* 1957, *Spiritual Disciplines,* 1960, *Man and Transformation,* 1964, and *The Mystic Vision,* 1969. General editor, "Myth and Man" series, Thames & Hudson, 1951-54. Member of editorial staff, *Dance Observer,* 1944-53.

Contributor:

(Author of introduction and commentary) Maud Oakes and Jeff King, *Where the Two Came to Their Father: A Navaho War Ceremonial,* Pantheon, 1943.

The Complete Grimm's Fairy Tales: Folkloristic Commentary, Pantheon, 1944, reissued, Random House, 1972.

James Joyce: Two Decades of Criticism, Vanguard, 1948.

Psychoanalysis and Culture, International Universities Press, 1951.

Basic Beliefs, Sheridan, 1959.

Culture in History, Columbia University Press, 1960.

Myth and Mythmaking, Braziller, 1960.

(Author of introduction) *Myths,* McGraw, 1974.

Cassettes:

"Imagery and Vision in James Joyce," Dolphin Tapes, 1968.

"World Mythology Series: World Mythology and the Individual Adventure," Dolphin Tapes, 1969.

"Myths of Alienation and Rapture," Dolphin Tapes, 1970.

"Myths, Personal Dreams, and Universal Themes," New Dimensions Foundation.

"Ancient Voices," New Dimensions Foundation.

"Beyond Dogma: The Vision Quest Experience," New Dimensions Foundation.

"Hermes, Alchemy and Voyages of Odysseus," Dolphin Tapes, 1971.

"The Myth of the Fool," New Dimensions Foundation.

"Mythological Musings: The Mythic Image," New Dimensions Foundation.

"Legends of Courtly Love and the Grail," Dolphin Tapes, 1983.

"The Hero's Journey," Dolphin Tapes, 1984.

■ Adaptations

"The Power of Myth: Joseph Campbell with Bill Moyers" (six-part series; includes "The Hero's Adventure," "The Message of the Myth," "The First Storytellers," "Sacrifice and Bliss," "Love and the Goddess," and "Mask of Eternity"), PBS-TV, May 23, 1988, (videocassette), 1988.

■ Work In Progress

Historical Atlas of World Mythology, Volume 3: *The Way of the Celestial Lights,* and Volume 4: *The Way of Man.*

■ Sidelights

Born March 26, 1904 in New York. "We had a stable with a cow and a horse out in Westchester. . . .My father, Charles W. Campbell, was in the hosiery business, importing and wholesale. My career as a mythologist began almost immediately, with Buffalo Bill's Wild West Show at Madison Square Garden. He came for two or three years, then he died and the group that replaced him was called the 101 Ranch. One of the Indians in the sideshow was Irontail, whose head had just appeared on the Indian-head nickel. He'd sit in profile to the people who filed by as they took their nickels out of their pockets, looked, *bowed their heads* and went on."[1]

From early on Indians held a special fascination for Campbell. "My brother was one year younger. One day my grandmother was wheeling the baby carriage with my sister in it down Riverside Drive—I guess I was five—and a lady stopped us and said, 'You're two nice little boys.' And I said, 'I have Indian blood in me.' And she looked amazed. My brother said, '*I* have dog blood.' I didn't know Charlie was interested in dogs!

"On Sundays, Dad would ask us what we wanted to do. We'd choose from the aquarium down in the Battery, the Bronx Zoo and the Museum of Natural History. And *there*—they have it to this day—in a magnificent room, with really grandiose totem poles, was an enormous Kwakiutl canoe from the northwest coast, and in it were these dummies of Indians paddling and another, in a bearskin, standing up. So I started reading Indian stories, legends, *The Kalevala*—that's *The Land of Heroes*, a Finnish folk epic by Elias Lonnrot. Those were days when Indians were hot from the warpath and Wounded Knee. And these wonderful books were coming out, very fresh, not contrived for children, just *great* retelling to boys of Indian tales, such as Lewis Henry Morgan's *League of the Iroquois*—a book Marx liked."[1]

"And then my parents had a place out in the woods where the Delaware Indians had lived, and the

Campbell in his office at Sarah Lawrence, during a pupil-don conference.

Iroquois had come down and fought them. There was a big ledge where we could dig for Indian arrowheads and things like that. And the very animals that play the role in the Indian stories were there in the woods around me. It was a grand introduction to this material."[2]

"When I was nine we moved up to New Rochelle and our house at Fifteen Pintard Avenue was right next to a vacant lot. Workmen started digging in the lot. My brother and I helped. When the building was finished it was the New Rochelle Public Library—it was *my* building!—and I was sitting on the stoop when they opened the door to the children's department for the first time. All these nice little books about Indians. Within a year I'd read all the American Indian books and was admitted to the stacks of the main library, where I began reading the annual reports of the Bureau of Ethnology."[1]

A continuing fascination with Indian lore, along with his religious upbringing, led Campbell to an important realization. "I was brought up as a Roman Catholic. Now, one of the great advantages of being brought up a Roman Catholic is that you're taught to take myth seriously and to let it operate on your life and to live in terms of these mythic motifs. I was brought up in terms of the seasonal relationships to the cycle of Christ's coming into the world, teaching in the world, dying, resurrecting, and returning to heaven. The ceremonies all through the year keep you in mind of the eternal core of all that changes in time. Sin is simply getting out of touch with that harmony.

"...It wasn't long before I found the same motifs in the American Indian stories that I was being taught by the nuns at school—creation, death and resurrection, ascension to heaven, virgin births—I didn't know what it was, but I recognized the vocabulary. One after another. I was excited. That was the beginning of my interest in comparative mythology."[2]

Attended the Canterbury Prep School in Connecticut before entering Dartmouth in 1921. After a successful freshman year studying mathematics and biology, Campbell came across Dmitri Merezhkovski's book, *The Romance of Leonardo da Vinci.* "The book simply overwhelmed me! I realized I didn't know a *goddamned thing* about literature, the arts or anything like that. Meanwhile, I was totally fed up with Dartmouth. So I left there and I switched to Columbia.

"...I switched my whole interest from biology and mathematics to the history of literature, history of art, of music, and so on. Again the courses were so easy I wasn't paying much attention to them. I became interested in playing in a jazz band. I had a family of saxes (C soprano, E-flat soprano—ah, that C melody!—alto and E-flat baritone) and guitars, ukuleles and so forth. We had a wonderful little band. Played for fraternity dances and junior proms. We'd augment the band and get it up to twelve pieces—that's *a lot of fun*, playing in a real band like that.

"We'd go down to the New Amsterdam to hear Paul Whiteman, our favorite. And the theater, what theater! Terrific! Every year a new play by George Bernard Shaw and Eugene O'Neill—the Ziegfeld Follies! The Greenwich Village Follies! And every week a whole new sheaf of music for us to play. Prohibition, I'd been brought up *in* prohibition, never had a drink in my life. Ask a girl to go to dance, that's as far as we went, and order ginger ale and for ten dollars have a glorious evening...."[1]

His passion for playing in the band took a dramatic turn when "...a whole new interest came into my life. In compulsory phys. ed. at Columbia, you had to run around a track. I've never been able to allow anybody to beat me at anything. So I used to come in first. Lapping kids all the way....

"So the track coach, Carl Merner, said, 'Have you ever run?' 'No.' 'Would you like to go out for track? You can go a faster mile than anybody we got in college right now.' 'Sure.'...Then the New York Athletic Club invited me to run on their team and I did. I ran my junior and senior years. I've got a box of championship medals that would cover a bed—mostly *gold.*

"Meanwhile, summers, my mother had been taking us traveling. I had very good parents. We took a trip across the United States, a boat in San Francisco, down the coast of Mexico, through the Panama Canal and up to Baltimore. Memorable! Brother Charles, Alice (my sister) and my mother. Then she took us to Europe and that was the summer of the 1924 Olympics. A great Olympics—Paavo Nurmi, what a runner! My father met us and we went to England and Scotland, Holland, Belgium, France, Switzerland, Italy—and gosh, I still remember every one of those cities, every place we went. What a wonderful introduction...."[1]

Graduated from Columbia in 1925. "...I'd just been elected captain of the team for the coming year, so I went back to Columbia to graduate school in order to run for another year. Well, what could I *take?* Nothing very serious! I couldn't read

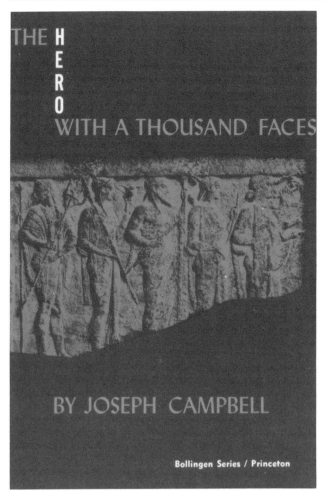

The book that first earned Campbell world-wide recognition and subsequently influenced generations of readers.

German or French that well. Knowing only English, I read for a graduate degree in English. I chose the Romantic period and the Middle Ages. Well, when I started reading the medieval material I became *so* excited. There were the old myth motifs again, which I remembered from my Indian days, particularly in the Arthurian stuff."[1]

Track provided Campbell with additional opportunity to travel. "...The N.Y.A.C. team was invited out to Golden Gate Stadium in San Francisco to run—and we ran away with everything. My roommate, Jackson Scholz, an Olympic runner and winner, told me about Hawaii. Well, I'm in California; why not Hawaii? So I get aboard a boat, full of myself—we had won everything!—and the boat drops anchor about a mile off the island in July. The island flowers are all blooming and the perfume comes a whole mile out: the whole island was a bouquet. Ecstasy. The boat comes in to dock, *Aloha* is being played by the band, there's this

crowd and above them is a staff with a pennant that says ALOHA JOE CAMPBELL! I thought, this is little enough for a guy like me! Track star, you know. But it was Jackson's friend trying to meet me.

"Well, fate. I stayed at the Courtland Hotel and, unknown to me, this was within one block of the home of Jean, the girl I married thirteen years later. She was a little thing then, going for dancing lessons, a *child.*

"Next year I went back for a master's degree. My thesis was 'The Dolorous Stroke,' a motif from Malory's *Morte d'Arthur.* They liked my thesis and gave me a traveling fellowship. I was absolutely fascinated by this material, and *still* running. I was twenty-two, twenty-three, years old. And the fellowship just came to me, as everything else did: this is a life of serendipity.

"I finally dropped track. You can't do serious scholarship and track at the same time."[1]

Videocassette cover for Part 3 of the PBS television series.

Campbell found himself in Europe at a very exciting time. He fell in love with Picasso and the writings of James Joyce. He met Jiddu Krishnamurti and was given a copy of Edwin Arnold's life of Buddha. He was also "soaking up medieval literature at the University of Paris, 1927, studying Old French and Provencal; I read nothing but French. But I found all the basic books were in German. They renewed my fellowship for a year in Munich and *there* the world opened up.

"I lived with a German family, spoke German and thought German. I bumped into an American student who was in philology like myself and he was working on Sanskrit. So I enrolled in Sanskrit, Buddhist studies and so forth with a *wonderful* Professor Oertel at the University of Munich. [All of this] was *far, far away* from where I was supposed to be in medieval French. But this thing just grabbed me.

"...I began to lose touch with my Ph.D. direction. Suddenly the *whole modern world* opened up! With a bang!"[1]

He also discovered the works of Freud and Jung which added a psychological dimension to the field of mythology. "I think the longer you live, the more Jung can say to you. I go back to him every so often, and things that I've read before always say something new. Freud never says something new to me anymore; Freud tells us what myths mean to neurotics. On the other hand, Jung gives us clues as to how to let the myth talk to us in its own terms, without putting a formula on it. So I've been with Jung since 1928, and that's a long spell."[3]

Having outgrown the narrow restrictions imposed by Columbia on his studies, Campbell abandoned his doctoral pursuit. "My decision to follow this course came one day in Paris while I was sitting in the little garden of Cluny, where the Boulevards St. Michel and St. Germain come together. It suddenly struck me: What in heaven's name am I doing? I don't even know how to eat a decent, nourishing meal, and here I'm learning what happened to vulgar Latin when it passed into Portuguese and Spanish and French."[3] Returning to America just in time for the 1929 stock market crash, "...I didn't have a job for five years.

"My father's hosiery business was in very bad condition in the Crash. I didn't know where I was. The world had blown open. I'm no longer in the Ph.D. bottle. I don't want to go on with my little Arthurian pieces. I had *much* more exciting things to do—and I didn't know what they were."[1]

Alone in New York City, Campbell discovered American literature and began writing short stories. "...Hemingway, Sinclair Lewis, the whole bunch. Hemingway just knocks me over, those early things of his—*In Our Time, Men without Women, The Sun Also Rises.* Like every callow young author, I wanted to write like him....

"Finally, in desperation, I thought, I'm going away. So Mother let me take the Model A Ford and start across the United States to try to find a job. That car drive across the States was simply something. A coupe, its maximum speed was sixty, and you felt you were rattling the hell out of it."[1]

Campbell wound up in Pacific Grove, California, where he befriended then-struggling novelist, John Steinbeck. "A beautiful time; we were all in heaven. The world had dropped out. We weren't the dropouts; the world was the dropout. We were in a halycon situation, no movement, just floating. Just great....So I'm coasting along, trying to find where I am, crazy on Spengler."[1] He also met Ed Ricketts an intertidal biologist and central character in Steinbeck's *Cannery Row.* "We'd go out and collect hundreds of starfish, sea cucumbers, things like that, between high and low tides, furnishing animals for biology classes and schools.

"Ed made an arrangement to go to Alaska on a small boat. Great! What else is there to do? So we cruised up the Inside Passage from Seattle to Juneau...well, the Inside Passage was gorgeous. We sat on the stern as that little launch went out into the waters of Puget Sound, off for six weeks, much of which we'd spend at an absolutely uninhabited island gathering animals while Ed made notes. The cost: twenty-five cents a day for the whole crew. We would pull into the port, all the canneries were closed, the fishing fleets immobilized—they'd *throw* salmon at us. Put your hand in the water and pull fish out. Just an idyll. And the towns were supposed to be dead and they were the most *living* things. There's nothing like living when you're not living with a direction but just enjoying the glory of the moment. That's what we were doing."[3]

"...Steinbeck and I trying to write....Oh, four months of just something glorious...."[1]

1932. Canterbury Prep School offered Campbell a teaching position. "Alaska and California dropped *like that* out of my life....Where was the next dollar coming from? Teaching—I don't ever want to teach boys that age again...."[1]

Jacket from the hardcover publication of the Campbell-Moyers television interviews.

"Then one of my short stories sold...for three hundred fifty dollars. So I retired. I don't know what the magazine was; I took the money and ran. [And] took a vow that I would never work for money."[1]

So at age thirty, Campbell moved to Woodstock, New York, where he read the classics "twelve hours a day" for two years. "...Living on nothing, a single young man, always available for dinner—I learned to live on that dinner. A couple with a great big dog named Fritz—a cross between a Doberman pinscher and a police dog, a big, powerful, amusing lunatic of an animal—had built a house in the woods, and they asked me to take care of Fritz and keep the house warm while they lived in New York for the winter. A buster of a winter, so cold!

"So I was cutting wood and I really just buckled into reading Joyce and Sanskrit, Spengler, Mann, Jung—the whole thing was coming together. And another great passion of mine, Leo Frobenius, a German Africanist whom nobody was to read

because the patron was Kaiser Wilhelm. But he was the person who opened up African studies. I was tremendously excited. I wasn't interested at all in a job. I could live on nothing and was having a wonderful time...."[1]

1934. "The Depression was still on. So in my mailbox came an invitation to teach at Sarah Lawrence. I drove down. They wanted me. I told them that if I was going to teach I'd like to give a course on comparative literature that started back with the old epics and came on down the line. They liked the idea. It was very, very nice—and besides, the girls were beautiful."[1]

"I taught a course on comparative mythology for thirty-eight years. I taught young people of every available creed. More than fifty percent of my students from the New York area were Jewish; many were Christians—Protestant, Catholic; there were Mormons and Zoroastrians and Buddhists. There wasn't much of a problem with the Buddhists, but all the others were somewhat stuck in their provincial traditions.

"It was the simplest thing; all I did was to point out the parallels and identities all over the place. You see, when there is a motif—such as that of the virgin birth—which occurs in American Indian mythologies, in Greek mythology, and so on, it becomes obvious that the virgin birth could not have referred to a historical event. It's a spiritual event that's referred to—even in the Christian tradition. One after another, these motifs became spiritualized instead of historicized...."[3]

"There was a fascinating moment in New York City when the Dalai Lama arrived, and the first welcome was at St. Patrick's Cathedral. There they were, the Catholic clergy, the Eastern Orthodox clergy, the rabbis, Protestant ministers, and so forth; and the whole sense of Buddhism is that all traditions intend the same end, and are ways to it. And the Dalai Lama, seeing these people there, made this point. Well, Cardinal Cooke had to let his members of the group know that that is not so: only the Catholics, we, have It. There they were, sitting around the table—rabbis, Protestant ministers, Catholic priests—putting on this show of accord, but each one holding his cards close and thinking he had the trump. But the only way you can go is by yielding the trump."[3]

Campbell lectured on all he had learned over those years of travel and scholarship. "One of our problems today is that we are not well acquainted with the literature of the spirit. We're interested in the news of the day and the problems of the hour.

It used to be that the university campus was a kind of hermetically sealed-off area where the news of the day did not impinge upon your attention to the inner life and to the magnificent human heritage we have in our great tradition—Plato, Confucius, the Buddha, Goethe, and others who speak of the eternal values that have to do with the centering of our lives. When you get to be older, and the concerns of the day have all been attended to, and you turn to the inner life—well, if you don't know where it is or what it is, you'll be sorry."[2]

He contended that modern young people are not being handed a practical mythology with rituals they can believe in. "They make them up themselves. This is why we have graffiti all over the city. These kids have their own gangs and their own initiations and their own morality, and they're doing the best they can. But they're dangerous because their own laws are not those of the city. They have not been initiated into our society."[2]

A young dancer from Hawaii, Jean Erdman, became one of Campbell's students. ". . .She asked to take a course with me. I took her on as a private student. I'm susceptible to female beauty, so I was in a mild high all the time, but I realized that some little person somewhere was maybe a notch higher, and that was Jean. When she left at the end of her second year, to go around the world with her family, then join Martha Graham's dance company—Martha had asked her to dance with her; Jean was a beautiful dancer—well, I had a feeling that maybe this was it. But I wasn't sure. I still called her Miss Erdman. What can I do to make it so she'll see me after she graduates? I gave her *The Decline of the West!* I kept in touch with her through the guise of instruction. Ha!"[1] They were married in 1938.

The publication of James Joyce's novel, *Finnegans Wake* afforded Campbell the opportunity to co-author his first book. "A chap I'd known at Columbia, Henry Morton Robinson—he'd been a young member of the faculty, then had resigned and become a free-lance writer (he later wrote the best seller *The Cardinal*)—came to our place one evening with his wife and said, 'How ya doing with *Finnegans Wake?*' 'Fine.' 'How about you and I doing a book on it?' We'd talked about Joyce for years, he was a good Joyce scholar, a very good Joyce scholar, but I didn't take his idea seriously. We were walking out to Rochambeau (it's now a Blimpies) and he argued me into it. We made an agreement, 1939. . . .And we started."[1]

"In Joyce's. . .*Finnegans Wake*, there is a mysterious number that constantly recurs. It is 1132. It occurs as a date, for example, and inverted as a house address, 32 West 11th Street. In every chapter, some way or another, 1132 appears. When I was writing *A Skeleton Key to 'Finnegans Wake,'* I tried every way I knew to imagine, 'What the dickens is this number 1132?' Then I recalled that in *Ulysses*, while Bloom is wandering about the streets of Dublin, a ball drops from a tower to indicate noon, and he thinks, 'The law of falling bodies, 32 feet per sec per sec.' Thirty-two, I thought, must be the number of the Fall; 11 then might be the renewal of the decade, 1, 2, 3, 4, 5, 6, 7, 8, 9, 10—but then 11, and you start over again. There were a number of other suggestions in *Ulysses* that made me think, 'Well, what we have here is perhaps the number of the Fall, 32, and Redemption, 11; sin and forgiveness, death and renewal.' *Finnegans Wake* has to do with an event that occurred in Phoenix Park, which is a major park in Dublin. The phoenix is the bird that burns itself to death and then comes to life renewed. Phoenix Park thus becomes the Garden of Eden where the Fall took place, and where the cross was planted on the skull of Adam: *O felix culpa* ('O Phoenix culprit!' says Joyce). And so we have death and redemption. That seemed a pretty good answer, and that's the one I gave in *A Skeleton Key.*

"But while preparing a class one evening for my students in comparative mythology, I was rereading St. Paul's Epistle to the Romans and came across a curious sentence that seemed to epitomize everything Joyce had had in mind in *Finnegans Wake*. St. Paul had written, 'For God has consigned all men to disobedience, that he may show his mercy to all.' You cannot be so disobedient that God's mercy will not be able to follow you, so give him a chance. 'Sin bravely,' as Luther said, and see how much of God's mercy you can invoke. The great sinner is the great awakener of God to compassion. This idea is an essential one in relation to the paradoxology of morality and the values of life.

"So I said to myself, 'Well, gee, this is really what Joyce is talking about.' So I wrote it down in my Joyce notebook: 'Romans, Chapter 11, verse 32.' Can you imagine my suprise? There was that same number again, 1132, right out of the Good Book! Joyce had taken that paradox of the Christian faith as the motto of the greatest masterwork of his life. And there he describes ruthlessly the depths of the private and public monstrosities of human life and

Campbell during the series of talks with Bill Moyers that were later presented on PBS-TV as "The Power of Myth."

action in the utterly sinful course of human history. It's all there—told with love."[2]

"...I wrote something like thirty thousand words about the first page and when I brought this to Rondo [Robinson], he said, 'For Christ's sake!! Are we gonna do the *Encyclopaedia Britannica?*' So he went at it with a meat-ax and finally I found a way to do this thing: stretches of narrative, what the real thread of the story was on which all of this had been structured or exploded out of. Worked on it *four years.* There were still cloudy areas we couldn't handle. And when we were finished he sent it to his publisher, Harcourt Brace. They didn't want it. We thought, What the hell, who wants it? Should we publish it ourselves? We knew it was valuable."[1]

"Well, one fine day I read in the paper, which I used to read in those days, that Thornton Wilder had a play going, 'The Skin of Our Teeth.' I'd done all my theatergoing in the Twenties, but somehow I thought I'd like to see that play. We got tickets. First row balcony, center. Hey, one quote after another from *Finnegans Wake!* 'Do you have a pencil?' I start copying it down on the program. So in the morning I phone Rondo in Woodstock.

'Rondo, "Skin of Our Teeth" is *Finnegans Wake.*' 'Oh?' 'Something oughta be done about it.' Monday he phones Norman Cousins and he says yes, so we wrote a piece and Cousins published it as *The Skin of Whose Teeth?* And it really rang a bell all over the country. Then the war came and Wilder went from captain to major to colonel almost, and we were just a pair of micks and Joyce wasn't the civilization we were fighting for, and they came down like a pack of wolves on us.

"We just waited. The play came out in book form and we found a word-for-word quote, four lines, and that did it. So Cousins says, 'What else have you guys got?' So we look at each other, and say, 'Let's give him Chapter One' [of *A Skeleton Key*]. So we did. Chapter One. Harcourt Brace sent it over to T. S. Eliot and Eliot says, 'Buy it!' They bought the book, the same bunch who'd rejected it."[1]

The already-busy scholar took on the translating of friend, Heinrich Zimmer's, lectures, and a new book. "...Zimmer's four volumes of lecture notes, all this had fallen on me, and I'm teaching. And just then the Bollingen Foundation was going to issue its first publication and they'd asked Zimmer to recommend someone to edit it and he advised that I do it. It was a Navaho book, *Where the Two Came to Their Father: A Navaho War Ceremonial,* 1943. Full circle! Back to Buffalo Bill.

"Believe me, I was sweating it out, working like hell in Woodstock, Jean working on her dances in a studio up there and teaching. Ha, twenty-three volumes! That's not bad. I could do it because Sarah Lawrence had no demand for publish or perish. I didn't have to publish a lot of junk in those official scrap baskets, *Publications of the Modern Languages Association* and *Journal of the American Oriental Society.* Who the hell reads 'em?"[1]

Campbell spent four years working on *The Hero with a Thousand Faces* which was published in 1949. It became his most influential work, selling 10,000 copies a year. The book describes the basic journey of the "Hero" who proves to be the same in stories, myths, religions, and legends of every culture. It tells how the hero receives a call to adventure, leaves the safety of his society, battles supernatural forces, and returns with the gift of enlightenment. A ritual which serves the needs of all people. "There are two ways of living a mythologically grounded life. One way is just to live what I call 'the way of the village compound,' where you remain within the sphere of your people. That can be a very strong and powerful and noble life....But if a person has had the sense of the Call—the feeling that there's an adventure for him—and if he doesn't follow that, but remains in the society because it's safe and secure, then life dries up. And then he comes to that condition in late middle age: he's gotten to the top of the ladder, and found that it's against the wrong wall.

"If you have the guts to follow the risk, however, life opens, opens, opens up all along the line. I'm not superstitious, but I do believe in spiritual magic, you might say. I feel that if one follows what I call one's 'bliss'—the thing that really gets you deep in the gut and that you feel is your life—doors will open up....

"If you follow your bliss, you'll have your bliss, whether you have money or not. If you follow money, you may lose the money, and then you don't have even that. The secure way is really the insecure way and the way in which the richness of the quest accumulates is the right way."[3]

Elaborating, he used the pursuit of the grail, the quest of Parzifal. "The problem of the grail quest is the re-vivification of what is known as the Waste Land. The Waste Land is a world where people live

not out of their own initiative, but out of what they think they're supposed to do. People have inherited their official roles and positions; they haven't earned them. This is the situation of the Waste Land: everybody leading a false life. T. S. Eliot used that idea in his poem, *The Waste Land....*The Waste Land is a place where the sense of the vitality of life has gone. People take jobs because they have to live, and then they find in mid-life that the job doesn't mean a thing."[3]

The book influenced a generation of artists, including filmmaker George Lucas and his "Star Wars" trilogy. Lucas eventually invited Campbell to Skywalker Ranch to view the films. "In the first stage of this kind of adventure, the hero leaves the realm of the familiar, over which he has some measure of control, and comes to a threshold, let us say the edge of a lake or sea, where a monster of the abyss comes to meet him. There are then two possibilities. In a story of the Jonah type, the hero is swallowed and taken into the abyss to be later resurrected—a variant of the death-and-resurrection theme. The conscious personality here has come in touch with a charge of unconscious energy which it is unable to handle and must now suffer all the trials and revelations of a terrifying night-sea journey, while learning how to come to terms with this power of the dark and emerge, at last, to a new way of life.

"The other possibility is that the hero, on encountering the power of the dark, may overcome and kill it, as did Siegfried and St. George when they killed the dragon. But as Siegfried learned, he must then taste the dragon blood, in order to take to himself something of that dragon power. When Siegfried has killed the dragon and tasted the blood, he hears the song of nature. He has transcended his humanity and reassociated himself with the powers of nature, which are the powers of our life, and from which our minds remove us.

"You see, consciousness thinks it's running the shop. But it's a secondary organ of a total human being, and it must not put itself in control. It must submit and serve the humanity of the body. When it does put itself in control, you get a man like Darth Vader in 'Star Wars,' the man who goes over to the consciously intentional side.

"The fact that the evil power is not identified with any specific nation on this earth means you've got an abstract power, which represents a principle, not a specific historical situation. The story has to do with an operation of principles, not of this nation against that. The monster masks that are put

Campbell observed, "The monster masks that are put on people in *Star Wars* represent the real monster force in the modern world."

on people in 'Star Wars' represent the real monster force in the modern world. When the mask of Darth Vader is removed, you see an unformed man, one who has not developed as a human individual. What you see is a strange and pitiful sort of undifferentiated face.

"Darth Vader has not developed his own humanity. He's a robot. He's a bureaucrat, living not in terms of himself but in terms of an imposed system. This is the threat to our lives that we all face today. Is the system going to flatten you out and deny you your humanity, or are you going to be able to make use of the system to the attainment of human purposes?...It can be done. By holding to your own ideals for yourself and, like Luke Skywalker, rejecting the system's impersonal claims upon you.

"['Star Wars'] is in a language that talks to young people, and that's what counts. It asks, Are you going to be a person of heart and humanity—because that's where the life is, from the heart—or are you going to do whatever seems to be required of you by what might be called 'intentional power?' When Ben Kenobi says, 'May the Force be with you,' he's speaking of the power and energy

of life, not of programmed political intentions....The Force moves from within. But the force of the Empire is based on an intention to overcome and master. 'Star Wars' is not a simple morality play, it has to do with the powers of life as they are either fulfilled or broken and suppressed through the action of man.

"I've heard youngsters use some of George Lucas' terms—'the Force' and 'the dark side.' So it must be hitting somewhere. It's a good sound teaching, I would say."[2]

Campbell expanded on these ideas, as well as many new ones in later works like *The Masks of God* series and *The Mythic Image*.

1972. Retired from teaching. "The day after I quit Sarah Lawrence, my last class, I boarded a plane to a conference in Iceland on altered states of consciousness and I've been on another course ever since...."[1]

He settled permanently in Hawaii with wife Jean, and focused on what would be the final project of his life, a four-volume series titled: *The Historical Atlas of World Mythology*. On October 30, 1987, after completing only the first two volumes, *The Way of the Animal Powers* and *The Way of the Seeded Earth*, Joseph Campbell died. "When you sit in meditation with your hands in your lap, with your head looking down, that means you've gone in and you're coming not just to a soul that is disengaged from God: you're coming to that divine mystery right there in yourself.

"Simply because [people] are all saying the same name for God, that doesn't mean they have the same relationship to That, or the same concept of what It is. And the concept of God is only a foreground of the experience. As Meister Eckhart wrote. . .in his sermon 'On Riddance,' the ultimate riddance, and the most difficult, is the getting rid of your god to go to God. Wow! That's the big adventure, isn't it? That's the ultimate adventure. That's what you have to strive for every minute of your life: to get rid of the life that you have planned in order to have the life that's waiting to be yours. Move. Move. Move into Transcendent. That's the whole sense of the adventure, I think."[3]

"I remember reading as a boy of the war cry of the Indian braves riding into battle against the rain of bullets of Custer's men. 'What a wonderful day to die!' There was no hanging on there to life. That is one of the great messages of mythology. I, as I now know myself, am not the final form of my being. We must constantly die one way or another to the selfhood already achieved."[2]

From May 23-June 27, 1988, PBS-TV broadcast a six-part series of conversations between Campbell and journalist Bill Moyers. Titled "Joseph Campbell and the Power of Myth," the interviews had been taped at Lucasfilm's Skywalker Ranch in San Rafael, California and the American Museum of Natural History during the last three years of Campbell's life. To the critics' surprise, the series drew two-and-one-half million viewers each week. Fifty thousand copies of a videocassette version were issued, and a book *The Power of Myth*, based on the series, was on the *New York Times* bestseller list for twenty-one weeks. In the introduction to the book, Moyers quotes an exchange that typifies the tone of the interviews and his genuine fondness for Campbell: "Once, as we were discussing the subject of suffering, he mentioned in tandem Joyce and Igjugarjuk. 'Who is Igjugarjuk?' I said, barely able to imitate the pronunciation.

'Oh,' replied Campbell, 'he was the shaman of a Caribou Eskimo tribe in northern Canada, the one who told European visitors that the only true wisdom "lives far from mankind, out in the great loneliness, and can be reached only through suffering. Privation and suffering alone open the mind to all that is hidden to others.'''

"'Of course,' I said, 'Igjugarjuk.'"

"'Joe let pass my cultural ignorance. We had stopped walking. His eyes were alight as he said, 'Can you imagine a long evening around the fire with Joyce and Igjugarjuk? Boy, I'd like to sit in on *that*.'"[2]

Footnote Sources:

[1] Donald Newlove, "The Professor with a Thousand Faces," *Esquire*, September, 1977.
[2] Joseph Campbell with Bill Moyers, *The Power of Myth*, Doubleday, 1988.
[3] Joseph Campbell (in Conversation with Michael Toms), *An Open Life*, Larson Publications, 1988.

■ **For More Information See**

Saturday Review of Literature, October 13, 1945 (p. 56ff).
New Yorker, May 7, 1949.
New York Times, June 26, 1949, March 22, 1987 (section 1, p. 62), December 4, 1987 (p. C-18), June 10, 1988.
Book World, November 21, 1971.
Time, January 17, 1972 (p. 50ff).
Parabola, spring, 1976 (p. 70ff), February, 1980 (p. 57ff), January, 1982 (p. 79ff).
New York Times Magazine, April 15, 1979 (p. 14ff).
San Francisco Sunday Examiner and Chronicle, September 23, 1979 (p. 16ff).
Los Angeles Times, October 14, 1980 (part 5, p. 1), January 13, 1984 (part 5, p.2), May 27, 1987 (part 5, p. 1).
Washington Post, April 17, 1981 (p. C-7).
Chronicle of Higher Education, March 21, 1984 (p. 5ff).
Publishers Weekly, August 23, 1985 (p. 74ff).
National Catholic Reporter, May 1, 1987 (p. 7ff).
San Francisco Chronicle, August 9, 1987 (p. 47).
"A Hero's Journey: The World of Joseph Campbell" (film), William Free, 1987.
Newsweek, November 14, 1988 (p. 60ff).

Obituaries:

San Francisco Chronicle, November 2, 1987 (p. A-9).
New York Times, November 2, 1987 (p. D-15).
Washington Post, November 4, 1987.
Chicago Tribune, November 5, 1987.
Time, November 16, 1987.

Robert Cormier

B orn January 17, 1925, in Leominster, Mass.; son of Lucien Joseph (a factory worker) and Irma (Collins) Cormier; married Constance B. Senay, November 6, 1948; children: Roberta S., Peter J., Christine J., Renee E. *Education:* Attended Fitchburg State College, 1943-44. *Home:* 1177 Main St., Leominster, Mass. 01453. *Agent:* Curtis Brown Ltd., 575 Madison Ave., New York, N.Y. 10022.

■ Career

Radio station WTAG, Worcester, Mass., writer, 1946-48; *Telegram & Gazette*, Worcester, reporter and columnist, 1948-55, writing consultant, 1980-83; *Sentinel* (now *Fitchburg-Leominster Sentinel and Enterprise*), Fitchburg, Mass., reporter, 1955-59, wire editor, 1959-66, associate editor and columnist, 1969-78; free-lance writer, 1966—. *Member:* L'Union St. Jean Baptiste d'Amerique.

■ Awards, Honors

Prize for Best News Writing from the Associated Press in New England, 1959, 1973; Bread Loaf Writers Conference Fellowship, 1968; Best Newspaper Column from K. R. Thomson Newspapers, Inc., 1974; *New York Times* Outstanding Book of the Year Award, 1974, for *The Chocolate War*, 1977, for *I Am the Cheese,* and 1979, for *After the First Death; The Chocolate War* was selected one of American Library Association's Best Books for Young Adults, 1974, *I Am the Cheese,* 1977, *After the First Death,* 1979, *The Bumblebee Flies Anyway,* 1983, and *Fade,* 1988; Maxi Award from *Media & Methods,* 1976, Lewis Carroll Shelf Award, 1979, and one of *School Library Journal's* Best of the Best Books 1966-1978, 1979, all for *The Chocolate War;* Doctor of Letters, Fitchburg State College, 1977; Woodward Park School Annual Book Award, 1978, for *I Am the Cheese.*

Eight Plus One was selected a Notable Children's Trade Book in the Field of Social Studies by the National Council for Social Studies and the Children's Book Council, 1980; ALAN (Assembly on Literature for Adolescents) Award from the National Council of Teachers of English, 1982, for significant contributions to the field of adolescent literature; *The Chocolate War, I Am the Cheese,* and *After the First Death* were each chosen one of American Library Association's Best of the Best Books, 1970-1983; *The Bumblebee Flies Anyway* was chosen one of *School Library Journal's* Best Books of the Year, 1983; Golden Pen Award, 1984, for *I Am the Cheese; Beyond the Chocolate War* was chosen one of *New York Times* Notable Books, 1985.

■ Writings

Novels, Except As Indicated:

Now and at the Hour, Coward, 1960.
A Little Raw on Monday Mornings, Sheed, 1963.
Take Me Where the Good Times Are, Macmillan, 1965.
The Chocolate War (ALA Notable Book; illustrated by Robert Vickery; with teacher's guide), Pantheon, 1974.
I Am the Cheese (ALA Notable Book; *Horn Book* honor list; illustrated by R. Vickery; with teacher's guide), Pantheon, 1977.
After the First Death (with teacher's guide), Pantheon, 1979.
Eight Plus One (short stories; with teacher's guide), Pantheon, 1980.
The Bumblebee Flies Anyway (ALA Notable Book; with teacher's guide), Pantheon, 1983.
Beyond the Chocolate War (*Horn Book* honor list), Knopf, 1985.
Fade, Delacorte, 1988.

Contributor:

Sixteen: Short Stories by Outstanding Writers for Young Adults, Delacorte, 1984.
Mark I. West, editor, *Trust Your Children: Voices against Censorship in Children's Literature*, Neal-Schuman, 1987.

Author of human interest column, "And So On," 1964-78, under pseudonym, John Fitch IV, and of a book review column, "The Sentinel Bookman," 1966-78, both for the *Fitchburg Sentinel;* also author of monthly human interest column, "1177 Main Street," *St. Anthony Messenger*, 1972-80. Contributor of articles and short stories to periodicals, including *McCall's, Redbook, St. Anthony's Messenger, New York Telegram, Scholastic Voice, Saturday Evening Post, Sign*, and *Woman's Day.*

■ Adaptations

"The Chocolate War" (record; cassette), Miller-Brody, 1982, (motion picture) Management Company Entertainment Group, 1988.
"I Am the Cheese" (record; cassette), Miller-Brody, 1982, (motion picture; starring Robert Wagner, Hope Lange, Don Murray, Robert MacNaughton, and Robert Cormier), Almi Films, 1983.
"After the First Death" (record; cassette), Miller-Brody, 1982.

■ Work In Progress

A novel.

■ Sidelights

Robert Cormier began his life in the French-Canadian section of Leominster, Massachusetts on January 17, 1925. "We lived in a three-story tenement. I remember my mother and father heating up the water so we could take baths. I had a great childhood, surrounded by a large, loving family. There was the loneliness of adolescence, but home was always a haven.

"When I was five, my three-year-old brother Leo died. In 1930 all of us kids had contracted measles, which was a common childhood disease. We all got over it except Leo, who developed pneumonia. In those days, they didn't have antibiotics, so he died. He was a golden-haired child. I remember his death and the little white coffin in the front parlor. But I was so young that a true, awful sense of loss didn't affect me. I felt that there was something weird going on, something terrible, because we moved out of the house the following week. My parents couldn't bear to be there. In fact, people moved a lot in those days. Every time another baby was born, you looked for a bigger tenement. We were eight children in all. We moved a lot."[1]

"The streets were terrible. I wasn't the physical type, the ball-playing type, and I never got chosen for the team. I was out under a tree, reading a book, probably. It was [the] Depression and it was bleak....I was a skinny kid living in a ghetto-type neighborhood wanting the world to know I existed. I'd listen to the radio programs at night, Jack Benny, or famous singers....I felt so unknown and so lost that I said, 'Someday I want them to know that I'm here. I exist.'

"...My heroes were in the library, in books. One of the greatest thrills was graduating from the childhood section to the adult section. Then you could go into the stacks behind the circulation desk....They gave me the adult card at a very early age because I zipped through all those children's books. I went from *Penrod and Sam* right into Thomas Wolfe....The book was *The Web and the Rock*. It was under new fiction; it had just been published. The book jacket said, 'This is a novel of man's longing in his youth.' It's about a boy from a small town who wanted to be a writer, and wanted to go to the big city (which was the rock), and become famous and have people know who he was. I said, 'That's me!' Then I realized there was someone else like me, who felt the same way.

"If Wolfe opened the door emotionally to me as a writer, Hemingway opened it stylistically. He made me realize that you didn't have to have the mountain torrent of prose. You could have a clear, thin stream. He used the simple word. I realized that the one great adjective or the one great verb can do it. You don't need all those other words. His stuff was like his music. The opening passage of *A Farewell to Arms* is like a simple melody, part of a great symphony. William Saroyan also wrote simply. Hemingway wrote these great romantic things, the war hero, the wounded war hero in *The Sun Also Rises*. But Saroyan wrote about people like me, in his neighborhood in Fresno, California—the Armenian neighborhood. There I was, in a French-Canadian one. I thought God, this stuff can be the stuff of drama. I don't have to imitate Wolfe and I don't have to be a war hero. I can write about what's happening right here on French Hill."[2]

"What's tough about the first few years of struggling with your writing is that you're imitating. You're influenced by Thomas Wolfe, so for several months you try to write like Thomas Wolfe. Then you discover William Saroyan and suddenly you're trying to write like William Saroyan. But it is all writing and learning the craft. Finally you develop your own voice."[1]

1943. Entered Fitchburg State College in Massachusetts. "I was very fortunate with my teachers. When I was a college freshman I had an art teacher...[who] read one of my theme papers, brought me up after class and said, 'The next time you write something I'd love to see it.' I was looking for an audience in those days. I had all these plots and emotions hanging around so I just went home that day and on the kitchen table, with pencil and paper wrote a story called 'The Little Things That Count,' and brought it into her. She read it, said she liked it, and then she said a puzzling thing to me, 'Do you mind if I hold onto it for awhile?' I said fine. Without telling me, she had it typed and sent it to a magazine.

"During the summer, her car pulled up in front of our house and she got out waving this check. She had sold the story for seventy-five dollars to a national Catholic magazine. It wasn't a particularly Catholic story but it was about a family living in a place like French Hill. So I had a teacher acting as an agent. I didn't give her ten percent but I did send her a bouquet of flowers—roses, red roses. Suddenly, I was a professional writer. Until then, I was a strange kid who was always in his room

Jacket of Cormier's 1974 novel.

scribbling. But with our American system of the dollar economy, the dollar society, as soon as you sell, you are a writer. My cousins and uncles and aunts who had thought that I was just a strange, eccentric little kid said, 'My God! He made seventy-five dollars by putting words on paper.' This was miraculous to them."[2]

"As soon as you start making money at something, certain people—not everybody—but certain people figure you're a success. You might have written a novel that was printed in some obscure magazine or had a short story in some other obscure literary quarterly, but it doesn't matter. I guess that's human nature. Maybe it's the same all over the world, but we put a great value on dollar-success in America. Often, that's why artists are neglected. Not too many people get rich writing, painting, or creating. They mostly exist on grants or have second jobs."[1]

While looking for a newspaper job, Cormier was sidetracked into working for radio station WTAG in Worcester, Mass. "I found the newspaper building and walked in the front door. In the foyer I was met with a doorway to the left and one to the right. I didn't think it mattered much, so I took the one to the right. As I was walking down the corridor, a man stopped me and asked if he could help. I said, 'I'm looking for a job writing.' He told me that I was at the radio station, but to come in and talk with him. He was the manager of the station owned by the newspaper. He hired me, so for the next two years I wrote commercials.

"I had to sit down at eight o'clock on a Monday morning and rhapsodize clever pieces about farm implements or three-piece suits. The minute commercials were a hundred words; the station breaks were thirty, and I had to get the information across. I wrote for the ear instead of the eye. It was very tough, but I learned about the use of words, and to write tightly. I still wanted to work for a newspaper, however, so I kept my eye out for an opening. After a couple of years I was able to transfer."[1]

1948. Started work as a reporter for the Leominster bureau of the Worcester *Telegram & Gazette*. "I became a reporter and was a reporter for most of my life and loved it...."[2]

1955. Began a stint with the *Fitchburg Sentinel*. "Writing for a newspaper after a while is very constricting. It's very formularized. There are just so many ways you can write a three-alarm fire or a two-car accident or cover court. I was lucky, I moved sideways into an editing position where I wrote headlines, which was a different kind of writing, but it was working with words....Then I became an associate editor. I started writing editorials, and then I wrote a human interest column which allowed me to create rather than write the standard, routine, ordinary story. So my newspaper work was very rewarding because I kept changing...."[2]

In 1959, a tragedy sparked his writing career. "On May 22, about 6:10 in the morning, my father died in my arms. A gentle man with a very dry wit, he would listen to people tell jokes and then come out with a devastating one-liner. My father was a hard worker. For forty years he worked in factories. He was my buddy. He was my protector. The day he died, I felt a hint of my own mortality."[1]

Now and at the Hour relates this experience. "I didn't think of it as a novel; it was written as therapy. I went through a terrible decline and started writing with a furious anger. A hurt. I wanted to put the whole world in bed with my father and have them know what it was like to die."[1]

"...I regarded myself as a novelist who was a reporter in order to support his family. There has to be a certain amount of obsession in being a writer, a certain amount of madness...."[2]

"I've always been able to get along on little sleep. After my kids were quiet, I'd write from about 10:30 until 2:30 in the morning. Then I'd get up at 6 or 6:30 and go to work. But I was lucky in that, for a good many years, I worked for an afternoon paper. I'd get out of work by two, come home, be with the kids, take a nap after supper, and be ready to write at night. My body would be tired but my mind would be alive.

"I resist going to sleep. I figure, you might as well be dead. There's so much going on late at night. It's quiet; you've got books; you've got music; you've got David Letterman. And your mind is sharp and alert. Somebody said that to go to heaven, you had to do two things you hated every day. I think I'm a candidate for heaven, because I hate to go to bed at night and I hate to get up in the morning."[1]

"I always knew I had choices. I'd get up from the supper table in the evening and there'd be a good television show on, and I'd say to myself, 'What are you, a television watcher or are you a writer?' Some men played golf, I wrote...."[2]

1960. *Now and at the Hour* published. "I'm always conscious of...wanting to affect the reader. You

By the time Adam was fifteen years old the government had changed his name, moved his parents, and wiped out his past.

But they couldn't erase his memory....

I AM THE CHEESE

by Robert Cormier
Now a Major Motion Picture

DELL ● 94060 ● U.S. $2.75 CAN. $3.75

Paperback cover for the 1977 ALA Notable Book.

either make the reader laugh or you make him angry or frightened. I use everything I can. I go for clarity and I keep to those simple words and simple sentences. But simplicity doesn't mean that a thing has to be without meaning or depth. I try to write and let the reader supply the emotion...."[2]

"But I certainly don't think of myself as a minimalist. I use similes and metaphors and try to create characters to the fullest extent I can. What I do probably goes back to, 'If you want to send messages, use Western Union.' I don't believe in beating people over the head. It's really the opposite of minimalism because if you set a scene and characters that are very real and something bad happens, the reader will react emotionally.

"There is room in the literary world for all kinds of styles and writings. I go from detective fiction to what I consider fine literature. There is room for everybody. Like everything else, it's a matter of individual taste."[1]

1963. Second novel, *A Little Raw on Monday Mornings*, published, followed by *Take Me Where the Good Times Are*. "I hate to let novels go when they are done. One of my novels, *Take Me Where the Good Times Are*, I actually wrote over completely after it was all done and ready to go to the publisher...."[3]

"Actually, I think of myself as a rewriter rather than a writer. I rewrite and rewrite and rewrite. With each novel, I fill a shopping bag with material that has been rewritten. I think for every page that appears finally in the finished product, there are probably three to four pages that don't. What makes my wife start climbing the walls is [the fact that] I don't throw anything away. I have boxes and boxes of manuscripts. These have now been collected at a college near my home.

"I had a growing family, yet I never had a door to my writing room. My writing was never off limits to the kids. I remember writing when they were very small crawling up my leg....

"The guy who went out and played golf probably saw less of his family....[Because of my insomnia,] I'd be there when they came home from dances or dates or movies. A lot of nights they'd just go to bed, 'Goodnight Dad,' and then up the stairs. Sometimes they didn't. My son and I would sit and talk....He will tell you things at one o'clock in the morning that he won't tell you at one o'clock in the afternoon, and you'll tell your son things at that hour that you wouldn't earlier. I think those insights helped when I began writing novels that started to appeal to young adults."[2]

Those insights were captured in Cormier's book *The Chocolate War*. "It was rejected by four publishers who wanted me to change the ending. One publisher specifically offered me a five thousand dollar advance and a lot of promotion if I'd come down to New York and talk about doing the same. It was seductive. After all, I had kids growing up and facing college. Since I was working full time, it had taken me two or three years to write the book on nights and weekends. I didn't want to rewrite the ending because I thought I'd have to rewrite the whole book; you just don't tack a happy ending onto a story. But I wasn't being that heroic. My agent had faith that it would be published as is, and ultimately it was. But it was a long year and a half, waiting for them to print it. You have to have faith and draw the line somewhere. You've got to say, 'I'll go this far, but no further.' Then you have to stick to it."[1]

The Chocolate War was based on the experience of his teenage son. "My son was going to a high school much like the high school in the book. They were having a chocolate sale and Peter refused to sell the chocolates. It was a family decision, a matter of principle....He was the only kid in the place who didn't sell the chocolates. Nothing happened to him but something happened to me. I used the thing all writers use: 'What if? What if there had been peer pressure; what if there had been faculty pressure?' The emotional content was there.

"Jerry Renault got terribly beaten up at the end of *The Chocolate War*. He was the protagonist, the kid readers identified with. But Jerry gave it the good fight. He went against society, *his* society at school. He was alone and he tried to beat the odds. What a

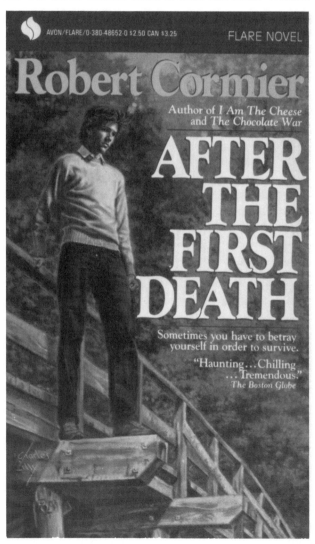

Softcover edition of Cormier's 1979 novel.

lot of kids respond to is that he tried. The fact that he failed was almost beside the point."[2]

"When I was writing *The Chocolate War*, I realized that, at the point when Jerry did fight back, he was descending to their level."[1]

"Some critics who feel that my books are too downbeat only look at the ending and say, 'Gee, that poor kid got beaten up and was kind of dispirited about it.' They forget about what came before: that he made the great effort. And to me that's always been the big thing.

"When [my son] brought those chocolates back the next day, I was apprehensive for him. I was fearful. I felt guilty that we had allowed him to do this. He was fourteen years old, a freshman in a new school, in a different city—these emotions got me to the typewriter. Then I saw a chance to explore themes, the individual against society, manipulation...."[2]

These themes have brought Cormier both success and controversy. "My youngest daughter got very upset when that stuff about *The Chocolate War* started. One of the newspaper headlines read: 'Cormier is a Corrupter of Children,' or something like that. My family knows what I'm trying to do. They've been very supportive. They grew up with me as a writer. They remember the good times when the checks came in, when we'd go out to dinner and celebrate. They remember the rejection slips that came in.

"I always liked being surrounded by family, friends, tradition. I still live in the same town where I was born. I think it's a great boost because I continually write about that area. I've invented, out of necessity, a place called Monument, which really is my home town of Leominster and also part of Fitchburg. It's a typical area, so I don't have to travel a thousand miles to do research."[1]

I Am the Cheese, another novel of psychological suspense which featured a teenage protagonist, was published and eventually adapted into a film that was released in 1983. "When *I Am the Cheese* was published, I never felt as though I'd written a young adult book. I write books with young people in them. I write with all the craft I can command. *The Chocolate War* had just seen some success and, for the first time, I really had a lot of literary and financial success. Then I wrote *I Am the Cheese* and said to my editor, 'I think I'm leaving the young adult field behind.' He said, 'Why not stretch their minds?' I agreed. You've got to stretch.

"*I Am the Cheese*, for instance, had first person present tense, third person past tense, flashbacks

Actor Robert MacNaughton sets out on a journey in the movie "I Am the Cheese."

within flashbacks. It had interrogations, questions, answers. It started as an experiment with first person present tense. I put a kid on a bike and tried to get a sense of forward movement on only trust. I still think of my writing as experimental even though it sometimes comes out conventional. I've been trying to speed it up or juggle all the levels in it. I love to have people think they're reading one kind of story and have them discover at a certain point in the book they're reading a different kind of story."[1]

"I remember Robert Frost said a marvelous thing...'Poetry is saying one thing and meaning another.' I try to apply that in my books....This upsets people. When I say, 'upsets people,' I'm talking about adults; it doesn't upset children.

"In *I Am the Cheese* this poor, traumatized, drugged kid has an awful future. But he's on that bicycle pumping away, peddling away. Kate, in *After the First Death*, has a terrible fate. Yet to the final moment she tried to rescue those kids, tried to start the bus. She even resorted to feminine wiles, which she hated doing because she was a feminist. My protagonists put up the good fight.

"I really think kids recognize this; that's why, although parents and adults are disturbed by these things, they're not. I never had a letter from a young person saying, 'This was too downbeat, this was awful.' They do say, 'I wish Kate hadn't died.' But add, 'We knew it was inevitable.'"[2]

"They have adults reviewing these books. By adult reviews, I mean somebody who hasn't had a teenager around for a long time, or is even aware what is going on in schools. A lot of people underestimate that intelligent teenager out there. These kids today, I'm talking about the sensitive intelligent kid, are really far ahead of a lot of adults. They have been exposed to so much. Anybody who writes down to these people is making a mistake. Sure I get letters with misspellings from kids who grope to express themselves because they've been short changed by the educational system. But there are kids out there who are naturals, and that's terrific. I think a lot of people who review the books with their patronizing attitude just haven't been around kids lately. Kids know what is going on in the world.

"Some people call my work political. It isn't, overtly, but I think I've developed a certain attitude toward government. It may be cynical; I think it's realistic. I don't have any illusions. I grew up in the era where you could tell the good guys from the bad guys. We were always the good guys. Now you're not quite sure. Yet the great thing is that I can write critical stuff about the government and nobody's going to knock on my door and drag me out of the house at midnight. So the system does work, but that doesn't mean it's perfect.

"Our society is so complex that people can be reduced to numbers or nonentities. There is a danger there. Look at the number system. From the moment of your birth, you have a social security number. Our youngest daughter was given gifts of money when she was born. So we went down to start a bank account for her. She was only three weeks old and they issued her a social security number. Then there's credit card numbers, zip codes, area codes. We've become so big: big schools, big technology, big defense. Everything is so big that the individual can be swallowed up by it."[1]

1979. *After the First Death*, a novel about terrorism on a school bus, published. The title is part of a line from a poem by Dylan Thomas: "After the first death, there is no other." "That line has always haunted me. There are so many kinds of deaths: death of innocence, death of idealism, ritual death, murder, assassinations. Once innocence dies, it can never die again. Once someone dies that first death, the rest may be routine. It may not have the same impact. That has always intrigued me. I knew that someday I would use that as the theme for a novel. There are all kinds of deaths after the first death. There are all kinds of first deaths."[1]

Besides its bleak ending, other aspects of the book followed the trademark Cormier style. To affect pace, suspense, and tension, he often weaves several plots together in a very cinematic way. "As a writer, I was probably affected more by movies when I was growing up than by books. Up to a certain point, I was reading trash—comic books and pulp magazines. The movies in the Thirties and Forties told stories. They moved: the play was the thing.

"My mother never went to the movies because of a religious vow, so I would come home, follow her around the house, acting out what had happened— scene by scene. That was my first real plunge into writing, even though it was verbal. It gave me a sense of structure. Of course, I was also reading like a mad man. I discovered Ellery Queen and the detective guys. They gave me a further sense of

structure in plotting. I disseminated all of this almost subconsciously. So when I started to embark on the novels that have really counted with audiences, I brought along all of this experience, especially in plotting. It was almost as if I was going by instinct."[1]

"When I write, I never think of segments as chapters; I think of them as scenes. I always visualize them in my mind. Then I try to get the scene down on paper as closely as I can. That's one thing that the readers don't see—what you have in your mind. The reader can only see what you get on the page.

"I don't even number my pages. There again, I don't think that I'm writing a novel. I also don't like to think in terms of writing ten or twelve pages a day. Usually I'm writing a scene, and it's always with the idea, 'I wonder what's going to happen?' Or sometimes I write about what's affected me emotionally the day before and that I don't want to lose. I'm very unorganized at first; but finally it comes into a structure where consciously I'm working on a novel per se.

"Even with these influences I don't think I [became] a professional writer until I learned my weaknesses and what I couldn't do. This forced me to compensate. I use a lot of similies and metaphors when I work, simply because it's my best way of describing a building or a scene....The inanimate things don't interest me....When I first started out writing and heard about figures of speech, I thought they were 'fancy writing,' but I realize they're not. Graham Greene showed me the use of metaphor to evoke emotion, scene and place."[4]

Cormier also learned to rely on other sources. "I'm very lucky, having been a reporter all those years in the same area, because I came to know a lot of cops, doctors, lawyers, and judges. If I have a problem, I can usually call somebody. Instead of going to a book to find out about guns, I can just call the cop I know. For instance, *After the First Death* had a military background. As a reporter, I had covered stories about an army installation about fifty miles from my house. I knew a young woman who worked there, so she refreshed my memory about the way things were. I seldom have to go to libraries."[1]

1983. *The Bumblebee Flies Anyway* is a novel about terminally sick young people who, despite their fate, still live and love. "My cousin is a doctor and he gave me most of the medical background for *The Bumble Bee Flies Anyway*. After doing all that research with him, I finally decided to leave out the medical stuff because I didn't want the book to read like a textbook. But it gave me a feeling of knowledge so that the reader felt I knew what I was talking about: When you see the tip of the iceberg, you know there's more underneath."[1]

"Parents have a tendency to tell young people, 'These are the happiest days of your life.' But young people know this isn't true....The fact is that teenagers do not live in a peppermint world of fun and frolic. Their world is vividly real, perhaps harsher and more tragedy prone than the everyday world their mothers and fathers inhabit.

"Teachers know this. Anyone who works with young people on a day-to-day basis knows this. They have witnessed the strength of 'young adults'—their resilience, their ability to absorb the blows teenage life delivers.

"They also aspire to happy endings. In their lives and in the books they read and the movies they see.

"But they don't flee friends who are unhappy or ignore books and movies that present them with tragedy. They already know that tragedy is part of existence."[5]

This view has drawn both criticism and praise. "What you have to realize is that, in all of these books, I've dealt with a specific situation. For instance, with Jerry at the end of the *The Chocolate War* people think that I'm telling everybody to give up. I'm not. For that particular time, at that particular moment, and with that particular kid, that's what happened. I wrote it that way because it seemed traumatically valid and honest.

"One other thing is that a lot of people confuse what I think with what my characters think, and the critics jump all over me. When Archie Costello in *The Chocolate War* says to one of the kids that he doesn't mind receiving Communion because he doesn't believe that the host is the personification of Christ; it's just a wafer of bread, people think that's what I believe. That's Archie talking, not me. Of course, ultimately, the entire feeling of my work does reflect my attitudes. I'm not trying to cop out."[1]

Cormier disputes the notion that his works are unrealistic in their violence and outlook. "You see 'Rambo' running with everyone shooting eight thousand bullets at him, never hitting him once. Wasn't 'Rambo' a Vietnam veteran? Look at their plight. They are hounded by mental problems, drug problems. Society still hasn't accepted them. Jesus, that's not 'Rambo'. You think of a Vietnam veteran and it's linked up with 'Rambo.' Or 'James Bond.' There is an air of complicity about it because people watch these things and have a sense that all is well with the world.

"Kids are drinking in this unreality. Particularly with television, which is the most pervasive influence: 'Use this detergent, it's better than the other,' 'Deodorants will make everybody love you.' The poor woman who is a little overweight feels out of place today because everybody is so beautiful. You see a family passing the ketchup around the table with these big smiles. Commercials create a phony, never-never land. And some people think life is really like this.

"But mostly it's the big lie. Mostly it's the big promise. So much of it is cynical and only for the buck. It is irresponsible. They're seducing the public into thinking that happiness depends on a new hairspray or a sleek car. It's the shortcut to happiness which turns out to be a blind alley.

"I think there is a good place in society for a cold-water book or a cold-water movie that shows things as they really are."[1]

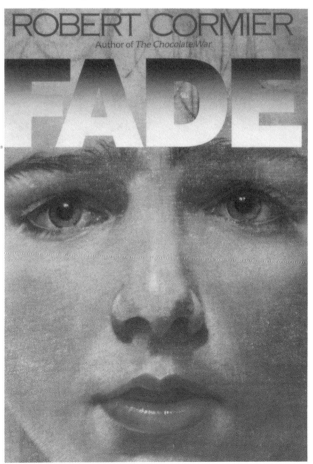

Dust jacket for the 1988 novel.

Cormier's books are on the shelves of English classrooms all over the country. "I'm really fortunate because my books are in schools. I always come back to my first premise: that I'm a storyteller. I want people to open my books and be engaged by the characters and the setting, to keep turning the pages so that when they close it, they feel they've had an emotional experience. On the second level, there are themes in the stories I hope will create pause for thought. If they just read *The Chocolate War* as a schoolboy's story in which a kid doesn't sell the chocolates, or if they read *I Am the Cheese* as a chase story about this kid on a bike going somewhere, and they just get the suspense out of it, fine. I'm hoping they will get more out of it, however. It still comes back to gathering around a fireplace with 'once upon a time.'"[1]

1985. *Beyond the Chocolate War* published, taking up where the *The Chocolate War* left off. "I don't like sequels, per se, but the kids hounded me. *The Chocolate War* left things up in the air. When I went to talk in schools and in the letters I received, they all wanted to know: 'Did Archie ever get the black marble?' and 'What happened to Jerry?' They were upset that I introduced minor characters and didn't follow up on them. So after years of being badgered, I thought, 'Let's find out what happens.' I started writing it very tentatively. Next thing I knew, I was involved with it again. But really, the readers made me do it."[1]

"...The young adult audience is a marvelous audience because it is so responsive. A thirty-eight-year-old adult would *never* call an author. Fifteen-year-old readers will because they identify with you, and you're their friend. They feel you know the shocks of recognition, 'I'll call him because I know he wouldn't mind.' This is a marvelous relationship to have with your readership."[2]

1988. *Fade*, his latest novel, published. "The book is based on something that happened in my family. My father's family photo was taken years and years ago. When the picture was developed, one of my uncles didn't show up. He just didn't emerge in the photograph. I remember hearing about that picture as a kid. It's long gone by now. My mother remembers it vaguely. That picture always made me wonder. Was it just a fluke or could it have been more than that? So I've written a novel which talks about the possibility of invisibility. It begins in 1938 with a thirteen-year-old kid.

"*I* was thirteen in 1938, so *Fade* draws upon those days. I write about a death, the coffins at home, and the wakes that went on for two or three days. I realized when I was writing it that I had buried all this stuff for a lot of years. The story takes place here in the French-Canadian section of Leominster. It goes on to 1988, through fifty years and three generations. Again I think it's a complex novel, but it's a story essentially of people fading in and out of your life. Is it possible to be invisible? Are we invisible sometimes? Desire fades; youth fades; so many things fade. Then there is the real problem of 'can somebody really become invisible or is it just a fantasy?'"[1]

The book was published in both adult and young adult trades, which delighted Cormier. "I don't think of my books as young adult books. The fact that my books have a 'YA' label on them has kept certain people from reading them, because they would never want to read what they call a 'YA' book. At the same time, I have to quickly point out that I owe so much success to that 'YA' label. But I do wish that the border between adult and young adult were less defined. You've got good writers like Paul Zindel writing for this field and I think that's what has happened in the last fifteen or twenty years. You have these wonderful writers who are now interested in writing about adolescents. Zibby O'Neal is a marvelous writer. There are so many writers attracted to the field that they just elevated the genre. Writers don't write these books as just 'young adult' books. Patricia MacLachlan who won the Newbery medal for *Sarah, Plain and Tall*—a book for all ages—didn't just sit down and condescend to the young reader. She was writing to the fullest of her powers.

"Each writer has a particular burden or particular thing he does. Judy Blume is terrific. To me, *Are You There God? It's Me, Margaret*, is a classic. It is not only a good story but it has probably helped some young people over different thresholds at a very sensitive time in their lives. That's what storytellers and great writers do. A lot of people are upset by what she writes. That's all right. A lot of people are upset by what I write.

"The barrier between children's books/young adult books/adult books is breaking down. Writers are rising above these labels. There is exciting stuff going on in children's literature and it's too bad it has to be labeled 'children's' literature. Even Maurice Sendak isn't kid's stuff. It's for everybody. To me, a good story is a good story, no matter who the protagonist is: the old man in Hemingway's *Old Man and the Sea*, Holden Caulfield in *Catcher in the Rye*.

John Glover and Ilan Mitchell-Smith starred in the 1988 movie "The Chocolate War."

"*The Chocolate War*, which is called a 'young adult' novel, is selling more today than it ever has. I'm sure it's not just kids reading it. Teachers have to like it to teach it. So an adult reads it in the first place."[1]

In the introduction of *Eight Plus One*, a book of short stories, Cormier told of a woman he had met while lecturing at a writer's conference. She had expected to meet a monster. She met instead "this other Robert Cormier. The guy you see walking down the street who has brought up a family and has tried to be one of the good guys, sometimes failing, but trying anyway."[1]

Footnote Sources:

[1] Based on an interview by Dieter Miller for *Authors and Artists for Young Adults.*
[2] From a taped interview produced by Random House/Miller Brody, 1982. Amended by Robert Cormier.
[3] Patricia J. Campbell, *Presenting Robert Cormier*, Twayne, 1985.
[4] Anita Silvey, "An Interview with Robert Cormier," *Horn Book*, May/June 1985. Amended by R. Cormier.
[5] R. Cormier, "Do We Underestimate Teenagers?," *Dell Catalog*, winter, 1984-1985.

■ For More Information See

Books:

Contemporary Literary Criticism, Volume XII, Gale, 1980, Volume XXX, 1985.
Robert Cormier, *Eight Plus One*, Pantheon, 1980.
Kenneth L. Donelson and Alleen Pace Nilson, *Literature for Today's Young Adults*, Scott, Foresman, 1980.
David Rees, *The Marble in the Water: Essays on Contemporary Writers of Fiction for Children and Young Adults*, Horn Book, 1980.
Betsy Hearne and Marilyn Kaye, editors, *Celebrating Children's Books: Essays on Children's Literature in Honor of Zena Sutherland*, Lothrop, 1981.
Fred Inglis, "Love and Death in Children's Novels," *The Promise of Happiness: Value and Meaning in Children's Fiction*, Cambridge University Press, 1981.

Contemporary Authors, New Revision Series, Volume 5, Gale, 1982.

Sally Holmes Holtz, editor, *Fifth Book of Junior Authors and Illustrators,* H. W. Wilson, 1983.

D. L. Kirkpatrick, editor, *Twentieth-Century Children's Writers,* St. Martin's, 1983.

Dictionary of Literary Biography, Volume LII, *American Writers for Children since 1960,* Gale, 1986.

Children's Literature Review, Volume XII, Gale, 1987.

Periodicals:

Library Journal, June 1, 1960 (p. 2203), September 1, 1963 (p. 3101), May 15, 1974 (p. 1480).

Kirkus Reviews, June 1, 1960, February 1, 1965 (p. 132), April, 1979 (p. 391), November 15, 1980 (p. 1469), September 1, 1983 (p. J172).

Leominster Daily Enterprise, July 28, 1960.

New York Herald Tribune Book Review, July 31, 1960 (p. 4).

Time, August 1, 1960 (p. 168).

Fitchburg-Leominster Sentinel and Enterprise, August 2, 1960 (p. 6), September 16, 1976 (p. 1), December 4, 1981.

Atlantic, September, 1960 (p. 118).

Catholic Library World, December, 1960 (p. 182), November, 1979 (p. 182).

Best Sellers, October 1, 1963 (p. 222), April 15, 1974, November, 1980 (p. 300).

America, May 15, 1965 (p. 717).

Commonweal, July 2, 1965.

John Fitch IV, "Staying Up Late—Comfort, Curse," *Fitchburg Sentinel,* October 20, 1970.

Publishers Weekly, April 15, 1974 (p. 52), March 7, 1977 (p. 100), July 24, 1987.

Booklist, July 1, 1974 (p. 1199), March 15, 1979 (p. 1141), September 15, 1980 (p. 110), September 1, 1983 (p. 37), March 15, 1985 (p. 1048).

American Libraries, October, 1974 (p. 492).

Times Literary Supplement, April 4, 1975 (p. 364), December 2, 1977 (p. 1415), December 14, 1979 (p. 125), November 25, 1983 (p. 1318), November 29, 1985.

New Statesman, May 23, 1975 (p. 694).

Junior Bookshelf, June, 1975 (p. 194), August, 1979 (p. 216), December, 1985 (p. 274).

Growing Point, July, 1975 (p. 2656), April, 1978.

English Journal, September, 1975, September, 1977 (p. 10), October, 1983 (p. 84), November, 1984.

Signal, September, 1975 (p. 146).

School Library Journal, May, 1977 (p. 78), March, 1979 (p. 146), September, 1980, November, 1982 (p. 33), September, 1983 (p. 132), April, 1985 (p. 96).

Horn Book, August, 1977 (p. 427), April, 1979 (p. 217), August, 1979 (p. 426), October, 1980 (p. 524), December, 1983 (p. 715), March/April, 1985 (p. 145), July/August, 1985 (p. 451).

World of Children's Books, fall, 1977 (p. 58).

Times Educational Supplement, November 18, 1977 (p. 34), January 13, 1984 (p. 42).

Newsweek, December 19, 1977 (p. 85), July 16, 1979 (p. 87), August 13, 1979 (p. 6).

Houston Chronicle, May 14, 1978 (p. 12).

Media & Methods, May/June, 1978 (p. 24), February, 1983 (p. 12).

Catholic Library World, July, 1978 (p. 6).

Lion and the Unicorn, fall, 1978 (p. 109), winter, 1979 (p. 125).

Washington Post Book World, May 13, 1979 (p. K3), January 11, 1981 (p. 7), November 6, 1983, June 9, 1985.

Christian Science Monitor, June 1, 1979 (p. 22), May 20, 1980 (p. 23).

Manchester Guardian, June 22, 1979.

R. Cormier, "Speech at Young Adult Services Division Luncheon" (recording), ALA Conference, Dallas, Tex., 1979.

Los Angeles Times, April, 1980 (p. 16).

Top of the News, spring, 1980 (p. 283), fall, 1980 (p. 79), winter, 1980 (p. 214, 283).

ALAN Review, spring, 1980 (p. 3), fall, 1980 (p. 79), winter, 1980 (p. 1, 31), fall, 1981 (p. 33), winter, 1985 (p. 8, 19, 43).

Boston Globe Magazine, November 16, 1980 (p. 17).

Boston, December, 1980 (p. 78).

Voice of Youth Advocates, December, 1980, December, 1983 (p. 278), December, 1984 (p. 245).

Bulletin of the Center for Children's Books, December, 1980, September, 1983.

John Dinolfo, "Exclusive: An Interview with Robert Cormier," *You and Your World,* teacher's edition, part 1, December 3, 1980, part 2, December 10, 1980.

Proceedings of the Eighth Annual Conference of the Children's Literature Association, March, 1981 (p. 50).

Children's Literature in Education, summer, 1981 (p. 74), summer, 1983 (p. 94), Volume 19, number 2, 1988 (p.67ff).

Wilson Library Bulletin, September, 1981 (p. 47), December, 1981 (p. 246ff), January, 1982 (p. 327), December, 1984.

Writer, June, 1982 (p. 6).

Worcester Sunday Telegram, July 1, 1982, July 18, 1982 (p. 8ff).

Fiction Writer's Market, May, 1983 (p. 500).

"Robert Cormier: His Novels Focus on the Teenage Years," *Read,* May 20, 1983.

Nicholas Basbanes, "Cormier Launches *Bumblebee,*" *Worcester Evening Gazette,* September 14, 1983.

New York Post, November 11, 1983 (p. 14).

Books for Keeps, September, 1985 (p. 14).

Times (London), November 14, 1985.

Children's Literature Association Quarterly, spring, 1986 (p. 42).

Frank McLaughlin, "Cheese, Chocolates, and Kids: A Day with Robert Cormier" (videotape), Robert E. Cormier Collection, Fitchburg (Mass.) State College, n.d.

Collections:

Robert E. Cormier Collection, Fitchburg State College, Fitchburg, Mass.

Jules Feiffer

Born January 26, 1929, in the Bronx, New York; son of David (who held a variety of jobs from dental technician to salesman) and Rhoda (a fashion designer; maiden name, Davis) Feiffer; married Judith Sheftel (a production executive with Warner Bros.), September 17, 1961 (divorced, 1983); married Jennifer Allen (a journalist), September 11, 1983; children: (first marriage) Kate; (second marriage) Halley. *Education:* Attended Art Students' League, 1946, and Pratt Institute, 1947-48, 1949-51. *Agent:* Robert Lantz, 888 Seventh Ave., New York, N.Y. 10106. *Office:* c/o Publishers-Hall Syndicate, 30 East 42nd St., New York, N.Y. 10017.

■ Career

Playwright, cartoonist, satirist. Assistant to Will Eisner (cartoonist), 1946-51; ghost-scripted "The Spirit," 1949-51; drew syndicated cartoon, "Clifford," 1949-51; held various art jobs, 1953-56, including a job making slide films, a job as writer for Terrytoons, and one designing booklets for an art firm; cartoons published in *Village Voice*, 1956—, published weekly in London *Observer*, 1958-66, 1972—, and regularly in *Playboy*, 1959—; cartoons syndicated by Publishers-Hall

Syndicate and distributed to over one hundred newspapers in the United States and abroad. Member of faculty, Yale University Drama School, New Haven, Conn., 1972-73. *Military service:* U.S. Army, Signal Corps, 1951-53; worked in a cartoon animation unit. *Member:* Authors League of America, Dramatists Guild (member of council), P.E.N., Writers Guild of America, East.

■ Awards, Honors

Academy Award (Oscar) from the Academy of Motion Picture Arts and Sciences for Best Short-Subject Cartoon, 1961, for "Munro"; Special George Polk Memorial Award, 1961; named most promising playwright of 1966-67 season by New York Drama Critics, London Theatre Critics Award for Best Foreign Play of the Year, 1967, and Outer Critics Circle Award, and Obie Award from the *Village Voice*, both 1969, all for "Little Murders"; Outer Critics Circle Award, 1970, for "The White House Murder Case"; Pulitzer Prize, 1986, for editorial cartooning.

■ Writings

Cartoons, Unless Otherwise Noted:

Sick, Sick, Sick: A Guide to Non-Confident Living, McGraw, 1958, published with introduction by Kenneth Tynan, Collins, 1959.
Passionella and Other Stories, McGraw, 1959.
The Explainers, McGraw, 1960.
Boy, Girl, Boy, Girl, Random House, 1961.
Feiffer's Album, Random House, 1963.

Hold Me!, Random House, 1963.

Harry, the Rat with Women (novel), McGraw, 1963.

(Compiler and annotator) *The Great Comic Book Heroes*, Dial, 1965.

The Unexpurgated Memoirs of Bernard Mergendeiler, Random House, 1965.

The Penguin Feiffer, Penguin (London), 1966.

Feiffer on Civil Rights, Anti-Defamation League, 1966.

Feiffer's Marriage Manual, Random House, 1967.

Pictures at a Prosecution: Drawings and Text from the Chicago Conspiracy Trial, Grove, 1971.

Feiffer on Nixon: The Cartoon Presidency, Random House, 1974.

Ackroyd, Simon & Schuster, 1977.

Tantrum: A Novel-in-Cartoons, Knopf, 1979.

Feiffery: Jules Feiffer's America from Eisenhower to Reagan, Knopf, 1982.

Marriage Is an Invasion of Privacy and Other Dangerous Views, Andrews, McMeel, 1984.

Feiffer's Children, Andrews & McMeel, 1986.

Ronald Reagan in Movie America: A Jules Feiffer Production, Andrews & McMeel, 1988.

The Collected Works of Jules Feiffer, Volume 1: *Clifford*, Fantagraphics Books, 1989.

Plays:

"The Explainers" (satirical review; based on book), first produced in Chicago at Playwrights Cabaret Theater, May 9, 1961.

Crawling Arnold (one-act; first produced in Spoleto, Italy at Gian-Carlo Menotti's Festival of Two Worlds), June 27, 1961, Dramatists Play Service, 1963.

"The World of Jules Feiffer," first produced in New Jersey at Hunterdon Hills Playhouse, 1962.

Little Murders (two-act comedy; first produced on Broadway at Broadhurst Theatre, April 25, 1967 [closed after seven performances]; first American play produced by Royal Shakespeare Co. in London at Aldwych Theatre, 1967; revived Off-Broadway at Circle in the Square, January 5, 1969), Random House, 1968.

"The Unexpurgated Memoirs of Bernard Mergendeiler," first produced in Los Angeles, Calif. at Mark Taper Forum, October, 1967, produced with other plays under title "Collision Course" Off-Broadway at Cafe au Go Go, May 8, 1968, published in *Collision Course*, edited by Edward Parone, Random House, 1968.

Feiffer's People: Sketches and Observations (first produced in Edinburgh, Scotland at International Festival of Music and Drama, August, 1968; produced in Los Angeles, Calif., 1971), Dramatists Play Service, 1969.

"God Bless," first produced in New Haven, Conn. by Yale School of Drama, October 10, 1968; produced by Royal Shakespeare Co. at Aldwych Theatre, 1968.

"Dick and Jane: A One-Act Play," first produced in New York at Eden Theatre as part of "Oh! Calcutta!," revised by Kenneth Tynan, June 17, 1969, published in *Oh! Calcutta!*, edited by K. Tynan, Grove, 1969.

The White House Murder Case: A Play in Two Acts [and] *Dick and Jane: A One-Act Play* ("The White House Murder Case" first produced in New York City at Circle in the Square, February 19, 1970), Grove, 1970.

(With others) "The Watergate Classics," first produced in New Haven, Conn. at Yale Repertory Theatre, November 16, 1973.

Knock-Knock (first produced in New York City at Circle in the Square, 1974), Hill & Wang, 1976.

Hold Me! (first produced in New York City at American Place Theatre, January 13, 1977), Dramatists Play Service, 1977.

"Grown-Ups" (first produced in New York City at Lyceum Theater, December 7, 1981), Samuel French, 1982.

"A Think Piece," first produced in Chicago at Circle Repertory Theatre, June 26, 1982.

"Elliot Loves" (first produced in Chicago, 1988), Grove, 1989.

"Feiffer's America," first produced in Evanston, Ill. at Northlight Theater, April 13, 1988.

"Carnal Knowledge," first produced in Houston, Tex. at Stages Repertory Theater, April 23, 1988.

Screenplays:

"Little Murders," Twentieth Century-Fox, 1971.

(With Israel Horovitz) *VD Blues*, PBS-TV, 1972, Avon, 1974.

"Popeye," Paramount Pictures, 1980.

Robin Williams and director Robert Altman's grandson, Wesley Ivan Hurt, starred in the 1980 Feiffer-scripted movie "Popeye."

(Adapter) "Puss in Boots," CBS/Fox Video, 1984.

"I Want to Go Home," Marvin Karmitz Productions, 1989.

Illustrator:

Robert Mines, *My Mind Went All to Pieces*, Dial, 1959.

Norton Juster, *The Phantom Tollbooth*, Random House, 1961.

Has contributed sketches to productions of DMZ Cabaret, New York; writer for "Steve Allen Show," 1964; author of episode "Kidnapped" for "Happy Endings" series for ABC-TV, August 10, 1975; contributor to periodicals, including *Ramparts*. Feiffer's books have been translated into German, Swedish, Italian, Dutch, French, and Japanese.

■ Adaptations

"Munro" (animated cartoon; based on a Feiffer story), Rembrandt Films, 1961.

"Crawling Arnold," WEAV-TV, 1963.

"The Apple Tree" (musical by Jerry Bock and Sheldon Harnick; consists of three playlets, one based on Feiffer's "Passionella"), first produced at Schubert Theater, October 18, 1966.

Harry, the Rat with Women (play), first produced at Institute of Arts, Detroit, Mich., 1966.

Carnal Knowledge (released by Arco Embassy, 1971), Farrar, Straus, 1971.

"Academy Award Winners: Animated Short Films" (includes Feiffer's "Munro"), Vestron Video, 1985.

"Grown-Ups" PBS-TV, May 9, 1986, (video), Warner Home Video, 1987.

■ Work In Progress

An Off-Broadway musical based on *Harry, the Rat with Women*, starring Sylvester Stallone, with music by Alan Mencken and book by Howard Ashman; script of "Terry and the Pirates," for Cinecorp; drama commissioned by the Philadelphia Festival of New Plays; cartoons.

■ Sidelights

Born in the Bronx, New York on January 26, 1929, Feiffer was the product of an unhappy marriage. "[My mother] was not meant to be married; there wasn't a moment of married life that wasn't cruel to her. She was a bohemian, but she lived in a time when independent women had to be much stronger and tougher of spirit...in order to go it alone. She would have been most happy with a career and friendships and no sex life and no children....[She] would have ended up in her 80s as a fairly delightful person with many, many friends, living an upper-middle class life...instead of being in poverty for most of her mature years and embittered and alienated from her children who were furious with her, because they felt unloved."[1]

"[My father was] a defeated man by the time I knew him. Maybe it was that, as an immigrant, he never made an adjustment to his country. Or maybe being surrounded by wheelers and dealers, he just never had the absence of ethics to be a successful businessman. He was a sweet man, my father. He lived by avoiding living."[2]

Feiffer discovered very early on that he did not blend well with other children, often isolating himself in his home in order to draw. "In a way, I've used my childhood...as a sort of lab try-out....As a kid I just wasn't there most of the time. I was hiding. The things I wanted to do had nothing to do with what was going on around me. My clock didn't tick with anybody else's time."[3]

"I have always been a dreadful competitor—a sore loser and a guilty winner. One of my great desires to grow up was that, as I understood it, adults did not have to take gym."[3]

"Growing up in the Bronx, as I did, during the Depression...I was almost always aware of this sense of victimization. First economic and then, in the forties, political, at the beginning of the witch hunts, which started long before Joe McCarthy. You felt this very strongly if your parents came, as mine did, from Eastern Europe, and the memory of the pogrom was still very strong in the family. There was always this undefined anxiety about

political danger, and a certain uneasiness about making any sort of dissent. As a kid I felt— silenced. I didn't get beat up a lot, because I was too much of a working coward, but I was miserable."[4]

"I had a very strong sense of where the power was. It wasn't with the kids, it was with the grown-ups, and I discovered it was almost impossible for a child's evaluation of a situation to be accepted over the contradictory evaluation of a grown-up...."

"I didn't seem to have a facility for anything except drawing. But even my drawings didn't look like everybody else's drawings...."[5]

Comic books, World War II, the Depression, and Feiffer, all got started "at roughly the same time. I was eight. *Detective Comics* was on the stands, Hitler was in Spain, and the middle class (by whose employment record we gauge depressions) was, after short gains, again out of work...."

"Eight was a bad age for me. Only a year earlier I had won a Gold Medal in the John Wanamaker Art Contest for a crayon drawing on oak tag paper of Tom Mix jailing an outlaw. So at seven I was a winner—and didn't know how to handle it. Not that triumph isn't at any age hard to handle, but the younger you are the more of a shock it is to learn that it simply doesn't change anything. Grownups still wielded all the power, still could not be talked back to, still were always right however many times they contradicted themselves. By eight I had become a politician of the grownup, indexing his mysterious ways and hiding underground my lust for getting even until I was old enough, big enough, and important enough to make a bid for it. That bid was to come by way of a career—(I knew I'd never grow big enough to beat up everybody; my hope was to, somehow, get to own everything and fire everybody). The career I chose, the only one that seemed to fit the skills I was then sure of—a mild reading ability mixed with a mild drawing ability—was comics.

"...Instead of being little and consequently ridiculed for staying in the house all day and drawing pictures, one was big, and consequently canonized for staying in the house all day and drawing pictures. Instead of having no friends because one stayed in the house all day and drew pictures, one grew up and had millions of friends because one stayed in the house all day and drew pictures. Instead of being small and skinny with no muscles and no power because one stayed in the house all day and drew pictures, one grew up to be less small, less skinny, still perhaps with no muscles,

Feiffer's first published comic strip, "Clifford." From *The Spirit* © by Will Eisner.

but with lots of power: a friend of Presidents and board chairmen; an intimate of movie stars and ball players—all because one stayed in the house all day and drew pictures.

"I swiped diligently from the swipers, drew sixty-four pages in two days, sometimes one day, stapled the product together, and took it out on the street where kids my age sat behind orange crates selling and trading comic books. Mine went for less because they weren't real.

"My interest in comics began on the most sophisticated of levels, the daily newspaper strip, and thereafter proceeded downhill. My father used to come home after work, when there was work, with two papers: the *New York Times* (a total loss) and the *World-Telegram*....''[6]

"...I had to steal newspapers, the *Daily News* and the Hearst press, from other neighbor's garbage cans or befriend kids who I didn't particularly like in order to get their papers. To see 'Terry and the Pirates,' we'd have to get the *Daily News,* which my family wouldn't allow in the house.

"I came from a New Deal Democratic family and they considered Captain Patterson, who ran the *News*, and Hearst to be anti-Semites and racist and all of those other things. And they weren't far off the mark....''[1]

The secret to acceptance in the Feiffer home was to remain unobtrusively successful. "Both my parents were concerned about me without having the faintest understanding or interest in my interests. And the only advice I got from them was bad advice because it was always conservative and cautious. My mother was very ambitious for me, but being an immigrant with memories of Polish pogroms, she was never far from feeling that if you offended the gentiles, they would throw you out of the country.''[2]

"It was obviously not the dream of most Jewish immigrants...to have their only son grow up to become a cartoonist.''[7]

"When I was a kid in high school, which were four very mixed-up, unhappy years, I still hadn't learned what to listen to or where I was going, obviously. And we'd always have to go into the auditorium and listen to some successful, famous graduate tell us about the wonderful times he had in high school. I was absolutely cut off from this. I didn't understand how this guy could ever be a former student or care. You know, he looked like the enemy—he had a moustache. And my boyhood dream was always to someday become successful

and famous and come back to my school and look around and tell them the way it really was.''[8]

"My idea of going to school was to mark time until I got into the comic-strip business. But I was never rebellious as a kid. It never occurred to me that I could be. I saw who had the guns. I assumed I was outnumbered from the start, so I went underground for the first 20 years of my life. I observed, registered things, but commented as little as possible.''[9]

At the age of fifteen, Feiffer attended the Art Students' League. "...My mother dragged me. I was a very shy kid, and very nervous, truly nervous about putting this talent that I fantasized a lot about on the line....[So] when she...took me by the hand and took me to the Art Students' League, I remember screaming bloody murder, I didn't want to go. But she thought I should study anatomy, and it was wonderful....''[1]

Shy a few credits for college, Feiffer found he would have to attend summer school. "I hated high school....I liked people in it, and I liked some teachers in it, but the whole notion of going back was anathema to me. So, I forgot about college, which is probably the best accident that ever happened to me [and] went to Pratt for one year. But Pratt at that time was very much under the influence of the Bauhaus school, and had a lot of transplanted Europeans, and its mode of thinking was towards abstract art about which I knew nothing and cared nothing....Certainly those teachers weren't going to make it more sympathetic to me, because they were overblown with their own self-importance, and belonged to that school of thought which was not unpopular in those years—that the more you demean the students, the more they learned. Well, the more I was demeaned, the more I disappeared, and so I vanished altogether from the day school, switched over to the evening school, where I ran into a wonderful teacher, wonderful perhaps because he actually worked in the field. He was an advertising art director for Grey Advertising named Lenny Kusokov. He was very sympathetic, and I learned a lot from him in a period of three years or so....''[1]

1946. Became an assistant to Will Eisner, one of his childhood idols. "He said I was worth absolutely nothing, but if I wanted to hang out there, and erase pages or do gofer work, that was fine, which I did a few weeks, and then he came upon bad times. I forget what was going on at the time, but he let virtually everyone go....He kept me around for $10 a week, just to fill in, to do blacks and rule

"Munro," Feiffer's strip about a drafted five-year-old.

borders and things like that....Then I got promoted to $20 a week and did more of the same. But the main reason he kept me on was because I was the only real fan he had.

"...At some point, we got into one of our arguments—and we got into a lot of them—about his stories. I said that his post-'46 stories weren't really up to his '39, '40, '42 stories. He had heard enough of this, and he said, if you think you can do better, write me a story. So I did. He liked it, and from that point on I was writing a lot of them....We worked well together, and when we didn't, he would win.

"...I was writing 'The Spirit' and laying it out. I thought that was worth $30 a week. He informed me that it really wasn't. So I threatened to quit. And to keep me on, he said he'd give me the back page of 'The Spirit' section, which then had a nice strip, but rather predictable and tired by then, called 'Jonesy' by a wonderful old cartoonist named Bernard Dribble. Stibble or Dribble. But I was a cut-throat competitor, so the hell with him, and I got the 'Clifford' page."[1]

1951. Against his will, Feiffer was drafted into the Army during the Korean War—"not having the courage to be a conscientious objector...."[7]

"...It was the first time I was truly away from home for a long period of time, and thrown into a world that was antagonistic to everything I believed in, on every conceivable level. In a war that I was out of sympathy with, and in an army that I despised. [An army that] displayed every rule of illogic and contempt for the individual and mindless exercise of power. [That] became my material."[1]

"I had never appreciated the luxury in being able to hate—the clear freedom in facing pure evil—and the Army was it....I was totally on my own in what you might consider a serious man's world, and discovered that reason, or even simple basic idiot logic, had very little to do with day-to-day existence."[3]

"After two years of discovering hate, I turned into a satirist."[11]

During that first year in the Army, Feiffer began the story of the five-year-old boy, "Munro." "...I did a couple of dummies [and] couldn't get it tight, I couldn't finish it. It was the first work of this kind that I had ever toyed with, and I didn't understand exactly what I was doing...what I was going after....It went along fine up until the last third and then I seemed to blow it....[By] the time I finished it [in 1953,] I was ready to get out of the Army....[Finally it] became clear that the answer was in a sense dictated right from the first ten pages...."[1]

Animators had a hard time dealing with Feiffer's anti-military stance. "This was at a time when McCarthyism was officially over, but the resultant suppression and fear were still very much hall-

Bob Dishy and Cheryl Giannini starred in the 1981 stage-production of "Grown-Ups."

marks of society. In fact, the blacklist in the entertainment industry didn't end until some years later, so the entertainment industry wasn't likely to take to anything with a message such as this."[1]

Publishers had a hard time reconciling the innocence of the form with the bleakness of the satire. "They also didn't know how to market it. They explained to me over and over that unfortunately I was not William Steig (who was famous) or James Thurber (who was famous) or Saul Steinberg or Robert Osborne (who were famous), therefore nobody would buy since nobody had heard of me, even though they thought the work was very good. I understood instantly the necessity of becoming famous in order to sell my work."[12]

October, 1956. Feiffer began drawing a weekly comic strip for the *Village Voice.* "...My approach to the *Voice* was totally cynical. I had been turned down over and over and over again by book publishers...[who all] thought I was terrific....'It's wonderful stuff, but there's no market for it.'...[It] was a Catch-22 situation. I had no name, so who was going to buy this work that looked like children's drawings, but was very adult materi-

al?...I had to figure out a way of becoming Steig, Steinberg or Thurber in order to get what I wanted into print. I thought of all sorts of things. I could kill somebody....I could commit suicide ....Suicide was not then established as a form of self-promotion, as it later became with several poets.

"But short of suicide or murder, I didn't know what to do until the *Voice* came along....[The] very people who were rejecting me read that paper, because it was hip, it was inside. It was very modestly circulated, but to all the right people. I was smart enough to know, even at the age of 27, which I was then, that if I could get the stuff they're turning down in print...they will change their minds, which is what happened."[1]

"...We cut a stiff deal. They would publish anything I wrote and drew as long as I didn't ask to be paid....[But] it worked just as I had fantasized....An editor said, 'Oh boy, this guy is good, he's in the *Voice*,' and accepted the same stuff his company had turned down when I had come to their offices as an unpublished cartoonist...."[12]

"...All my advisers advised me to never do anything for free—get paid for everything, they said. Before I started doing the cartoons in the *Voice* I got paid for everything; I was doing more and more work and earning less—probably because I was doing things I hated to do—things I got no enjoyment from. I was quickly turning into a hack. I'd wanted to become a cartoonist since I was a child. I loved to draw, I loved to invent fantasies, and I loved to combine words with pictures. But after being a professional for several years the word 'love' went out the window. I was doing it because I *had* to, because it was the only way I could make a living, the way most people do their jobs—because they know of no way to get out.

"Becoming an amateur again—going to the *Village Voice* and saying 'I just want to get in print somehow'—re-created the element of love in the work, and revived the pleasure of being an *amateur,* of doing something for the hell of it. It was easily the most valuable lesson I've learned in my career.

"So—be warned of the good advice of others. Be warned when they tell you that your attitude is immature....All *good* advice is necessarily *safe* advice, and though it will undoubtedly follow a sane pattern, it will very likely lead one into total sterility: one of the crushing problems of our time."[13]

Now that Feiffer had the job, he was struggling for style. In dealing with reproduction, he would stiffen up. He couldn't handle a brush well; he couldn't handle a pen. He could handle a pencil but you can't reproduce in pencil. Finally he stumbled on a technique of using wooden dowels that gave him a dry line approximating pencil. He'd draw those in poster and black ink, diluted. "...That gave me a line that I liked for a while. But it took forever....In those years I was very influ-

enced by William Steig and Osborn, and the closer I could get my work to look like them, the happier I would be. I must have been doing the weekly strip for...six months to maybe a year, before I hit on the drawing style I liked...."[1]

1956. While continuing with the *Voice*, he took a monetary job at Terrytoons. "I met people I really liked, and whose talents I respected....There was a man I never heard of named Ernie Pintoff doing a cartoon called 'Flea Bits' which I think is still a

Cartoon from Feiffer's 1988 book.

brilliant piece of work. There was a man I never heard of named Bob Blechman, who was going up on the same train I was, working on an animated version of 'The Juggler of Our Lady.' There was a lot of talent around. So, for the first time, I felt that I was among constituents, that there were peers around. They put me...to coming up with the morning animated series that would replace 'Tom Terrific' when that ran out, so it would run four or five minutes a day. So I designed a series called 'Easy Winners' about a bunch of kids living in a neighborhood like the Bronx. Something that would have been vaguely autobiographical...a kind of spin-off of 'Clifford.'...They all loved it....Then some muckety-muck from CBS was coming who had to O.K. it....He came in a three-piece suit, very expensive looking, and very well coiffed, and I knew I was dead.

"...The storyboards are pinned up by push-pins on the wall, and it looks like a comic strip....My idea of a comic strip is you read a comic strip. That's not the way it works in animation. The people who come in to O.K. it...expect to be performed for. And you get these 50- or 60-year old animators who quack like ducks and jump up and down and flap their wings [acting] out the drawings. So you have a middle-aged animator, or a story layout man flapping his wing, and then being his own laugh-track, so as to encourage the clod who's looking on to think this is amusing, because how would he know? He wouldn't know from the drawings and he wouldn't know from the performance. But from his laugh and from the laughs of the claque in attendance....

"I didn't quack once, and I was kind of mumbling. I could see my support system...all around me, grinning, beaming, [but] by the time I had finished the last drawing, I was standing alone and they were all surrounding this guy from CBS.

"...And he said, well, it's a little too *New Yorker*-ish....The worst curse word in the world. And then he said, what I mean is—and this is a direct quote I will never forget—'It's a little closer to Dostoevsky than it is to *Peter Pan*'....That afternoon they cancelled the series....

"...The next day I went in and quit, and I got a $50 a week raise to stay on. By that time I knew that my days there were numbered, but I needed the money, and I would take it until something else came along. What came along was Mr. Hefner offering me 500 bucks a month to do a cartoon for *Playboy*."[1]

1961. "Munro," made into an animated cartoon, won an Academy Award. "The Explainers," a musical revue based on his cartoons, was directed by Paul Sills and produced by Chicago's Playwrights of the Second City. "I was quite dissatisfied with seeing the cartoons acted out. They were much too one-dimensional. At the same time I became interested in seeing if I could write for the stage, and do a full-length play, rather than these little vignettes....

"Transferring the cartoons to live action, whether on stage or on film, presents very difficult problems...."[14]

On September 17, 1961, Feiffer married Judy Sheftel. A few years later his daughter, Kate, was born. "I didn't want a kid, I'd never liked kids. Then they showed me Kate at the hospital. Wow! Five seconds and I was won for life."[15]

"It wasn't funny when my baby threw a spoon on the floor the first time. But when I put it back on the table, when I watched her examine it, when she threw it on the floor again, when I picked it up again, I began to see that it was funny.

"We were embroiled in a comedy routine. It was a team. I was the straight man. The baby was the clown. There were an infinite variety of pauses and expressions, but it was all part of the same gag. If it wasn't such a gag, you'd want to kill the baby."[5]

Begun originally as a novel, Feiffer's first full-length play, "Little Murders," was produced on Broadway in 1967. "[I] realized that whatever the fate of the play, I was stuck as a playwright. I felt as at home with a play as with the cartoon."[16]

"Once you fall in love with the form, you can't fall out of love with it, whatever the travail. Also, it's fun. The production process, the collaboration in the rehearsal process—I take lots of pleasure in that."[17]

"...I structured 'Little Murders' to look and sound in many ways like a darkened version of a traditional Broadway comedy. You had this kooky family and their upright daughter who stands for all truth and strength and energy and all the basic verities of apple pie. She's the darling of the family, and she brings home this guy who is some kind of weirdo radical extremist who stands for none of the things the family does. What we've learned from years of Broadway theater is that this nut can get off wonderful lines and do terrific takeoffs on and insults of the family. The audience loves this as long as, according to tradition, by the climax of the play he admits that he's wrong about everything,

The March 5, 1989 issue of the *Daily News Magazine* (N.Y.) featured the famous cartoonist. (Photo by Joyce Ravid.)

the family forgives him, he discovers the error of his ways and goes into business with the father. Or he reveals that he was just kidding. But the sense in the traditional scenario is, 'None of this is serious, folks.' None of this titillation, none of the leg-pulling of the audience, none of the nose-tweaking—none of this is for real."[12]

1969. "Little Murders" re-opened at Circle in the Square and ran for 400 performances.

Feiffer expanded the range of his career when he wrote his first screenplay, "Carnal Knowledge," in 1969. The film, released in 1971, explored very abusive male/female relationships. "...I wrote 'Carnal Knowledge' originally as a play, and I sent it to [director, Mike] Nichols. I had originally sent 'Little Murders' to Nichols, and I'd never heard from him about it. So I was surprised when, within twenty-four hours, he called up to tell me how he loved the play but he thought it wasn't a play but a movie, that we could shoot it just as it was written (which turned out to be grossly untrue); also that the role of the lawyer from the Bronx could only be played by a young actor who was in a new movie I should see called 'Easy Rider.' Jack Nicholson. So I went to see 'Easy Rider' and thought, 'This is weird.' And Nichols said that the other part could only be played by Art Garfunkel, who had never acted in a movie until something Nichols was then finishing called 'Catch-22.' I thought that was weird, too. And then he suggested Candice Bergen, who I didn't think could do it. And Ann-Margret, to whom I objected strongly.

"It generally went that way. I had learned a bit about casting from the Broadway version of 'Little Murders.' I was directly involved in several awful mistakes in casting on that, so when Arkin was going to do 'Little Murders,' the one demand I made was that he not consult me on casting, and he didn't. Every time I heard that so-and-so was going to be cast in a particular part, I said, 'That's awful. That's a terrible mistake.' And his choices turned out to be perfectly right. So, when 'Carnal Knowledge' was being cast, every time I thought Nichols was making a mistake, I figured I still had a bad sense of casting (I am much better at casting my friends' plays than my own). I didn't quite stay out of it, but I made leaps of faith with Mike that paid off."[12]

1971. Separated from his wife.

1973. "Carnal Knowledge" was banned in Georgia due to Supreme Court obscenity ruling. "Movies, which in the past were made to please banks, will in the future be made to please courts. Different prints for different towns. New, fast, cheap forms of editing and splicing. Detachable scenes. Perforated prints. Tear along line A for Albany, Ga.; insert for Albany, N.Y.

"Automatic bleeping equipment. Federal financing of a community bleeping system. Publishers bringing out novels in spiral notebooks. Plays going on the road with a company censor, editing and revising from town to town.

"A system of culture defenders, much like public defenders, whose role it is to tour the court circuit and arbitrate low-profile obscenity back into the work. 'Okay, we'll excise three mother— if you give us back two ass—.' Artists creating works for men in black robes. The growth, in and out of government, of an obscenity bureaucracy: lawyers, researchers, librarians, file clerks, microfilm makers; Talmudic authorities on community standards. Community standard boards spawning like draft boards."[18]

"...The Supreme Court finally ruled nine to nothing that it was not obscene. It proved that if you have several million dollars and a major movie company behind you, you can retain your First Amendment rights."[19]

Feiffer also encountered opposition from feminists. Joan Mellen claimed: "No contemporary film offers as vicious a portrait of female sexuality....All the women in this film are shallow, crass or stupid. [Feiffer and Nichols'] tone and the absence from their film of women at least as articulate as the men amounts to a smug assent, a silent endorsement."[20]

Molly Haskell found "One intelligent-romantic woman of that film, Candice Bergen, [but she] cannot be envisioned beyond the moment she outlives her romantic usefulness to the men, and so disappears from the movie. [The Ann-Margret character] is presented as a harridan so that Nicholson can emerge with more dignity and sympathy than he deserves. We get an image that purports to indict the men, but that insidiously defends them, not least through the satisfaction they take in degrading the women."[20]

Feiffer has argued that his intent was otherwise. "...There was an easy point to be made in 'Carnal Knowledge,' and I set out to do that, and that is that heterosexual men of my generation were raised to dislike women. And that's what the story of that play and that movie is about. And I think that's unarguable. It would have been arguable 20 years ago, but I think most people have come around to that point of view.

Elliott Gould starred in the 1971 Twentieth Century-Fox film "Little Murders." Screenplay by Jules Feiffer.

"I think it was simply the cultural norm. Boys knew at an early age that they weren't supposed to play with girls because they were sissies, and were supposed to shove girls around, which would prove they were boys, [until] the point where they were supposed to start dating girls, or they were fags. The complicated code was in place, not just in my early childhood, but from my father's early childhood and his father's. It was in place a long, long time ago. Generations. And there were efforts, since the days of the women's movement, to break out of that. And there are some small areas where it is. . . .''[1]

Having completed "Knock, Knock" in 1971, Feiffer went through five producers before the play was done. ". . .Nobody would put it on. . . .I'd sent it to all sorts of directors. Arkin, who turned it down. Nichols. Nobody seemed to want to do it. And then I found Marshall Mason with the Circle Rep, and he wanted to do it, but we still couldn't get it financed, or find a producer.''[1]

"Knock-Knock" opened at Circle in the Square in 1974 and moved to Broadway in 1976. "[It] deals with an emotion that I share in common with many in its audience. At the very moment we feel that change is necessary, there is that digging-in-at-the-heels resistance. All of us do it—we see it happen continually in families, in race relations, in relationships between men and women. You want to behave differently and can't.''[21]

"The only real interest I have in theater is to create the drama between the actors, the stage and the members of the audience. So it's a two-way dialogue, not just between two people on stage, but between the two people and individual members of the audience, who are reacting to what's being said.''[22]

1980. Feiffer's film, "Popeye" was released. ". . .My love of 'Popeye' really started late. In some bookstore or other, I ran into the Bill Blackbeard collection of 1936 Popeyes that Woody Gelman put out. And it was a revelation to me, because I had not remembered 'Popeye' as being that witty. . . .But more importantly, it created a kind of universe, and had a philosophy that seemed to be apt for our time. . .a social-Darwinian world . . . .There was something Kafkaesque in that world, and there was something Beckett-like. . . .[His] use of time—certain sequences could stretch on for days and days, where virtually nothing happened, [yet] it was so full of events.

"Then I got a call from Robert Evans maybe a year or so later, saying he was doing a movie of 'Popeye,' and was I interested in doing the screenplay. . . .I said, it depends, if you want to do Max Fleischer's 'Popeye' I am not your man. If you want to do Segar's 'Popeye' no one else can write it but me. He said, 'I want to do any "Popeye" you want to do.' So that's how it started. . . .There was great enthusiasm for the project from the beginning. Dustin Hoffman was originally supposed to

play Popeye. . . .He read the first fifty pages of the script, loved it.

". . .Evans loved the first draft. Dustin hated it. At one point it became a question of him or me. Evans stayed with the script, which he supported completely. Dustin pulled out. You don't get many cases of a Hollywood producer losing his financing in order to stay with a script. . . .A year or so later Robin [Williams] became a hit in 'Mork and Mindy' and Evans suggested him for the part, and that's how the film got off the ground again. Otherwise it would have been still on the shelf.''[1]

1981. Feiffer's autobiographical play, "Grown-Ups," opened at the Lyceum Theatre to rave reviews. It is the story of Jake, a young *New York Times* reporter, whose parents place more importance on his success than on his work. ". . .My mother had died in February of 1973. I knew that I could handle that because I'd spent eighty-five years in psychotherapy talking about my mother and working out all of our problems. Except that the day that she was buried, I couldn't go to the funeral because I had a fever of 104 and no voice. Something had gone wrong. Since I couldn't get a refund on my psychotherapy, I decided that this needed looking into in some other way. I had started another novel, but I'd stopped working on it and didn't really want to work on anything. I had simply quit everything. The best thing about a contract is that, whatever personal breakdown you may be having, you have to stop it in order to earn your living. So I did the work I was supposed to do, and then went back to my breakdown.

"I decided after a couple of months that this was kind of silly, and I'd better find out what's going on here and learn a little about who I am and was in regard to this woman and her life and history with me. So maybe I'd better write a family play. There was a problem: I am cursed with instant boredom and immediately move into nap-time when I touch on anything directly autobiographical. When I start telling people about something that's really happened, I lose interest instantly because I know the ending. I see no point in telling it. So I had to create characters who were related to me and my family but weren't simply photographs or paste-ups of those people.

"The parents in 'Grown-Ups' I made as close to my parents as I could. In the first draft of the play, I had a hard time recreating their voices. When I finished it, I realized that I hadn't written the Feiffers but Portnoy's parents. They were the conventional Jewish parents of modern-day novels

Daniel Seltzer in the 1976 Off-Broadway production of "Knock Knock." (Photo by Martha Swope.)

and plays. They weren't my parents. So I went through my files and was fortunate enough to discover letters that my parents had written to me from the Forties through the Fifties. In going over those letters, I rediscovered their voices. I remembered again how they talked, how they sounded, and I started jotting down notes. Then I rewrote the play with the real parents.

"After I revised the script, I put it all on tape to hear what it sounded like. It was chilling. I shuddered with the realization that I had raised Dave and Rhoda Feiffer from the dead. It was scary and wonderful and moving, but the one thing it wasn't was a play. It was just an act of memory. So I had to go back like a playwright and do the difficult job of cutting all the stuff that was nice writing as I

wrote it but turned out not to be so nice when it was all put together. So I did that and then decided, for personal reasons, that it was simply too potent a piece of work to put on the stage at that particular time. My first child was seven or eight years old then, and I really didn't like the idea of her seeing this on stage until she was older. So I waited seven years. . . ."[12]

"How would my parents have reacted if they saw it? I think they would have been mortally offended and would have prayed desperately for its success."[2]

June, 1982. "A Think Piece," a play which focuses on the trivialities of daily life, opened at Circle Repertory Theatre. The protagonist is a woman "concerned with her unimportance. She has a stable home life, a husband, two daughters, an apartment on the East Side, a dog, and two sisters who visit her frequently. Although there are no problems immediately visible, Betty exists in a state of constant crisis."[7]

"Not life and death. Not cancer. Not poverty. Not the bomb. But that she can't get the children to walk the dog. That she has to get the children to school. Who does the shopping? Who parks the car?....The decisions in her mind have all the weight that...Margaret Thatcher gave to the decision to invade the Falklands."[23]

"Ordinary life is often dominated by trivia, the moment-to-moment traumas: You can't find the kids when the school bus is here. The stove doesn't work and company is coming to dinner. And all the time you are hearing enormous, pulsating Alfred Hitchcock music pounding in your head. Neck muscles tighten. Lips clamp together in a straight line. It may be comedy, but it ain't funny because it's happening to us."[5]

"Everybody has gone through the struggle: A balances B balances C. We go over and over it in our minds, and when we finally come to a decision, it has made it for itself, or has more to do with external circumstances. 'A Think Piece' is about a woman trying to get hold of her thought processes."[23]

In 1983, Feiffer divorced his wife and married Jennifer Allen. On November 20, 1984, his daughter, Halley, was born.

April 17, 1986. Received the Pulitzer Prize for editorial cartooning. "I've only wanted what all nice Jewish boys want....To be honest, collect paychecks and get a few prizes, and actually I've done pretty well.

"The Pulitzer certainly helps me to go on, because often you feel you're having no effect, and that nothing will change....Now, at least, I have won a prize. So I can continue to feel this way, and still get on with it."[24]

"As wonderful as winning the award was the response from friends and strangers. It reaffirmed the reason I've been doing the cartoons all these years...and gave me a sense of rejuvenation. One assumes there's an audience out there, but it's not always evident."[25]

Throughout his career as a playwright and screenwriter, Feiffer has remained dedicated to his weekly strip. The dream is "to get to the very core of people...to reduce the story of mankind to eight panels."[8]

The differences between playwrighting and cartooning have presented more pleasures than problems for Feiffer. "...The use of the language is very different, and what it has to say....I love that....If I do cartoons about men and women, it's usually about what's not working and how it falls apart. And it has to be succinct, it has to be pithy, it has to make a point, and it better be fun. And it's got to be in six panels. In theater, I have much more range, and it doesn't have to be funny. It can be anything I damn please....

"Normally, the assumption is that when you move out of cartooning into a second profession which is taken more seriously, then you'll forget the cartooning. I found it was just the reverse. Because the more I got into theater the more important retaining the cartoon became....

"...There is something that's exciting to me about going from one form to another...."[1]

Throughout his career as a playwright, Feiffer has been accused of writing characters that are less deeply developed, more like cartoon characters. "The irony of all this is that during all the years when I was doing only the cartoons, what was being said and written about me was that I wasn't really a cartoonist—that these were little plays or little short stories. So in my cartoons, I'm a writer, and in my stage work, I'm a cartoonist."[26]

With a career that has touched many mediums, Feiffer allows each piece of work to lead him into a new direction. "I can only understand my career when the latest piece of work is finished. Then I can connect it to the last thing I did. There's a kind of trail that I'm following, and I don't know what the hell it is."[26]

Footnote Sources:

1. Gary Groth, "Memories of a Pro Bono Cartoonist," *Comics Journal*, August, 1988.
2. Michiko Kakutani, "In Writing 'Grown-Ups,' Jules Feiffer Found He Really Liked His Parents," *New York Times*, December 15, 1981.
3. Julius Novick, "Jules Feiffer and the Almost-in-Group," *Harper's*, September, 1961.
4. Tom Burke, "Feiffer: If at First You...," *Boston Globe*, January 26, 1969.
5. Marian Christy, "Conversations," *St. Louis Post-Dispatch*, November 3, 1985.
6. Jules Feiffer, compiler, *The Great Comic Book Heroes*, Dial, 1965.
7. Mimi Leahey, "Jules Feiffer Writing a Serious Play,"*Other Stages*, June 17, 1982.
8. Eve Auchincloss and Nancy Lynch, "An Interview with Jules Feiffer," *Mademoiselle*, January, 1961.

[9] Robin Brantley, "'Knock Knock' 'Who's There?' 'Feiffer,'" *New York Times Magazine*, May 16, 1976.

[11] Rex Reed, "Breaking All the Rules—and Winning," *Sunday News*, February 15, 1976.

[12] Christopher Durang, "Jules Feiffer, Cartoonist—Playwright," *Dramatists Guild Quarterly*, winter, 1987.

[13] Roy Newsquist, "Jules Feiffer," *Counterpoint*, Rand McNally, 1964.

[14] Jordan R. Young, "The Screenplay According to Jules Feiffer," *Millimeter*, April, 1981.

[15] "The Prolific Pen of Jules Feiffer," *Life*, September 17, 1965.

[16] Samuel G. Freedman, "Jules Feiffer's West Side Story," *New York Times*, May 3, 1987.

[17] Helen Dudar, "Jules Feiffer on the Tyranny of Trivia," *New York Times*, June 20, 1982.

[18] J. Feiffer, "Art for Court's Sake," *New York Times*, August 5, 1973.

[19] "Can Great Books Make Good Movies? Seven Writers Just Say No!," *American Film*, July/August, 1987.

[20] Stephen J. Whitfield, "Jules Feiffer and the Comedy of Disenchantment," *From Hester Street to Hollywood*, edited by Sarah Blacher Cohen, Indiana University Press, 1983.

[21] Holly Hill, "Master Satirist at Work," *Westchester Weekend*, May 7, 1976.

[22] John Lahr, "Jules Feiffer," *Behind the Scenes: Theater and Film Interviews from the Transatlantic Review*, edited by Joseph McCrindle, Holt, 1971.

[23] Jerry Tallmer, "Jules Feiffer, Thinking Person's Playwright," *New York Post*, June 28, 1982.

[24] Clarke Taylor, "Feiffer Surviving on Anxiety," *Los Angeles Times*, May 8, 1986.

[25] David Astor, "An Unexpected Pulitzer for Jules Feiffer," *Editor and Publisher*, May 31, 1986.

[26] John Engstrom, "Has Feiffer Switched Pens?," *Horizon*, November, 1981.

■ For More Information See

Mademoiselle, January, 1958 (p. 70).

Village Voice, May 14, 1958, April 13, 1967 (p. 5), May 4, 1967, October 25, 1976.

Mayfair, September, 1958.

Time, February 9, 1959 (p. 36), May 26, 1961, June 28, 1963.

New Republic, June 6, 1960 (p. 17ff).

Realist, February, 1961.

Cue, March 18, 1961 (p. 11).

New York Post, March 29, 1961 (p. 46), January 13, 1976, February 19, 1976, May 21, 1987.

Horizon, November, 1961.

Commentary, November, 1961, December, 1964 (p. 52ff).

Newsweek, November 13, 1961 (p. 93), May 8, 1967.

Harper's, June, 1962 (p. 74ff), February, 1968 (p. 48).

"Jules Feiffer," *Current Biography*, H. W. Wilson, 1962.

Holiday, June, 1963 (p. 66ff).

New York Times Book Review, June 30, 1963.

Saturday Evening Post, October 3, 1964 (p. 38ff).

Look, January 11, 1966 (p. 60).

New York Times, February 26, 1967 (p. 15), April 23, 1967, April 27, 1967, October 12, 1968, November 28, 1972, February 10, 1976 (p. 42), July 24, 1981 (p. C-2).

Ramparts, May, 1968 (p. 36), August, 1969 (p. 23ff).

Lydia Joel, "Happy Holidays to You and Jules Feiffer," *Dance*, December, 1968.

Plays and Players, January, 1969 (p. 35ff).

Evergreen Review, February, 1969.

Transatlantic Review, summer, 1969.

"Jules Feiffer," broadcast on Artists in America series, PBS-TV, 1971.

Graphis, Volume 28, number 159, 1972/73 (p. 76ff).

Carolyn Riley, editor, *Contemporary Literary Criticism*, Volume II, Gale, 1974.

"The Dancer Tripping the Light Fantastic Is Really the Cartoonist on a Fantastic Trip: Jules Feiffer," *People Weekly*, November 1, 1976.

Nation, July 1, 1978 (p. 19), December 30, 1978 (p. 734ff), July 11-18, 1981 (p. 39).

David Badder and Bob Baker, "Jules Feiffer," *Film Dope*, September, 1978.

"Jules Feiffer," *Dictionary of Literary Biography*, Volume 7, Gale, 1981.

Los Angeles Times, January 18, 1981, November 7, 1982 (part V, p. 1), March 20, 1983.

Focus on Film 37, March, 1981 (p. 10).

Frank D. Gilroy, "Broadway Playwrighting: An Impossible Dream?," *Dramatists Guild Quarterly*, spring, 1981.

James Vinson, editor, *Contemporary Dramatists*, 3rd edition, St. Martin's, 1982.

Progressive, January, 1983 (p. 28).

Wilson Library Bulletin, November, 1985 (p. 50).

James Harney, "New York's Prize City," *Daily News*, April 18, 1986.

Esquire, July, 1986 (p. 60).

Video, May, 1987 (p. 15).

Jerry Tallmer, "Feiffer's Fun and Prophecy," *New York Post*, May 21, 1987.

Variety, May 11, 1988 (p. 137).

Daily News Magazine, March 5, 1989 (p. 11ff).

Paula Fox

Born April 22, 1923, in New York, N.Y.; daughter of Paul Hervey (a writer) and Elsie (de Sola) Fox; married Richard Sigerson, 1948 (divorced, 1954); married Martin Greenburg (a professor), June 9, 1962; children: (first marriage) Adam, Gabriel. *Education:* Columbia University, 1955-58. *Residence:* Brooklyn, N.Y. *Agent:* Robert Lescher, Lescher & Lescher, 67 Irving Place, New York, N.Y. 10003.

■ Career

Author. Worked as a teacher at the Ethical Culture School in New York, N.Y.; University of Pennsylvania, Philadelphia, professor of English literature, 1963—. *Member:* P.E.N., Authors League of America, Authors Guild.

■ Awards, Honors

National Book Award Finalist, Children's Book Category, 1971, for *Blowfish Live in the Sea*, and 1979, for *The Little Swineherd and Other Tales*; National Institute of Arts and Letters Award, 1972; Guggenheim Fellow, 1972; Newbery Medal from the American Library Association, 1974, for *The Slave Dancer*; Hans Christian Andersen Medal,

1978; *A Place Apart* was selected one of *New York Times* Outstanding Books, 1980; American Book Award for Children's Fiction Paperback, 1983, for *A Place Apart*; Brandeis Fiction Citation, 1984; Rockefeller Foundation Fellowship Grant, 1984; Child Study Children's Book Award from the Bank Street College of Education, and one of *New York Times* Notable Books, both 1984, Newbery Honor Book, and Christopher Award, both 1985, and International Board on Books for Young People Honor List for Writing (USA), 1986, all for *One-Eyed Cat*; *The Moonlight Man* was selected one of *New York Times* Notable Books, 1986, and one of Child Study Association of America's Children's Books of the Year, 1987; Silver Medallion from the University of Southern Mississippi, 1987.

■ Writings

Maurice's Room (illustrated by Ingrid Fetz), Macmillan, 1966, reissued, 1985.
A Likely Place (illustrated by Edward Ardizzone), Macmillan, 1967.
How Many Miles to Babylon? (illustrated by Paul Giovanopoulos), David White, 1967, reissued, Bradbury, 1980.
Poor George (adult), Harcourt, 1967.
The Stone-Faced Boy (ALA Notable Book; illustrated by Donald A. Mackay), Bradbury, 1968.
Dear Prosper (illustrated by Steve McLachlin), David White, 1968.
Portrait of Ivan (illustrated by Saul Lambert), Bradbury, 1969, reissued, 1985.

The King's Falcon (*Horn Book* honor list;
  illustrated by Eros Keith), Bradbury, 1969.
Hungry Fred (illustrated by Rosemary Wells),
  Bradbury, 1969.
Blowfish Live in the Sea, Bradbury, 1970.
Desperate Characters (adult), Harcourt, 1970,
  reissued, Nonpareil, 1980.
The Western Coast (adult), Harcourt, 1972.
Good Ethan (Junior Literary Guild selection;
  illustrated by Arnold Lobel), Bradbury, 1973.
The Slave Dancer (ALA Notable Book;
  illustrated by E. Keith), Bradbury, 1973.
The Widow's Children (adult), Dutton, 1976.
The Little Swineherd and Other Tales
  (illustrated by Leonard Lubin), Dutton, 1978.
A Place Apart, Farrar, Straus, 1980.
One-Eyed Cat, Bradbury, 1984, large print
  edition, Cornerstone Books, 1987.
A Servant's Tale (adult), North Point Press,
  1984.
The Moonlight Man, Bradbury, 1986.
Lilly and the Lost Boy, Orchard Books, 1987.
The Village by the Sea, Orchard Books, 1988.

Has also written for television.

■ Adaptations

"Desperate Characters" (motion picture),
  Paramount, 1970.
"One-Eyed Cat" (cassette; filmstrip with
  cassette), Random House.

■ Work In Progress

Two adult books—one entitled

The God of Nightmares, takes place in New
  Orleans during the 1940s.

■ Sidelights

Paula Fox is one of the most highly-regarded
writers currently working in the United States. Her
books for children and young adults are regularly
cited for their intelligence, originality and social
consciousness. Her adult novels have been praised
for their exquisite craftsmanship, keen observations and uncompromising integrity. Critic Irving
Howe has written that *Desperate Characters* is a
masterpiece in a major line of American fiction,
along with *Billy Budd, The Great Gatsby, Miss
Lonelyhearts* and *Seize the Day.* Among the awards
Fox has received for her work are the Newbery
Medal, the Hans Christian Andersen Medal, a
Guggenheim Fellowship, National Institute of Arts

and Letters Award, and National Endowment for
the Arts Fellowship.

"There are a good many autobiographical details in
my books, mostly having to do with place: the
Cuban sugar plantation where I spent part of my
childhood with my grandmother; Spanish Harlem,
where my cousins lived; the Hudson Valley and
Brooklyn Heights, where I have lived. I have never
written—and do not intend to write—the 'story of
my life.' Yet my childhood was in many ways
uncommon, and I have written about parts of that.

"My father was an itinerant writer. In the 20s,
when I was born, he was trying to earn a living as a
play fixer, which meant that he was hired to
rewrite ailing plays so that they could open in New
York City. In one tryout in Boston, he told me
years later, a play he had 'fixed' opened and closed
the first night. The cast, which included Louis
Calhern, realized in the middle of the first act that
there were only three people in the audience.
Calhern advanced to the proscenium and suggested they join the cast so they wouldn't feel so
lonely.

"My father wrote several plays of his own, one of
which ran for nine months, a fairly respectable run
for that period. At some point, he went to Provincetown, where he was part of a group of writers
and actors who established the Provincetown Theater. Then he and my mother went to Hollywood,
where he worked for M-G-M, and after that to the
British-Gaumont studios in England."[1]

But Fox did not live with her parents. "As for me,
my home for the first six years of my life was with a
Congregational minister who had been a newspa-
perman...before he had found his vocation in the
ministry. He was an ardent historian of the Revolutionary period in American history, particularly as
it unfolded in the Hudson Valley, where he spent a
large part of his life. Every morning he went to his
study, and over the years there issued from his
Remington typewriter sermons, items for a column
he wrote for a local newspaper called 'Little-
Known Facts about Well-Known People,' essays on
battles that had taken place in defense of the
Hudson Heights and a book on George Washington. A volume of his poems had also been published—mostly sonnets, a form for which he felt a
special reverence. He wrote his poems by hand. In
the nursing home where he spent his last days, the
old Remington was close by on the floor next to his
bed, and there was writing paper and pen on the
bedside table along with the paraphernalia of
sickness.

"I lived with him and his invalided mother in a Victorian house on a hill that overlooked the Hudson River....The house had been built by the minister's father in the 1890s on a site he had picked out as he stood at the bow of an Albany-bound boat on his first trip through the Hudson Highlands. Like other houses of that period, it seemed to unfurl from its own turreted roof. Its exterior had a massive, brooding air, a look of depth and temperament. In strong winds, the outer branches of surrounding trees scraped against the upper windows, making a sound as evocative as certain strains of music and which still, for me, is somehow bound up with history, with the past. When there was an electric storm, of which there were many during the humid Hudson Valley summers, the three of us would sit in the front hall near the entrance doors so that if lightning struck and set the house on fire, we could escape quickly....While his mother dozed in her wheelchair, and the storm roared and wheeled around us, he told me stories....

"Often he would read something to me from his own work. He talked of the difficulties of writing a sonnet. I could hardly have understood, but the word sonnet itself stirred me. He knew many poems by heart and would recite them to me before I went to sleep. He taught me to read, and I memorized a poem myself, 'If' by Rudyard Kipling.

"There were books in nearly every room of that house. Even in the bathroom, on a shaky small rattan table, there was a volume of poems by Eugene Field. Among them was 'Little Boy Blue,' which when he read it to me, caused me to grieve so he would not read it again. Gingerly, I would open the book; an intimation of the power of words had touched me....

"When I was five, I had my first experience of being a ghost writer—of sorts. I was on my way outdoors one day when, as I passed his study, the minister called out to ask me what he should preach about the following Sunday. 'A waterfall,' I said, because at that moment I had been thinking about a picnic we had recently had on the banks of a stream fed by a cascade whose spray had dampened us and our lunch.

"I can still recollect the startled pleasure I felt that Sunday when, sitting in the corner of a pew, I realized that his sermon was, indeed, about a waterfall. Of course I knew nothing of metaphors or themes. But, for an instant, I grasped consciously what had been implicit in every aspect of my life with the minister—that everything could count, that a word, spoken as meant, contained in itself an energy capable of awakening imagination, thought, emotion, just as in the Chinese soapstone I often held in my hand, there was the concentrated essence of an earthquake.

"I think it was soon after the minister had preached his sermon on a waterfall that I told him I hoped I would be a writer when I grew up. He told me, with great seriousness, that he hoped so, too.

"When I left the minister's care, I was taken first to California for a couple of years, then to a sugar plantation in central Cuba. I didn't think about becoming a writer for a very long time, and I didn't find much to read. But he had given me substantial provisions, and they helped me through lean years."[2]

In Cuba, Fox attended a one-room school and learned to speak Spanish fluently. When Batista began his revolutionary rise to power, Fox was sent to New York. She rarely lived in one place for more than a year and hardly ever saw her parents.

Hardcover jacket for the 1980 novel.

By the time she was twelve she had gone to a total of nine schools. "I learned young that public libraries are places of refuge and stability amid chaos and confusion."[1]

Fox went to work at a variety of jobs, including machinist for Bethlehem Steel, reader for a movie production company, and punctuator of fifteenth-century Italian madrigals for a music publisher. "I knew I wanted to travel and was able to find jobs that would enable me to do so. In London I read manuscripts for Victor Gollancz, mostly novels by Irish mythologists that were so terrible they defy description. Right after the war, I became a 'stringer' for a small leftist, labor-oriented British news agency and covered Poland: the devastation wrought by the war, the concentration camps, the first efforts at recovery, the first elections. I remember meeting with the group of architects charged with rebuilding Warsaw, of which scarcely anything remained. I was taken to the concentration camp in Breslau. I remember taking a Polish aristocrat to lunch one day (it took me a month to pay off that bill!). He had been in one of the camps; his wife had lost her mind there and did not survive. 'Let me tell you a story about class,' he said with light irony. 'I tried to escape and was shot in the leg. The first thing I asked when I came out of the anesthetic was, "Will I be able to ride a horse again?"'"

"I had the opportunity then to expatriate, but somehow couldn't face the enormity and finality of such an act. Not that I'm in the least bit nationalistic, but I couldn't see giving up my citizenship or leaving the States definitely.

"Eventually I returned to New York, married, had two sons, attended Columbia University and taught at a school for emotionally disturbed students and then English to Spanish-speaking children. I also taught for a few years at Ethical Culture. I had wanted to be a writer, but for a long time it remained a shining, but elusive, goal. When my kids were about four months and two years old, my first husband and I divorced. I was teaching, my children were beyond the kind of constant custodial care they required when they were young, and I found myself with the time to write."[1]

Maurice's Room, Fox's first book tells the story about a boy who is such an avid collector that only he and one friend can enter his bedroom safely. Essentially Maurice succeeds in creating a world apart. "I was off and running. The books just seemed to pour out of me."[1]

How Many Miles to Babylon? was in many ways a breakthrough book for Fox. It was one of the first contemporary books for young adults to deal with the harsh realities of life for a black child in the inner city. Margot Hentoff of the *New York Times Book Review* wrote: "There is a dual sense of isolation; both the isolation of a lonely childhood and the further isolation of an impoverished urban existence. And like the hero of a *nouveau roman*, James moves through this dream city, accepting what he sees. . . .

"There is a plot. Perhaps too dense a plot. . . .But what is rare and valuable about this book is its unblunted vision of the way things are, and its capacity to evoke the sense of what it is to live as so many do live in this city, in this time."[3]

Ruth Hill Viguers of *Horn Book* felt that the writing was "subtle, making the understated story almost nightmarish in its excitement. Against the background, suggested rather than described, Jimmy is a small bewildered victim of an almost overwhelming situation. A story with great impact, it is far more important for young people who have no knowledge of Negro ghettos than it is for children for whom the setting may be all too familiar."[4]

The readership of *The King's Falcon* about a monarch who had no desire to rule, included college students, particularly those engaged in anti-Vietnam protests and the "counter-culture." "Of course they read it as a pacifist allegory, which in many ways, I suppose, it is. It goes to show that one can not always accurately predict what age-groups will be attracted to a given book. I thought I had written *The King's Falcon* for younger readers. It pleases me greatly that it has drawn readers of different ages."[1]

Fox is frequently asked to differentiate between literature intended for adults and literature intended for children. "That is a difficult and teasing question. As Coleridge said, 'difference is not division.' But there is a perfectly apparent difference between children and adults: whereas we all live in time, children haven't lived in time as long. Children have everything adults have, with the exception of judgment, which comes only over the course of time. So there are certain things you don't write about for children, because it does not conform to the knowledge they have acquired. I would not write an explicitly detailed sexual book for children, or one about dismembering a corpse. 'Appropriate' is a word that has currency here; and by 'appropriate' I do not mean 'prudish.' It means that you don't write about teenage pregnancies in a book for six-year-olds. Because those readers simply cannot understand.

"And yet, children know about pain and fear and unhappiness and betrayal. And we do them a disservice by trying to sugarcoat dark truths. There is an odd kind of debauchery I've noticed, particularly in societies that consider themselves 'democratic' or 'liberal': they display the gory details but hide meaning, especially if it is ambiguous or disturbing."[1]

Fox's recent book *The Moonlight Man* for young readers is a good case in point. The book takes place over a summer vacation during which a teenager lives with her divorced father. A "n'er-do-well" by his own standards, "the moonlight man" is nevertheless a beguiling, even seductive, person. After a very difficult, disillusioning visit, father and daughter take their leave of one another. "See you," says the girl. "Not if I see you first," replies her dad.

"Oh, I hope no one ever asks me the precise meaning of that last line. But it seemed to me the absolute sum of everything that is true about that

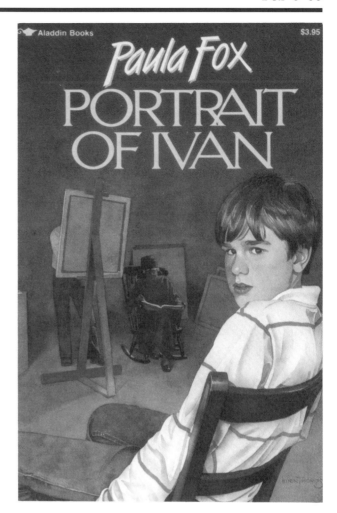

Cover for the 1987 paperbound reissue.

Dust jacket for Fox's 1970 novel.

man. The line has that wicked charm he radiates, and like many of his actions, is nearly impossible to 'read.' Given those characters, how on earth could I have written a 'happy' story about them? It would have rung completely false.

"One thing is certain: the criteria for artistry and integrity must be every bit as high in books for children as for adults. We must never, ever try to pull the wool over children's eyes by 'watering down' powerful stories. Contrary to popular belief, children are not easily fooled; they know if a story is authentic, or not. And for this they deserve our respect and the best literature that can be made available."[1]

Fox published *Desperate Characters*, her first book intended for adults, in 1970. The reviews were admiring, calling attention to Fox's craftsmanship, subtlety, grasp of complex and sometimes contradictory relationships, and extraordinary powers of observation. The book gained readers slowly and steadily, and ten years after its initial publication was reissued with an afterword by Irving Howe, who placed the book in a line of masterpieces in the American short-novel genre.

Howe explains: "The strength of [the book] lies in its prose, which we should see not as some autonomous beauty or pretty decoration, but sentence by lapidary sentence as the realization of a mind committed to the hardness of its own truth....*Desperate Characters* is a book about civilization, its fragility and its costs—I should add that, in its hard way, it is also about injustice. It captures, to some extent, a mood of the late 1960s, the anxiety of cultivated liberated people that 'everything is going to hell' and the threatening hordes are at the gate. Those who felt this were far from right, yet not entirely wrong, either; and it is the complicatedness, perhaps even the hopelessness, of the Bentwoods' responses, shown as settling into no easy formulas of acceptance or rejection, that may be one reason for Paula Fox's severity of tone. Some readers have spoken of that tone as one of resignation, but I would call it a gritty stoicism, a determination to fight for one's morale. The civilization depicted here is flawed, and without sufficient joy or energy. But it is a civilization, and even with its quotient of middle-class guilt and failure, it embodies the achievement of generations in giving us whatever it is we have."[5]

The years during which Fox wrote *Desperate Characters* were a time of explosive experimentation in fiction, indeed in all the arts. Yet in writing her novel about creeping social chaos, she chose to observe the classical unities and to make a strictly linear narrative. "I've never been part of any trend. I don't think I ever could be, or in fact would I wish to be. In the case of *Desperate Characters*, I think that the very stern simplicity allows for much more drama than what Coleridge called the 'madness prepense of pseudo-poesy.' Raging and screaming hasn't nearly the intensity for me that George Eliot has, for example. I think too that the classical form throws the contemporary setting into relief. As far as I'm concerned, an artist preoccupied with being 'modern' is well on the road to an early death. To be 'modern' is to be dead. But you can be at once classical and new.

"Story remains critical for me. Stories last—just think of the old, in fact ancient, tales that are so central a part of our lives. Style is ephemeral, and the more it calls attention to itself for its own sake, the more ephemeral it usually is."[1]

Fox may be most widely known for *The Slave Dancer*, easily her most controversial work. It is an historical novel about a white thirteen-year-old street musician who is kidnapped and forced to work on a slave ship. Jessie, the protagonist, is confronted with a series of moral tests on board ship, and although he never willingly commits any wrongful act toward the slaves, the experience profoundly, and even tragically, changes him. *The Slave Dancer* received the coveted Newbery Medal for the most distinguished work of fiction for young people published in a given year. However, the reviews were far from unanimous, and there were demonstrations against the book on the evening of the awards ceremony.

Among the book's supporters was C.S. Hannabuss, writing in *Children's Book Review*: "In a concise and carved style, Paula Fox once again gets into a child and looks out on a harsh and dangerous world. For the nightmare of the voyage is shown in the very moments of realisation, growing fear and panic and disgust gripping the reader too at deep levels of consciousness. The ship is an evil place, and cruelty and degradation and fever and greed are its crew. The boy's groping understanding and the power of suggesting by few words both generate involvement to an unusual degree, involvement which like life itself has to be worked at and worked through. Jesse's horror of the fetid hold, the hatreds among the crew, the hypocrisy of the Mate and the crazed bravado of the Captain, and the terribly just fate of the ship build on one another to a crescendo that must be resolved....This story...extends the belief that [Paula Fox] is one of the most exciting writers practising for children and young people today."[6]

Anita Moss, one of the most highly-respected scholars in the field of children's literature writes in the same vein: "*The Slave Dancer* is historical fiction at its finest, for Fox has meticulously researched every facet of the slave trade and of the period. More important she allows the reader to perceive the true horror of showing the sights, sounds, and details of it as they are filtered through Jesse's consciousness. Like Joseph Conrad's *Heart of Darkness*, *The Slave Dancer* takes the reader on a voyage that reveals a haunting glimpse into the abyss of human evil...*The Slave Dancer* is clearly Fox's masterpiece, and it is fast becoming a classic in American children's literature."[7]

A number of critics who attacked *The Slave Dancer* did so out of a belief that the story was racist and/or promoted racist viewpoints. Albert Schwartz of *Interracial Books for Children* said, "The Black people *are* only pathetic sufferers. No 'fight back' qualities whatever are found in these characterless, chained objects on the ship....For them the author presents no balance....White readers who empathize with the misery of the Black Experience can feel virtuous. To feel virtuous is to feel superior. To put it into the terms of an R. D. Laing 'Knot' or paradox: 'I feel bad that this is happening to them. I feel good that I feel bad.' But by thus feeling compassion, whites are relieved of the need to change society.''[8]

''No matter what the author's intent,'' says Binnie Tate of *Interracial Books for Children*, ''[*The Slave Dancer*] presents grave problems for those of us concerned with eliminating children's materials which help perpetuate racism....

''As the story develops the author attempts to portray the slave ship's captain and crew as villains, but through the characters' words, she excuses the captors and places the blame for the slaves' captivity on Africans themselves. The author slowly and systematically excuses almost all the whites in the story for their participation in the slave venture and by innuendo places the blame elsewhere....''[9]

Julius Lester, writing in the *New York Times Book Review*, took a slightly different approach in his attack. ''What saves [this] book from being a failure is the quality of [the] writing, which is consistently excellent. With such good writing, it is too bad that the book as a whole does not succeed. This novel describes the horrors of The Middle Passage, but it does not re-create them, and if history is to become reality, the reader must live that history as if it were his own life. In *The Slave Dancer* we are only spectators and we should have been fellow sufferers—as slave traders and slaves.''[10]

''I was under the impression that the reception of *The Slave Dancer* was an unmitigated success. Not long after the book came out I was at a party when a woman approached and said, 'My goodness, you're calm! I'd be a total wreck.' Well, I was a total wreck when I found out what was going on. And on the evening of the Newbery Award, when I learned that there were plans for a sort of demonstration, I literally thought I would die. There I was in my evening gown, shaking like a leaf. But I gave my speech, and afterwards one or two of the previously hostile critics approached me, to let me know I was 'forgiven.''[1]

Fox's Newbery Award acceptance speech may be considered an important part of her literary oeuvre, so lucidly, profoundly and elegantly does she analyze the writer's task. ''Nearly all the work of writing is silent. A writer does it alone. And the original intention—that first sudden stirring of

one's imagination—is made up of many small, almost always humble, things. Because a major effort of writing is reflection, which is silent and solitary, I place thought under the heading of the experiences I had while I was writing *The Slave Dancer*.

''By thought, I do not mean the marshalling of one's intellectual forces to refute an argument or to bring about a temporary victory over what agitates and bewilders us. All such victories are, I believe, transient. By thought, I mean that preoccupation with what we feel and why we feel it, and the enormous effort we must make to educe from a tangle of impressions and fleeting images the nature of those feelings. In this sense, thought is the effort to recognize.

''It is an effort carried about against formidable enemies: habit; inertia; the fear of change and what it will entail; the wish to preserve our idiot corners of safety, of being 'right' and self-righteousness—the most dangerous enemy of all, full of a terrible energy that would turn us away from pondering

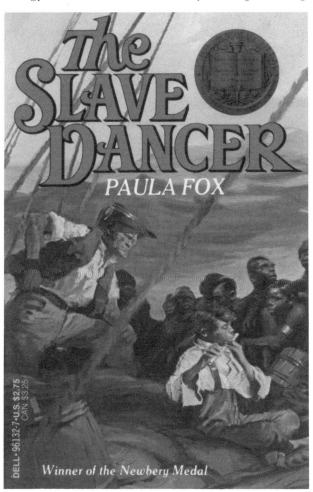

Softcover edition of the 1974 Newbery award winner.

the mystery of existence towards its own barren pleasures.

"This effort to recognize is an effort to connect ourselves with the reality of our own lives. It is painful; but if we are to become human, we cannot abandon it. Once set on that path of recognition, we cannot forswear our integral connections with other people. We must make our way towards them as best we can, try to find what is similar, try to understand what is dissimilar, try to particularize what is universal.

"Once we accept the responsibility of our connection with others, we must accept that we are like them even in our differences; and if in one instance, we are not a victim, we can be in another. And if in one instance we do not persecute, in another we will. And if we have not experienced the ultimate shame and anguish of captivity, of utter helplessness, we have experienced—at some time in our lives—something approximate to it, something from which we can construe a sense of what it is like to be other than ourselves....I write to discover, over and over again, my connections with myself, with others. Each book deepens the question. It does not answer it....

"There are those who feel that slavery debased the enslaved. It is not so. Slavery engulfed whole peoples, swallowed up their lives, committed such offenses that in considering them, the heart falters, the mind recoils. Slavery debased the enslavers....

"There are others who feel that black people can be only humiliated by being reminded that once they were brought to this country as slaves. But it is not the victim who is shamed. It is the persecutor, who has refused the shame of what he has done and, as the last turn of the screw, would burden the victim with the ultimate responsibility of the crime itself....

"I wrote *The Slave Dancer* as a never-quite-to-be-freed captive of a white childhood in a dark condition. When I read a footnote in a book, the title of which I can't now recall, that said that slaver crews often kidnapped youthful street musicians and signed them on ships as slave dancers— for such were they called—something consonant with, or peculiar to, my own sense of myself set me on the course of writing my book.

"Writing *The Slave Dancer* was the closest I could get to events of spirit and flesh which cannot help but elude in their reality all who did not experience them. Still, the effort to draw nearer is part of the effort of writing. It is not so different from the

effort to understand our own infancies which become fictions because we cannot consciously recall them. Yet a few powerful images maintain their grip on our imaginations for all of our lives. If we are able to invoke even fragments of those images, we can, sometimes, despite formidable differences in circumstance, rouse them up in others. Little though we may have in common, there is enough for us to take on the truest obligation we have—recognition of the existence of that which is other than ourselves."[11]

"This notion that we must 'identify' with characters in books, that we must be able to see the particulars of our lives in their lives and vice versa—which Julius Lester affirms—drives me up a wall. It is tantamount to saying we are unable to feel compassion, unable to bear witness, and unable to register feelings about what we have seen. This mania for identifying is right out of the sentimental slop jar of American culture. The whole point of reading is to find out about others. This insistence on always finding evidence and reflections of oneself is a result of a deep-seated denial of the reality of others. My thoughts go immediately to Maxim Gorki's three-volume autobiography, *My Life,* in which he says outright and repeatedly that reading saved his life, that had he not read about *other lives, other places, other options* and *other ambitions,* he never would have survived the horrible, dank interiors he lived in with his violent relatives. Books may well be the best way to surmount the physical, economic, social and spiritual confines of a given individual life."[1]

Fox's next book, *The Widow's Children,* drew admiring, if not altogether enthusiastic reviews. As the reviewer for *Newsweek* put it in a little vignette:
"Here. Read this novel. Please."
"Is it any good?"
"First rate."
"Will I like it?"
"Not a chance. It's for admiring, not liking."
"Oh. Well, I like to like a book."[12]

The Widow's Children takes place over the course of one evening and the following day. The "widow" of the title is the grandmother who has that afternoon died in a nursing home. The widow's daughter, the redoubtable Laura, knows and tells no one at the family dinner cum farewell party for her and her husband, who are leaving on an extended trip. It is an evening of heavy liquor, ancient rivalries, and high domestic theatre. Lau-

Fox's 1987 novel featured this jacket.

Jacket from the 1986 Bradbury edition.

ra's secret lends an extraordinary charge to the dinner, even by the melodramatic standards of the family.

The *Newsweek* reviewer goes on to say: "Mortification, humiliation, unattended gasps for recognition—Fox spares her characters no distress. . .but how is a reader to rise to this story? Fox's brilliance has a masochistic aspect: I will do this so well, she seems to say, that you will hardly be able to read it. And so she does, and so do I, who admire her work, find myself muttering in the street—'admirable, not likable.'"[12]

"People are always saying my work is 'depressing.' But what does that mean? They said *Desperate Characters* was depressing too, and it's been reissued twice. I'm so used to having the word '*depressing*' tied to me I feel like a dog accustomed to the tin can around its neck. The charge can still make me angry, not because of how it might reflect on my work, but because of what it tells me about reading in this country. Is *Anna Karenina* depressing? Is *Madame Bovary*? 'Depressing,' when applied to a literary work is so narrow, so confining, so impoverished and impoverishing. This yearning for the proverbial 'happy ending' is little more than a desire for oblivion."[1]

Ten years (and several books) after the publication of *The Slave Dancer*, Fox published *A Servant's Tale*, and in the process was once again exposed to the racism and ethnic bias ingrained in American culture. "There are two stories connected to this novel. *A Servant's Tale* is set on a sugar plantation in Cuba. Many of the events are entirely invented, but the place, and a good deal of the history is not, including the sorry attempt at revolution there. The book was rejected by an editor at Farrar, Straus because he said he had 'never heard of a revolution like that.' Well, I lived through that revolution! I was there! The point here is that the editor could not allow for what he didn't know. The irony is that the very arrogant position he took was really born of ignorance. We're back to that characteristically American mania for identification with books: the editor was saying, 'If this book isn't about me and what I know, it can't be any good. So I'll banish it.'

"The second story takes place immediately after *A Servant's Tale* was published and was being circulated for reviews. It happened that I knew someone on the editorial board of the *New York Times Book Review*, and he told me the following story. At the weekly book review meeting, the editor-in-chief said, 'There's a book by a very fine black writer I think we should review. It's called—, the author is—, the editor at this point fumbled around in his pockets, fishing for a little piece of paper. Oh yes, *A Servant's Tale* by Paula Fox. Well, my friend had all he could do not to burst into loud guffaws. The editor-in-chief had jumped to the conclusion that a book about a servant would perforce be written by a black. Particularly if that author had previously written something about slaves. It's a funny story, but its message is very discouraging.

"It seems that American consciousness is completely bound up with real estate; we have no pre-capitalist history here. The first thing the European settlers did upon arriving was to 'strike a deal' with the Indians for land. The American spirit, if you will, derives from that original real estate transaction. The recent trend in so-called minimalist writing reflects this perfectly. I do not hold with those critics who affirm that the minimalism in recent fiction is an important philosophical statement. I am not convinced that so-called minimalist writers have chosen to use a limited part of the language. Rather, I think the work is semi-literate and that those authors are using as many words as they know.

"A favorite American myth is that we have an open, democratic society. I think our society is rigidly divided. The vignette about the *Times Book Review* illustrates it. The perception is that there are black writers who write about such-and-such, white writers who would never write about what the black writers do, Spanish-American writers who have their territory, and on and on. And of course, 'white knight' publications who in their infinite bounty deign to favor with a review a few authors out of the so-called mainstream.

"In our culture, writers increasingly 'make it' on the basis of being 'personalities.' Reading and writing take time, quiet and solitude, all of which are grossly devalued in this country. It isn't merely that ours is a visual culture: look at the horrendous quality of visual imagery on television. I could accept, I think, that the visual was becoming a pre-eminent form of literacy. But the common fund of visual imagery that pervades television and the media is execrable and lacks complexity and reso-

nance. It consists mostly of flashes, demanding mere seconds of our attention.

"This was really brought home to me when I was teaching in the early and mid-seventies. My students were of the first generation to be raised on television. Because our classes were three hours, which I found impossibly long, I spent a good deal of time reading to them. And they were mesmerized, they couldn't get enough. For they had not been read to. They'd been plunked down in front of the TV instead. They had very little in the way of a common literary currency, their cultural points of reference were not tales, myths, poems, novels or plays—they were TV shows and, especially, TV commercials.

"It isn't like this everywhere. In Europe, for example, writers are held in great esteem. The assumption is that good writing, in and of itself, has value. I remember when I was finally able to quit my teaching job and devote myself full-time to writing. People asked me, 'But what will you do?'

"'I'm going to write books,' I would say. And they would reply, 'Yes, but what will you DO?'

"People have this idea that a life spent writing is essentially a life of leisure. Writing is tremendously hard work. There is nothing more satisfying, but it is work all the same. Even after years of experience and a good number of books published, it can still be painfully difficult.

"I generally don't work from an outline (although for *A Servant's Tale* I had a kind of blueprint), but do keep notebooks. I write down everything that comes to mind in no apparent order. I dream a lot, and everything I see, dream, feel and think seems to relate to the book. I keep pads all over the house, so that even when I'm chopping onions, if something occurs to me, I can easily jot it down. It is very easy to lose ideas and impressions—writing them down 'solidifies' them. I work every day, starting in the morning because that's when my energy is best. Usually I put in about four hours of writing, though when I'm finishing a book I'll work straight through until evening. I need a lot of time around my writing periods. If I know I have an afternoon appointment, for example, I'm somewhat distracted all morning and don't work as well as I might."[1]

Fox's conversation is studded with quotes, paraphrases and references to her favorite writers. "I love George Eliot, James Joyce, D. H. Lawrence, and E. M. Forster. Tolstoy is another hero, and Flannery O'Connor a heroine. O'Connor gets better and better to me: as time passes she becomes more immediate. There are several Italian writers who mean a lot to me. Alberto Moravia is one. He is very hard and cold and very brilliant. His greatest work, I think, is *The Conformist.* Hard to believe, but it is out of print in this country. Cesare Pavese, too, is enormously important; his autobiography *This Business of Living* is a cornerstone for me. Elsa Morante's *History: A Novel* is a stupendous effort depicting Italy during its fascist period. The title alone expresses her ambition. In Europe, it is considered the finest novel to come out of Italy since the war—its first edition sold out within hours. Here, sales languished and reviews carped about the book's considerable length. Here, it seemed, Morante's ambition was held against her.

"It is the work of other writers and the examples of their lives that provide the deepest encouragement and the most abiding inspiration. In some ways, the work is harder now than it was. I am more conscious of craft now and much more deliberate in my efforts. And at times I'm weary of myself, tired of my own mind. Yet, to an extent we are all prisoners of ourselves, even though we write to lessen that bondage. And perhaps, on balance, the enterprise is easier. I no longer feel that people are looking over my shoulder with every sentence I write. Even the parrot who used to look over my shoulder is gone now. Early in my career, I was hungry for attention, for praise, for awards. I am less vain now. I have my work to do, and I do it. Come what may."[1]

Footnote Sources:

[1] Based on an interview by Marguerite Feitlowitz for *Authors and Artists for Young Adults.*

[2] Paula Fox, "A Childhood of Sermons and Sonnets," *New York Times Book Review,* July 12, 1981.

[3] Margot Hentoff, *"How Many Miles to Babylon?" New York Times Book Review,* September 24, 1967.

[4] Ruth Hill Viguers, *Horn Book,* October, 1967.

[5] Irving Howe, "On *Desperate Characters," New Republic,* April 19, 1980.

[6] C. S. Hannabuss, *Children's Book Review,* winter, 1974-75.

[7] Anita Moss, "Paula Fox," *Dictionary of Literary Biography,* Volume 52, Gale, 1986.

[8] Albert V. Schwartz, *Interracial Books for Children,* Volume 5, number 5, 1974.

[9] Binnie Tate, *Interracial Books for Children,* Volume 5, number 5, 1974.

[10] Julius Lester, *New York Times Book Review,* January 20, 1974.

[11] Lee Kingman, editor, *Newbery and Caldecott Medal Winners 1966-1975,* Horn Book, 1975.

[12] "Books," *Newsweek,* September 27, 1976.

■ For More Information See

Books:

Sheila Egoff and others, editors, *Only Connect: Readings on Children's Literature,* Oxford University Press, 1969.

John Rowe Townsend, *A Sense of Story: Essays on Contemporary Writers for Children,* Lippincott, 1971, revised and enlarged edition published as *A Sounding of Storytellers: New and Revised Essays on Contemporary Writers for Children,* Lippincott, 1979.

Contemporary Literary Criticism, Gale, Volume II, 1974, Volume VIII, 1978.

Children's Literature Review, Volume I, Gale, 1976.

Doris de Montreville and Donna Hill, *Fourth Book of Junior Authors and Illustrators,* H. W. Wilson, 1978.

D. L. Kirkpatrick, editor, *Twentieth-Century Children's Writers,* St. Martin's, 1978, new edition, 1983.

Lina Mainiero, editor, *American Women Writers: A Critical Reference Guide from Colonial Times to the Present,* Ungar, 1980.

Dictionary of Literary Biography, Volume LII: *American Writers for Children since 1960: Fiction,* Gale, 1986.

Periodicals:

Atlantic Monthly, December, 1967.

Horn Book, August, 1969, April, 1970, December, 1970 (p. 623), April 1974, August, 1974, October, 1977 (p. 514ff), April, 1984 (p. 219ff), August, 1984 (p. 496ff).

New York Times Book Review, February 1, 1970, October 8, 1972, October 3, 1976, November 9, 1980, May 8, 1983 (p. 12ff), November 11, 1984, November 18, 1984.

New Leader, February 2, 1970.

New Yorker, February 7, 1970, November 1, 1976.

New York Times, February 10, 1970, September 22, 1972, September 16, 1976.

Newsweek, March 16, 1970, December 1, 1980.

Saturday Review, September 19, 1970 (p. 34), January 23, 1971, October 16, 1976.

New York Review of Books, October 5, 1972, October 28, 1976, June 27, 1985.

New Statesman, November 8, 1974, December 4, 1981.

Interracial Books for Children, Volume 5, number 5, 1974.

Time, October 4, 1976.

Washington Post Book World, October 31, 1976, February 8, 1981, September 23, 1984.

New Republic, January 15, 1977.

Critique: Studies in Modern Fiction, Volume 20, number 2, 1978 (p.33ff).

Perry Nodelman, "How Typical Children Read Typical Books," *Children's Literature in Education,* number 12, winter, 1981 (p. 177ff).

Lois R. Kuznets, "The Fresh-Air Kids, or Some Contemporary Versions of Pastoral," *Children's Literature,* number 11, 1983 (p. 156ff).

Ms., October, 1984.

Nation, November 3, 1984.

Commonweal, January 11, 1985.

Alleen Pace Nilsen and Kenneth L. Donelson, *Literature for Today's Young Adults,* 2nd edition, Scott, Foresman, 1985.

Times Literary Supplement, February 21, 1986.

School Library Journal, November, 1987 (p. 33ff), May, 1988 (p. 48ff).

Jacqueline S. Weiss, "Paula Fox" (videocassette), Profiles in Literature Series, Temple University, 1987.

Gabriel Garcia Marquez

Surname pronounced Gar-*see*-a Mar-*kez*; born March 6, 1928, in Aracataca, Colombia; son of Gabriel Eligio Garcia (a telegraph operator) and Luisa Santiaga Marquez (Iguaran); married Mercedes Barcha, March 21, 1958; children: Rodrigo, Gonzalo. *Education:* Attended Universidad Nacional de Colombia, 1947-48, and Universidad de Cartegena, 1948-49. *Address:* P.O. Box 20736, Mexico City D.F., Mexico. *Agent:* Agencia Literara Carmen Balcelos, Diagonal 580, Barcelona 11, Spain. *Office:* Apartado Postal 20736 Deleyacion Alvaro bregon 01000, Mexico.

■ Career

Worked as a journalist in Latin America, Europe, and the United States, 1947-65; writer, 1965—. Fundacion Habeas, founder, 1979, president, 1979—. *Member:* American Academy of Arts and Letters (honorary fellow).

■ Awards, Honors

Colombian Association of Writers and Artists Award, 1954, for short story "Un dia despues del sabado"; Premio Literario Esso (Colombia), 1961, for *La mala hora;* Chianchiano Award (Italy), 1969, Prix de Meilleur Livre Etranger (France), 1969, and Romulo Gallegos Prize (Venezuela), 1972, all for *One Hundred Years of Solitude;* honorary doctorate, Columbia University, 1971; Neustadt International Prize for Literature from *Books Abroad,* 1972; Common Wealth Award for Literature from the Bank of Delaware, 1980; Nobel Prize for Literature, 1982.

■ Writings

La hojarasca (novel), Ediciones Sipa (Colombia), 1955, translation by Gregory Rabassa, published as "Leaf Storm" in *Leaf Storm and Other Stories,* Harper, 1972.

El coronel no tiene quien le escriba (novella), Aguirre Editor (Colombia), 1961, translation by J. S. Berstein, published as "No One Writes to the Colonel" in *No One Writes to the Colonel and Other Stories,* Harper, 1968, original Spanish editon published with *La increible y triste historia de la candida Erendira y de su abuela desalmada* (novella), Libreria del Colegio (Buenos Aires), 1975.

La mala hora (novel), Talleres de Graficas "Luis Perez" (Spain), 1962, translation by G. Rabassa, published as *In Evil Hour,* Harper, 1979.

Cien anos de soledad (novel), Editorial Sudamericana (Argentina), 1967, translation by G. Rabassa, published as *One Hundred Years of Solitude,* Harper, 1970.

Isabel viendo llover en Macondo (novella), Editorial Estuario (Argentina), 1967, translation by G. Rabassa, published as "Monologue of Isabel Watching It Rain in Macondo" in *Leaf Storm and Other Stories*, Harper, 1972.

(With Mario Vargas Llosa) *La novela en America Latina: Dialogo*, Carlos Milla Batres (Peru), 1968.

Relato de un naufrago, Tusquets Editor (Spain), 1970, published as *The Story of a Shipwrecked Sailor*, Random House, 1986.

El otono del patriarca (novel), Plaza & Janes Editores (Spain), 1975, translation by G. Rabassa, published as *The Autumn of the Patriarch*, Harper, 1976.

Cronica de una muerte anunciada (novel), Oveja Negra, 1981, translation by G. Rabassa, published as *Chronicle of a Death Foretold*, J. Cape, 1982, Knopf, 1983.

(With P. Mendoza) *El olor de la guayaba* (title means, "The Fragrance of Guava"), Oveja Negra (Colombia), 1982.

El amor en los tiempos del colera, Oveja Negra, 1984, translated by Edith Grossman, published as *Love in the Time of Cholera*, Knopf, 1988.

La Aventura de Miguel Littin Clandestino en Chile, Oveja Negra, 1986, translated by Asa Zatz, published as *Clandestine in Chile: The Adventures of Miguel Littin*, Holt, 1986.

El General en su Laberinto, Oveja Negra, 1989.

Omnibus Volumes:

Los funerales de la Mama Grande (short stories), Editorial Universidad Veracruzana (Mexico), 1962, translation by J. S. Berstein of title story published as "Big Mama's Funeral" in *No One Writes to the Colonel and Other Stories*, Harper, 1968.

No One Writes to the Colonel and Other Stories, Harper, 1968.

La increible y triste historia de la candida Erendira y de su abuela desalmada (short stories), Barral Editores (Spain), 1972, translation by G. Rabassa of title story published as "Innocent Erendira and Her Heartless Grandmother" in *Innocent Erendira and Other Stories*, Harper, 1978.

Leaf Storm and Other Stories, Harper, 1972.

El negro que hizo esperar a los angles (short stories), Ediciones Alfil (Uruguay), 1972.

Ojos de perro azul: nueve cuentos desconocidos (short stories), Equisditorial (Argentina), 1972, translation by G. Rabassa of title story published as "Eyes of a Blue Dog" in *Innocent Erendira and Other Stories*, Harper, 1978.

Cuando era feliz e indocumentado (journalistic pieces; title means "When I Was Happy and Undocumented"), Ediciones El Ojo del Camello (Venezuela), 1973.

Todos los cuentos de Gabriel Garcia Marquez: 1947-1972 (title means "All the Stories of Gabriel Garcia Marquez: 1947-1972"), Plaza & Janes Editores, 1975.

Cronicas y reportajes (journalistic pieces), Oveja Negra, 1978.

Periodismo militante (journalistic pieces), Son de Maquina Editores (Colombia), 1978.

Innocent Erendira and Other Stories (includes translation of stories from several collections), Harper, 1978.

De viaje por los paises socialistas: 90 dias en las "Cortina de hierro" (journalistic pieces), Ediciones Macondo (Colombia), 1978.

Obra periodistica (journalistic pieces), Volume I: *Textos costenos*, Bruguera, 1981.

Collected Stories, translated by G. Rabassa and S. J. Bernstein, Harper, 1984.

Plays:

"Diatribe of Love against a Seated Man," first produced in Buenos Aires, Argentina at Cervantes Theater, August, 1988.

Author of weekly syndicated column in Spanish-language newspapers.

■ Adaptations

Two of Garcia Marquez' works have been adapted into motion pictures: "Erendira," Les Films du Triangle, 1984, and "Chronicle of a Death Foretold," 1987.

■ Sidelights

1928. Born in Aracataca, Colombia. "...Everyone knows that I was born with the umbilical cord tangled around my neck almost strangling me. This was the origin of my terrible claustrophobia."[1]

"...I happen to come from the Caribbean part of Colombia, which is a fantastic place—completely different from the Andean part, the highlands. During the colonial period of Colombian history, all the people who considered themselves respectable went to the interior—to Bogota. On the coast, all that were left, were bandits—bandits in the good sense—and dancers, adventurers, people full of gaiety. The coastal people were descendants of pirates and smugglers, with a mixture of black slaves. To grow up in such an environment is to have fantastic resources for poetry. Also, in the Caribbean, we are capable of believing anything, because we have the influences of all those different cultures, mixed in with Catholicism and our own local beliefs. I think that gives us an open-mindedness to look beyond apparent reality....Growing up, I heard wonderful stories of people who were able to move chairs by simply looking at them. There was a man in Aracataca who had the facility for deworming cows—for healing their infections—by standing in front of the beasts. He would stand in front of the cow and the worms would start coming out of the head of the cow. Now, it's true that I once saw that....That seemed marvelous to me as a child, and it still does."[2]

Until the age of eight, Garcia Marquez lived with his grandparents, Colonel Nicolas Ricardo and Dona Tranquilina. "It's a story that's common in the Caribbean. My parents were poor. My father worked as a telegraphist. When my father wanted to marry the daughter of Colonel Nicolas Marquez, her family opposed it; my father had a reputation for going with too many women. So, after the wedding, my father took a job in another town far from Aracataca. When my mother became pregnant with me, in a gesture of reconciliation, my grandparents said, 'Come have the baby in our house.' Which she gladly did. After a while, my mother returned to the village my father was working in, and so my grandparents said, 'Leave Gabriel with us to raise.' The family was poor and, as I said, extended families are common in the Caribbean. Later on, when my parents returned to Aracataca, I went on living with my grandparents—where I was mostly very happy.

"...In the Caribbean, it's perfectly natural to live with grandparents and aunts and uncles. It *is* true that for the longest time, my mother was a stranger to me. I remember one morning being told to dress up because my mother was coming for a visit. I have no memory of her before that. I remember going into a room, and there were many women sitting there and I felt disconcerted, because I didn't know which one was my mother. She made some kind of gesture that made me realize that it was she. And she wore a dress from the Twenties, really from the Twenties, with a long waistline and a straw hat. She looked like Louise Brooks. Then she embraced me and I became very frightened, because I felt I didn't love her. I'd heard one was supposed to love one's mother very much, and it seemed evil that I didn't. Later on, when my parents moved to Aracataca, I remember going to their house only when I was sick. I'd have to stay overnight, and I would be given a purgative of resin oil. It's not a pleasant memory."[2]

Both Garcia Marquez's grandmother and grandfather were instrumental in building his character which eventually influenced his style of writing. "...My grandfather...was the only person I communicated with in the house. The world of the women—it was so fantastic that it escaped me. But my grandfather brought me back to reality by telling me stories about tangible things—items from the newspapers, war stories from the time he was a colonel on the liberal side in the Colombian civil wars. Whenever my grandmother or my aunts

Cover from the paperback edition of the multi-award-winning novel.

said something particularly wild, he'd say, 'Don't listen to that. Those are women's beliefs.' My grandfather also had a great practical sense—which I think I inherited from him. Among my friends, it is often said that I'm one of the few writers they know who ha[s] a practical sense. It is that practical sense that I use for politics. And also for everyday life. I have a great sense of safety. I am very worried about preventing accidents—I take precautions so that they don't happen. I prefer stairs to elevators. I prefer *anything* to planes. That practical sensibility is not typical of poets. And if, someday, I become a patriarch, a patriarch in the political sense, it will be for that reason—not because I have real power. My friends always consult me on practical matters, and that is something I got from my grandfather."

"...When he spoke of the civil wars, he spoke of them as almost pleasant experiences—sort of youthful adventures with guns. Nothing like the wars of today. Oh, certainly, the civil wars had many terrible battles and many, many deaths. But during that time, my grandfather also had a great many love affairs and he also fathered a great many children.

"...The exact number will never be known...According to my mother, there were seventeen. She was one of the two children who came from the marriage.

"...My grandmother was a very, very jealous woman. But when she'd hear of one of those children being born...she took it into her household. My grandmother said that the family blood couldn't just wander out there, lost. Anyway, she loved all those children a lot. There was a point in that house when you couldn't tell which children came from the marriage and which didn't. My grandmother was also a very strong woman. When my grandfather went off to the war, she didn't have any news of him for a year. She took care of the house and the security of the family until, one might, there was a knock on the door. In the dark, in the early hours of the morning, someone said, 'Tranquilina, if you want to see Nicolas, come to the door now.' And so she ran and opened the door and she could see these men on horseback passing, but she didn't see him. All she saw was the horses leaving town. It was a year later before she received any further news of him."[2]

"The style of my books is almost entirely that of my grandmother. Whenever she did not want to answer a question, she would invent fantasies so that I wouldn't be saddened by the truth of things.

It was almost impossible for me to distinguish where reality left off and imagination took over; my head was full of images. The world of my childhood caused me to lose my fear of doing some things in literature, because anything is possible—just as it had been in my childhood."[1]

"...She was a fabulous storyteller who told wild tales of the supernatural with a most solemn expression on her face. As I was growing up, I often wondered whether or not her stories were truthful. Usually, I tended to believe her because of her serious, deadpan facial expression. Now, as a writer, I do the same thing: I say extraordinary things in a serious tone. It's possible to get away with *anything* as long as you make it believable. That is something my grandmother taught me."[2]

1936. Grandfather died. "After the death of my grandfather, nothing really interesting happened to me any more."[3]

"[He was] the person I've probably got on best with in my life and with whom I've had the best understanding. But looking back nearly fifty years later I feel he probably never realized it. I don't know why but this notion, which I first thought about when I was an adolescent, has always upset me. It's very frustrating, like having to live with a gnawing uncertainty which should have been cleared up but never will now because my grandfather died when I was eight. I didn't see him die because I was in another town a long way from Aracataca at the time, and I wasn't even given the news but heard people in the house where I was staying talk about it. It had no effect on me at all, as I remember; yet as an adult whenever anything happens to me, particularly if it's something good, I feel the only thing missing to make me completely happy is for my grandfather to know. So all my happy moments as an adult have been slightly spoilt by this germ of frustration, and always will be."[4]

The memories of Aracataca and his childhood home would continue to haunt Garcia Marquez as did the supernatural tales woven in the night by his grandmother. "My most constant and vivid memory is not so much of the people but of the actual house in Aracataca where I lived with my grandparents. It's a recurring dream which persists even now. What's more, every single day of my life I wake up with the feeling, real or imaginary, that I've dreamt I'm in that huge old house. Not that I've gone back there, but that I *am* there, at no particular age, for no particular reason—as if I'd never left it. Even now in my dreams that sense of

Irene Papas as the outrageously wicked grandmother in the film version of "Erendira."

night-time foreboding which dominated my whole childhood still persists. It was an uncontrollable sensation which began early every evening and gnawed away at me in my sleep until I saw dawn breaking through the cracks in the door. I can't define it very well, but I think that sense of foreboding was rooted in the fact that, at night, all my grandmother's phantoms, portents and invocations took shape. That was our relationship, a kind of invisible thread keeping us both in touch with the world of the supernatural. During the day my grandmother's magic world fascinated me—I was absorbed in it, it was my world. But at night it terrified me. Even now, when I'm asleep alone in a strange hotel in some part of the world, I often wake up in a panic, shaken by this terrible fear of being alone in the dark, and it always takes me several minutes to calm down and go back to sleep. My grandfather, on the other hand, represented absolute security in my grandmother's uncertain world. My anxieties disappeared when he was there. I felt I was on firm ground again, back in the real world. The strange thing was that I wanted to

be like my grandfather—realistic, brave, safe—but I could not resist the constant temptation to peep into my grandmother's territory."[4]

Following his grandfather's death, he was sent to live with his parents. "...I had problems at first, because my system for communicating with adults had been different, almost supernatural. In my parents' house I encountered the concrete reality of people who had seven children and who expected the eighth the next year, then the ninth, and so on."[1]

"The most distinctive feature of my relationship with my mother, since I was quite a small boy, has been its seriousness. It's probably the most serious relationship I've ever had. I believe there's nothing she and I can't tell each other and no subject we can't talk about, but we've always treated one another with a certain almost professional formality, rather than any intimacy. It's difficult to explain, but that's how it is. Perhaps it comes from my having gone to live with her and my father when I was already old enough to think for myself. . . .For her my arrival must have meant that there was one of her numerous children (all the others were younger than me) to whom she could really talk and who would help her sort out her domestic problems. She had a tough, unrewarding life, sometimes in extreme poverty.

". . .I already had a very solid paternal image—my grandfather's image. My father was not only unlike my grandfather, he was almost the exact opposite. His personality, his idea of authority, his whole view of the world and of his relationship with his children, were completely different. It's very likely that at that age I was affected by the sudden change, so that until adolescence I found our relationship very difficult to cope with. It was mostly my fault. I was never sure how to behave with him. I didn't know how to please him and mistook his strictness for lack of understanding. In spite of all this, I think we both managed it well because we never ever had a serious quarrel.

"On the other hand, I feel I owe much of my vocation for literature to him. In his youth he used to write poems, not always clandestinely, and when he was a telegraph operator in Aracataca he played the violin very well. He's always loved literature and is an avid reader. . . .My father reads anything and everything he can get his hands on—the best literature, all the newspapers and magazines, advertising hand-outs, refrigerator manuals, anything. I don't know anyone more bitten by the literature bug. . . ."[4]

"My father was trying a lot of different things to make a living. The situation was so terrible that my parents were waiting for a miracle—hoping to win the lottery, or something like that. I realized I couldn't stay there for long or we would all sink together, so when I was twelve I decided to apply for a scholarship. I had to take an exam in Bogota. The 700-mile, eight-day voyage by ship cost more than our family's budget for three months, but my parents arranged it somehow.

"The last leg of the trip was by train, and one of the most hopeless memories I have is an image of myself, alone in a station, sitting on a metal trunk, thinking, 'Now what do I do?' There were other students in the station, so I went with them to a *pension*. The next day I got in an enormous line to register for the scholarship test; there were 3,000 of us, and only 300 would be chosen.

"Then something absolutely providential happened. On the train a shy man had asked if I would copy the lyrics of a song we were singing because he was sure the girl he would marry would like it.

Now that man walked up and asked what I was doing in the long line. He turned out to be in charge of scholarships for the whole country. He gave me a scholarship to a school an hour outside of Bogota."[1]

By the time Garcia Marquez finished high school in Bogota in 1946, he had earned the reputation of being a writer, but it wasn't until he entered law school at the Universidad Nacional in Bogota (1947) that he began his first short stories. ". . .Before I could read or write I used to draw comics at school and at home. The funny thing is that I now realize that when I was in high school I had the reputation of being a writer, though I never in fact wrote anything. If there was a pamphlet to be written or a letter of petition, I was the one to do it because I was supposedly the writer. When I entered college I happened to have a very good literary background in general, considerably above the average of my friends. At the university in Bogota, I started making new friends and acquaintances, who introduced me to contemporary writers. One night a friend lent me a book of short stories by Franz Kafka. I went back to the pension where I was staying and began to read *The Metamorphosis*. The first line almost knocked me off the bed. I was so surprised. The first line reads, 'As Gregor Samsa awoke that morning from uneasy dreams, he found himself transformed in his bed into a gigantic insect. . . .' When I read the line I thought to myself that I didn't know anyone was allowed to write things like that. If I had known, I would have started writing a long time ago. So I immediately started writing short stories. They are totally intellectual short stories because I was writing them on the basis of my literary experience and had not yet found the link between literature and life. The stories were published in the literary supplement of the newspaper *El Espectador* in Bogota and they did have a certain success at the time—probably because nobody in Colombia was writing intellectual short stories. What was being written then was mostly about life in the countryside and social life."[5]

". . .That's when I first became interested in the novel. . .when I decided to read all the most important novels ever written.

". . .Starting with the Bible: a fabulous book where fantastic things happen all the time. I dropped everything, including my law degree, and dedicated myself entirely to reading novels. To reading novels and writing.

"All of a sudden I understood how many other possibilities existed in literature outside the rational and extremely academic examples I'd come across in secondary school text books. It was like tearing off a chastity belt. Over the years, however, I discovered that you can't invent or imagine just whatever you fancy because then you risk not telling the truth and lies are more serious in literature than in real life. Even the most seemingly arbitrary creation has its rules. You can throw away the fig leaf of rationalism only if you don't then descend into total chaos and irrationality."[4]

1950. Joined the staff of *El Heraldo,* a newspaper in Barranquilla, where he became acquainted with men who shared his intense study and interest in literature. "It was an absolutely astonishing period for me and a period of discovery not only about literature but about life. We'd go on until dawn getting drunk and talking about literature. Every night at least ten books I hadn't read would come up in the conversation. The next day they'd all be lent to me. They had them all....Also, one of the group was a bookseller and we used to help him make up the orders. Whenever a crate of books arrived from Buenos Aires, we'd go quite mad...."[4]

Through his ferocious reading, Garcia Marquez discovered the masters: Sophocles, Hemingway, Faulkner, and Woolfe, who became his teachers. "I don't know who said that novelists read the novels of others only to figure out how they are written. I believe it's true. We aren't satisfied with the secrets exposed on the surface of the page: we turn the book around to find the seams. In a way that's impossible to explain, we break the book down to its essential parts and then put it back together after we understand the mysteries of its personal clockwork. The effort is disheartening in Faulkner's books, because he doesn't seem to have an organic system of writing, but instead walks blindly through his biblical universe, like a herd of goats loosed in a shop full of crystal. Managing to dismantle a page of his, one has the impression of springs and screws left over, that it's impossible to put back together in its original state. Hemingway, by contrast, with less inspiration, with less passion and less craziness but with a splendid severity, left the screws fully exposed, as they are on freight cars. Maybe for that reason Faulkner is a writer who has had much to do with my soul, but Hemingway is the one who had the most to do with my craft—not simply for his books, but for his astounding knowledge of the aspect of craftsmanship in the science of writing. In his historic interview with George Plimpton in *The Paris Review,* he showed...that one of the chief difficulties is arranging the words well; that when writing becomes hard it is good to reread one's own books, in order to remember that it always was hard; that one can write anywhere so long as there are no visitors and no telephone; and that it is not true that journalism finishes off a writer, as has so often been said—rather, just the opposite, so long as one leaves it behind soon enough. 'Once writing has become the principal vice and the greatest pleasure,' he said, 'only death can put an end to it.' Finally, his lesson was the discovery that each day's work should only be interrupted when one knows where to begin again the next day. I don't think that any more useful advice has ever been given about writing. It is, no more and no less, the absolute remedy for the most terrible specter of

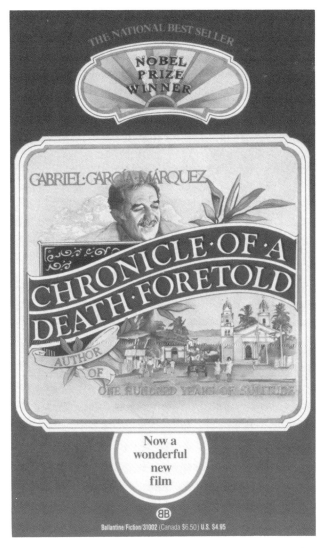

Paperback edition of the novel described as "a sort of metaphysical murder mystery."

writers: the morning agony of facing the blank page."[6]

During 1950 Garcia Marquez returned to Aracataca—a trip that provided the inspiration for his novel, *Leaf Storm*. "...My mother asked me to accompany her to Aracataca, where I was born, and to sell the house where I spent my first years. When I got there it was at first quite shocking because I was now twenty-two and hadn't been there since the age of eight. Nothing had really changed, but I felt that I wasn't really looking at the village, but I was *experiencing* it as if I were reading it. It was as if everything I saw had already been written, and all I had to do was to sit down and copy what was already there and what I was just reading. For all practical purposes everything had evolved into literature: the houses, the people, and the memories. I'm not sure whether I had already read Faulkner or not, but I know now that only a technique like Faulkner's could have enabled me to write down what I was seeing.

"The atmosphere, the decadence, the heat in the village were roughly the same as what I had felt in Faulkner. It was a banana plantation region inhabited by a lot of Americans from the fruit companies which gave it the same sort of atmosphere I had found in the writers of the Deep South. Critics have spoken of the literary influence of Faulkner, but I see it as a coincidence: I had simply found material that had to be dealt with in the same way that Faulkner had treated similar material.

"From that trip to the village I came back to write *Leaf Storm*, my first novel. What really happened to me in that trip to Aracataca was that I realized that everything that had occurred in my childhood had a literary value that I was only now appreciating. From the moment I wrote *Leaf Storm* I realized I wanted to be a writer and that nobody could stop me and that the only thing left for me to do was to try to be the best writer in the world.

"...When I was working for *El Espectador* in Bogota, I used to do at least three stories a week, two or three editorial notes every day, and I did movie reviews. Then at night, after everyone had gone home, I would stay behind writing my novels. I liked the noise of the Linotype machines, which sounded like rain. If they stopped, and I was left in silence, I wouldn't be able to work."[5]

1955. Went to Geneva as a correspondent for *El Espectador*. A high point of his newspaper career occurred in 1956 when a sailor, Louis Alejandro Velasco, came to the *El Espectador* staff with an offer to tell the story of his survival at sea. Velasco

was turned over to Garcia Marquez. "It wasn't questions and answers. The sailor would just tell me his adventures and I would rewrite them trying to use his own words and in the first person, as if he were the one who was writing. When the work was published as a serial in a newspaper, one part each day for two weeks, it was signed by the sailor, not by me. It wasn't until twenty years later that it was published and people found out I had written it."[5]

"There's not a single invented detail in the whole account. That's what's so astonishing. If I had invented that story I would have said so, and been very proud of it too....He told me his story in minute detail. As his cultural level was only fair he didn't realize the extreme importance of many of the details he told me spontaneously, and was surprised at my being so struck by them. By carrying out a form of psychoanalysis I helped him remember things— for instance, a seagull he saw flying over his raft—and in that way we succeeded in reconstructing his whole adventure. It went like a bomb! The idea had been to publish the story in five or six installments in *El Espectador* but by about the third there was such enthusiasm among the readers, and the circulation of the paper had increased so enormously, that the editor said to me, 'I don't know how you're going to manage, but you must get at least twenty installments out of this.' So then I set about enriching every detail."[7]

First novel published. *Leaf Storm*, a story told through the monologues of three characters attending a wake, takes place in Macondo, a mythical land based on Aracataca which provides the setting for many of his stories. Garcia Marquez has called *Leaf Storm* the favorite of his novels. "The only character who resembles my grandfather is the unnamed colonel in *Leaf Storm*. In fact, that character is a minutely detailed copy both of his personality and the way he looked. However, this is perhaps a subjective judgement because the colonel isn't described in the novel and the reader's image of him will probably be different in the novel and the reader's image of him will probably be different from mine. My grandfather lost an eye in a way I thought too dramatic to put in any novel: he was looking at a beautiful white horse from his office window when he suddenly felt something in his left eye; he put his hand over it and lost his eyesight quite painlessly. I don't remember the incident, but as a child I often heard it talked about and my grandmother always ended by saying, 'He had nothing left in his hand but tears.' This physical defect was transposed to the colonel in *Leaf Storm*—he is lame. I don't know if I put it in the novel but I've always had in mind that his lameness was the result of a war wound. My grandfather attained the rank of colonel in the revolutionary Forces of the Liberal Party during the Thousand Days' War in Colombia in the early part of this century. My most vivid memory of him relates to this. Just before he died a doctor was examining him in bed (I don't know why exactly) and he suddenly noticed a scar near my grandfather's groin. 'That was a bullet,' said my grandfather. He'd often talked to me about the civil war and it was he who stimulated an interest in that historical period which comes across in all my books, but he'd never told me that that scar had been made by a bullet. When he told the doctor that, to me it was like the revelation of something legendary and heroic."[4]

1958. Returned to South America and married his childhood sweetheart, Mercedes Barcha. "I met Mercedes in Sucre, a town just inland from the Caribbean coast, where both our families lived for several years and where she and I spent our holidays. Her father and mine had been friends

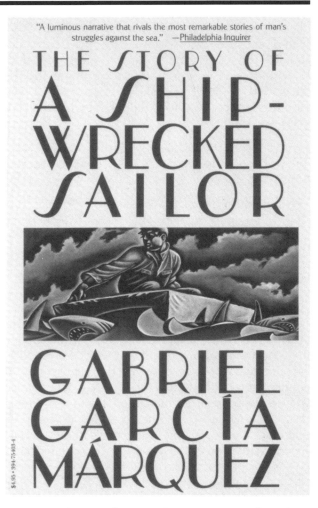

Paperback cover for one of Garcia Marquez's early works.

since they were boys. One day, at a students' dance, when she was only thirteen, I asked her to marry me. Looking back I think the proposal was a metaphorical way of getting round all the fuss and bother you had to go through in those days to get a girlfriend. She must have understood it this way because we saw each other very sporadically, and always very casually, but I think neither of us had any doubt that sooner or later the metaphor would become fact."[4]

"I'm convinced that everyone has a totally secret and personal part of his personality that is never communicated or revealed. Mercedes and I, for instance have a very good relationship....Yet we are both aware that we have obscure areas that neither person can enter. And we've been respectful of that, because we know there's no way to fight it. For instance, I don't know how old Mercedes is. I didn't know her age when we married, and she was very young then. When we travel, I *never* look at her passport or identity card. On airplanes, I'll

Jacket from the 1988 Knopf publication.

fill out our landing cards and leave blank the section on hers that requires the birth date. Of course, this is a game. But it's a game that represents very well how there are impenetrable areas that none of us can ever go near. I am absolutely sure that it is impossible to know a person completely."[2]

1959. During the Cuban Revolution, Garcia Marquez headed the Cuban News Agency, "Prensa Latina," in Bogota, Cuba, and New York.

1961. Published *No One Writes to the Colonel*, the story of an aging colonel who spends fifteen years waiting for his pension check.

1962. Published *In Evil Hour*, a novel in which anonymous notes revealing secrets and making accusations of a variety of misdeeds, begin to appear mysteriously on the doors in the town. "...When I finished *In Evil Hour*, I saw that all my views were wrong again. I came to see that in fact my writings about my childhood were *more* political and had more to do with the reality of my country than I had thought....I had an idea of what I always wanted to do, but there was something missing and I was not sure what it was until one day I discovered the right tone—the tone that I eventually used in *One Hundred Years of Solitude*. It was based on the way my grandmother used to tell her stories."[5]

1965. Left journalism for full-time writing. "When I was a reporter writing my books on Sundays I dreamed of being a full-time writer, working all day and every day. I published four books, but I had to continue working in journalism until my fifth became a success before I could devote myself to writing. But it can't be done. You have to wait until a book calls you, and you develop a bad conscience because you think that you should be working all the time. I found that the worst thing that can happen to a writer is to become a full-time writer, because you begin to lose contact with reality. You begin to live in fiction, and you begin to grow old."[8]

1967. Published *One Hundred Years of Solitude*. "...In previous attempts to write [it], I tried to tell the story without believing in it. I discovered that what I had to do was believe in them myself and write them with the same expression with which my grandmother told them: with a brick fact."[5]

Though confronted with an initial struggle, the work soon became easy as Garcia Marquez heard his grandmother's voice weaving fantastic tales in his head. "...I remember quite distinctly the day

that with enormous difficulty I finished the first sentence and I asked myself, terrified, what the hell came next....But from that point on the whole thing became a kind of frenzy, and very enjoyable as well.

"I'd been writing from nine in the morning to three in the afternoon every day for eighteen months. I knew for sure that this was the last day, but the book came to its natural conclusion at the wrong time, at about eleven in the morning. Mercedes wasn't at home and I couldn't get hold of anyone on the phone to tell them about it. I remember my total bewilderment as if it were yesterday. I didn't know what to do with the time left over and began inventing things to help me survive until three in the afternoon."[4]

"I knew that it would be a book that would please my friends more than my others had. But when my Spanish publisher told me he was going to print eight thousand copies I was stunned, because my other books had never sold more than seven hundred. I asked him why not start slowly, but he said he was convinced that it was a good book and that all eight thousand copies would be sold between May and December. Actually they were all sold within one week in Buenos Aires."[5]

"I have lost track of the total sales of the book. Seven years ago the Sudamericana edition alone, published in Buenos Aires, had sold two million copies, and demand hasn't fallen off. It has been translated into twenty-five languages so far. But the most important thing is neither its favorable critical reception nor its popular success. For me, what matters is that *One Hundred Years of Solitude* has passed from one generation to another."[1]

Many critics have read interpretations into *One Hundred Years of Solitude* which Garcia Marquez insists do not exist. "...I merely wanted to tell the story of a family who for a hundred years did everything they could to prevent having a son with a pig's tail, and just because of their very efforts to avoid having one they ended by doing so. Synthetically speaking, that's the plot of the book, but all that about symbolism...not at all. Someone who isn't a critic said that the interest the novel had aroused was probably due to the fact that it was the first real description of the private life of a Latin American family...we go into the bedroom, the bathroom, the kitchen, into every corner of the house. Of course I never said to myself, 'I shall write a book that will be interesting for that reason,' but now that it's written, and this has been said about it, I think it may be true. Anyway it's an interesting concept. . . ."[7]

Despite the continous offers to make the film version of *One Hundred Years of Solitude,* Garcia Marquez maintains that he will never allow the movie to be made. "Producers keep offering me enormous sums for the rights, but I refuse. The last offer, I believe, was, $2,000,000. I don't want to see it turned into a movie, because I want readers to go on imagining the characters as they see them. That isn't possible in the cinema. In movies, the image is so definite that the spectator can no longer imagine the character as he wants to, only as the screen imposes it on him.

"When I studied the way movies were made, I realized there are limitations in the form that do not exist in literature. I've become convinced that the novelist's work is the freest work that exists. You are totally your own master."[2]

Due to the tremendous success and popularity of the novel, Garcia Marquez has had to contend with the trappings of fame as well as its rewards. ". . .In general I think you usually do write for someone. When I'm writing I'm always aware that this friend is going to like this, or that another friend is going to like that paragraph or chapter, always thinking of specific people. In the end all books are written for your friends. The problem after writing *One Hundred Years of Solitude* was that now I no longer know whom of the millions of readers I am writing for; this upsets and inhibits me. It's like a million eyes are looking at you and you don't really know what they think.

"I think that the idea that I'm writing for many more people than I ever imagined has created a certain general responsibility that is literary and political. There's even pride involved, in not wanting to fall short of what I did before."[5]

"For several years I had my friends divided into the pre-*One Hundred Years of Solitude* friends and those that came afterwards. I was implying by this that the former seemed more dependable because we'd become friends for many different reasons but not because I was famous. I've found over the years that this was a mistake. There are multiple, unfathomable reasons for friendship and the attraction stimulated by fame is as valid a reason as any other. This works both ways of course. I too have got to know many famous people I could never have met before, and I've got to know them because they're famous and for no other reason. Afterwards we've become friends because of an affinity which had nothing to do with their fame or mine. In this sense, fame is a positive thing. It offers valuable opportunities for striking up friendships which would not have been possible otherwise. Nevertheless, in spite of the affection I feel for my new friends, I do still think of my old friends of the pre-*One Hundred Years of Solitude* days as a band apart, a kind of secret society indestructibly bound together by shared nostalgia."[4]

With the passage of time and the pressures of fame, writing has become a more difficult task. "When I became a professional writer the biggest problem I had was my schedule. Being a journalist meant working at night. When I started writing full-time I was forty years old, my schedule was basically from nine o'clock in the morning until two in the afternoon when my sons came back from school. Since I was so used to hard work, I felt guilty that I was only working in the morning; so I tried to work in the afternoons, but I discovered that what I did in the afternoon had to be done over again the next morning. So I decided that I would just work from nine until two-thirty and not do anything else that might come up. I have another problem in that I can only work in surroundings that are familiar and have already been warmed up with my work. I cannot write in hotels or borrowed rooms or on borrowed typewriters. This creates problems because when I travel I can't work. Of course, you're always trying to find a pretext to work less. That's why the conditions you impose on yourself are more difficult all the time. You hope for inspiration whatever the circumstances. That's a word the romantics exploited a lot. My Marxist comrades have a lot of difficulty accepting the word, but whatever you call it, I'm convinced that there is a special state of mind in which you can write with great ease and things just flow. All the pretexts—such as the one where you can only write at home—disappear. That moment and that state of mind seem to come when you have found the right theme and the right ways of treating it. And it has to be something you really like, too, because there is no worse job than doing something you don't like.

"One of the most difficult things is the first paragraph. I have spent many months on a first paragraph, and once I get it, the rest just comes out very easily. In the first paragraph you solve most of the problems with your book. The theme is defined, the style, the tone. At least in my case, the first paragraph is a kind of sample of what the rest of the book is going to be. That's why writing a book of short stories is much more difficult than writing a novel. Every time you write a short story, you have to begin all over again."[5]

Writing a novel begins with finding the proper structure. "The image grows in my head until the whole story takes shape as it might in real life. The problem is that life isn't the same as literature, so then I have to ask myself the big question: How do I adapt this, what is the most appropriate structure for this book? I have always aspired to finding the perfect structure. One perfect structure in literature is that of Sophocles' *Oedipus Rex*. Another is a short story, 'Monkey's Paw,' by an English writer, William Jacobs.

"When I have the story and the structure completely worked out, I can start—but only on condition that I find the right name for each character. If I don't have the name that exactly suits the character, it doesn't come alive. I don't see it.

"Once I sit down to write, usually I no longer have any hesitations. I may take a few notes, a word or a phrase or something to help me the following morning, but I never work with a lot of notes. That's what I learned when I was young. I know writers who have books full of notes and they wind up thinking about their notes and never write their books."[9]

"Inspiration is when you find the right theme, one which you really like; that makes the work much easier. Intuition, which is also fundamental to writing fiction, is a special quality which helps you to decipher what is real without needing scientific knowledge, or any other special kind of learning. The laws of gravity can be figured out much more easily with intuition than anything else. It's a way of having experience without having to struggle through it. For a novelist, intuition is essential. Basically it's contrary to intellectualism, which is probably the thing that I detest most in the world—in the sense that the real world is turned into a kind of immovable theory. Intuition has the advantage that either it is, or it isn't. You don't struggle to try to put a round peg into a square hole."[5]

1971. Received an Honorary Doctorate from Columbia University, and was granted a temporary visa to the United States. "...What I find completely puzzling and disconcerting is not the honor nor the recognition—although such things can be true—but that a university like Columbia should decide to choose me out of twelve men from the whole world. The last thing I ever expected in this world was a doctorate of letters. My path has always been anti-academic; I never graduated as doctor of law from the university because I didn't want to be a 'doctor'—and suddenly I find myself in the thick of the academic world. But this is something quite foreign to me, it's off my beat. It's as if they gave the Nobel Prize to a bullfighter.

"My first impulse was not to accept it, but then I took a plebiscite among my friends and none of them could understand what reason I had for refusing. I could have given political reasons, but they wouldn't have been genuine, because we all know, and we have heard declared in university speeches, that imperialism is not their prevailing system. So that to accept the honor wouldn't involve me politically with the United States, and there was no need to mention the subject. It was rather a moral question. I always react against ceremonies—remember that I come from the most ceremonious country in the world—and I asked myself, 'What should I be doing in a literary academy in cap and gown?' At my friends' insistence I accepted the title of *doctor honoris causa* and now I'm delighted, not only at having accepted it, but also on behalf of my country and Latin America. All this patriotism one pretends not to care about suddenly does become important."[10]

1975. Published *Autumn of the Patriarch.* Told from a variety of different points of view, the story consists of episodes in the life of an aging Latin American dictator. "...I stopped writing *The Autumn of the Patriarch* in Mexico in 1962 when I'd done almost three hundred pages, and the only thing that survived was the name of the main character. I took it up again in Barcelona in 1968, worked on it a lot for six months and left it again because I couldn't come to grips with certain moral aspects of the central figure, a very old dictator. About two years later I bought a book on hunting in Africa because I was interested in the prologue by Hemingway. The prologue wasn't worth much but I went on to read the chapter on the elephants, and there was the solution to the novel. Certain elephant customs explained my dictator's morality perfectly."[4]

"In every novel, the character is a collage: a collage of different characters that you've known, or heard about or read about. I read everything that I could find about Latin American dictators of the last century, and the beginning of this one. I also talked to a lot of people who had lived under dictatorships. I did that for at least ten years. And when I had a clear idea of what the character was going to be like, I made an effort to forget everything I had read and heard, so that I could

Dust jacket for the 1984 Harper edition.

invent, without using any situation that had occurred in real life. I realized at one point that I myself had not lived for any period of time under a dictatorship, so I thought if I wrote the book in Spain, I could see what the atmosphere was like living in an established dictatorship. But I found that the atmosphere was very different in Spain under Franco from that of a Caribbean dictatorship. So the book was kind of blocked for about a year. There was something missing and I wasn't sure what it was. Then overnight, I decided that the best thing was that we come back to the Caribbean. So we all moved back to Brarranquill in Colombia. I made a statement to the journalists which they thought was a joke. I said that I was coming back because I had forgotten what a guava smelled like. In truth, it was what I really needed to finish my book. I took a trip through the Caribbean. As I went from island to island, I found the elements which were the ones that had been lacking from my novel."[5]

"I'm extremely fascinated by power. Nothing secret about it. I think it is quite obvious in many of my characters. . . .Of course it's the *raison d'etre* for *The Autumn of the Patriarch.* Power is without a doubt the highest form of human ambition and will, and I can't understand how it is that other writers aren't more intrigued by something which affects and sometimes determines their entire lives."[4]

"The more power you have, the harder it is to know who is lying to you and who is not. When you reach absolute power, there is no contact with reality, and that's the worst kind of solitude there can be. A very powerful person, a dictator, is surrounded by interests and people whose final aim is to isolate him from reality; everything is in concert to isolate him."[5]

". . .I've always thought absolute power is the highest and most complex of human achievements and, therefore, it is the essence of man's nobility and of his degradation. As Lord Acton said, 'All power corrupts and absolute power corrupts abso-

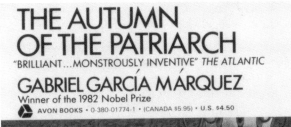

Softcover of the 1976 English translation.

lutely.' This has to be an enthralling subject for a writer."[4]

Critics have attributed the term "magic realism" to the manner in which he treats reality, particularly in *Autumn of the Patriarch* and *One Hundred Years of Solitude*.

1982. Awarded Nobel Prize for Literature. He awaited the presentation with some reluctance. "I envy the chemists and the Peace Prize winners. They don't have to say a word and everyone applauds anyway. I've heard that the Swedish Academy is a solemn clan out to make me over. And I have to wear a tail coat, a colonial costume, an upper-class outfit from the nineteenth century. I will feel terrible."[11]

On the other hand, the occasion was a "...great opportunity. I must try and break through the cliches about Latin America. Superpowers and other outsiders have fought over us for centuries in ways that have nothing to do with our problems. In reality we are all alone."[11]

1984. Published *Love in the Time of Cholera*. "This book was a pleasure. It could have been much longer, but I had to control it. There is so much to say about the life of two people who love each other. It's infinite.

"Also, I had the advantage of knowing the end beforehand. Because in this book, the end was a problem. It would have been in poor taste if one or even both of the characters died. The most wonderful thing would be if they could go on loving forever. So the reader is given the consolation that the boat with the lovers will keep on with its journey, coming and going. Not only for the rest of their lives, but forever.

"...Those two years when I was writing it was a time when I was almost completely happy. Everything went well for me. People spend a lifetime thinking about how they would really like to live. I asked my friends and no one seems to know very clearly. To me it's very clear now. I wish my life could have been like the years when I was writing *Love in the Time of Cholera*.

"I would get up at five-thirty or six in the morning. I need only six hours of sleep. Then I quickly listened to the news. I would read from six to eight, because if I don't read at that time I won't get around to it anymore. I lose my rhythm. Someone would arrive at the house with fresh fish or lobster or shrimp caught nearby. Then I would write from eight till one. By midday, Mercedes would go to the beach and wait for me with friends. I never

quite knew who to expect; there were always people coming and going. After lunch I had a little siesta. And when the sun started going down I would go out on the street to look for places where my characters would go, to talk to people and pick up language and atmosphere. So the next morning I would have fresh material I had brought from the streets."[12]

"I think aging has made me realize that feelings and sentiments, what happens in the heart, are ultimately the most important. But in some way, all my books are about love. In *One Hundred Years* there is one love story after another. *Chronicle of a Death Foretold* is a terrible drama of love. I think there is love everywhere. This time love is more ardent. Because two loves join and go on.

"I think...that I could not have written *Love in the Time of Cholera* when I was younger. It has practically a lifetime's experience in it. And it includes many experiences, my own and other peoples. Above all, there are points of view I didn't have before...."[9]

"It is not surprising that a man who claims his heart as his greatest weakness has felt compelled to write a love story....I need to be loved a great deal. My great problem is to be loved more, and that is why I write.

"...If I had not become a writer, I'd want to have been a piano player in a bar. That way, I could have made a contribution to making lovers feel even more loving toward each other. If I can achieve that much as a writer—to have people love one another more because of my books—I think that's the meaning I've wanted for my life.

"...I am the shyest man in the world. I am also the kindest man. On this I accept no argument or debate."[2]

"...It always amuses me that the biggest praise for my work comes for the imagination, while the truth is that there's not a single line in all my work that does not have a basis in reality. The problem is that Caribbean reality resembles imagination."[5]

Footnote Sources:

[1] Gabriel Garcia Marquez, "The Making of a Classic," *Atlas World Press Review*, July, 1979.
[2] Claudia Dreifus, "Playboy Interview: Gabriel Garcia Marquez," *Playboy*, February, 1983.
[3] Wolfgang A. Luchting, "Gabriel Garcia Marquez: The Boom and the Whimper," *Books Abroad*, winter, 1970.
[4] Plinio Apuleyo Mendoza and G. Garcia Marquez, *The Fragrance of Guava*, Verso Editions, 1983.

5 George Plimpton, editor, *Writers at Work: The 'Paris Review' Interviews*, 6th series, Viking, 1984.
6 G. Garcia Marquez, "Gabriel Garcia Marquez Meets Ernest Hemingway," *New York Times Book Review*, July 26, 1981.
7 Rita Guibert, *Seven Voices: Seven Latin American Writers Talk to Rita Guibert*, Vintage Books, 1973.
8 Herbert R. Lottman, "Gabriel Garcia Marquez," *Publishers Weekly*, May 13, 1974.
9 Marlise Simons, "Garcia Marquez on Love, Plagues and Politics," *New York Times Book Review*, February 21, 1988.
10 William Kennedy, "The Yellow Trolley Car in Barcelona and Other Visions," *Atlantic Monthly*, June, 1973.
11 M. Simons, "A Talk with Gabriel Garcia Marquez," *New York Times Book Review*, December 5, 1982.
12 M. Simons, "The Best Years of His Life: An Interview with Gabriel Garcia Marquez," *New York Times Book Review*, April 10, 1989.

■ For More Information See

Books:

Luis Harss and Barbara Dohmann, *Into the Mainstream: Conversations with Latin-American Writers*, Harper, 1967.
Mario Vargas Llosa, *Garcia Marquez: Historia de un deicido*, Barral Editores, 1971.
David P. Gallagher, *Modern Latin American Literature*, Oxford University Press, 1973.
Current Biography 1973, H. W. Wilson, 1974.
Selden Rodman, *Tongues of Fallen Angels*, New Directions, 1974.
Contemporary Literary Criticism, Gale, Volume II, 1974, Volume III, 1975, Volume VIII, 1978, Volume X, 1979, Volume XV, 1980, Volume XXVII, 1984.
John Wakeman, editor, *World Authors, 1950-1970*, H. W. Wilson, 1975.
David W. Foster, compiler, *A Dictionary of Contemporary Latin American Authors*, Center for Latin American Studies, Arizona State University, 1975.
George R. McMurray, *Gabriel Garcia Marquez*, Ungar, 1977.
Gordon Brotherson, *The Emergence of the Latin American Novel*, Cambridge University Press, 1979.
V. S. Pritchett, *The Myth Makers*, Random House, 1979.
Regina Janes, *Gabriel Garcia Marquez: Revolutions in Wonderland*, University of Missouri Press, 1981.
Dictionary of Literary Biography Yearbook: 1982, Gale, 1983.
D. Foster, editor, *Gabriel Garcia Marquez*, Twayne, 1984.
Leonard S. Klein, editor, *Latin American Literature in the Twentieth Century*, Ungar, 1986.
Alok Bhalla, editor, *Garcia Marquez and Latin America*, Sterling, 1987.
George R. McMurray, *Critical Essays on Gabriel Garcia Marquez*, G. K. Hall, 1987.

Periodicals:

Atlantic Monthly, May, 1968 (p. 52ff), January, 1973 (p. 50ff).
New York Times Book Review, September 29, 1968, March 8, 1970 (p. 5ff), February 20, 1972 (p. 1), October 31, 1976 (p. 1ff), July 16, 1978 (p. 3ff), September 16, 1978, November 11, 1979, November 16, 1980, October 22, 1982 (p. 1), October 29, 1982 (section 3, p. 23), December 11, 1982 (p. 1), February 6, 1983, March 25, 1983 (section 3, p. 25), March 27, 1983 (p. 1), April 7, 1985 (p. 1ff), April 27, 1986 (p. 11), April 10, 1988 (p. 1).
Nation, December 2, 1968 (p. 600ff), May 15, 1972, October 25, 1975 (p. 412ff), September 5, 1981 (p. 184), November 6, 1982 (p. 453).
Saturday Review, December 21, 1968, March 7, 1970 (p. 34ff).
Washington Post Book World, February 22, 1970, November 25, 1979, March 27, 1983, November 18, 1984 (p. 3).
Newsweek, March 2, 1970, December 3, 1979, November 1, 1982 (p. 81ff).
Commonweal, March 6, 1970.
Time, March 16, 1970 (p. 96), November 1, 1982 (p. 88), March 7, 1983 (p. 78ff).
New York Review of Books, March 26, 1970 (p. 3), January 24, 1980.
National Observer, April 20, 1970.
Studies in Short Fiction 8, winter, 1971 (p. 159ff).
Harper's, February, 1972 (p. 98ff), July, 1984 (p. 29), January, 1985 (p. 13).
Books Abroad, winter, 1973 (p. 10ff), summer, 1973 (p. 466ff).
Southwest Review, summer, 1973.
New Yorker, June 3, 1974 (p. 32ff), March 27, 1978 (p. 34ff), April 17, 1978 (p. 30ff), May 20, 1985 (p. 118ff).
New York Times, May 8, 1976 (p. 22), January 12, 1977 (p. 8), July 11, 1978, November 6, 1979, May 22, 1980 (p. 2), March 27, 1981, June 14, 1982 (section 3, p. 30), October 22, 1982 (p. 1), October 29, 1982 (section 3, p. 23), December 11, 1982 (p. 1), February 6, 1983, March 25, 1983, October 6, 1983 (section 2, p. 3), April 27, 1984 (p. C8), December 7, 1985 (p. 18), April 26, 1986 (p. 10), June 5, 1986 (p. C26).
Hispania, September, 1976.
Virginia Quarterly Review, spring, 1977 (p. 366ff).
New Republic, April 9, 1977, October 27, 1979, May 2, 1983 (p. 36), February 4, 1985 (p. 32ff).
Times Literary Supplement, April 15, 1977, September 10, 1982 (p. 965), November 28, 1986 (p. 1333).
Hudson Review, summer, 1977 (p. 299).
New Statesman, May 18, 1979, February 15, 1980, November 14, 1986 (p. 31).
Chicago Tribune Book World, November 11, 1979, November 7, 1982.
Review, number 24, 1979, September/December, 1981.
Rolling Stone, May 29, 1980 (p. 43ff).
El Pais, January 22, 1981.
Paris Review, winter, 1981.

World Press Review, April, 1982 (p. 61), February, 1983 (p. 61), February, 1988 (p. 34).
Los Angeles Times, October 22, 1982.
Washington Post, October 22, 1982.
Detroit News, October 27, 1982.
New York Times Biographical Service, October, 1982 (p. 1303ff).
Publishers Weekly, November 5, 1982 (p. 16).
National Review, November 12, 1982 (p. 1392), June 10, 1983 (p. 699ff).
Christian Century, November 17, 1982 (p. 1159ff).
World Literature Today, winter, 1982 (p. 48ff).

Christian Science Monitor, January 27, 1983 (p. B7).
Chicago Tribune, March 6, 1983.
Los Angeles Times Book Review, April 10, 1983.
Commentary, May, 1983 (p. 59ff).
Variety, October 12, 1983 (p. 4).
Enrique Fernandez, "Welcome to Maconda: The Seductive Life of Garcia Marquez," *Village Voice,* July 3, 1984.
American Film, July-August, 1984 (p. 12).
Midwest Quarterly, summer, 1985 (p. 467ff).
Maclean's, July 28, 1986 (p. 50).
Voice Literary Supplement, December, 1986 (p. 22).

E. L. Konigsburg

Born Elaine Lobl, in New York, N.Y.; daughter of Adolph (a businessman) and Beulah (Klein) Lobl; married David Konigsburg (an industrial psychologist); children: Paul, Laurie, Ross. *Education:* Carnegie Institute of Technology (now Carnegie-Mellon University), B.S. (with honors), 1952; University of Pittsburgh, graduate study, 1952-54; also attended Art Students' League, 1962-66. *Address:* c/o Atheneum Publishers, 115 Fifth Ave., New York, N.Y. 10003.

■ Career

Shenago Valley Provision Co., Sharon, Pa., bookkeeper, 1947-48; Bartram School, Jacksonville, Fla., science teacher, 1954-55, 1960-62; writer, 1967—.

■ Awards, Honors

Book World's Children's Spring Book Festival Honor Book, 1967, and Newbery Honor Book from the American Library Association, 1968, both for *Jennifer, Hecate, Macbeth, William McKinley, and Me, Elizabeth;* Newbery Medal, and Lewis Carroll Shelf Award, both 1968, and William Allen White Award, 1970, all for *From the Mixed-Up*

Files of Mrs. Basil E. Frankweiler; Carnegie-Mellon Merit Award, 1971; National Book Award finalist, 1974, for *A Proud Taste for Scarlet and Miniver;* American Library Association Best Book for Young Adults, 1975, for *The Second Mrs. Giaconda,* and 1976, for *Father's Arcane Daughter;* American Book Award finalist, 1980, for *Throwing Shadows; About the B'nai Bagels, Jennifer, Hecate, Macbeth, William McKinley, and Me, Elizabeth, Journey to an 800 Number,* and *A Proud Taste for Scarlet and Miniver* were all chosen Children's Books of the Year by the Child Study Association of America, 1986.

■ Writings

Jennifer, Hecate, Macbeth, William McKinley, and Me, Elizabeth (ALA Notable Book; *Horn Book* honor list; self-illustrated), Atheneum, 1967 (published in England as *Jennifer, Hecate, Macbeth and Me,* Macmillan, 1968).

From the Mixed-Up Files of Mrs. Basil E. Frankweiler (ALA Notable Book; *Horn Book* honor list; Junior Literary Guild selection; self-illustrated), Atheneum, 1967.

About the B'nai Bagels (self-illustrated), Atheneum, 1969.

(George) (self-illustrated), Atheneum, 1970 (published in England as *Benjamin Dickinson Carr and His (George),* Penguin, 1974).

Altogether, One at a Time (short stories; illustrated by Gail E. Haley, Mercer Meyer, Gary Parker, and Laurel Schindelman), Atheneum, 1971.

A Proud Taste for Scarlet and Miniver (ALA Notable Book; Junior Literary Guild selection; self-illustrated), Atheneum, 1973.

The Dragon in the Ghetto Caper (self-illustrated), Atheneum, 1974.

The Second Mrs. Giaconda (illustrated with museum plates), Atheneum, 1975.

Father's Arcane Daughter, Atheneum, 1976.

Throwing Shadows (short stories; ALA Notable Book; Junior Literary Guild selection), Atheneum, 1979.

Journey to an 800 Number, Atheneum, 1982 (published in England as *Journey by First Class Camel*, Hamish Hamilton, 1983).

Up from Jericho Tel, Atheneum, 1986.

■ Adaptations

"From the Mixed-Up Files of Mrs. Basil E. Frankweiler" (record; cassette), Miller-Brody/Random House, 1969, (motion picture), starring Ingrid Bergman, Cinema 5, 1973, released under new title "The Hideaways," Bing Crosby Productions, 1974.

"Jennifer and Me" (television movie; based on *Jennifer Hecate, Macbeth, William McKinley, and Me, Elizabeth*), NBC-TV, March 3, 1973.

"The Second Mrs. Giaconda" (play), first produced in Jacksonville, Fla., 1976.

(Contributor) *Expectations 1980* (braille anthology), Braille Institute, 1980.

"Jennifer, Hecate, Macbeth, William McKinley, and Me, Elizabeth" (cassette), Listening Library, 1986.

About the B'nai Bagels and *From the Mixed-Up Files of Mrs. Basil E. Frankweiler* are available as Talking Books. *From the Mixed-Up Files of Mrs. Basil E. Frankweiler* is also available in Braille.

■ Sidelights

Born in New York City, the second of three daughters and reared in mill towns in Pennsylvania. "Growing up in a small town gives you two things: a sense of your place and a feeling of self-consciousness—self-consciousness about one's education and exposure, both of which tend to be limited. On the other hand, limited possibilities also means creating your own options. A small town allows you to grow in your own direction, without a bombardment of outside stimulation. You can get a sense of yourself in relation to yourself not to a host of accomplished others. It is important to break out of small town prejudices, however. It is easy to be arbitrary with little basis

for comparison. Where I grew up, for instance, women over forty who dyed their hair or girls who wore black before the age of sixteen were considered immoral. All through high school, my father would not allow me to wear make-up. These 'rules' were established as principles of morality. Later I was to learn (as I had always suspected) that morality was concerned with larger issues."[1]

As a child Konigsburg "...used to read in the bathroom a lot. It was the only room in our house that had a lock on the door, and I could run water in the tub to muffle the sounds of my sobbing over Rhett Butler's leaving Scarlett. Reading was tolerated in my house, but it wasn't sanctioned like dusting furniture or baking cookies. My parents never minded what I read, but they did mind *when* (like before the dishes were done) and *where* (there was only one bathroom in our house)."[2]

"...There was no one to guide my reading, consequently I read a lot of trash along the *True Confessions* line. I have no objection to trash. I've read a lot of it and firmly believe it helped hone my taste. Besides, I had problems with a lot of the books I read. Nothing I picked up told me anything about the world in which *I* was living."[1]

"[In] *Mary Poppins...* you get a good glimpse of upper-middle-class family life in England a quarter of a century ago, a family that had basis in fact....Read *The Secret Garden*, and you find another world that I know about only in words. Here is a family living on a large estate staffed by servants who are devoted to the two generations living there. Here is a father who has no visible source of income. He neither reaps nor sows; he doesn't even commute....Families of this kind had a basis in fact, but fact remote from me.

"I have such faith in words that when I read about such families as a child, I thought that they were the norm and that the way I lived was subnormal, waiting for normal.

"Where were the stories then about growing up in a small mill town where there was no one named Jones in your class? Where were the stories that made having a class full of Radasevitches and Gabellas and Zaharious normal? There were stories about the crowd meeting at the corner drugstore after school. Where were the stories that told about the store owner closing his place from 3:15 until 4:00 P.M. because he found that what he gained in sales of Coca-Cola he lost in stolen Hershey Bars? How come that druggist never seemed normal to me? He was supposed to be grumpy but lovable; the stories of my time all said so."[3]

"I drew a lot as a child and was an excellent student for as long as I can remember. I graduated valedictorian from Farrell High School and wanted to go away to college. My high school had no guidance department and no one in my family had ever gone to university. I devised a plan whereby I would work for a year, earn enough for two semesters of tuition and board, go back to work to finance another academic year, and so on until I finished my degree. No one had ever told me about scholarships. Right after high school, I got a job as a bookkeeper in a wholesale meat plant."[1]

It was while working there that she met her future husband, David Konigsburg, an industrial psychologist. "The following year I enrolled at Carnegie Institute of Technology in Pittsburgh as a chemistry major. If I had in mind eventually to be a writer and artist, the notion was so deeply submerged that I was unaware of it. Besides, if you were the first person in your family to go to college, you didn't say you were going away to become a writer. You said you were going away to become a *something*— a librarian, a teacher, a chemist, a *something*. I chose chemistry because I was good at it and there would be jobs waiting when I finished. In Farrell, I never met anyone who made his living from the arts. One day late in my freshman year as I was walking across campus, my English professor stopped me and inquired about my plans. When I told him that I would be returning to my job for another year, he said, '*Miss* Lobl, I think that this school would not choose to lose students of your *ilk*.' Thanks to his intervention, I was able to get a scholarship. I had jobs all through school—in the library, managing a laundry service in the dormitory—and I remained *enrolled*.

"An interesting thing about that time is that my closet friends and dormitory mates were women from other small towns in Pennsylvania—bright, ambitious, capable women, set on doing something with their education. We're still in touch with each other.

"College was a crucial 'opening up' for me. I worked hard and did well. However, the artistic side of me was essentially dormant. My close college friends never even knew that I could write and loved to draw. Chemistry majors spend long hours in the lab; some of our courses were full-day labs, and there was not a lot of time for much besides work and school work."[1]

Softcover of the 1979 Junior Literary Guild selection.

Graduating with honors, she then married Konigsburg, and continued her education at graduate school at the University of Pittsburgh. "I'm convinced that, had I not been such a disaster in the lab, I could have made a contribution to chemistry, something creative. I had the mind for it, but not the temperament. There was all that awful lab work to get through. And there was no one to tell me that it is only in the higher reaches that science and art are one."[4]

Konigsburg moved with her husband to Jacksonville, Florida, where she taught science at a private girls' school. "I began to supsect that chemistry was not my field. Not only did I always ask my students to light my Bunsen burner, having become match-shy, but I became more interested in what was going on inside them than what was going on inside the test tubes.

"I had the mind for chemistry, but not the temperament. There were rumblings of this in my head much earlier, I believe, but I wasn't listening."[1]

Konigsburg left teaching shortly before the birth of son Paul. Soon after her second child, Lauri, was born, she took up painting in local adult education classes. "I had good luck in that I won the first art competition I entered. There were mostly Jacksonville artists in the show, but the judge had some renown. Not long afterward, we moved to New York. I was so ready! Just as getting an education was critical exposure for me, New York was a kind of graduate school. I took Saturdays 'off': in the morning I attended drawing classes at the Art Students' League; in the afternoon I explored the galleries, museums and streets of Manhattan."[1]

Her writing began when her youngest child went to school. "I learned that no one respects the housewife's time. I had waited in every pediatrician's office, every dentist's office, and even at the shoe store for my boys to be fitted for orthopedic shoes. Once when I telephoned a supermarket and asked to speak to the butcher, I was not allowed. They would give him the message and I could call back to find out what he said. His time, too, was more valuable than mine. I realized that no one would value my time except me. So I decided that I would take the mornings—not make a bed, not do the dishes—and write. This turned out to be easier than I expected. We had just moved to Port Chester, New York, where I knew no one, so I was spared the endless round of telephone calls from friends, neighbors and acquaintances. I kept my writing a secret except from my family. When my kids came home for lunch, I would often read them what I'd written and watch their reactions."[1]

"...When I realized that my kids' growing up was very different from my own, but was related to this middle-class kind of child that I had seen when I had taught at the private girls' school, I recognized that I wanted to write something that reflected their kind of growing up, something that addressed the problems that come about even though you don't have to worry if you wear out your shoes whether your parents can buy you a new pair, something that tackles the basic problems of who am I? What makes me the same as everyone else? What makes me different?"[4]

"[I wanted to] describe what life is like in these suburbs. Tell how it is normal to be very comfortable on the outside but very uncomfortable on the inside. Tell how funny it all is. But tell a little something else, too. What can it hurt? Tell a little something else—about how you can be a nonconformist and about how you can be an outsider. And tell how you are entitled to a little privacy. But for goodness' sake, say all that very softly. Let the telling be like fudge-ripple ice cream. You keep licking vanilla, but every now and then you come to something darker and deeper and with a stronger flavor. Let the something-else words be the chocolate."[3]

1967. Atheneum published her first two books, *Jennifer, Hecate, Macbeth, and Me, Elizabeth*, inspired by her daughter's efforts to find new friends when the family moved to Port Chester, New York, and *From the Mixed-Up Files of Mrs. Basil E. Frankweiler*. "The idea for [*Mixed-Up Files*]...came from three experiences; two of them were reading experiences.

"I read in the *New York Times* that the Metropolitan Museum of Art in New York City had bought a statue for $225. At the time of the purchase they did not know who had sculptured it, but they suspected that it had been done by someone famous in the Italian Renaissance; they knew that they had an enormous bargain. (The statue, by the way, is called The Lady with the Primroses; it is not an angel, and it was not sculptured by Michelangelo.)

"Shortly after that article appeared in the paper I read a book that told the adventures of some children who upon being sent by ship from their island home to England are captured by pirates. In the company of the pirates, the children became piratical themselves; they lost the thin veneer of civilization that they had acquired in their island home.

"The third thing that happened was a picnic that our family took while we were vacationing at Yellowstone Park. After buying salami and bread and chocolate milk and paper cups and paper plates and paper napkins and potato chips and pickles, we looked for a place to eat. There were no outdoor tables and chairs, so when we came to a clearing in the woods, I suggested that we all eat there. We all crouched slightly above the ground and began to spread out our meal. Then the complaints began: the chocolate milk was getting warm, and there were ants over everything, and the sun was melting the icing on the cupcakes. This was hardly having to rough it, and yet my small group could think of nothing but the discomfort.

"I thought to myself that if my children ever left home, they would never become barbarians even if they were captured by pirates. Civilization was not a veneer to them; it was a crust. They would want at least all the comforts of home plus a few dashes of extra elegance. Where, I wondered, would they ever consider running to if they ever left home? They certainly would never consider any place less elegant than the Metropolitan Museum of Art.

"Yes, the Metropolitan Museum of Art. All those magnificent beds and all that elegance. And then, I thought, while they were there, perhaps they would discover the secret of a mysterious bargain statue and in doing so, perhaps they could discover a much more important secret, the need to be different—on the inside where it counts."[5]

Konigsburg illustrated both novels, as she has for most of her books, using her children as models. "The illustrations probably come from the kindergartener who lives inside, somewhere inside me, who says, 'Silly, don't you know that it is called *show and tell?* Hold up and show and then tell.' I have to show how Mrs. Frankweiler looks and how Jennifer looks. Besides, I like to draw, and I like to complete things, and doing the illustrations answers these simple needs."[3]

1968. While moving back to Jacksonville, Florida, Konigsburg received the news that she had made children's book history. *From the Mixed-Up Files of Mrs. Basil E. Frankweiler* won the Newbery Medal and *Jennifer, Hecate, Macbeth, and Me, Elizabeth* was the Newbery runner-up. In her acceptance speech she said: "Chemistry was my larval stage, and those nine years at home doing diaper service were my cocoon. And you see standing before you today the moth I was always meant to be. (Well, I hardly qualify as a butterfly.) A moth who lives on words. . . .

"I think about words a lot. I need words. I need written-down, black-on-white, printed words. . . .I spread words on paper for the same reasons that Cro-Magnon man spread pictures on the walls of caves. I need to see it put down. . . .Thus, first of all, writing it down adds another dimension to reality and satisfies an atavistic need.

". . .I need words for this reason: to make record of a place, suburban American, and a time, early autumn of the twentieth century. . . .

"My phylogenetic need, adding another dimension to reality, and my class and order need, making record, are certainly the wind at my back, but a family need is the directed, strong gust that pushes me to my desk. And here I don't mean *family* in the taxonomic sense. I mean *family* that I lived in when I was growing up and *family* that I live in now.

"Winning the Newbery Medal has made a difference, and it has not made a difference, too. Both—making and not—have happened in the right places.

"Professionally, it has meant a happy difference. Had I not won the Newbery, I don't know if I would have had the courage to experiment. . . .Receiving the award has given me the strength to go on from where I was when I got it, and I am grateful for that.

"I can best explain how it has not made a difference by relating an incident. Sometime after I had won, a teacher approached my daughter, Laurie, and asked, 'How does it feel to live with a famous mother?' 'Famous?' Laurie replied. 'My mother's just a mother. Why, I'd never argue with anyone famous, and I argue with my mother every day!'

"So you see, winning couldn't send me altogether into orbit. My kids demand that my feet stay on the ground."[3]

Konigsburg's next novel was *About the B'nai Bagels.* In this book, the bagels, a baseball team

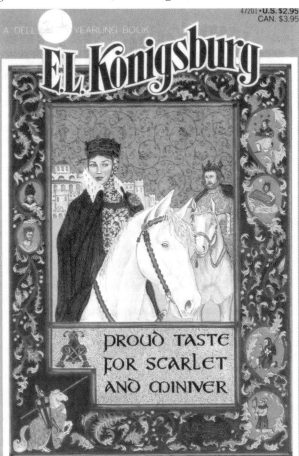

Softcover edition of the 1973 novel.

Jacket from the multi-award-winning novel, written and illustrated by Konigsburg.

sponsored by a suburban Jewish Community Center, has lost it's coach. The mother of one of the boys steps in—an unprecedented move, as the coaches had always been men—and fields a championship team. "I was trying to write a story about a mother invading her child's 'alone' time. I was having trouble, couldn't get a handle on it. Then one day, we went to a JCC basketball game....One of the players was dribbling in, but couldn't make his shot because his older brother, who was on the opposing team, was guarding him very closely. Their mother stood up in the stands and yelled, *'Peetuh, leave your brother alone!'* Well, this woman unlocked the story for me, and set the tone for Bessy, the mother in my book. I love this character—she's so full of life and so funny—still, the underlying theme of *The B'nai Bagels* is a kid's need for privacy."[1]

Rich in details of Jewish secular culture, this book has been called by reviewers a "Jewish Diaspora story." Another underlying theme is anti-semitism. "My kids were living that. Gentile children would line up across the sidewalk, blocking them, taunting them, as they tried to get to Hebrew School....Being Jewish is very important to me. As with many things, however, one must find one's own way within a larger context."[1] With characteristic humor, she added, "I love being Jewish, but I have some trouble with the synagogue."[1]

Konigsburg is routinely praised for the depth, wit, and sophistication of her novels. Her protagonists exhibit an extraordinary capacity for growth, even when that growth cannot be achieved without pain. Her books tend to be classified by libraries, teachers, and the press as "young adult" novels. "I have serious reservations about the young adult genre. I think there's too much trash being published under that label, too much of the sort of thing I used to read in *True Confessions*—though, as I've said, I'm not against reading trash....But I do object to trash masquerading as literature. You might say I like my trash pure and simple. What bothers me most is that too many young adult novels are not extensions of a personal history or imagination but are 'novelizations' of television. They display sit-com humor, deal with the disease of the month or a current social disorder. I feel more at home in the category of 'children's books,' which is an older, more literary tradition."[1]

"I bring all of my adulthood to my writing for children. I make an effort to help them hear the language of my culture, a culture that reaches into the past and spreads over the present. And I also make an effort to expand the perimeter of their language, to set a wider limit to it, to give them a vocabulary for alternatives, perhaps. Because language not only tells you the shape of a culture; it helps shape it."[6]

Konigsburg's work focuses on, what is sometimes referred to as, the middle-aged child. ". . .I think that it is the age at which the pull of the peer group is so strong a child can lose his sense of self. If his need to be part of the group is so strong, he's going to pull in that direction and he's going to lose what I call *(George)* in one of my books. George is a little old man who lives inside Benjamin Dickinson

Carr, and I think that if you lose touch with that inner self because your peer pressure is so great, you suffer a serious loss. I think that there is never a stronger pull than in a child between the ages of ten and fourteen. It's a difficult, difficult age and that makes it fascinating. It's exasperating and fascinating."[7]

"To the publishing world the middle-aged child is the child from ages eight through twelve. A child whose reading habits are post-Dr. Seuss but pre-*The Sensuous Woman.* The child rated G through PG. . . .My acceptance of the term has come about as a result of establishing a relationship between the child, aged eight through twelve, and the Middle Ages. The Middle Ages of Western Civilization. Those dark centuries of history from the time of the collapse of the Roman Empire until that great rebirth, the Renaissance. Those so-called one thousand years without a bath.

"I started making the parallel when we lived in the suburbs of New York, and I took my children to the Cloisters, the branch of the Metropolitan Museum

Ingrid Bergman starred in the 1973 movie "From the Mixed-Up Files of Mrs. Basil E. Frankweiler."

of Art that is devoted exclusively to medieval art. One of the works of art that fascinated my oldest son was a rosary bead. It is a giant as far as rosary beads go—about the size of a golf ball. It is hinged, and it is displayed opened up. There, within that tiny realm, is carved a three-dimensional scene of Christ's crucifixion, complete with Mary and Joseph of Arimathea and troops of Roman soldiers. The whole carving is so exquisite that one can read the expressions on the faces of the people, faces no bigger than a saccarine tablet, quarter grain.

"My son was so impressed with this bead that he decided to carve one for his favorite teacher of the moment. His favorite teacher of the moment was his Hebrew teacher. He knew that she would appreciate Moses on Mt. Sinai more than she would appreciate Christ on Calvary. So that was the scene he decided upon. He borrowed a paring knife from me and stole a small piece of pine from some construction site and went to work. There you have the mind of a middle-aged child—he was eight at the time. He wanted to carve a rosary bead for a teacher of Hebrew. He wanted to do something beautiful, and he stole to do it. His thinking was truly Middle Aged or medieval. The contradictions exist side by side. There was no blending of the right of what he wanted to do with the wrong of it. There was no blending of the concepts of Christian Jew. For him *Jewish* and *rosary bead* existed side by side.

"Once I established this basic parallel, I began to find others. Examine the art of the Middle Ages, and you find literal interpretations of 'the light of God' and the 'mouth of Hell.' A middle-aged child listens literally and interprets literally, too. Look at a painting or a piece of sculpture from the Middle Ages, and it is hard to find perspective. A middle-aged child lacks perspective in his philosophy as well as his art. A middle-aged child outlines his pictures in bold black crayon and unashamedly fills in the spaces with bright primary colors. Compare that to a piece of thirteenth-century stained glass. Even the spelling bears comparison. Chaucer spells *eat* E-T-E, and the middle-aged child rightly asks, 'Well, if E-T-E doesn't spell *eat*, what in heck does it spell?'

"And abiding, superseding, almost bellowing, over all this is Faith. The people of the Middle Ages were believers. They believed in ghosts and angels and demons and fairies, and so do middle-aged kids. The people of the Middle Ages traveled miles and miles to view the relics of Thomas Becket at Canterbury because they believed in the healing power of relics. How different is this from the good luck ring worn by a child of ten?

"By the time I was convinced that the term middle-aged child is accurate, I was thoroughly in love with the Middle Ages. Then I went to see the play *Becket* by Jean Anouilh, the play that tells of the clash between Henry II and his Archbishop of Canterbury, Thomas Becket. I discovered nothing in the play to contradict my hypothesis, but I did find something that contradicted some other observations I had made: Henry II who reigned in England from 1154 to 1189 was one of the all time great kings of that country. He laid the foundation for the whole of the English Common Law. He started a civil service, a corporate policy whereby men were chosen according to ability rather than birth and paid in coin rather than land. He was a strong king, a powerful executive, and I knew it, but I was bothered by the depiction of his wife in the play. She is portrayed as a whiny, no-talent nag.

"I have observed a lot of executives in my time— and what is a medieval king but an executive in drag?—and I've known a lot of executive wives. And I have noticed that executive wives are strong ladies. To stay with a man of vitality and ego requires a woman of character.

"So I checked up on the wife of Henry II. Her name was Eleanor of Aquitaine. And what a woman she turned out to be. What a woman! She was a woman who, at a time when wives were considered chattel, was in essence everything that woman's liberation is in slogans."[8]

Konigsburg resolved to write about Eleanor, and did so in *A Proud Taste for Scarlet and Miniver*, which she also illustrated. "Eleanor of Aquitaine was the lady who was wife not to one king, but to two. She divorced Louis VII of France and married Henry of England. She was thirty at the time, and he was eighteen, and you can't tell me that that's not doing your own thing. She was the mother, not of one king but two. You know her sons by name: Richard the Lion Heart and King John, that same John who signed a great charter at Runnymede in 1215. Eleanor of Aquitaine was the lady who was responsible for lifting a minor Saxon king by the name of Arthur from the dusty pages of a history book and handing him over to her troubadours who in turn imbued him with grace and chivalry, bedecked him with honor, and seated him at a Round Table with a bunch of noble if sometimes lecherous knights. Eleanor of Aquitaine was the lady responsible for establishing the rules of Court-

A detail from a da Vinci drawing illustrated this 1975 dust jacket.

ly Love, rules that caused a gentleman to rise when a lady entered a room. Rules that took a Woodstock and a revolution, a sexual revolution, to change.

"Besides awakening me to new and even deeper interest in the Middle Ages, my investigations of Eleanor of Aquitaine served another purpose. Her era serves as a radioactive tracer by which I can track events forward and backward. The time of her personal history, the years 1122 to 1204, marks the time when European art was changing from Romanesque to Gothic. A time when the Crusades, those greatest cultural exchanges of all times, were at their peak. A time when the great universities were beginning; her husband Henry started Oxford. It was a time when the middle class was just starting to knock on the doors of nobility, money in hand, ready to pay admission for upward movement.

"The Age of Eleanor of Aquitaine is a watershed.

"I wanted to write about this queen, this woman's libber, for children. I wanted to do it accurately, but I didn't want to invent a small child character

and plop him into the twelfth century. I felt I didn't need to do that. Eleanor of Aquitaine already had an age in common with children: the Middle Ages. So I have written a book of a bastard genre. There are no made-up characters in my book. Everyone who inhabits the pages had lived. But I have chosen to have him live both then in the 1170s and now in the 1970s. They speak in phrases that are historically documented as well as others blatantly invented. But there is over, under and throughout all this mixture of historical fact and fiction—even some fantasy—a truth. A true portrait of Eleanor of Aquitaine, a portrait of a liberated woman."[8]

Eleanor of Aquitaine is only one of Konigsburg's many brainy, feisty, and witty female characters. Her girls don't have it easy, they surmount complex conflict. Yet Konigsburg holds that the creation of her characters doesn't start with an overtly feminist agenda. "I didn't realize how consistently feminist my female characters were until I read it in a review. Not that I object! I'm not a very brave

Dust jacket by Konigsburg for her 1976 novel.

person in social situations. I always think of brilliant rejoinders *after* the party. Perhaps my witty female characters are a form of 'revenge.'"[1]

Konigsburg is vehemently outspoken against censorship of any form in reading material. "...I think there is room for everything. I hate to see anything being called inadmissible; it may not appeal to me but it's my judgment to open that book and read it or not open it at all. As for children, my whole idea about censorship is that if a child reads something with understanding, he's ready for it, and if he reads it without understanding, what does it hurt?"[7]

She has had personal experience with censorship. Certain textbook editors and publishers have attempted to expurgate her novels to make excerpts "suitable" for inclusion in sixth-grade readers. School librarians have removed her books from shelves. Administrators have requested Konigsburg to change certain words and after her refusal, forbade teachers and librarians from ordering her books. An incident particularly grating to her involved a textbook company's desire to print a chapter from *From the Mixed-Up Files of Mrs. Basil E. Frankweiler.* Hiding from the guards in the museum, the brother and sister take refuge in the bathrooms and remain undetected by standing on the toilet seats. The publisher relinquished the chapter when Konigsburg refused to delete mention of the toilets.

Another instance involved her story, "Momma at the Pearly Gates," from a collection entitled *Altogether, One at a Time.* A school system deemed the story "inappropriate" for its libraries because it contained the word "nigger." "[The story] takes place in the 1940s, a time when the term *black* was unknown to the blacks as well as to the whites of eastern Ohio [where the characters live]....I have read 'Momma at the Pearly Gates' to audiences of children of mixed races, and they have never had any doubt about how cleverly Momma picks up Roseann's weapon, the word *nigger* and cudgels her with it....I predict that Black Americans will feel patronized...and cheated. Cheated of a black heroine who triumphs over being called nigger to become the heroine of her own story....What [censors] are showing...readers is contempt....I say that anyone who looks at the word 'nigger' in 'Momma at the Pearly Gates,' like anyone who looks at the word 'nigger' in *Huckleberry Finn* and who does not see beyond that word, who refuses to see where the author's sentiments lie, is showing contempt for that author. And anyone who properly sees where that author's sentiments lie and does

not trust others to do so is showing contempt for them...."[9]

Konigsburg generally spends a year to a year and a half writing a book, unless a lot of research is involved, in which case the work takes considerably longer. "I'm very hard on myself, revising and rewriting as I go along. By the time I send in a manuscript, I've been over it a number of times with a fine-toothed comb. Several of my books have gone directly from manuscript to galleys."[1]

When Konigsburg begins a book, character and plot germinate at the same time. "The plot couldn't happen unless it happened to those people, and unless there were those people, those things wouldn't be happening. So it goes together; I can't really separate them.

"Before I begin, I have some characters that are bothering me. They begin living in me somewhere and when I know where they're going and when I know a major incident along the way, I start writing. Somewhere in the course of writing the characters take over and often begin writing their own dialogue....

"[I tell] myself the story as I'm telling it to others. That's a kind of magic that happens when your characters become so alive that you write something, and review it the next day, and you think, 'Oh, did I write that?' It's almost as if you're a conduit for what's happening. Although I'm a very disciplined person...I still believe in inspiration. I don't believe that you can only write when inspired, but I believe in something called inspiration—when my Muse or whatever it is visits."[7]

"I'm at my desk every day when I'm...at home. I get up, get dressed, and go to my office, which is my son's old bedroom. I used to be very rigid about my mornings and not even answer the phone....But now that my children are gone from home, I do take necessary calls. My friends are all very nice; they know that I don't like to take personal calls in the morning. I find now that I go back in the afternoon; it splashes over. A lot of that is catching up with mail. I travel a lot—I enjoy speaking, and there's always mail connected with that and mail connected with other things."[4]

"Because I work alone in that office...I can go for months at a time without having a good talk about books—good talk to me always implies a certain amount of gossip—so I like to talk to people to whom books are important. Very often those are people who get books into the hands of children. In their passage to the reader, children's books pass through one, and sometimes two, more filters than do adult books. Besides the editor at the publishing house and the reviewer in the media, there is the teacher or the librarian or the parent who controls what a child has available to read. That control can be one of purse strings; there is not enough money in any household or in any institution to buy everything that is published. I like to talk to these people about the creative process as it applies to children's fiction. Now that many more children's books are in paperback, children themselves have greater control over what they have access to read. Now that my books are coming out in mass-market paperback, I see from the mail that is coming in that with more titles available, more are being read."[4]

To young people who aspire to be writers or artists, Konigsburg advises, "*Finish.* The difference between being a writer and being a person of talent is the discipline it takes to apply the seat of your pants to the seat of your chair and finish. Don't talk about doing it. Do it. Finish."[1]

Her contemplation of the creative process has had it's fullest expression in her novel about Leonardo Da Vinci, *The Second Mrs. Giaconda.* Central to the book is Leonardo's relationship with Salai, a fetching young thief who was the artist's lover, assistant, and companion. "In his notebooks Leonardo complains of Salai; he calls him *glutton, thief, mulehead, liar.* He lists items that Salai stole and the dates on which he stole them. Yet, Leonardo kept this young man with him for more than twenty years. He helped pay his sister's dowry, and he remembered him in his will. Why did Leonardo do that?. . ."[10]

"Every great work of art, every work of genius, has a wild element. Some artists carry that wild element within them. Michelangelo did; Rembrandt did; Beethoven did; but Leonardo did not.

"Leonardo, the bastard son, the uneducated, defensive, self-conscious, inhibited genius, needed Salai to supply that irreverence, that wild element, that all-important something awful that great works of art have. Salai gave Leonardo a necessary sense of unimportance. We all need a child to do that; Salai in many ways was a perpetual child. . . .

"Young readers give me what Salai gave Leonardo: a highly developed sense of unimportance. We match up quite well. Just as Salai lacked reverence toward important works, so do young readers. They provide me with a wild element, and that is why they are a challenge to write for. And because they are that challenge, I like to write for them.

Should you ask why I write for children, I would tell you that writing for them makes me research history and human emotions. Writing for children makes me research deeply, beyond and beneath the slick, sexy explanations you first come across.

"And writing for children demands a certain kind of excellence: the quality that Salai helped to give to Leonardo, the quality that young readers demand, as Renaissance viewers demanded it—that works of art must have weight and knowing beneath them, that works of art must have all the techniques and all the skills; they must never be sloppy but must never show the gears. Make it nonchalant, easy, light. The men of the Renaissance called that kind of excellence *sprezzatura.*

"And because Salai appreciated this quality, Leonardo kept him with him. And because children demand it subliminally and appreciate it loudly, and because I do, too, I write for children."[10]

"I can tell you that there is no greater compliment than having your work cherished by. . .someone who has read a lot and chooses your book out of a vast experience of reading. There is also no greater compliment than hearing from a young man in Pennsylvania, 'I never liked reading until I read you.' And. . .imagine, the joy of being *chosen* by someone who otherwise reads only assignments. So I guess you could say that I love all my readers, for I do. I think they are wonderful, and I like it when they think that I am. Don't we all want to be wonderful to someone?"[4]

Footnote Sources:

[1] Anne Commire, editor, *Something about the Author,* Volume 48, Gale, 1987.
[2] E. L. Konigsburg, "A Book Is a Private Thing," *Saturday Review,* November 9, 1968.
[3] Lee Kingman, editor, *Newbery and Caldecott Medal Books, 1966-1975,* Horn Book, 1975.
[4] Linda Metzger and Deborah A. Straub, editors, *Contemporary Authors: New Revision Series,* Volume 17, Gale, 1986.
[5] John Rowe Townsend, editor, *A Sounding of Storytellers,* Lippincott, 1979.
[6] E. L. Konigsburg, "The Double Image, Language as the Perimeter of Culture," *Library Journal,* February 15, 1970.
[7] Linda T. Jones, "Profile: Elaine Konigsburg," *Language Arts,* February, 1986.
[8] E. L. Konigsburg, "The Genesis of a Proud Taste for Scarlet and Miniver" (pamphlet), *Atheneum,* 1973.
[9] E. L. Konigsburg, "Excerpts from My Bouboulina File," *Library Quarterly,* Volume 51, number 1, 1981.
[10] E. L. Konigsburg, "Sprezzatura: a Kind of Excellence," *Horn Book,* June, 1976.

■ For More Information See

Books:

Martha E. Ward and Dorothy A. Marquardt, *Authors of Books for Young People*, 2nd edition, Scarecrow, 1971.

Miriam Hoffman and Eva Samuels, *Authors and Illustrators of Children's Books: Writings on Their Lives and Works*, Bowker, 1972.

Doris de Montreville and Donna Hill, editors, *Third Book of Junior Authors*, H. W. Wilson, 1972.

Lee Bennett Hopkins, *More Books by More People*, Citation Press, 1974.

Lee Kingman, editor, *Newbery and Caldecott Medal Books: 1966-1975*, Horn Book, 1975.

Ann Block and Carolyn Riley, editors, *Children's Literature Review*, Volume I, Gale, 1976.

Paul Heins, editor, *Crosscurrents of Criticism: Horn Book Essays 1968-1977*, Horn Book, 1977.

D. L. Kirkpatrick, *Twentieth-Century Children's Writers*, St. Martin's, 1978, 2nd edition, 1983.

John Rowe Townsend, *A Sounding of Storytellers: Essays on Contemporary Writers for Children*, Penguin Books, 1979.

Lina Mainiero, *American Women Writers: A Critical Reference Guide from Colonial Times to the Present*, Volume 2, Ungar, 1980.

Jim Roginski, compiler, *Newbery and Caldecott Medalists and Honor Book Winners*, Libraries Unlimited, 1982.

Periodicals:

Library Journal, October 15, 1967, March 15, 1968, May 15, 1971 (p. 1805).

New York Times Book Review, November 5, 1967 (p. 44), February 25, 1968, March 30, 1969 (p. 30), November 8, 1970, May 30, 1971 (p. 8), October 14, 1973 (p. 8), November 4, 1973, October 5, 1975, November 7, 1976, December 9, 1979, May 30, 1982.

Publishers Weekly, February 26, 1968.

School Library Journal, March, 1968, February, 1970, October, 1973 (p. 117), November, 1986 (p. 30ff).

Top of the News, April, 1968.

PTA April, 1968 (p. 32ff).

Times Literary Supplement, October 3, 1968, April 3, 1969, July 2, 1971, April 4, 1975, March 25, 1977, June 16, 1983.

Chicago Tribune Children's Book World, November 8, 1970.

Saturday Review, November 14, 1970.

Horn Book, December, 1970 (p. 619ff), August, 1971 (p. 384), April, 1973 (p. 179), February, 1978 (p. 79ff), April, 1980.

E. L. Konigsburg, "Forty Percent More Than Everything You Want to Know about E. L. Konigsburg" (pamphlet), Atheneum, 1974.

Christian Science Monitor, May 1, 1974 (p. F1).

E. L. Konigsburg, "How I Came to Love a Thief and Write the Second Mrs. Giaconda" (pamphlet), Atheneum, 1978.

Learning Today, fall, 1981.

Washington Post Book World, April 11, 1982.

Children's Literature Association Quarterly, spring, 1983 (p. 6ff).

Times (London), June 16, 1983.

Other:

"E. L. Konigsburg" (videocassette), Profiles in Literature, Temple University, 1983.

Collections:

University of Pittsburgh, Pennsylvania.

C. S. Lewis

Born Clive Staples Lewis, November 29, 1898, in Belfast, Ireland; died of heart failure, November 22, 1963, in Oxford, England; son of Albert James (a solicitor) and Flora Augusta (Hamilton) Lewis; married Joy Davidman Gresham (a poet and novelist; died, 1960), 1956; children: (stepsons) David Gresham, Douglas Gresham. *Education:* Attended Malvern College, one year; afterwards privately tutored; University College, Oxford, A.B. (classics; first class honors), 1922, A.B. (English; first class honors), 1923. *Home:* Cambridge, England.

■ Career

Novelist, Christian apologist, scholar and critic of English literature. Oxford University, Oxford, England, lecturer, 1924; Magdalene College, Oxford, fellow and tutor in English literature, 1925-54; Cambridge University, Cambridge, England, professor of Medieval and Renaissance English, 1954-63. University of Wales, Cardiff, Ballard Matthews lecturer, 1941, University of Durham, Durham, England, Riddell lecturer, 1942, Trinity College, Cambridge, Clark lecturer, 1944. *Military service:* British Army, Somerset Light Infantry, 1917-19; became second lieutenant. *Member:* British Acade-

my (fellow, 1955), Royal Society of Literature (fellow, 1948), Athenaeum, Sir Walter Scott Society (president, 1956).

■ Awards, Honors

Hawthornden Prize, 1936, for *The Allegory of Love*; Gollancz Memorial Prize for Literature, 1937; D.D. from St. Andrews University, 1946; Docteur es Lettres from Laval University, 1952; honorary fellow, Magdalene College, Oxford, 1955, and University College, Oxford, 1958; Carnegie Medal Commendation from the British Library Association, 1955, for *The Horse and His Boy*; Carnegie Medal, 1957, for *The Last Battle*; D.Litt. from the University of Manchester, 1959; Lewis Carroll Shelf Award, 1962, for *The Lion, the Witch and the Wardrobe*; honorary doctorate from the University of Dijon, 1962, and University of Lyon, 1963.

■ Writings

Poetry:

Spirits in Bondage, Heinemann, 1917, published as *Spirits in Bondage: A Cycle of Lyrics*, Harcourt, 1984.
(Under pseudonym Clive Hamilton) *Dymer*, Dutton, 1926, reissued, Macmillan, 1950.

Novels:

Out of the Silent Planet, John Lane, 1938, reissued, Macmillan, 1970.

Perelandra: A Novel, John Lane, 1943, reissued, Macmillan, 1968, new edition published as *Voyage to Venus*, Pan Books, 1960.

That Hideous Strength: A Modern Fairy-Tale for Grown-ups, John Lane, 1945, reissued, Macmillan, 1968.

The Great Divorce: A Dream, Bles, 1945, Macmillan, 1946, reissued, 1963.

Till We Have Faces: A Myth Retold, Bles, 1956, Harcourt, 1957, reissued, Time, 1966.

Space Trilogy (contains *Out of the Silent Planet*, *Perelandra*, and *That Hideous Strength*), Macmillan, 1975.

The Dark Tower and Other Stories, edited by W. Hooper, Harcourt, 1977.

Novels; For Young People:

The Lion, the Witch, and the Wardrobe: A Story for Children (ALA Notable Book; illustrated by Pauline Baynes), Macmillan, 1950, study edition, 1979, new edition (illustrated by Michael Hague), 1983, large print edition, G. K. Hall, 1986, reissued, Macmillan, 1988.

Prince Caspian: The Return to Narnia (illustrated by P. Baynes), Macmillan, 1951, large print edition, G. K. Hall, 1986, reissued, Macmillan, 1988.

The Voyage of the "Dawn Treader" (illustrated by P. Baynes), Macmillan, 1952, large print edition, G. K. Hall, 1986, reissued, Macmillan, 1988.

The Silver Chair (illustrated by P. Baynes), Macmillan, 1953, large print edition, G. K. Hall, 1986, reissued, Macmillan, 1988.

The Horse and His Boy (illustrated by P. Baynes), Macmillan, 1954, large print edition, G. K. Hall, 1986, reissued, Macmillan, 1988.

The Magician's Nephew (ALA Notable Book; illustrated by P. Baynes), Macmillan, 1955, reissued, Macmillan, 1988.

The Last Battle: A Story for Children (ALA Notable Book; illustrated by P. Baynes), Macmillan, 1956, large print edition, G. K. Hall, 1986, reissued, Macmillan, 1988.

The Complete Chronicles of Narnia (a collection of the above books; illustrated by P. Baynes), seven volumes, Penguin, 1965, large print edition, G. K. Hall, 1986, reissued, Macmillan, 1988.

Theological Works:

The Pilgrim's Regress: An Allegorical Apology for Christianity, Reason and Romanticism, Dent, 1933, Sheed & Ward, 1935, new edition (illustrated by M. Hague), Eerdmans, 1981.

The Problem of Pain, Centenary Press, 1940, Macmillan, 1943, reissued, 1968.

The Screwtape Letters, Bles, 1942, Macmillan, 1943, new edition with the addition of *Screwtape Proposes a Toast*, Macmillan, 1964, revised edition, 1982.

Broadcast Talks: Reprinted with some Alterations from Two Series of Broadcast Talks, Bles, 1942, published in America as *The Case for Christianity*, Macmillan, 1943, reissued, 1968.

Christian Behaviour: A Further Series of Broadcast Talks, Macmillan, 1943.

Beyond Personality: The Christian Idea of God, Bles, 1944, Macmillan, 1945.

Miracles: A Preliminary Study, Macmillan, 1947, reissued, 1968.

The Weight of Glory and Other Addresses, Macmillan, 1949, revised edition, 1980 (published in England as *Transposition and Other Addresses*, Bles, 1949).

Mere Christianity (revised and enlarged edition of *The Case for Christianity, Christian Behavior*, and *Beyond Personality*), Macmillan, 1952, reissued, 1986.

Surprised by Joy: The Shape of My Early Life (autobiographical), Bles, 1955, Harcourt, 1956, reissued, Macmillan, 1981.

Reflections on the Psalms, Harcourt, 1958.

Shall We Lose God in Outer Space?, S.P.C.K., 1959.

The Four Loves, Harcourt, 1960.

The World's Last Night and Other Essays, Harcourt, 1960, reissued, 1973.

(Under pseudonym N. W. Clerk) *A Grief Observed*, Faber, 1961, Seabury, 1963, large print edition, Walker, 1985.

Beyond the Bright Blur, Harcourt, 1963.

Letters to Malcolm: Chiefly on Prayer, Harcourt, 1964.

Christian Reflections, edited by W. Hooper, Eerdmans, 1967.

God in the Dock: Essays on Theology and Ethics, edited by W. Hooper, Eerdmans, 1970 (published in England as *Undeceptions: Essays on Theology and Ethics*, Bles, 1971).

The Grand Miracle, Ballantine, 1983.

The Seeing Eye and Other Selected Essays from Christian Reflections, Ballantine, 1986.

Literary Criticism:

The Allegory of Love: A Study in Medieval Tradition, Clarendon Press, 1936, Oxford University Press, 1958.

Dust jacket for the 1977 collection of Lewis' work.

(With Eustace M. W. Tillyard) *The Personal Heresy: A Controversy,* Oxford University Press, 1939, reissued, 1965.

Rehabilitations and Other Essays, Oxford University Press, 1939, reissued, Folcroft, 1980.

A Preface to "Paradise Lost": Being the Ballard Matthews Lectures, Delivered at University College, North Wales, 1941, Oxford University Press, 1942, reissued, 1970.

Hamlet: The Prince or the Poem?, H. Milford, 1942, reissued, Folcroft, 1973.

The Abolition of Man; or, Reflections on Education, Oxford University Press, 1943, Macmillan, 1947, reissued, 1967.

(Author of commentary) Charles W. S. Williams, *Taliess in through Logres, [and] The Region of the Summer Stars, [and] Arthurian Torso,* Oxford University Press, 1948, Eerdmans, 1974.

The Literary Impact of the Authorized Version, Athlone Press, 1950, revised edition, Fortress, 1967.

English Literature in the Sixteenth Century, Excluding Drama, Clarendon Press, 1954, Oxford University Press, 1975.

Studies in Words, Cambridge University Press, 1960, 2nd edition, 1967.

An Experiment in Criticism, Cambridge University Press, 1961.

The Discarded Image: An Introduction to Medieval and Renaissance Literature, Cambridge University Press, 1964.

Spenser's Images of Life, edited by Alistair Fowler, Cambridge University Press, 1967.

Selected Literary Essays, edited by W. Hooper, Cambridge University Press, 1969.

Shelly, Dryden, and Mr. Eliot in Rehabilitations, R. West, 1973.

The Visionary Christian: One Hundred Thirty-One Readings from C. S. Lewis, selected by Chad Walsh, Macmillan, 1981.

Selected Works:

They Asked for a Paper: Papers and Addresses, Bles, 1962.

Poems, edited by W. Hooper, Bles, 1964, Harcourt, 1965.

Letters of C. S. Lewis, edited by W. H. Lewis, Harcourt, 1966, reissued, 1975.

Of Other Worlds: Essays and Stories, edited by W. Hooper, Bles, 1966, Harcourt, 1967.

Studies in Medieval and Renaissance Literature, edited by W. Hooper, Cambridge University Press, 1966, reissued, 1980.

Letters to an American Lady, edited by Clyde S. Kilby, Eerdmans, 1967.

A Mind Awake: An Anthology of C. S. Lewis, edited by C. Kilby, Bles, 1968, Harcourt, 1969.

C. S. Lewis: Five Best Books in One Volume, Iversen Associates, 1969.

Narrative Poems, edited by W. Hooper, Bles, 1969, Harcourt, 1972.

The Joyful Christian: One Hundred Readings from the Work of C. S. Lewis, Macmillan, 1977.

On Stories: And Other Essays on Literature, edited by W. Hooper, Harcourt, 1982.

The Business of Heaven: Daily Readings from C. S. Lewis, Harcourt, 1984.

Letters to Children, edited by Lyle W. Dorsett and Marjorie Lamp Mead, Macmillan, 1985.

(With others) *The Collier Christian Library,* three volumes, Collier, 1988.

Other:

(Editor) *George MacDonald: An Anthology,* Centenary Press, 1945, Doubleday, 1962, reissued, Macmillan, 1978.

Essays Presented to Charles Williams, Eerdmans, 1966.

Present Concerns, Harcourt, 1987.

Recordings:

"Love" (talks recorded by the author for broadcast on American radio), Creative Resources, 1971. Contributor to the proceedings of the British Academy and to *Essays and Studies by Members of the English Association.*

■ Adaptations

Cassettes; Records:

"The Chronicles of Narnia: The Lion, the Witch and the Wardrobe," Caedmon, 1978.

"The Chronicles of Narnia: Prince Caspian," Caedmon, 1979.

"The Chronicles of Narnia: The Voyage of the 'Dawn Treader,'" Caedmon, 1979.

"The Chronicles of Narnia: The Silver Chair," Caedmon, 1980.

"The Chronicles of Narnia: The Horse and His Boy," Caedmon, 1980.

"The Chronicles of Narnia: The Magician's Nephew," Caedmon, 1981.

"The Chronicles of Narnia: The Last Battle," Caedmon, 1981.

Cassettes:

"Out of the Silent Planet," Books on Tape.

"Perelandra," Books on Tape.

"Philia," Word Books.

"Storge," Word Books.

"That Hideous Strength," Books on Tape.

"The Four Loves," Catacomb.

Recordings:

"The Four Loves," Word Books.

"Agape" (title means "Divine Love"), Word Books.

Films:

"The Lion, the Witch, and the Wardrobe," Lord & King Associates, (animated television special) CBS-TV, April 1-2, 1979.

"The Chronicles of Narnia" (series), PBS-TV, 1989.

Theater:

"Narnia the Musical," first produced in New York City at St. Stephens Church, September 29, 1986.

"The Lion, the Witch and the Wardrobe," first produced in Chicago, Ill. at the Lifeline Theater, December, 1986.

■ Sidelights

November 29, 1898. Lewis was born in Belfast, Northern Ireland. His father, Albert, was a lawyer, and his mother, Flora, the daughter of a clergyman. "My parents had only two children, both sons, and I was the younger by about three years. Two very different strains had gone to our making. My father belonged to the first generation of his family that reached professional station. His grandfather had been a Welsh farmer; his father, a self-made man, had begun life as a workman, emigrated to Ireland, and ended as a partner in the firm of Macilwaine and Lewis, 'Boiler-makers, Engineers, and Iron Ship Builders.' My mother was a Hamilton with many generations of clergymen, lawyers, sailors, and the like behind her; on her mother's side, through the Warrens, the blood went back to a Norman knight whose bones lie at Battle Abbey.

"The two families from which I spring were as different in temperament as in origin. My father's people were true Welshmen, sentimental, passionate, and rhetorical, easily moved both to anger and to tenderness; men who laughed and cried a great deal and who had not much of the talent for happiness. The Hamiltons were a cooler race. Their minds were critical and ironic and they had the talent for happiness in a high degree—went straight for it as experienced travelers go for the best seat in a train. From my earliest years I was aware of the vivid contrast between my mother's cheerful and tranquil affection and the ups and downs of my father's emotional life, and this bred in me long before I was old enough to give it a name a certain distrust or dislike of emotion as something uncomfortable and embarrassing and even dangerous."[1]

Both parents "by the standards of that time and place, were bookish or 'clever' people."[1] His mother had been a promising mathematician in her youth and had her young son tutored in French and Latin. His father "was fond of oratory and had himself spoken on political platforms in England as a young man; if he had had independent means he would certainly have aimed at a political career. In this, unless his sense of honor, which was fine to

Paperback cover for Lewis' 1938 novel.

Another cover from Lewis' "Space" series.

the point of being Quixotic, had made him unmanageable, he might well have succeeded, for he had many of the gifts once needed by a Parliamentarian—a fine presence, a resonant voice, great quickness of mind, eloquence, and memory."[1]

He was "almost without rival, the best *raconteur* I have ever heard. What neither he nor my mother had the least taste for was that kind of literature to which my allegiance was given the moment I could choose books for myself....If I am a romantic my parents bear no responsibility for it....My mother, I have been told, cared for no poetry at all."[1]

The other blessing of his life's beginning, Lewis said, was his brother: "Though three years my senior, he never seemed to be an elder brother; we were allies, not to say confederates, from the first. Yet we were very different. Our earliest pictures (and I can remember no time when we were not incessantly drawing) reveal it. His were of ships

and trains and battles; mine, when not imitated from his, were of what we both called 'dressed animals'—the anthropomorphized beasts of nursery literature. His earliest story—as my elder brother he preceded me in the transition from drawing to writing—was called *The Young Rajah*. He had already made India 'his country'; Animal-Land was mine.

"I do not think any of the surviving drawings date from the first six years of my life which I am now describing, but I have plenty of them that cannot be much later. From them it appears to me that I had the better talent. From a very early age I could draw movement—figures that looked as if they were really running or fighting—and the perspective is good. But nowhere, either in my brother's work or my own, is there a single line drawn in obedience to an idea, however crude, of beauty. There is action, comedy, invention; but there is not

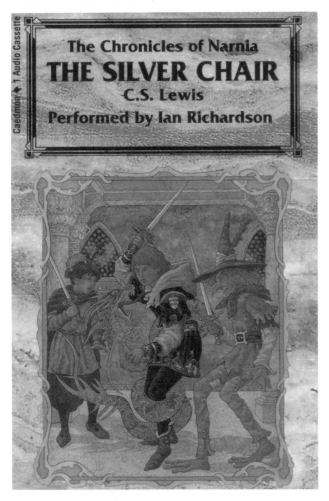

Cover from Caedmon's audio cassette.

even the germ of a feeling for design, and there is a shocking ignorance of natural form. Trees appear as balls of cotton wool stuck on posts, and there is nothing to show that either of us knew the shape of any leaf in the garden where we played almost daily.

"This absence of beauty, now that I come to think of it, is characteristic of our childhood. No picture on the walls of my father's house ever attracted—and indeed none deserved—our attention. We never saw a beautiful building nor imagined that a building could be beautiful.

"My earliest aesthetic experiences, if indeed they were aesthetic, were not of that kind; they were already incurably romantic, not formal. Once in those very early days my brother brought into the nursery the lid of a biscuit tin which he had covered with moss and garnished with twigs and flowers so as to make it a toy garden or a toy forest. That was the first beauty I ever knew. What the real garden had failed to do, the toy garden did. It made me aware of nature—not indeed, as a

storehouse of forms and colors but as something cool, dewy, fresh, exuberant. I do not think the impression was very important at the moment, but it soon became important in memory. As long as I live my imagination of Paradise will retain something of my brother's toy garden. And every day there were what we called 'the Green Hills'; that is, the low line of the Castlereagh Hills which we saw from the nursery windows. They were not very far off but they were, to children, quite unattainable. They taught me longing— *Sehnsucht;* made me for good or ill, and before I was six years old, a votary of the Blue Flower."[1]

By the time he was four years old, he had decided to change his name from Clive Staples to Jack, refusing to answer to any other name. Thus, he became known as Jack by his family and friends for the rest of his life.

"In. . .my seventh year, the first great change in my life took place. We moved house. My father, growing, I suppose, in prosperity, decided to leave the semidetached villa in which I had been born and build himself a much larger house, further out into what was then the country. The 'New House,' as we continued for years to call it, was a large one even by my present standards; to a child it seemed less like a house than a city. My father, who had more capacity for being cheated than any man I have ever known, was badly cheated by his builders; the drains were wrong, the chimneys were wrong, and there was a draft in every room.

"None of this, however, mattered to a child. To me, the important thing about the move was that the background of my life became larger. The New House is almost a major character in my story. I am a product of long corridors, empty sunlit rooms, upstairs indoor silences, attics explored in solitude, distant noises of gurgling cisterns and pipes, and the noise of wind under the tiles. Also, of endless books.

"My father bought all the books he read and never got rid of any of them. There were books in the study, books in the drawing room, books in the cloakroom, books (two deep) in the great bookcase on the landing, books in a bedroom, books piled as high as my shoulder in the cistern attic, books of all kinds reflecting every transient stage of my parents' interest, books readable and unreadable, books suitable for a child and books most emphatically not. Nothing was forbidden me. In the seemingly endless rainy afternoons I took volume after volume from the shelves. I had always the same certainty of finding a book that was new to

Joss Ackland starred in the television special "Shadowlands," the love story of C. S. Lewis and Joy Gresham, whom he married late in life. Presented on PBS-TV, October 29, 1986.

me as a man who walks into a field has of finding a new blade of grass."[1]

Brother Warren was sent off to an English boarding school and Lewis' life was becoming one of increasing solitude, though it was a solitude always at his command rather than—with parents, a grandfather, gardener and maids—a lack of people to talk to. "I soon staked out a claim to one of the attics and made it 'my study.' Pictures, of my own making or cut from the brightly colored Christmas numbers of magazines, were nailed on the walls. There I kept my pen and inkpot and writing books and paintbox....Here my first stories were written, and illustrated, with enormous satisfaction. They were an attempt to combine my two chief literary pleasures—'dressed animals' and 'knights in armor.' As a result, I wrote about chivalrous mice and rabbits who rode out in complete mail to kill not giants but cats. But already the mood of the systematizer was strong in me....

"There came a night when I was ill and crying both with headache and toothache and distressed because my mother did not come to me. That was because she was ill too; and what was odd was that there were several doctors in her room, and voices and comings and goings all over the house and doors shutting and opening. It seemed to last for hours. And then my father, in tears, came into my room and began to try to convey to my terrified mind things it had never conceived before. It was in fact cancer and followed the usual course; an operation (they operated in the patient's house in those days), an apparent convalescence, a return of the disease, increasing pain, and death. My father never fully recovered from this loss.

"Children suffer not (I think) less than their elders, but differently. For us boys the real bereavement had happened before our mother died. We lost her gradually as she was gradually withdrawn from our life into the hands of nurses and delirium and morphia, and as our whole existence changed into something alien and menacing, as the house became full of strange smells and midnight noises and sinister whispered conversations. This had two further results, one very evil and one very good. It divided us from our father as well as our mother. They say that a shared sorrow draws people closer together; I can hardly believe that it often has that effect when those who share it are of widely different ages. If I may trust my own experience, the sight of adult misery and adult terror has an effect on children which is merely paralyzing and alienating. Perhaps it was our fault. Perhaps if we had been better children we might have lightened

our father's sufferings at this time. We certainly did not.

"His nerves had never been of the steadiest and his emotions had always been uncontrolled. Under the pressure of anxiety his temper became incalculable; he spoke wildly and acted unjustly. Thus by a peculiar cruelty of fate, during those months the unfortunate man, had he but known it, was really losing his sons as well as his wife. We were coming, my brother and I, to rely more and more exclusively on each other for all that made life bearable; to have confidence only in each other. I expect that we (or at any rate I) were already learning to lie to him. Everything that had made the house a home had failed us; everything except one another. We drew daily closer together (that was the good result)—two frightened urchins huddled for warmth in a bleak world."[1]

Years later, Lewis drew upon the memory of his mother's illness for his story *The Magician's Nephew*. Digory's mother nearly died, but Alsan intervened before it was too late. "My mother's death was the occasion of what some (but not I) might regard as my first religious experience. When her case was pronounced hopeless I remembered what I had been taught; that prayers offered in faith would be granted. I accordingly set myself to produce by will power a firm belief that my prayers for her recovery would be successful; and, as I thought, I achieved it. When nevertheless she died I shifted my ground and worked myself into a belief that there was to be a miracle. The interesting thing is that my disappointment produced no results beyond itself. The thing hadn't worked, but I was used to things not working, and I thought no more about it.

"With my mother's death all settled happiness, all that was tranquil and reliable, disappeared from my life. There was to be much fun, many pleasures, many stabs of Joy; but no more of the old security. It was sea and islands now; the great continent had sunk like Atlantis."[1]

1908. Lewis set off with his brother for school in England. "We are in low spirits. My brother, who has most reason to be so, for he alone knows what we are going to, shows his feelings least. He is already a veteran. I perhaps am buoyed up by a little excitement, but very little. The most important fact at the moment is the horrible clothes I have been made to put on. Only this morning—only two hours ago—I was running wild in shorts and blazer and sand shoes. Now I am choking and sweating, itching too, in thick dark stuff, throttled by an Eton collar, my feet already aching with unaccustomed boots."[1]

They parted on shipboard, the father "deeply moved,"[1] Lewis "mainly embarrassed and self-conscious."[1] The older brother conducted a tour of the ship and the younger one felt "an agreeable excitement."[1]

Lewis took an immediate dislike to England, before he even saw the school: "The strange English accents with which I was surrounded seemed like the voices of demons. But what was worse was the...landscape....Even to my adult eye the main line still appears to run through the dullest and most unfriendly strip in the island. But to a child who had always lived near the sea and in sight of high ridges it appeared as I suppose Russia might.... The flatness! The interminableness!... Everything was wrong; wooden fences instead of stone walls and hedges, red brick farmhouses instead of white cottages, the fields too big, haystacks the wrong shape....I have made up the quarrel since; but at that moment I conceived a hatred for England which took many years to heal."[1]

As for the school: "The only stimulating element in the teaching consisted of a few well-used canes which hung on the green iron chimney piece of the single schoolroom....Oldie (the headmaster) lived in a solitude of power, like a sea captain in the days of sail....He was a big, bearded man with full lips like an Assyrian king on a monument, immensely strong, physically dirty....The curious thing is that despite all the cruelty (Oldie practiced on his students) we did surprisingly little work. This may have been partly because the cruelty was irrational and unpredictable; but it was partly because of the curious methods employed. Except at geometry (which he really liked) it might be said that Oldie did not teach at all....

"You may ask how our father came to send us (to this school). Certainly not because he made a careless choice. The surviving correspondence shows that he had considered many other schools before fixing on Oldie's; and I know him well enough to be sure that in such a matter he would never have been guided by his first thoughts (which would probably have been right) nor even by his twenty-first (which would at least have been explicable). Beyond doubt he would have prolonged deliberation till his hundred-and-first; and they would be infallibly and invincibly wrong. This is what always happens to the deliberations of a simple man who thinks he is a subtle one."[1]

Softcover edition of the 1956 novel.

When the school of the mad Englishman failed, Lewis was sent temporarily to a local Irish school, whose population was more socially "mixed" than at most English schools, and where Lewis described the children as "always 'moving on' or 'hanging about'—in lavatories, in storerooms, in the great hall. It was very like living permanently in a large railway station."[1]

From here he was moved to Wyvern, a school his brother had loved but which he detested. Part of his antipathy he attributed to his face, which seems to have perpetually cast him for flogging and for upper-classmen demands to "get that look off your face."[1]

The final wearying element, in addition to the flogging system for underclassmen, was the games—games which Lewis detested but in which he feigned interest. He would later declare: "The truth is that organized and compulsory games had, in my day, banished the element of play from school life almost entirely. There was no time to play (in the proper sense of the word). The rivalry was too fierce, the prizes too glittering, the 'hell of failure' too severe."[1]

1916. As a scholarship candidate he sent his first impressions of Oxford to his father: "This is Thursday and our last papers are on Saturday morning....This place has surpassed my wildest dreams; I never saw anything so beautiful, especially on these frosty nights; though in the Hall of Oriel where we do our papers it is fearfully cold at about four o'clock on these afternoons. We have most of us tried, with varying success, to write in our gloves."[2]

His studies were supported by stipends from home and the letters home were filled with reports of expenses as he "panned out" his funds. He was advised to join the Officers Training Corps—the brightest result of which was a later exemption from a mathematics examination, which his brother suggests he would have had difficulty passing—and he made a gradual transition from college to military life.

Winter, 1917. Lewis was stationed in France, with one of his cadet friends, E. F. C. ("Paddy") Moore, whose home he had visited on leave before going to the front. By April of 1918 Lewis was wounded and transferred to a London hospital; his friend Paddy was missing and presumed dead. That June, Lewis wrote to his father: "It seems that now-a-days one is sent from hospital to be kept for some time in a convalescent home before going on leave. Of course I have asked to be sent to an Irish one, but there are only a few of these, and they are already crowded; we must not therefore expect too much, but wherever I am I know that you will come and see me.

"You know I have some difficulty in talking of the greatest things; it is the fault of our generation and of the English schools. But at least you will believe that I was never before so eager to cling to every bit of our old home life and to see you. I know I have often been far from what I should be in my relation to you, and have undervalued an affection and generosity which an experience of 'other people's parents' has shown me in a new light. But, please God, I shall do better in the future. Come and see me, I am homesick, that is the long and short of it...."[2]

Lewis' father ignored his son's appeal, choosing instead to remain at home. "One would have thought it impossible for any father to resist an appeal of this kind, coming at such a moment."[2] Brother Warren observed years later. "But my father was a very peculiar man in some respects: in

none more than in an almost pathological hatred of taking any step which involved a break in the dull routine of his daily existence. Jack [C. S. Lewis] remained unvisited, and was deeply hurt at a neglect which he considered inexcusable."[2]

He returned to Oxford to resume a pattern of life that was essentially unchanged throughout the rest of his life. Lewis was an excellent scholar, taking a First in Honours (1920), a First in Greats (1922), and a First in English (1923), and also won the Chancellor's Prize for an English Essay.

"I...am quite sure that an academic or literary career is the only one in which I can hope ever to go beyond the meanest mediocrity,"[2] he wrote to his father in 1922. "The Bar is a gamble...and in business of course I should be bankrupt or in jail very soon...."[2]

When the first possibility of being elected to a fellowship at Magdalene had presented itself, Lewis reported the interview to his father, noting "I need hardly say that I would have coached a troupe of performing bagbirds in the quadrangle,"[2] but Lewis was elected. Even before, he had had run-ins with unprepared undergraduates, and re-created this dialogue with a scholarship candidate for his father:

"SELF 'Well S., what Greek authors have you been reading?'

"S[TUDENT] (cheerfully) 'I can never remember. Try a few names and I'll see if I get on to any.'

"SELF (a little damped) 'Have you read any Euripides?'

"S. 'No.'

"SELF 'Any Sophocles?'

"S. 'Oh yes.'

"SELF 'What plays of his have you read.'

"S. (after a pause) 'Well—the Alcestis.'

"SELF (apologetically) 'But isn't that by Euripides?'

"S. (with genial surprise of a man who finds 1 where he thought there was only a 10/-note) 'Really. Is it now? Then by jove I *have* read some Euripides.'

"What idiots can have sent him in for a Scholarship? However, he is one of the cheeriest, healthiest, and most perfectly content creatures I have ever met with...."[2]

There was also the pleasant society of other scholars: "(On Monday I have no pupils at all, so) it

From the "Wonderworks" series of "The Lion, the Witch and the Wardrobe," which premiered on PBS-TV, January, 1989.

has become a regular custom that Tolkien should drop in on me of a Monday morning and drink a glass. This is one of the pleasantest spots in the week. Sometimes we talk English School politics; sometimes we criticize one another's poems; other days we drift into theology or 'the state of the nation'; rarely we fly no higher than bawdy or puns...."[2]

1928. A book on Erasmus had been scrapped for a book "about medieval love poetry and the medieval idea of love"—Lewis was thirty, and the book begun, which would be published in 1936, was *The Allegory of Love:* "I have actually begun the first chapter of my book. This perhaps sounds rather odd since I was working at it all last Vac., but you will understand that in a thing of this sort the collection of the material is three quarters of the battle. Of course like a child who wants to get the painting before he has really finished drawing the outline, I have been itching to do some actual *writing* for a long time. Indeed—you can imagine it as well as I—the most delightful sentences would come into one's head; and now half of them can't be used because, knowing a little more of the

subject, I find they aren't true. That's the worst of facts—they do cramp a fellow's style...."[2]

The work was done mostly in one of Lewis' favorite haunts, the Bodleian Library, a place that "if only one could smoke and if only there were upholstered chairs...would be one of the most delightful places in the world."[2] Even without these provisions, Lewis treasured working there: "I sit in 'Duke Humphrey's Library,' the oldest part, a Fifteenth Century building with a little mullioned window on my left hand through which I look down on the garden of Exeter, where these mornings I see the sudden squalls of wind and rain driving the first blossoms of the fruit trees and snowing the lawn with them....This room...is full of books which stand in little cases at right angles to the wall, so that between each pair there is a kind of little 'box'—in the public-house sense of the word—and in these boxes one sits and reads. By a merciful provision, however many books you send for, they will be left on your chosen table at night for you to resume work next morning; so that one gradually accumulates a pile as comfortably as in one's own room...."[2]

September, 1929. Father died. Lewis had helped nurse him through his last illness and wrote of the experience to a friend: "My father and I are physical counterparts: and during these days more than ever I notice his resemblance to me."[2]

1939. Another war had begun in Europe. Lewis plunged into the requirements of wartime life with philosophic good humor, writing his brother, who had been recalled to service: "One of the most reminiscent features of the last war has already reappeared, i.e. the information which always comes too late to prevent you doing an unnecessary job. We have just been informed that New Building will not be used by Govt. and that the Fellows' rooms in particular will be inviolable; so that we *are* going to have a Term and quite a lot of undergraduates up. . . .

". . .The main trouble of life at present is the blacking out which is done (as you may imagine) with a most complicated Arthur Rackham system of odd rags—quite effectively, but at the cost of much labour. Luckily I do most of the rooms myself, so it doesn't take nearly as long as if I were assisted. . . ."[2]

1940. The idea of *Screwtape* was first mentioned to his brother. ". . .I was struck by an idea for a book which I think might be both useful and entertaining. It would be called 'As one Devil to another' and would consist of letters from an elderly retired devil to a young devil who has just started work on his first 'patient.' The idea would be to give all the psychology of temptation from the other point of view."[2]

October, 1941. The manuscript was completed and he sent it on to Sister Penelope (with whom he also spoke on a BBC series): "I enclose the MS of *Screwtape*. If it is not a trouble I should like you to keep it safe until the book is printed (in case the one the publishers have has got blitzed)—after which it can be made into spills or used to stuff dolls or anything. . . .

"Writing a book is much less like creation than it is like planting a garden or begetting a child; in all three cases we are only entering as *one* cause into a causal stream which works, so to speak, in its own way. I would not wish it to be otherwise. . . ."[2]

It was during the fifties that Lewis wrote his seven-volume fantasy for children, "The Chronicles of Narnia," the first of which, *The Lion, the Witch, and the Wardrobe* told the story of the freeing of a kingdom held in bondage by a wicked witch; this was followed by "P.[rince] Caspian,. . .The Voyage *of the 'Dawn Treader'*: Then *The Silver Chair*: then *The Horse and His Boy*. . . .Next autumn [1955], will come *The Magician's Nephew*, and, the year after, *The Last Battle* (at least I think that will be the name, but I might change it) which will finish off the series. Peter gets back to Narnia in it. I am afraid Susan does not. . . .She is rather fond of being too grownup. I am sorry to say that side of her got stronger and she forgot about Narnia.

". . .I didn't start with four real children in mind: I just made them up."[3]

In these seven stories Lewis created a world called Narnia that can only be entered by children and only at certain times. The books, which have often been called fairy tales, allegories or parables, were published from 1951 to 1956 and were well received by critics, adults and children, although J. R. R. Tolkien was among those who were critical of his friend's stories, apparently because he thought them too allegorical. Lewis himself explained his purpose in writing the tales: "I thought I saw how stories of this kind could steal past a certain inhibition which had paralysed much of my own religion in childhood. Why did one find it so hard to feel as one was told one ought to feel about God or about the sufferings of Christ? I thought the chief reason was that one was told one ought to. . . .But supposing that by casting all these things into an imaginary world, stripping them of their stained-glass and Sunday school associations, one could make them for the first time appear in their real potency? Could one not thus steal past those watchful dragons? I thought one could."[4]

The actual writing of the Narnia books began with an image. "I see pictures. . . .I have no idea whether this is the usual way of writing stories, still less whether it is the best. It is the only one I know: images always come first.

"Some people seem to think I began by asking myself how I could say something about Christianity to children. . . .I couldn't write in that way at all. Everything began with images; a faun carrying an umbrella, a queen on a sledge, a magnificent lion. At first there wasn't even anything Christian about them; that element pushed in of its own accord.

"I did not say to myself 'Let us represent Jesus as He really is in our world by a Lion in Narnia': I said 'Let us *suppose* that there were a land like Narnia and that the son of God, as He became a Man in our world, became a Lion there, and then imagine what would happen.' If you think about it, you will see that it is quite a different thing."[3]

In one of his numerous letters to children, Lewis listed the rules for writing well.

"1) Always try to use the language so as to make quite clear what you mean, and make sure your sentence couldn't mean anything else.

"2) Always prefer the plain direct word to the long vague one. Don't 'implement' promises, but 'keep' them.

"3) Never use abstract nouns when concrete ones will do. If you mean 'more people died,' don't say 'mortality rose.'

"4) In writing. Don't use adjectives which merely tell us how you want us to feel about the thing you are describing. I mean, instead of telling us a thing was 'terrible,' describe it so that we'll be terrified. Don't say it was 'delightful,' make *us* say 'delightful' when we've read the description. You see, all those words (horrifying, wonderful, hideous, exquisite) are only saying to your readers 'Please will you do my job for me.'...

"5) Don't use words too big for the subject. Don't say 'infinitely' when you mean 'very'; otherwise you'll have no word left when you want to talk about something *very* infinite."[2]

1953. Lewis met Joy Davidman Gresham, an American, with whom he had corresponded. Warren Lewis describes the relationship as "at first undoubtedly intellectual: "Joy was the only woman whom he had met...who had a brain which matched his own in suppleness, in width of interest, in analytical grasp, and above all in humor and sense of fun. Further, she shared his delight in argument for argument's sake, whether frivolous or serious, always good-humoured yet always meeting him trick for trick as he changed ground. A woman of great charity, she had an unbounded contempt for the sentimental. Setting herself high standards, she could laugh at the seeming absurdities to which they sometimes carried her. With all this, she was intensely feminine."[2]

There was one added element to which Lewis alluded openly in a letter to an acquaintance in 1956 asking for prayers. "I am likely very shortly to be both a bridegroom and a widower, for (Joy) has cancer."[2]

Their married happiness—and it was a very real one—endured not for the few weeks physicians originally gave her to live, but for three years: Joy Lewis died in June, 1960. "To lose one's wife after a very short married life may, I suspect, be less miserable than after a long one. You see, I had not grown *accustomed* to happiness. It was all a 'treat,' I was like a child at a party. But perhaps earthly happiness, even of the most innocent sort, is addictive. The whole being gets geared to it. The withdrawal must be more like lacking bread than lacking cake...."[2] Lewis himself was suffering from a crippling bone disease.

A television special "Shadowlands," presented on PBS-TV, October 29, 1986, depicted the love story of C. S. Lewis and Joy Gresham.

Autumn had always been the magical season for Lewis, the season he first sensed to his delight in *Squirrel Nutkin*. His last published note, dated 27 October 1963, was to the young writer, Jane Douglass, to whom he'd once recommended the mental "mouth-wash"[2] of good books to counteract "the baneful influence"[2] of women's magazines. He wrote Douglass: "...Autumn is really the best of the seasons; and I'm not sure that old age isn't the best part of life. But of course, like autumn, it doesn't last."[2]

November 22, 1963. Died of heart failure, one week before his sixty-fourth birthday, in the home where he and Warren Lewis lived. "For we—even our poets and musicians and inventors—never, in the ultimate sense, *make*. We only build. We always have the materials to build from."[5]

Footnote Sources:

[1] C. S. Lewis, *Surprised by Joy: The Shape of My Life*, Harcourt, 1956.
[2] W. H. Lewis, editor, *Letters of C. S. Lewis*, Harcourt, 1966.
[3] Lyle W. Dorsett and Marjorie Lamp Mead, *C. S. Lewis: Letters to Children*, Macmillan, 1985.
[4] *Contemporary Authors*, Volumes 81-84, Gale, 1979.
[5] Virginia W. Bass, editor, *Young in Heart*, Caslett, 1967.

■ For More Information See

Current Biography Yearbook, H. W. Wilson, 1944.
Chad Walsh, *C. S. Lewis: Apostle to the Skeptics*, Macmillan, 1949, reissued, Folcroft, 1974.
John W. Montgomery, "The Chronicles of Narnia and the Adolescent Reader," *Religious Education*, September/October, 1959.
Horn Book, October, 1963 (p. 459, 470), October, 1966 (p. 533).
Muriel Fuller, editor, *More Junior Authors*, H. W. Wilson, 1963.
Current Biography Yearbook, H. W. Wilson, 1964.
Clyde S. Kilby, *The Christian World of C. S. Lewis*, Eerdmans, 1964.
H. H. Kruener, "Tribute to C. S. Lewis," *Religion in Life*, summer, 1965.
Roger Lancelyn Green, *Tellers of Tales*, F. Watts, 1965.

Jocelyn Gibb, editor, *Light on C. S. Lewis,* Harcourt, 1965.

Richard B. Cunningham, *C. S. Lewis: Defender of the Faith,* Westminster Press, 1967.

C. S. Kilby, editor, *Letters to an American Lady,* Eerdmans, 1967.

Use of English, winter, 1968 (p. 126), spring, 1977 (p. 16).

Brian Doyle, *The Who's Who of Children's Literature,* Schocken Books, 1968.

David C. Hill, *Messengers of the King,* Augsburg, 1968.

Margery Fisher, R. L. Green, and Marcus Crouch, *Henry Treece, C. S. Lewis and Beatrix Potter,* revised edition, Bodley Head, 1969.

Peter Kreeft, *C. S. Lewis,* Eerdmans, 1969. Martha E. Ward and Dorothy A. Marquardt, *Authors of Books for Young People,* Scarecrow, 1971.

Miriam Hoffman and Eva Samuels, *Authors and Illustrators of Children's Books,* Bowker, 1972.

Douglas Gilbert and C. S. Kilby, *C. S. Lewis: Images of His World,* Eerdmans, 1973.

Contemporary Literary Criticism, Gale, Volume 1, 1973, Volume 3, 1975, Volume 6, 1976.

Paul Kocher, *Master of Middle-Earth,* Houghton, 1973.

Children's Literature in Education, March, 1973 (p. 3), summer, 1977 (p. 51).

C. D. Linton, "C. S. Lewis Ten Years Later," *Christianity Today,* November 9, 1973.

Kathryn Ann Lindskoog, *The Lion of Judah in Never-Never Land: The Theology of C. S. Lewis Expressed in His Fantasies for Children,* Eerdmans, 1974.

Corbin S. Carnell, *Bright Shadow of Reality: C. S. Lewis and the Feeling Intellect,* Eerdmans, 1974.

Richard Purtill, *Lord of the Elves and Eldils: Fantasy and Philosophy in C. S. Lewis and J. R. R. Tolkien,* Zondervan, 1974.

Virginia Haviland, *Children and Literature: Views and Reviews,* Lothrop, 1974.

R. L. Green and Walter C. Hooper, *C. S. Lewis: A Biography,* Harcourt, 1974.

W. Hooper, *Past Watchful Dragons: The Narnian Chronicles of C. S. Lewis,* Macmillan, 1974.

Carolyn Keefe, *C. S. Lewis: Speaker and Teacher,* Zondervan, 1974.

R. Green, "C. S. Lewis and Andrew Lang," *Notes and Queries,* May, 1975.

J. Neuleib, "Technology and Theocracy: The Cosmic Voyages and Wells and Lewis," *Extrapolation,* May, 1975.

Anne Arnott, *The Secret Country of C. S. Lewis,* Eerdmans, 1975.

R. P. Tripp, editor, *Essays on C. S. Lewis,* Society for New Languages Study, 1975.

Susan C. Poskanzer, "Thoughts on C. S. Lewis and the Chronicles of Narnia," *Language Arts,* May, 1976.

B. Murphy, "Enchanted Rationalism: The Legacy of C. S. Lewis," *Christianity and Literature,* winter, 1976.

Peter J. Schakel, editor, *The Longing for a Form: Essays on the Fiction of C. S. Lewis,* Kent State University Press, 1977.

Sheldon Vanauken, *A Severe Mercy,* Harper, 1977.

Humphrey Carpenter, *The Inklings: C. S. Lewis, J. R. R. Tolkien, Charles Williams, and Their Friends,* Allen & Unwin, 1978, Houghton, 1979.

Gilbert Meilander, *The Taste for the Other: The Social and Ethical Thought of C. S. Lewis,* Eerdmans, 1978.

Children's Literature Review, Volume 3, Gale, 1978.

James T. Como, editor, *"C. S. Lewis at the Breakfast Table" and Other Reminiscences,* Macmillan, 1979.

Martha C. Sammons, *A Guide through Narnia,* H. Shaw, 1979.

P. J. Schakel, *Reading with the Heart: The Way into Narnia,* Eerdmans, 1979.

Chad Walsh, *The Literary Legacy of C. S. Lewis,* Harcourt, 1979.

Paul F. Ford, *Companion to Narnia,* Harper, 1980.

C. S. Kilby and M. L. Mead, editors, *Brothers and Friends: The Diaries of Major Warren Hamilton Lewis,* Harper, 1982.

W. Hooper, *Through Joy and Beyond: A Pictorial Biography of C. S. Lewis,* Macmillan, 1982.

L. W. Dorsett, *And God Came In: The Extraordinary Story of Joy Davidman, Her Life and Marriage to C. S. Lewis,* Macmillan, 1983.

W. Hooper, editor, *Boxen: The Imaginary World of the Young C. S. Lewis,* Harcourt, 1984.

William Griffin, *Clive Staples Lewis: A Dramatic Life,* Harper, 1986.

W. Griffin, *Rum Thing: An Imaginative Biography of C. S. Lewis,* Harper, 1986.

Brian Sibley, *C. S. Lewis: Through the Shadowlands,* Revell, 1986.

Celia Van Oss, *Christian Childhoods: An Anthology of Personal Memories,* Crossroad, 1986.

Martin Moynihan, translator, *C. S. Lewis Letters: A Study in Friendship,* Servant, 1988.

Collections:

Bodleian Library at Oxford University.

Marion Wade Collection at Wheaton College, Wheaton, Illinois.

Arnost Lustig

B orn December 21, 1926, in Prague, Czechoslovakia; came to the United States in 1970; son of Emil and Therese (Lowy) Lustig; married Vera Weislitz, July 24, 1949; children: Josef, Eva. *Education:* College of Political and Social Science, Prague, Czechoslovakia, M.A., 1951; Degree in Political and Social Sciences, 1954. *Home:* 4000 Tunlaw Rd. N.W., Washington, D.C. 20007. *Agent:* Elaine Markson Literary Agency, Inc., 44 Greenwich Ave., New York, N.Y. 10011. *Office:* Department of Literature, American University, Washington, D.C. 20016.

■ Career

Radio Prague, Prague, Czechoslovakia and *Jewish Gazette*, Prague, Arab-Israeli war correspondent, 1948-49; Czechoslovak Radio Corp., reporter in Europe, Asia, and North America, 1950-68; Barrandov Film Studios, Prague, screenwriter, 1960-68; writer in Israel, 1968-69; Jadran Film Studio, Zagreb, Yugoslovakia, screenwriter, 1969-70; University of Iowa, Iowa City, member of International Writing Program, 1970-71, visiting lecturer in English, 1971-72; Drake University, Des Moines, Iowa, visiting professor of English, 1972-73; American University, Washington, D.C., visiting profes-

sor of literature, 1973-75, assistant professor of literature, 1976-77, associate professor of literature, 1977—. Head of the Czechoslovak film delegation to the San Sebastian Film Festival, 1968; member of the jury, Karlovy Vary International Film Festival, 1968; member of the jury, Neustadt International Prize for Literature. Visitor at Kibutz Hachotrim, Israel, 1968-69. Lecturer in film and literature at universities in Czechoslovakia, Israel, Japan, Canada, and the United States. *Member:* Authors Guild, Authors League of America, P.E.N., Film Club (Prague), Union of Czechoslovak Writers.

■ Awards, Honors

First Prize from the Oberhausen Film Festival, 1961, and Best Short Story from the University of Melbourne (Australia), and First Prize from Amsterdam's Film School Festival, both 1962, all for "A Bite to Eat"; Best Book of the Year from Mlada Fronta Publishing House (Czechoslovakia), 1962 for *Diamonds of the Night*; First Prize from the Locarno Film Festival, 1963, for "Transport from Paradise"; First Prize from the Mannheim Film Festival, and from the Pesaro Film Festival, both 1964, both for "Diamonds of the Night"; First Prize of Czechoslovak Radio Corp., 1966, for radio play, "Prague Crossroads," and 1967, for radio play, "A Man the Size of a Postage Stamp"; Award from Dr. Vit Nejedly Competition from the Defense Ministry in Prague, for several literary works concerned with anti-fascist themes; First Prize at Monte Carlo Film Festival, 1966, and eight other international prizes, all for television film of "A

Prayer for Katerina Horovitzova''; Clement Gottwald State Prize, 1966, and National Book Award finalist, and B'nai B'rith Award, both 1974, all for *A Prayer for Katerina Horovitzova*; Second Prize of San Sebastian Film Festival, 1968, for the film, ''Dita Saxova''; Prize from Prague Spring Music Festival, 1968, for symphonic poem ''Night and Hope.''

National Jewish Book Award, 1980, for *Dita Saxova* and 1986, for *The Unloved*; Emmy Award for News and Documentary Outstanding Individual Achievement, 1985, for PBS film ''The Precious Legacy''; honorary doctor of Hebrew Letters from Spertus College of Judaica, 1987.

■ Writings

In English:

Nac a nodeje (short stories), Nase Vojsko, 1958, translation by George Theiner, published as *Night and Hope*, Dutton, 1962.

Demanty noci (short stories), Mlada Fronta, 1958, translation by Irish Urwin, published as *Diamonds of the Night*, Artia, 1962.

Dita Saxova (novel), Ceskoslovensky Spisovatel, 1962, translation by G. Theiner, published as *Dita Saxova*, Hutchinson, 1966, translation by Jeanne Nemcova, Harper, 1979.

Modlitba pro Katerinu Horovitzovou (novel), Ceskoslovensky Spisovatel, 1964, translation by J. Nemcova, published as *A Prayer for Katerina Horovitzova*, Harper, 1973.

The Unloved: From the Diary of Perla S., Arbor House, 1985.

Nikoho neponizis, Nase Vojsko, 1963, published as *Indecent Dreams*, Northwestern University Press, 1988.

Collected Works; ''Children of the Holocaust'' Series:

Darkness Casts No Shadow, translation by J. Nemcova, Inscape, 1976, 2nd revised edition, Northwestern University Press, 1986.

Night and Hope, Inscape, 1976, new edition, Northwestern University Press, 1985.

Diamonds of the Night, translation by J. Nemcova, Inscape, 1978, 2nd revised edition, Northwestern University Press, 1986.

Other:

Ulice ztracenych (title means ''The Street of Lost Brothers''), Mlada Fronta, 1949.

Muj znamy Vili Feld (novel; title means ''My Acquaintance Willi Feld''), Mlada Fronta, 1949.

Bile brizy na podzim (title means ''The White Birches in September''), Ceskoslovensky Spisovatel, 1966.

Horka vune mandli (title means ''The Bitter Smell of Almonds''), Mlada Fronta, 1968.

Milacek (title means ''Darling''), Ceskoslovensky Spisovatel, 1969.

■ Adaptations

Screenplays:

''Transport from Paradise'' (based on *Night and Hope*), Studio Barrandov (Prague), 1963.

''Diamonds of the Night,'' Studio Barrandov, 1964.

''Dita Saxova,'' Studio Barrandov, 1968.

Television Scripts:

''The Blue Day,'' T.V. Prague, 1960.

''A Prayer for Katerina Horovitzova,'' T.V. Prague, 1965.

(With Ernest Pendrell) ''Terezin,'' ABC-TV, 1965.

''Stolen Childhood,'' for TV-Rome, 1966.

(Co-screenwriter) ''The Precious Legacy,'' PBS-TV, 1984.

(With Robert Gardner) ''The Triumph of Memory,'' PBS-TV, 1988.

Radio Scripts:

''Prague Crossroads,'' Radio Prague, 1966.

''A Man the Size of a Postage Stamp,'' Radio Prague, 1967.

Also author of text for Otmar Macha's symphonic poem, ''Night and Hope.'' Libretto for ''Beadle of Prague'' Cantata, music by H. Berlinski. Also author of unproduced screenplays, ''The Golem'' with Zbynek Brynych, ''The Excursion'' with Jan Kadar, ''The Street of Lost Brothers'' with Jan Nemec, ''The White Birches in the Fall'' with Jaromil Jires, and a screenplay about the International Writers Program at the University of Iowa. Author of a short filmscript, ''A Bite to Eat,'' directed by J. Nemec, 1960. Correspondent for literary magazines in Czechoslovakia, 1950-58; editor, *Mlady svet* (youth magazine; title means ''The Young World''), 1958-60.

■ Work In Progress

Screenplay adaptation of ''The Unloved''; new screenplay, ''A Prayer for Katerina Horovitzova''; a book of short stories, *Don Juan in Iowa City.*

■ Sidelights

Arnost Lustig was born on December 21, 1926 in Prague, Czechoslovakia. After he had completed seven years of schooling, the Nazis prohibited the education of Jewish children, and he became an apprentice tailor and leather-worker. In 1942, he was sent with his parents to Theresienstadt concentration camp where he dug tracks for railroads and air-raid shelters for a German hospital. Two years later, he was transferred to Auschwitz-Birkenau (where his father died in the gas chambers), then to Buchenwald. "Nine out of ten survivors of Auschwitz-Birkenau gain safe distance from it during the day, but at night when the will is suspended they inevitably return to it....Auschwitz-Birkenau...[is] with them. In them."[1]

In the spring of 1945, Lustig escaped from the train carrying him to his death in Dachau when an American plane dive-bombed the engine, mistaking the train for a military transport. Lustig returned to Prague and participated in the anti-Nazi uprising of May, 1945.

Years after his internment, Lustig returned to the former concentration camp. "...A new horror took possession of me. Auschwitz-Birkenau as a museum, as a giant reservation commemorating human brutality, does not evoke in one's imagination even a shadow of the fear, anxiety, and hopelessness which a single moment of this death factory induced while still in full operation. Auschwitz-Birkenau, this empty, silenced camp, the largest man ever built for man, has the effect of a calm burial ground. The dead do not talk. The land is almost beautiful, whether grassy or covered with snow. Memory that serves the living betrays the dead. It is not in the power of the living to give voice to the dead. Time works against the innocent. Time toys with what happened yesterday. Time clears the mind to gain space for what will happen tomorrow. The image of the dead a person has who loiters in a cemetery is no image of the dead but only their faded picture.

"I rage at my impotence to express in words the weakness of memory....Balzac is supposed to have said that evil which is too great can never be punished. How to bring this to terms with the four million dead who saw their last sun, stars, and moon here, with the mothers who saw the last of their children? How at least to breathe afterlife into them? Each one had been someone—my mother, my father, my brother, my sister....

Darkness casts no shadow
Arnost Lustig

"A terrible tale – told simply, directly, beautifully through the eyes of children: MOVING BEYOND WORDS."
—Barbara Bannon, *Publishers Weekly*

Hardcover jacket from the 1976 edition of the first book in the "Children of the Holocaust" series.

"Once I was a prisoner here. Why do I feel the same way as those who were never here, never saw Auschwitz-Birkenau? How can I call back to life the feeling of the dead?

"Was I really at the ramp when the orchestra, made up of the finest musicians of occupied Europe, played the French hit *J'attendrai* for those who were going to the gas, for those servicing the crematoria, for the workers at the Buna Werke or in the Auto Union or in the delousing station? Once a trio sang the German version of a hit for those who had attempted to escape. *'Komm zurueck, denn ich warte auf dich, denn du bist fuer mich all mein Glueck'*: Come back to me, I am waiting for you—for you who are my happiness.

"In the orchestra I had a friend, Ota S., who used to play at the Esplanade Hotel in Prague and in the Est Bar. While he was playing, he watched his wife and three little boys go to the crematorium. On the day that his family was murdered, he was playing 'A Jew Had a Little Wife' and a song about a young man's unrequited love and a song about a wedding under the sky and how merry the wedding guests were and about how the bride and bridegroom's parents danced.

"Was I really standing here in the wind when two friends of mine, the older T. and the younger T., in a soccer game against eleven SS men, were told to play as best they could but not to win, and to remember that any injury they might inflict on the Germans, or even on themselves, would send them into the chimney? Surviving, they received a loaf of German commissary bread and a half-pound of blood pork pate. I watched the older T.'s clothes and shoes until they were through playing. It was almost like home—two teams, dressing rooms, lines, a field, goals, and a round ball. However, as Tadeusz Borowski later wrote, between the starting and final whistle of the referee, a stone's throw from the soccer field, three thousand people went to the gas.

"Was I really in the Gypsy camp, which SS men 'cleaned out' the night and day before we arrived from Terezin, 'the city Adolf Hitler gave the Jews;—and where only a few Gypsy children escaped death by digging themselves into the ground like worms and where the Gypsy boys stoned us as if we had caused their parents' deaths?

"Did I really talk with the twins Pavel and Peter on whom Dr. Mengele performed experiments and whom he castrated? Back in Terezin, at the Home for Youth, the twins gave me three ounces of sugar in exchange for a collection of poems by the Catholic poet Otakar Brezina. When I asked where their parents were, they replied that they had flown through the chimney in Crematorium No. 2 as if telling me they had taken the Orient Express to Istanbul.

"I remember little Rene G. from Prague who felt privileged because his sister was allowed to serve in the SS bordello and could bring him milk, bread, and sugar. He knew he would live only as long as his sister was there. But the gas and the chimney and the ashes would greet the two of them as soon as she was used up.

"I remember how in September 1944 I got through the gate onto the ramp in Auschwitz-Birkenau. We felt what animals feel during a solar eclipse or a forest fire or an approaching earthquake; within several minutes, all children under fifteen, women and men above forty, the sick, and the ones with glasses or grey hair were in bathrooms where Zyklon B came out of the sprinklers instead of water. In half an hour, a greasy fire was flashing from Chimneys No. 2 and No. 3, followed

by smoke which gave off the pungent smell of human bones like from a glue or soap factory. Mothers waiting their turn had to watch their toddlers being thrown like chickens into the furnace. On the bathroom wall was written: *Baths of Eternal Forgetting.*

"I understand how difficult it is to write about this in primers and textbooks for children who were born years after the time when the swastika flag fluttered above Auschwitz-Birkenau headquarters. Sometimes I wish that all men and women wherever they live on earth, would have to visit Aushwitz-Birkenau for a day, an hour, or even a single second during the time when Hitler, Himmler, Eichmann, or Baldur von Schirach swelled with pride at what they had commissioned German architects, planners, and builders to do....Auschwitz-Birkenau must be at the beginning of all questions that torment us, and instead of providing answers it can only lead to further questions.

"I remember an afternoon in September 1944 when I stood in the Gypsy camp by the high-voltage wires, surrounded by bare Polish plains and forests. A thin transparent fog enveloped the ground and the people. It penetrated the soul. We could see Crematoria No. 2 and No. 3 where our relatives were burning. From the other side, smoke came from large pits where the dead from Hungary, for whom there were not enough furnaces, were burning in their own fat. A purple fire was flashing from the chimneys, soon glowing a deeper purple before turning into evil-reeking black smoke. Everything stank. The smoke became a cloud, and slowly a black rain—ashes—dropped down from it. Like everyone else I wished the wind would lift or the earth reverse its direction. The ashes had a bitter taste. Also the gas in the shower rooms had the bitter smell of almonds. These ashes were not from coal or burnt wood, rags or paper.

"They fell on us—mute, deaf, relentless ashes, in which human breath, shrieks, and tears could be felt. I stood at a concrete fence post with white porcelain insulators, taking it all in like an hallucination. A tune from Johann Strauss's 'Die Fledermaus' was going through my head. But this was no dream. It was real.

"A couple of days earlier I had heard it at a cabaret with my father, in the attic of the fire station in Terezin. Now my father was soap. Ashes. Smoke tasting of bones. The fog, as white as swan's wings, turned black, and song, sky, and ashes fused into one. The curve of the melody and the plait of the

Jacket from the 1985 Overlook Press edition.

Dust jacket from the 1976 edition of Lustig's first book.

lyrics suddenly acquired a new meaning: *Glueck-lich ist, wer vergisst, was doch nicht zu aendern ist.* Happy the one who forgets what cannot be changed. I was singing. My friends dragged me into the hut before prisoner count so I would live at least until the next day.

"It was exactly what the men of the SS wanted for those who still lived in Auschwitz-Birkenau: to feel as insane and lonely, as lost and helpless, as in a nightmare, to regard the absurd as normal and the normal as absurd. But the loneliness among the dead is still better than the loneliness of the living. Sometimes I would go to the concrete fence post and wires just as one might visit a cemetery, save only that our dead did not have graves. I would only catch the ashes in the palm of my hand or watch the chimney smoke day and night.

"Once, standing by the wires again, I saw a little herd of completely naked women. It was October and a cold wind blew on them as they each carried shoes and a bundle of effects under their arms.

Their heads were shaven bare. The last twenty wore transparent shirts. All were barefoot.

"Since my father had become soap, ashes, and the echo of Strauss's 'Die Fledermaus,' I could not get rid of the thoughts that it would perhaps be better if my mother joined him. That way I would not have to watch her walk barefoot on the muddy October ground, through the wet patches of snow. I watched the chilled women, one after another, to see if my mother was among them. I felt relief when I went over the naked ones with my eyes to find that she was not there, and then over the ones in shirts to see that she was not walking among them either. Only when the last two came into view did I see that the next to the last was my mother.

"I was glad she failed to notice me. She did not even watch where she was going. I was sad that she had not been sent to the bath of eternal forgetting. Before they stole her clothes, shoes, and under-wear and shaved her head, she had been beautiful.

I was unable to call to her. The wires began to attract me again. A touch would have been enough. I did not want to imagine what was in store for my mother apart from torture, gas, fire. I watched until she disappeared into the fog. I woke up the next day with the consoling thought that she must have frozen before she reached the end of the road between the wires. Snow and rain kept falling. In my mind, I buried my mother too with the song in which one is happy when he forgets what cannot be changed. I did not want her to be with me once I became so terribly lonely again.

"I remember a day which seemed to me like a miracle. I was now a slave leaving Auschwitz-Birkenau to work for one meal a day at what used to be the Hugo Schneider Aktiengesellschaft, making kitchen utensils, but was now the Hassag munitions factory. It was October 28, 1944, a sunny day. The young SS guard with steely blue eyes and blond hair on duty in the train, who went with us till we reached our inland destination, had a clear expression of disgust at the corners of his mouth. I assumed that it was directed against us, since he had been brought up to regard us as the clean regard vermin. But the disgust of the young SS soldier was for the camp which he was as glad to leave as we were. He told me to sit next to him and then asked me how long I had been there. Without waiting for an answer, he told me that compared to him I knew only a fraction of what Auschwitz-Birkenau was like. His face expressed many kinds of exhaustion. The fatigue of a man who worked a lot, which in Auschwitz-Birkenau meant killed a lot; the fatigue of a man who had not slept for many nights and even lying in bed could not fall asleep; and finally, the fatigue of a man for whom life was a burden, a disgust, because it had lost its sense and beauty, its value and balance, as men had lost the ability to distinguish between cowardice and courage. I would be lying if I said I pitied him. Mostly the men of the SS were cold-blooded killers, good at their trade. The word compassion was as rare in their vocabulary as were blanks in their firearms. The guard had no one to talk to. It was not a trick, a caprice, nothing but the spur of the moment. Both of us were leaving hell, he told me, and as soon as the transport arrived, he would ask the SS command for a transfer. That meant the Eastern Front. For a man of the SS in the retreating German army that meant almost certain death. If his transfer request was rejected, he had a last alternative; he would kill himself. At no price would he return to serve at Auschwitz-Birkenau. We both knew of things that took place in Auschwitz-Birkenau that could not be expressed even if one spent years describing them—and even then they would be but shadows to those who had not been there. Even those who were there have no language for it.

"His face haunts me to this day, as our freight car passes through the gate across which *Arbeit macht frei* is written and we know we are leaving hell, where the last words are fire and ashes. He was confiding to me in German, which I had learned to understand, that if he told his father what he did for the SS in Auschwitz-Birkenau he would never talk to him as a German again; if he told his mother she would kill herself; and if he told his grandmother or grandfather, who lived in the same household, they would die of shame.

"He was not much older than I. I was seventeen going on eighteen, and I had seen what a man living for a thousand years could not have seen. I told him how to commit suicide. You pour water in the barrel, put the nozzle in your mouth, and pull the trigger.

"In the middle of a clear day I can close my eyes and see shadows. They are not specters but the hunched figures of men and women, children and old people. It is the ramp in Auschwitz-Birkenau, the baths where *Disinfection* is written in German. They are going to the gas. This is the Germany I carry within me. This is the Germany I carry within me even though I wish I could be more like my mother, who spoke its language before Auschwitz-Birkenau became the measure of everything German for her."[1]

Years later, "...during the spring of 1963, I came home in the evening and my wife was crying. When I asked her why she is crying, she told me this: having been asked by a West German court, eighteen years after World War II, to write whether her parents had turned in their wedding rings to the Reichsbank, as had been ordered for all Jews in German's territory, she replied that yes, her parents had turned those rings in to a Prague branch of the Reichsbank in 1941. To that, today's German court replied that unfortunately it has not been documented that her parents turned in those rings because there is no mention about it in existing German papers and therefore her request for her parents' wedding rings is rejected.

"That day I came home with the intention to write a story about American Jews who got in the hands of the German army during the American troops disembarkment on Sicily in the year 1943. That evening, both these incidents seemed devilish to the same degree. And so I connected both stories in a story about a devil. I began writing at seven P.M. that day, continued through the night and whole next day. In the evening of that day I was done. The following ten days I could not sleep. I had the impression I had been constantly meeting the devil.

"The result is this story *A Prayer for Katerina Horovitzova*, my personal payment for the six million dead of whom each represents to me one innocently killed human being, father, brother, sister, friend. Every one of them had been someone. I reject Balzac's wisdom, saying that if evil is massive enough it cannot be punished, for a great evil exceeds the framework of criminal law. Such evil must be punished and my attempts to punish and try is this story."[2]

Lustig grew up eith those haunting memories, and spent the next two decades as a journalist and screenwriter in postwar Communist Czechoslovakia, encouraged by the glimmers of freedom demonstrated by the liberal era of Dubcek. "I was in love with my country, to tell the truth. It's a beautiful country, a very romantic country. Prague is a mystical and romantic city. Just to walk through the streets makes you feel something special. And I felt it. If somebody had told me in the first half of 1968 that I would leave, I would have laughed at him. The idea of leaving my country was not in the least milli-millimeter of my mind.

"People in Czechoslovakia love to read, and if you are a writer, they like you. This is the only country where a poet can make a living, because people stand in line for books of poetry. This was a good country for writers. For instance, I didn't write on very popular themes. I wrote on suffering in camps, about the war, but they published over a half million copies in ten years. And this is a small nation of ten million people. Hemingway is published in Prague—150,000 copies; Fitzgerald—200,000 copies. Everybody knows who Faulkner is, sometimes more than they do [in the U.S.]. Steinbeck, whom I met once in Prague, is a favorite of Czech readers, because they know his best books.

"So to live in such a country, you don't have to be a hero; it is enough to be a writer. You feel that your life has meaning; you are working as well as you can, and people are reading your work. You don't need more. You can make a living. For a writer, it is not good to be very poor, but neither is it good for him to be very rich. Somewhere midway. This was my situation in Prague when we left. I felt like a prince."

With the Soviet invasion in 1968, however, "almost no books were published except by mistake." For instance, 22,000 copies of a collection of three of Lustig's novels were published in 1970, and were banned almost immediately, even though one of the novels had been reprinted seven times since 1964. "Suddenly the regime thought that my descriptions of Nazi concentration camps might be an allegory for life under the present regime in Czechoslovakia. For what can you publish in these countries, if you try to be as honest as possible, yet want to avoid a situation comparable to jumping on the tail of a snake so that he can still whirl around to bite you with his teeth? The only way is to write about the past. . . .

"Once everything was lost, when the country was invaded, I was declared by the last congress of the Communist party an 'enemy of the state,' an 'imperialist agent,' a 'Zionist.' They said all my

Jacket from the 1978 edition of Lustig's second book.

books and films were paid for by some world conspiracy, and my books were confiscated."

Lustig left Prague after the Soviet occupation in August of 1968 to live for a year in Israel and a year in Zagreb. In the summer of 1970 he was invited to the International Writing Program at the University of Iowa. "Being an exile you have to start all over again, from the bottom of life—you have no money, no country, just your hands. And for such a person [the U.S.] is very good. You have to prove yourself to survive. It was your Jack London who said that in literature, only the best survive. So far I have survived a lot, and hope I can go on surviving."[3]

"Under those circumstances it is better to be in a strange country, to start again, and to prove to yourself that you are a real writer. To be a writer under the best circumstances is not so difficult. To remain a writer under worse circumstances is, I think, a good test for a writer.

"Every writer has a duty to be as good as he can as a writer, to tell stories he likes in the best way he can. What he likes—this is his personal approach to life. I like stories about brave people, about how they survived under the worst cirumstances. I like people who are fighting for their fate, and who are better in the end, richer, in a sense, than they were in the beginning. I think that each writer has a certain duty—to imagine himself in theory as perhaps the last human being under certain circumstances and that perhaps his testimony will be the last one. He is obliged to deliver that testimony."

Lustig won the 1986 National Jewish Book Award for *The Unloved: From the Diary of Perla S.*, a novel drawing on much of his experience surviving the Nazi death camps. "I was afraid to publish this book. I really was waiting five years to publish it because it's about a seventeen-year-old prostitute, and I thought, my God. For me this prostitute is a very moral person. I wanted someone with the innocence of a half-child, half-woman, someone who is the last and can become the first. She is selling her body to save her life, so she will not die from hunger."[4]

Diane Cole, critic for the *Jewish Week* feels that "Lustig is a deceptively simple writer. His novels and short stories chronicle the Holocaust and its aftermath in a precisely rendered, reportorial style that is all the more chilling for its detailed, documentary-like realism. He tells his stories the way a photographer would, impartially and objec-

tively, and his devastating images force us to become witnesses, too.

"In such previous works as *A Prayer for Katerina Horovitzova, Darkness Casts No Shadow, Night and Hope, Dita Saxova* and *The Unloved: From the Diary of Perla S.*, Lustig focused mainly on the wartime experiences of Eastern European Jewry. In *Indecent Dreams*, his latest work to appear in English, Lustig widens his camera lens further to present the war from several other points of view as well."[5]

"In all my books, both those already published and those I am still working on, it is my aim to paint a truthful portrait of my generation. The war was a great school for this generation, a school for which people paid a high price. We grew up during the German occupation, which taught us the value of human solidarity. Our hopes were stronger than anything else. In the midst of a hell which sharply delineated people's characters, there lived men and women whose behaviour deserves to be recorded in legends or poems. They ought to be alive today, but they are not with us any more. It is therefore our duty to bring them back to life in stories in which people can learn to love them. . . .

"The stories I best like reading are those which show that life is an intesting privilege, that man is indestructible, because even though he may lose all his loved ones and all his earthly possessions, he still retains hope. The value of any human being is frequently impossible to assess at first sight. If he is incapable of saying anything out of the ordinary, let us not at once assume that there's nothing in him. How often during the war did we find that a seemingly insignificant, unassuming chap risked his life for his fellows, that someone who gave every impression of being a coward behaved like a hero, and vice versa. Literature, I think, should disclose these things for us.

"Every one of us daily seeks, loses or discovers the meaning of his life on the basis of his everyday experience. Every one of us who wants to know where he stands on this planet of ours has to find a place for himself in which he would have an objectively justified feeling of usefulness. I've worked in a quarry, in the mines, as a railway fireman. I have machine-tooled iron, carried cement, varnished doors, made handbags and sewed trousers. I have been a news correspondent. Now at last I have found a place for myself which gives me a feeling of usefulness: literature."

Lustig's books and stories have been translated into more than twenty languages, including German,

Spanish, Japanese, Polish, Hebrew, Hindi, Esperanto, French, Estonian, Norwegian, Italian, and Yiddish.

Footnote Sources:

[1] Arnost Lustig, "Auschwitz-Birkenau," translated by Josef Lustig, *Yale Review*, spring, 1983.

[2] A. Lustig, *A Prayer for Katerina Horovitzova*, Harper, 1973.

[3] "PW Interviews: Arnost Lustig," *Publishers Weekly*, February 21, 1977.

[4] Cathryn Donohoe, "A Survivior's Lucky Road to Liberty," *Insight*, June 16, 1986.

[5] Diane Cole, "Victories for Conscience," *Jewish Week*, June 3, 1988.

■ For More Information See

Booklist, November 1, 1973.
Best Sellers, October 15, 1973.
Kirkus Reviews, August 1, 1973.
New York Times Book Review, October 21, 1973.
Proteus, spring, 1974.
Choice, fall, 1974.
Southwest Review, winter, 1974.
Washingtonian, May, 1977.
World Literature Today, autumn, 1979 (p. 636).
Byron L. Sherwin and Susan G. Ament, *Encountering the Holocaust: An Interdisciplinary Survey*, Impact Press, 1979.

David Mamet

S urname pronounced *Mam*-it; born November 30, 1947, in Chicago, Ill.; son of Bernard Morris (an attorney) and Lenore June (a teacher; maiden name, Silver) Mamet; married Lindsay Crouse (an actress), December 21, 1977; children: Willa, Zosia. *Education:* Attended Neighborhood Playhouse School of the Theater, 1968-69; Goddard College, B.A., 1969. *Politics:* "The last refuge of the unimaginative." *Religion:* "The second-to-last." *Agent:* Rosenstone/Wender, 3 East 48th St., New York, N.Y. 10017. *Office:* St. Nicholas Theater Company, 2851 North Halstead St., Chicago, Ill. 60657.

■ Career

Playwright, theatrical director, and screenwriter. Marlboro College, Marlboro, Vt., teacher, 1969-70; Goddard College, Plainfield, Vt., instructor, 1971-72; St. Nicholas Theater Company, Chicago, Ill., founder, 1973, artistic director, 1973-76, member of board of directors, 1973—; Goodman Theater, Chicago, associate artistic director and playwright-in-residence, 1978-79. Special lecturer in drama, Marlboro College, 1970; artist-in-residence in drama, Goddard College, 1971-73; faculty member, Illinois Arts Council, 1974; visiting lecturer in drama, University of Chicago, 1975-76, 1979; teaching fellow, Yale University, 1976-77; guest lecturer, New York University, 1981. Has also worked at a canning plant, a truck factory, a real estate agency, and as a window washer, office cleaner, and taxi driver. *Military service:* Merchant Marines. *Member:* Dramatists Guild, Writers Guild of America, Actors Equity Association, P.E.N., United Steelworkers of America, Randolph A. Hollister Association.

■ Awards, Honors

Joseph Jefferson Award for Best New Chicago Play, 1975, for *Sexual Perversity in Chicago,* and 1976, for *American Buffalo;* Obie Award from the *Village Voice,* for Best New Playwright, 1976, for *Sexual Perversity in Chicago* and *American Buffalo,* and for Best American Play, 1983, for *Edmond;* Children's Theater Grant from the New York State Council on the Arts, 1976; Rockefeller Grant, 1976; Columbia Broadcasting System Fellowship in Creative Writing, 1976; New York Drama Critics' Circle Award for Best American Play, 1977, for *American Buffalo,* and 1984, for *Glengarry Glen Ross;* Outer Critics Circle Award for Contributions to the American Theater, 1978. *A Life in the Theatre* was selected one of New York Public Library's Books for the Teen Age, 1980; Society of West End Theater's Best Play Award, 1982-83, for *Glengarry Glen Ross;* Academy Award (Oscar) Nomination for Best Adapted Screenplay from the Academy of Motion Picture Arts and Sciences, 1983, for "The Verdict"; Antoinette Perry (Tony) Award nomination from the

League of New York Theaters and Producers, for Best Play, 1984, for *Glengarry Glen Ross*, and for Reproduction of a Play, 1984, for *American Buffalo*; Pulitzer Prize in Drama, and Joseph Dintenfass Award, both 1984, both for *Glengarry Glen Ross*; American Academy and Institute of Arts and Letters Award for Literature, 1986.

■ Writings

Warm and Cold (juvenile; illustrated by Donald Sultan), Solo Press, 1984, Grove, 1988.
Goldberg Street (collection of dramatic sketches), Grove Press, 1985.
Writing in Restaurants (essays), Viking, 1986.
(With Lindsay Crouse) *The Out* (juvenile), Kipling Books, 1987.
(With Shel Silverstein) *Things Change*, Grove, 1988.

Plays:

American Buffalo (two-act; first produced in Chicago at Goodman Theater Stage Two, October 23, 1975; produced Off-Off-Broadway at St. Clements, January 23, 1976; produced on Broadway at Ethel Barrymore Theater, February 16, 1977), Grove, 1977.
A Life in the Theatre (one-act; first produced in Chicago at Goodman Theater Stage Two, February 3, 1977; produced Off-Broadway at Theater de Lys, October 20, 1977), Grove, 1978.
Sexual Perversity in Chicago [and] *Duck Variations* ("Duck Variations" [one-act], first produced in Plainfield, Vt., at Goddard College, 1972; produced Off-Off-Broadway at St. Clements, May 27, 1975; "Sexual Perversity in Chicago" [one-act], first produced in Chicago at Organic Theater, summer, 1974; produced Off-Off-Broadway at St. Clements, September 29, 1975; both produced Off-Broadway at Cherry Lane Theater, June 16, 1976), Grove, 1978.
The Water Engine: An American Fable [and] *Mr. Happiness* ("The Water Engine" [two-act], first produced as a radio play on the program "Earplay" by Minnesota Public Radio, 1977; stage adaptation produced in Chicago by St. Nicholas Theater Company, May 11, 1977; produced Off-Broadway at New York Shakespeare Festival Public Theater, December 20, 1977; "Mr. Happiness," first produced with "The Water Engine" on Broadway at Plymouth Theater, March 6, 1978), Grove, 1978.

The Revenge of the Space Pandas; or, Birky Rudich and the Two-Speed Clock (one-act for children; first produced in Chicago by the St. Nicholas Theater Company, November, 1977), Dramatic Publishing, 1978.
The Woods (two-act; first produced in Chicago by St. Nicholas Theater Company, November 11, 1977; produced Off-Broadway at New York Shakespeare Festival Pubic Theater, April 25, 1979), Grove, 1979.
Reunion [and] *Dark Pony* ("Reunion" [one-act], first produced with "Sexual Perversity in Chicago" in Louisville, Kentucky at Actors' Theater of Louisville, October 12, 1976; "Dark Pony" [one-act], first produced with "Reunion" in New Haven, Conn. at Yale Repertory Theater, October 14, 1977; both produced Off-Broadway with "The Sanctity of Marriage" at Circle Repertory Theater, October 18, 1979), Grove, 1979.
Lakeboat (one-act; first produced in Marlboro, Vt., at Marlboro Theater Workshop, 1970; revised version produced in Milwaukee, Wis. at Milwaukee Repertory Theater, April 24, 1980), Grove, 1981.
Edmond (first produced in Chicago at Goodman Theater, June, 1982; produced Off-Broadway at Provincetown Playhouse, October 27, 1982), Grove, 1983.
Glengarry Glen Ross (two-act; first produced on the West End at National Theater, October, 1983; produced in Chicago at Goodman Theater, January 27, 1984; produced on Broadway at John Golden Theater, March 25, 1984), Grove, 1984.
Three Children's Plays: The Poet and the Rent, The Frog Prince, [and] The Revenge of the Space Pandas; or, Binky Rudich and the Two-Speed Clock ("The Poet and the Rent" first produced in New York City at Circle Repertory Theater, 1979; "The Frog Prince" first produced in Chicago, 1977; "The Revenge of the Space Pandas; or, Binky Rudich and the Two-Speed Clock" first produced in Chicago by the St. Nicholas Theater Company, November, 1977), Grove, 1986.

Unpublished Plays:

"Mackinac" (juvenile), first produced in Chicago at the Bernard Horwich Jewish Community Center.
"Marranos," first produced in Chicago at the Bernard Horwich Jewish Community Center.

Paul Newman starred in the 1982 movie "The Verdict." The film received five Oscar nominations including ones for Newman as "Best Actor" and Mamet for "Best Screenplay Adaptation."

"Squirrels" (one-act), first produced in Chicago by the St. Nicholas Theater Company, 1974.

"All Men Are Whores," first produced in New Haven at Yale Cabaret, 1977.

"Lone Canoe; or, the Explorer" (musical), music and lyrics by Alaric Jans, first produced in Chicago at Goodman Theater, May, 1979.

"The Sanctity of Marriage" (one-act), first produced Off Broadway with "Reunion" and "Dark Pony" in New York City at Circle Repertory Theater, October 18, 1979.

"Shoeshine" (one-act), first produced Off-Off-Broadway at Ensemble Studio Theater, December 14, 1979.

"A Sermon" (one-act), first produced Off-Off-Broadway at Ensemble Studio Theater, May, 1981.

"Five Unrelated Pieces," first produced Off-Off-Broadway at Ensemble Studio Theater, May, 1983.

"The Disappearance of the Jews" (one-act), first produced in Chicago at Goodman Theater, June 14, 1983.

"Prairie du chien," first produced in 1985.

"The Shawl," first produced in 1985.

"Speed-the-Plow," first produced on Broadway at the Royale Theater, May 3, 1988.

Screenplays:

"The Postman Always Rings Twice" (adaptation of novel by James M. Cain), Paramount, 1981.

"The Verdict" (adaptation of novel by Barry Reed), Twentieth Century-Fox, 1982.

"The Untouchables," Paramount, 1987.

The House of Games, Orion, 1987, Grove, 1987.

(With Shel Silverstein; also director) "Things Change," Columbia, 1988.

Radio Plays:

"Cross Patch," first produced on WNUR-Radio, March 4, 1985.

"Goldberg Street," first produced on WNUR-Radio, March 4, 1985.

Also translator and adapter of plays *Red River* by Pierre Laville, and *The Cherry Orchard* by Anton Chekhov. Author of episode, "Wasted Weekend," for "Hill Street Blues," NBC-TV, January 13, 1987. Contributing editor, *Oui*, 1975-76.

■ Work In Progress

A screenplay for "The Autobiography of Malcolm X."

■ Sidelights

David Mamet was born and raised in Chicago, November 30, 1947. "We have some strange local mythology. No Chicagoan makes gangster jokes or thinks of the City as particularly violent (which it isn't). (Al Capone *did* say, 'You get a lot farther with a kind word and a gun than you do with a kind word,' but this must be classed with philosophy rather than humor.) We do make Police jokes and take pride in considering the Chicago Police Force *haimishly* corrupt (which it isn't), and we take *great* pride in our excellent Fire Department."[1]

"...I came from a very bourgeois background—my father was a lawyer,...but in Chicago I was always exposed to a wider variety of lives. Summer jobs, the steel mills, factories, that kind of thing...."[2]

"...In the days prior to television, we liked to wile away the evenings by making ourselves miserable, solely based on our ability to speak the language viciously...."[3]

Mamet's parents divorced in 1957. "I don't see how anyone can escape a stormy adolescence. I think some of my anger, perhaps unconscious, comes out in my plays, in the gut language. But to me men trying to communicate speak that way. And what I use fits my meter.

"What I write about is what I think is missing from our society. And that's communication on a basic level. I've been in Freudian analysis and it helped some, but what I mean is nonprofessional communication. Nobody talks to an uncle or a grandmother any more."[4]

Moved with his mother to the North side of Chicago into a development called Olympic Fields.

Robert Duvall, John Savage, and Kenneth McMillan in Mamet's 1977 stage production "American Buffalo."

Joe Mantegna, James Tolkan, and Robert Prosky in the 1984 Broadway production of "Glengarry Glen Ross."

"We lived in a model home so small, it makes [a table for two] look like f—ing Switzerland...."[5]

Attended the prestigious Frances Parker School, but was a poor student who rebelled against the repression of his bourgeois background. "...There was nothing to do. I was fourteen years old, I was trying to get into trouble.

"I am very happy to be part of that august group now, but not when I was fourteen."[5]

Worked as busboy at Chicago's "Second City" Comedy club, and also acted at Hull House, an innovative community theater. An uncle who was director of broadcasting for the Chicago Board of Rabbis provided him with his first television job. "[I acted in] one of those religious TV shows that are on at six o'clock in the morning, you know, with titles like 'Thank God It's Purim.'"[5]

1964. Accepted at Goddard College in Vermont, to study acting. "Didn't your mother tell you to have something to fall back on? Mine did. Had I listened to her I would be writing advertising copy today."[5]

"We don't understand actors in this country. We don't treat them with the respect due their dili-

gence and their devotion and their outward-directness and their social consciousness. My God, these are people who are laboring, who get their enjoyment from bringing beauty to the stage, so that other people can come and sit in the audience and participate in the works of a writer."[6]

"We are told the Theatre is always dying. And it's true. But rather than being decried, it should be understood. The theatre is an expression of our dream-life—of our unconscious aspirations.

"It is not the theatre which is dying, but men and women—society. And as it dies a new group of explorers, artists, arises whose reports are disregarded, then enshrined, then disregarded.

"We live in an illiterate country. The mass-media—the commercial theatre included—pander to the low and the lowest of the low in the human experience. They, finally, debase us through the sheer weight of their mindlessness.

"Every re-iteration of the idea that *nothing matters* debases the human spirit. Every re-iteration of the idea that there is no drama in modern life, there is only dramatization; that there is no tragedy, there is only unexplained misfortune, debases us. It

Madonna, Ron Silver, and Joe Mantegna in a scene from the stage production of "Speed-the-Plow."

denies what we know to be true. In denying what we know we are as a nation which cannot remember its dreams—like an unhappy person who cannot remember his dreams and so denies that he *does* dream—we deny that there are such things as dreams.

"Who is going to speak up? Who is going to speak for the American Spirit? For the human spirit? Who is capable of being heard? Of being accepted? Of being believed? Only that person who speaks without ulterior motives, without hope of gain, without even the desire to *change*, with only the desire to *create*.

"The artist. The actor. The strong, trained actor dedicated to the idea that the theatre is the place we go to hear the truth, and equipped with the technical capacity to speak simply and clearly."[7]

To satisfy requirements for an advanced degree at school, Mamet wrote "Camel," a satire based on his experience as a busboy.

1968. Moved to New York City to study at the Neighborhood Playhouse School of the Theater. "I lived in New York for about a year and a half. I took time out from my graduate work at Goddard

to study acting. I had a great time. I worked my ass off as a student. I also worked for about a year with 'The Fantasticks' off-Broadway. I ran the lights and I was house manager for a while. It was a wonderful experience."[8]

1969. Graduated from Goddard and applied for a short-term teaching post at Marlboro College. "I was working. . .driving a cab. Since I had had some experience as an actor, I wrote a letter to some of my friends at Marlboro College, asking if they wanted an actor for their summer theater. They said no, but the fellow who ran the drama department was leaving on sabbatical and he asked me if I would like to teach. I said I'd love to. He wrote back asking if I had anything specific to recommend me, and I said I had just written a new play. I hadn't, but he said that was great and that I could come to Marlboro and produce it. In the interim, I worked on a bunch of notes concerning my stint in the Merchant Marines and made them into a second play called *Lakeboat.*"[8]

1970. Returned to Chicago. "I did everything in the way of work, and I guess I met a lot of people. I worked in restaurants, as a busboy and a short-order cook, I drove cabs, and I worked in a boiler room.

"A boiler room is a room with a lot of phones and a lot of people who work these phones, trying to sell people worthless land in Arizona and Florida. You follow up leads, like responses to a TV ad or something like that, and make appointments over the phone, so a salesman can go out and seal the deal.

"The area I used to work in, Petersen Avenue,...was full of marginal businesses like rodent control outfits and siding firms. At lunch time, all the pseudo-businessmen from the neighborhood, all those guys in silver sharkskin suits used to meet at Jimmy Wong's Chinese restaurant."[9]

1971. "[Goddard College] hired me for a short term and I started teaching an acting class. I ended up staying for two years as an artist-in-residence and wrote about three or four more plays. It was probably the most precipitous point in my career as a playwright, because it gave me a laboratory to constantly produce. It was invaluable."[8]

1972. Back in Chicago, he staged his next play, *Duck Variations* at The Body Politic, an experimental theater. Mamet made the rounds of local theaters and completed the transition from actor to playwright. "I wasn't a good enough actor. My perceptions of what was required of a great actor so far outdistanced my ability to fulfill those requirements that I wasn't happy anymore. The same was not true of writing, so I naturally gravitated towards that."[6]

"I never really wanted to be a writer. I never spent any conscious time devoted to the philosophy or technique of writing until I'd been writing for a long time. Sherwood Anderson talks in one of his stories about how he was writing advertising copy for a living and one day he just started writing a story. instead. And he looked at it and said, 'My God, that's writing. I can do that. How about that.'"[3]

1974. Mamet, along with several actor/director friends who worked in small Chicago theaters, resurrected the St. Nicholas Theater Company in Chicago. Served as playwright-in-residence. "We worked twelve hours a day. It was a great education. No wonder [we] are rising to some sort of manhood and womanhood. We've paid a price."[5]

The Company premiered *Sexual Perversity in Chicago*, a one-act satire about the singles' scene. "One critic in Chicago says I write the kind of plays where a character wakes up in Act One and

Joe Mantegna and Lindsay Crouse in a scene from the 1987 Orion Pictures film, "House of Games."

finally gets around to putting on his bathrobe in Act Three.

"The first thing I learned is that the exigent speak poetry. They don't speak the language of newspapers. I heard rhythms and verbal expressions that dealt with an experience not covered in anything I'd ever read. Then I read Mencken, and became fascinated by the notion of a native American language. And then through my dad—he was interested in semantics—I read Stanislavski. That's when I first learned the correlation between language and action, that words *create* behavior, which is obviously crucial if you want to become a playwright.

"Actually, my main emphasis is on the rhythm of language—the way action and rhythm are identical. Our rhythms describe our actions—no, our rhythms *prescribe* our actions. I became fascinated—I still am—by the way, the way the language we use, its rhythm, actually determines the way we behave, more than the other way around. Everything I am as a playwright I feel I owe to Stanislavski—I mean..., every playwright should be forced to read him just on consonants and vowels alone!"[2]

Mamet's sensitivity for language earned *Sexual Perversity in Chicago* the Joseph Jefferson Award for the best new Chicago play and was followed with an even bigger success, *American Buffalo*, which premiered in Chicago in 1975. The play dealt with a robbery, planned but never executed. "The play is about the American ethic of business. About how we excuse all sorts of great and small betrayals and ethical compromises called business. I felt angry about business when I wrote the play. I used to stand at the back of the theater and watch the audiences as they left. Women had a much easier time with the play. Businessmen left it muttering very vehemently about its inadequacies and pointlessness. But they weren't really mad because the play was pointless—no one can be forced to sit through an hour and a-half of meaningless dialogue—they were angry because the play was about *them*."[10]

"I was certainly writing about a society outside the law, which means the theme would probably be more focused there. But I think in a larger sense we're all outside the law. It's about the same thing Nixon and all those people were doing. It's not that much more sophisticated."[8]

"In New York, the delinquent classes still subscribe to the myth of mobility, but only within their own class structure. The only way people can break out is to go to college. For those who don't go to college, there's nothing for them to do—nothing meaningful, I mean. In New York, they exist only to steal from the corporate classes."[9]

But the "corporate classes" perform their own sleight-of-hand. "The corporate classes perform busy-work, make-believe work; but they still call it work. But what's the difference between a man who works as a censor for CBS and makes $250,000 and a man who works as a guard in a record shop for $2.50 an hour? Both are performing imaginary jobs. Neither man's work has any value. The economic realities of our lives are based on the flimsy and transparent lie that anyone can get ahead by fealty to a nation or corporation."[9]

"There's really no difference between the *lumpenproletariat* [phony wage-earners] and stockbrokers or corporate lawyers who are the lackeys of business. Part of the American myth is that a difference exists, that at a certain point vicious behavior becomes laudable. The job of the theater today, is to look at some of the assumptions upon which our society functions."[10]

"The proclamation and repetition of first principles is a constant feature of life in our Democracy. Active adherence to these principles, however, has always been considered un-American.

"We recipients of the boon of Liberty have always been ready, when faced with discomfort, to discard any and all first principles of liberty; and, further, to indict those who do not freely join with us in happily abrogating those principles.

"Freedom of speech, religion, and sexual preference are tolerated only until their exercise is found offensive, at which point those freedoms are haughtily revoked—and we hear, 'Yes, but the Framers of the Constitution (or Christ, or Lincoln, or whatever Saint we are choosing to invoke in our support) surely didn't envision an instance as extreme as *this!*'

"We tolerate and repeat the teachings of Christ, but explain that the injunction against murder surely cannot be construed to apply to *war*; and that against theft does not apply to *commerce*. We sanctify the Constitution of the United States, but explain that freedom of choice is meant to apply to all except women, racial minorities, homosexuals, the poor, opponents of the Government, and those with whose ideals we disagree."[11]

Sexual Perversity in Chicago and *American Buffalo* won Mamet an Obie Award as most promising new playwright.

Mamet with actress-wife, Lindsay Crouse, at work on the film, "House of Games."

A double bill of *Duck Variations* and *Sexual Perversity in Chicago* at St. Clement's Theater, introduced Mamet to New York audiences. Both plays soon moved up to Off-Broadway at the Cherry Lane Theater.

1976. Wrote *A Life in the Theater,* a play about play-making. "It's a play about actors. Everybody in this country loves the idea of the theater, but everyone is ambivalent about actors and treats them with, at best, a bemused tolerance. Yet when you stop and think about it, actors are the only essential element of the theater."[6]

"Theater people are seen as interesting but not constructive creatures. In contrast, people automatically treat doctors as laudable. There are probably as many charlatans in the medical profession as there are in theater. People in the theater are always told to make themselves clear. But nobody says to a doctor, 'What do you mean? Make yourself clear, bozo!' Who questions doctors, lawyers and stockbrokers. . .?"[10]

1977. Unfortunately *The Water Engine,* Mamet's play about an inventor, ran only two weeks on Broadway. *American Buffalo,* starring Robert Duval enjoyed a run at the Ethel Barrymore Theater in New York. "Broadway is basically a whore house. I've had terrible experiences with commercial producers. I've never met one I liked. What they're trying to do is antithetical to what the theatrical artist is trying to do."[12]

Rehearsed his play *Reunion* at the Yale Repertory Theater. "*Reunion* is a play about a father and daughter who haven't seen each other in twenty years, since the girl was five years old and the parents divorced. It's followed by a short afterpiece called *Dark Pony,* which is a flashback to the father and daughter when she was four and he was thirty. And it's written in fourteen very short, inconclusive scenes between the two of them.

"They really have virtually no common ground except the biological one, and perhaps the hint of something ineluctable in their mutual nature, and that's what they're trying to establish."[6]

Cover of the published screenplay.

Met Lindsay Crouse, actress daughter of playwright Russell Crouse, who was appearing in the play. "My life got really frantic the past year as a promising playwright. Even jogging didn't help because I was overcome with exhaustion instead of exhilaration. Then I met someone, and we really hit it off. She's an actress. Suddenly I loosened up. We communicate."[4]

He married Crouse on December 21, 1977. "Lindsay is a great woman. She's someone I can admire, look up to, learn from. I think I've become somewhat nicer since I married Lindsay. I kind of fell in love with her from seeing her in the movies—from seeing 'Slapshot.' I was thrilled when I heard she was going to be in my play. I always admired her work. She was real pretty, very talented and smart as a whip. And very funny. It was a very simple and straightforward showbiz romance. She just had nothing to do with other women I'd known. I knew I wanted to marry her immediately. Her feelings didn't enter into it. It's like her feelings were her own concern. We seemed to understand each other instantly. It's like you always ask your mother, how will I know? And she says, well, you'll just know. You always think your mother is nuts. But it's actually true. Or at least it was in our case. Tolstoy said all happy families are alike. . . .

"We viciously critize each other's work. I'm more vicious than she is. She is a great help to me. She reads everything that I write. She edits. She has a longtime classical education. She tells me about things I just never learned. For writers block, she just says, sit down and write. She's very understanding, she knows the only cure for it is to sit down and write. What I do for her is I scream at her a lot. My problem is that I taught acting for so many years. She's a great student, she can really do anything and she has a great desire to please and let me know how much she appreciates what I'm trying to say. Sometimes I think I'm too overbearing. I talk too much. But I think what I'm trying to help her do is to help her try to analyse a script. Nobody wins our fights. That's the thing about being married. You find out very quickly that you can't possibly win a fight. Because the point is not to make your point. Anytime you make a point you create resentment. The point is to resolve your differences and continue living with each other and loving each other."[13]

1979. Attracted by the title, *Sexual Perversity in Chicago,* Hollywood producers asked Mamet to adapt it for the screen. "As a callow youth with hay sticking out of my ears many years ago, I sold both the play and the screenplay for about $12 and a mess of porridge. The property was purchased by a bunch of speculators who subsequently sold it to another bunch of speculators who kicked me off the screenplay. When they purchased the property, they purchased the good and bad parts of the play and of the title. . . ."[14]

Ironically, Hollywood was too prudish to keep the original title, and later changed it to "About Last Night," which starred Rob Lowe and Demi Moore.

Hollywood was a shock to Mamet's Chicagoan sensibilities. "[The Chicago literary tradition] carries with it a certain intolerance for the purely ornamental and a great support for the idea of brashness and the application of the individual intellect. Chicago is: 'Have a good time, get a girl, have a beer.' There's also the idea of completion, of production. You don't have guys sitting around in cafes with cigarettes trembling—'Oh, my God, I'm a writer, but I can't write.' Well, in Chicago, the answer is, 'Go home, you sissy. If you're a writer, write.' "[3]

"The East views Los Angeles as the poor man's hell, and New York is considered by the movie industry to be the cultural capital of New England. A great deal of talent languishes underpaid and underemployed in the East, and most movies are garbage. This is unfortunate.

"Los Angeles *is* the poor man's hell. It is a city full of producers and those who would like to be. And the only idea a producer ever came up with was 'see if he'll settle for less.' "[15]

Through his wife, Mamet was offered another film to write. In 1981 he adapted James M. Cain's *The Postman Always Rings Twice,* for the screen. Directed by Bob Rafelson, it starred Jack Nicholson and Jessica Lange. "When I submitted the first draft, there were a number of people—Rafelson wasn't one of them—who said, 'What is this? It doesn't make any sense!' I answered, 'You're nuts! It's the best screenplay you've seen in the last five years!' But then it dawned on me that I wrote it the way I wrote my plays. I never write any adverbs. To me, the dialogue is self-explanatory. So I added 'savagely' or 'feelingly' after each character's name—and they said it was a great screenplay."[16]

"In a play the only way you have to convey the action of the plot is through the action of the characters, what they say to each other. With a movie, the action has to be advanced narratively. To advance it through the dialogue is just boring; it is not the proper exploitation of the form. It has to be advanced, showing the audience what's happening, narrating to them the state of mind of the protagonist, which is the worst kind of playwriting.

"From what I can see in the writing and directing, film is getting things structured so that it succeeds in spite of itself. You're taking the element of luck out. You also are taking out the elements of feeling and sensitivity, so you're relying absolutely on the structure of the script. The script makes the audience ask what happens next and makes the audience care about the answer to that question. Rafelson was teasing me about structure, and what I was doing was adding to the project, I think a vision of the characters; my construction of their actions, my construction of what they wanted."[17]

"I'm of the Aristotelian school: characters are nothing but habitual action. You don't create a character: you describe what he does. To me, it's the story of a drifter [Jack Nicholson] who's happy living by his wits and off the land until he meets this woman [Jessica Lange]. He tries to exploit her and leave her, but can't. He finds himself bound to her. And to have her, to be able to keep her, he commits a murder. It's the story of a man who gets caught up in spite of himself."[16]

Despite the difficult adjustments, Mamet enjoyed his work on the film. "My own experience in Hollywood was very good. Rafelson is a great perfectionist, in terms of planning and logistics. We spent almost a year working on the structure of the script, trying to make it fascinating and give the audience a treat. Someone once asked Vakhtangov, the Russian stage director, 'How is it that every time you stage a play it becomes a hit? It's impossible!' And he replied, 'I always imagine that the audience is there with me at the rehearsal; I put myself in their place.' To a great extent, that's what Bob does. He's not patronizing. He *becomes* part of the audience. We must have done ten drafts of the damn screenplay! When I was on the set, I was rewriting scenes that were to be shot the next day."[16]

1982. Wrote the screenplay for "The Verdict," which starred Paul Newman in the role of a lawyer. "I grew up in a house full of lawyers. My father is a lawyer, my step-father, my step-sister and step-brother. I was closest to my father's practice. He believes very much in the law. He practiced labor law and I was brought up to believe strongly in the efficacy of a good lawyer."[18]

His play, *Edmond*, ran at the Provincetown Play-house (New York City). It dealt with one of Mamet's favorite themes. "The American Dream has gone bad. It was basically raping and pillage. The idea was that if you got out there, as long as there was something to exploit—whether it was the wild west, the Negroes, the Irish, the Chinese in California, the gold fields, or the timberland—one had the capacity to get rich. This capitalistic dream of wealth turns people against each other. They fight each other to get something for nothing.

"But we are finally reaching a point where there is nothing left to exploit. There are no more races left to colonialize, no more free land to rape. The dream has nowhere to go so it *has* to start turning in on itself. All those considerable talents that the white race has been living by since the birth of Christ and before, the emotionlessness, the viciousness, and the acquisitiveness that have sustained them, they now turn against each other and they do it individually and on a mass scale.

"This is what *Edmond* is about."[19]

1983. His preoccupation with these themes culminated in his play, *Glengarry Glen Ross*, the story of crooked, desperate real estate salesmen. It opened on Broadway and won a Pulitzer Prize in 1984. "Well, hell, you know we're doing American theater, with American actors. It belongs on Broadway.

"The business of America is business. We're a nation of entrepreneurs. [I wanted to write a play] about those guys you see on planes. They all sit together, and you can never understand what they're talking about, and they all have these papers filled with columns and figures. They're all named Bob. And when they laugh, it's 'Ha *ha!*'—this imitation laugh.

"They all use words to influence actions. They build what's called a line of affirmatives. A customer is never allowed to say no: 'You'd like to make money, wouldn't you?' they say. Another great trick is not answering objections: 'That's an excellent point. Let's talk about that later.'"[5]

"I have the first act of about two hundred and fifty plays in my trunk. I'll be involved in about five or six projects and then something else will begin to interest me. I find it very unprofessional to keep accruing beginnings. Sometimes I really have to force myself to finish a project."[8]

"That's why people love [*Glengarry Glen Ross*]. Because I finally had the will to write a second act. I wrote a million episodic plays, I can write them with my left hand. So what? Who cares? Fortunately, I got sick of it before [the audience] did. What matters is keeping people in their seats."[5]

Despite criticisms of his style and profane use of language, Mamet definitely kept his audience in its seat. "There are, however, two types of criticism. There's the sort that's frequently used by friends and casual theatergoers. It's their way of co-opting the piece. They'll come up after the play and say, 'I wish you'd done this or that.' That's healthy because they identify with the piece, they've been given a license to participate.

"Then, there's the supposedly non-emotional sort sometimes practiced in the press. That's a fiction, of course. Dealing with a play non-emotionally simply distances the critic."[10]

Though critics have compared *Glengarry Glen Ross* to *Death of a Salesman*, Mamet doesn't like the comparison. "When I saw [*Death of a Salesman*] I was surprised....I was humbled. It's like the guy said, mediocrity sees nothing higher than itself, but talent recognizes genius instantly. What a work of art! There were great hearts up there on stage. That's what the theater should be. Stanislavski said the task of the actor is to bring to the stage the life of the human soul, and that's what those guys did.

"...I wrote Arthur Miller a letter...saying I felt a little bit of an idiot, proclaiming that thirty years after everyone in the world had proclaimed it. I sat in the theater and I said, 'My God, that's my life story. That's my relationship to my father.' And then I looked around and realized that everybody in that theater was having the same perception. Of course, the two plays [*Salesman* and *Glengarry*] come out of very different traditions....

"I wrote a play once called 'All Men Are Whores' and in it a guy said that men are the puppy dogs of the universe and that they'll do anything for some affection. Especially in this country, men are never forced to confront themselves, and so they have no rock-bottom self-respect. We'll do anything to get some, because we feel there's nothing that can be taken from us. We've learned to define ourselves *solely* in terms of our work, and in an economy that's crumbling and where there's no certainty, what's left?"[20]

1985. Two radio plays. "Cross Patch" and "Goldberg Street" premiered on WNUR-Radio at Northwestern University. Mamet was no stranger to radio. *Edmond* and *The Water Engine* had already been broadcast. "You can do anything on the radio. You are bounded only by your creative imagination. Stan Freberg once did a radio commercial for radio advertising, a dialogue between a television advertising executive and a radio advertising executive. The radio executive says, 'Here's my ad: You

take Lake Michigan and drain it. Bombers of the Royal Canadian Air Force fly over, laden with whipped cream. They drop the whipped cream in the lake until the lake is full. A huge helicopter circles Chicago carrying a forty-five-ton cherry and drops it on the top of the whipped cream, as the tops of the Chicago skyscrapers explode and paint the evening sky with fireworks from horizon to horizon. Do *that* on TV!

"Writing for the radio teaches there is no such thing as 'production values.' The phrase means, 'pour money on it,' and it has been the ruin of television, movies, and the professional stage. It is the triumph of the general, the celebration of nothing to say.

"This is why radio is a great training ground for dramatists. More than any other dramatic medium, it teaches the writer to concentrate on the essentials, because it throws into immediate relief that to characterize the people or scene is to take time from the story, which is to weaken the story. A lesson I learned working for the radio is that this is the way all great drama works: by leaving the endowment of characters, place, and especially action up to the audience.

"In the same way, good drama has no stage directions. It is the interaction of the characters' objectives expressed solely through what they say to each other—not through what the author says about them. The better the play, the better it will fare on the radio. Put *A Streetcar Named Desire*, *Waiting for Godot*, *Long Day's Journey into Night*, *King Lear* on the radio, and what do you miss? Nothing.

"Our enjoyment is increased by the absence of the merely descriptive. (A note here,...to beginning playwrights—a lesson from radio: don't write stage directions. If it is not apparent what the character is trying to accomplish by saying the line, telling us how the character said it, or whether or not he or she moved to the couch, isn't going to aid the case. We might understand better what the character means, but we aren't particularly going to care.)"[21]

Undertaking several new projects, Mamet wrote an episode for the television series, "Hill Street Blues," and adapted the television series, "The Untouchables," into a screenplay. "The Paramount people said they wanted me to write 'The Untouchables' as a native and loyal Chicagoan and I'm interested in anything about the mythos of Chicago.

Kevin Costner in the famous Union Station shoot-out scene from the movie, "The Untouchables." Screenplay by David Mamet, 1987.

"[Eliot] Ness was a straight-arrow fellow. He was a young guy when he took over in Chicago—twenty-nine years old. He's like a classic FBI agent—a Melvin Purvis—or a frontier sheriff."[22]

"My experience as a screenwriter is this: A script usually gets worse from the first draft on. This may not be a law of filmmaking, but in my experience it is generally true.

"'The Untouchables' may have been a bit of an exception. I met with [director] Brian De Palma three or four times, and he and Art Linson, the film's producer, had some ideas for cuts and restructuring that definitely aided the script.

"Inevitably, however, De Palma, Linson, and I disagreed about several aspects of the film and, as usually happens, we got to the point where someone said to me: 'Look, we disagree, and (in effect) you are the employee, so do *you* want to make the script changes which we require, or would you like us to do them, and do them badly?'

"On films in the past, this mixture of flattery and aggressiveness usually brought me around, like other screenwriters, with a sigh, to make the requested changes. On 'The Untouchables,' however, in the final and minor instances where I disagreed with the director and producer, I said, 'Fine, you screw it up. Spare me.'

"I said the above for a number of reasons: one, that I have gotten to the point as a writer where I am tired of being finessed; and, two, that I was directing my *own* movie, and had no sympathy to waste on the plight of others."[23] He made his directing debut with "House of Games," a film about a woman's dangerous attraction to sleazy Chicago characters.

Mamet found the experience of directing to be quite different from that of screenwriting. "[As a director], the amount of deference with which one is treated is absolutely *awesome*. One is deferred to by the crew because of the legitimate necessity of the chain of command in this sort of an enterprise, and by a great deal of the outside world because of supposed and real abilities to bestow favors, contracts, jobs, orders, et cetera.

"This deference was awfully refreshing after several years' acquaintanceship with Hollywood in the position of a writer (where, I should point out, I was treated, if one wants to judge by local standards, exceedingly well).

"One of my most treasured Hollywood interchanges follows: I made a suggestion to a producer and he responded, 'The great respect that I have for your talent doesn't permit me to sit here and listen to you spout such bullshit.'

"It is nice to be treated with deference, and, I think, even nicer to be treated with *courtesy;* which, I think we can all say, is almost universally lacking in Hollywood transactions.

"The downside of all that jolly deference and courtesy one receives as a film director is, of course, that one has to *direct* the movie.

"So, prior to directing 'House of Games,' I resolved, once again, to try to overcome my natural laziness, my natural aversion to tasks I would characterize as 'routine,' or 'uncreative,' and to apply myself to a series of detailed outlines: of the actions of the characters, of the rhythm of the movie as an expression of the proximity of the protagonist to her goal, and, finally, of the shots, shot by shot, of the entire film.

"So that's what I did. Once again, subscribing to my 'mountain climbing' theory of creative endeavor—get an absolutely firm foothold, and then make a small excursion to another absolutely firm foothold.

"Directing is, I think, a lot like being a night watchman over something one finds personally priceless: One must be unstinting in vigilance over a very long period of time, and it *does* get draining.

"Day by day, during the shooting, I tried to follow the plan, the outline of the movie. Each day, after shooting, I would watch the dailies with Mike Hausman, the producer, Juan Ruiz-Anchia, the cinematographer, and Trudy Ship, the editor.

"At the beginning of shooting, fresh and decisive, I would shoot an average of three and a half takes, and print no more than two. As the shooting went on and I got more and more fatigued, I started to shoot more and print more and more takes. . . .

"When in my 'keep printing this shot until Kodak hollers "Uncle"' stage, I'd sit watching the dailies with ten or twenty of the cast and crew, and as I'd printed six takes and couldn't remember the first when I'd seen the sixth, I'd ask for hands on who liked which takes best. Every time I'd ask for a vote, I'd get a few giggles, a few hands, and a lot of nervousness, and then it came to me that I was the

director, and that it wasn't funny. The people in the cast and crew were working hard enough at *their* job and I shouldn't, even in jest, be asking them to do mine.

"There is a condition called hypothermia, and it occurs when the body can't keep itself warm. Two of the symptoms are inability to think clearly, and panic; and it's no joke—it happened to me once alone in the woods in winter and I was lost and very lucky to stumble across a road before I froze to death.

"A situation very like this state of mind is brought about, I'm sure, by stress as well as cold; and if Eisenstein had lived longer and spent more time in Hollywood, he might have talked less about the Theory of Montage, and more about healthy eating, and what to have on the Craft service table."[23]

1987. "The Untouchables," starring Kevin Costner and featuring Robert DeNiro was released to great success. "House of Games," which starred his wife, Lindsay, opened and received critical acclaim. "One of the advantages of working with my wife is I get to work with a good actress.

"She's very opinionated, too. You want to know how we resolved differences? We stayed up late and talked about them until we accepted her point of view."[24]

Began directing his next film, "Things Change," a gangster comedy. "It's about this old shoeshine guy, an Italian immigrant, played by Don Ameche. The mob asks him to take a jail rap for one of their guys who's a dead ringer for him. The old guy agrees, and they take him to Tahoe for his last weekend, where he's treated like a Mafia don."[25]

1988. Directed a benefit for homeless Vietnam veterans which involved such stars as Al Pacino, Don Ameche, Michael J. Fox, among others, performing works by writers like David Rabe, Dalton Trumbo, and Shakespeare, and original poetry written by Vietnam vets. "This is one of the most exciting things I've ever done. Assembling all this magnificent material with all these terrific actors on a bare stage, for one night only. It's a very old-style theatrical evening, people coming together to talk about something of importance to them."[26]

"Speed the Plow" opened on Broadway. It starred Ron Silver, Joe Mantegna, and shockingly, pop-star Madonna who played the role of a producer's secretary. In the play, Mamet levels his satire at a familiar target: Hollywood. "My favorite new one is that studio executives' secretaries call me in Vermont and tell me that so-and-so can't talk to me now. Remember, I've never called *them*. They just want to let you know they're very busy!

"[But] I've got no kick with Hollywood. In fact, I've got to stop talking about Hollywood. It's like talking about Rudolf Hess. Sure he was a war criminal, but...."[27]

"I think it's a great time to be a young person in the theatre. Because all bets are off, as in times of social upheaval, in the twenties in Germany, the sixties in Chicago, the period from 1898 to 1920 in Russia. Traditionally, this is a time when new theatrical forms arise. That's what all this garbage about performance art is about, to a large extent, it's young people in the culture experimenting, casting about for a new form.

"...I think we're going to start putting people in jail again for what they write. People have been subconsciously afraid of expressing themselves because the times are so tenuous. And the reality will follow that feeling. So that will be exciting.

"It's like the weather. People get oppressed by the heat and humidity, it's got to rain before it's going to clear up. There are ebbs and flows in any civilization. Nothing lasts forever. We had a good time. We had Tennessee Williams. We had the hula hoop. We had the Edsel. All kinds of good stuff. The Constitution. To name but a few. Shelley Winters. Now you've got to pay the piper. Big deal."[27]

Footnote Sources:

[1] David Mamet, "My Kind of Town," *Horizon*, November, 1981.
[2] "David Mamet, Remember That Name," *Village Voice*, July 5, 1976.
[3] Samuel G. Freedman, "The Gritty Eloquence of David Mamet," *New York Times Magazine*, April 21, 1985.
[4] Robert Wahls, "Jogging with Mamet," *New York Daily News*, October 23, 1977.
[5] Jennifer Allen, "David Mamet's Hard Sell," *New York*, April 9, 1984.
[6] Jaques le Sourd, "All Work Is David Mamet's Play," *White Plains Reporter Dispatch* (N.Y.), October 16, 1977.
[7] D. Mamet, "A Tradition of the Theater as Art," *New York Theater Review*, February, 1979.
[8] Mark Zweigler, "David Mamet: The Solace of a Playwright's Ideals," *After Dark*, August, 1976.
[9] Marilyn Stasio, "Hunting the Buffalo," *Cue*, March 19-April 1, 1977.
[10] Richard Gottlieb, "The 'Engine' That Drives Playwright David Mamet," *New York Times*, January 15, 1978.
[11] D. Mamet, "First Principles," *Theater*, summer, 1981.
[12] William B. Collins, "David Mamet: Broadway Is Only Another Bad Word," *Philadelphia Inquirer*, October 1, 1978.
[13] Jan Cherubin, "Two on an Island," *New York Daily News*, December 15, 1980.
[14] Anne Thompson, "Cinematic Perversity in Hollywood," *Village Voice*, July 8, 1988.
[15] D. Mamet, "Mamet in Hollywood," *Horizon*, February, 1981.
[16] Dan Yakir, "The Postman's Words," *Film Comment*, March-April, 1981.
[17] Jean Vallely, "David Mamet Makes a Play for Hollywood," *Rolling Stone*, April 3, 1980.
[18] Twentieth Century-Fox Publicity Release, n.d.
[19] Mimi Leahey, "The American Dream Gone Bad," *Other Stages*, November 4, 1982.
[20] Mary Cantwell, "David Mamet: Bulldog of the Middle Class," *Vogue*, July, 1984.
[21] D. Mamet, "Air Plays," *Horizon*, May/June, 1982.
[22] S. G. Freedman, "Mamet's Next Subject Is Good Guy Eliot Ness," *New York Times*, July 30, 1985.
[23] D. Mamet, "I Lost It at the Movies," *American Film*, June, 1987.
[24] Michael Segell, "Lindsay Crouse," *Cosmopolitan*, November, 1987.
[25] Jack Kroll, "The Profane Poetry of David Mamet," *Newsweek*, October 19, 1987.
[26] Fox Butterfield, "David Mamet Lends a Hand to Homeless Vietnam Veterans," *New York Times*, October 10, 1988.
[27] David Savran, "Trading in the American Dream," *American Theater*, September, 1987.

■ For More Information See

New Yorker, November 10, 1975, October 31, 1977 (p. 115ff), January 16, 1978 (p. 69ff), October 29, 1979 (p. 81), June 15, 1981, November 7, 1983, June 29, 1987 (p. 70ff).
Chicago, February, 1976 (p. 8ff), May, 1979 (p. 12).
Newsday, June 17, 1976, August 22, 1976 (p. 4ff), December 16, 1986 (part II, p. 13).
New York Times, July 5, 1976 (p. 7), October 16, 1977 (p. D-7), January 15, 1978 (section 2, p. 1), March 17, 1978 (section IV, p. 40ff), March 18, 1979, April 26, 1979, May 10, 1979 (p. C-22), May 26, 1979, June 3, 1979, October 19, 1979, July 20, 1980 (section 2, p. 6), March 20, 1981, May 29, 1981, June 5, 1981, February 17, 1982, May 17, 1982, June 17, 1982, October 24, 1982, October 28, 1982 (p. C-20), December 8, 1982, May 13, 1983, October 9, 1983 (p. 6), November 6, 1983, March 26, 1984 (p. C-17), March 28, 1984, April 1, 1984, April 18, 1984, April 24, 1984, September 30, 1984, December 14, 1986, October 11, 1987 (section 2, p. 25), October 16, 1987 (p. C-10), October 20, 1988 (p. C-10).
Village Voice, July 5, 1976 (p. 101ff), October 25, 1988 (p. 62).
Time, July 12, 1976, February 28, 1977 (p. 54), April 9, 1984 (p. 105).
After Dark, August, 1976 (p. 42ff).
Sunday News (N.Y.), February 13, 1977 (section III, p. 3).

Newsweek, February 28, 1977 (p. 79), March 23, 1981, November 8, 1982, December 6, 1982, April 9, 1984 (p. 109).

Saturday Review, April 2, 1977 (p. 37).

W, November 11-18, 1977 (p. 24ff).

Daily News (N.Y.), December 22, 1977 (p. 7), July 8, 1984, September 7, 1986.

Contemporary Literary Criticism, Gale, Volume IX, 1978, Volume XV, 1980.

Us, January 10, 1978.

Boston Phoenix, February 28, 1978 (section 3, p.1).

New York Times Magazine, March 12, 1978 (p. 24ff), April 20, 1988 (p. 52).

Harper's, May, 1978 (p. 79ff).

Dramatist's Quarterly, autumn, 1978 (p. 30ff).

Horizon, October, 1978 (p. 96ff).

New York Arts Journal, November-December, 1978 (p. 21).

Nation, May 19, 1979 (p. 581ff), April 4, 1981, October 10, 1981, April 28, 1984 (p. 522ff).

Hollins Critic, October, 1979 (p. 1ff).

People Weekly, November 12, 1979 (p. 60), December 20, 1982.

Los Angeles Times, November 27, 1979, June 25, 1984.

Current Biography 1978, H. W. Wilson, 1979.

"David Mamet," *Performing Arts Journal,* Volume V, number 3, 1981.

D. Mamet, "Final Cut," *In Cinema,* March, 1981.

Chicago Tribune, March 20, 1981, March 27, 1984.

Washington Post, August 2, 1981, March 7, 1983, August 25, 1983, August 26, 1983.

Marcia Savin, "Writers' Cramp," *Other Stages,* November 5, 1981.

Steven H. Gale, "David Mamet: The Plays, 1972-1980," *Essays on Contemporary American Drama,* edited by Hedwig Bock and Albert Wertheim, Max Hueber, 1981.

Dictionary of Literary Biography, Volume VII: *Twentieth-Century American Dramatists,* Gale, 1981.

Richard Christiansen, "The Young Lion of Chicago Theater," *Chicago Tribune Magazine,* July 11, 1982.

New Republic, December 20, 1982 (p. 24ff), May 7, 1984 (p. 27ff), November 7, 1988 (p. 26).

Ruby Cohn, *New American Dramatists 1960-1980,* Grove, 1982.

Robert Becker, "Don Sultan with David Mamet," *Interview,* March, 1983.

Christian Science Monitor, March 21, 1984 (p. 21).

Esquire, March, 1985 (p. 110).

Chicago Sun Times, March 6, 1985 (p.49).

Sports Illustrated, November 4, 1985 (p. 68).

Mademoiselle, November, 1985 (p. 136).

Guido Almansi, "David Mamet, a Virtuoso of Invective," *Critical Angles: European Views of Contemporary American Literature,* edited by Marc Chenetier, Southern Illinois University Press, 1986.

New York Post, January 6, 1987, January 13, 1987.

Vogue, February, 1987 (p. 298).

Harper's Bazaar, September, 1987 (p. 85).

Life, October, 1987 (p. 65).

San Francisco Chronicle, October 16, 1987 (p. E- 1).

Vanity Fair, April, 1988 (p. 32ff).

Variety, September 7, 1988 (p. 25).

Seven Days, October 26, 1988 (p. 43).

New York, November 7, 1988

Garry Marshall

Born Garry Marciarelli, November 13, 1934, in New York, N.Y.; son of Anthony W. (a television producer) and Marjorie Irene (a dance instructor; maiden name, Ward) Marciarelli; married Barbara Sue Wells (a nurse), 1963. *Education:* Northwestern University, B.A. 1956. *Office:* Henderson Productions, 10067 Riverside Dr., Toluca Lake, Calif. *Publicist:* c/o Nancy Seltzer and Associates, 8845 Ashcroft Ave., Los Angeles, Calif. 90048.

■ Career

Producer, director, and writer. Drummer in Chicago, Ill., 1958; *Daily News*, New York, N.Y., reporter, 1958-59; free-lance comedy writer, New York, N.Y., 1958-60. Writer of over 100 television scripts, variety shows, and fifteen pilots, including comedy writer for "The Jack Paar Show," "The Tonight Show," 1960-62, "The Joey Bishop Show," 1962-64, "I Spy," 1966, "Bill Dana Show," and "Gomer Pyle"; writer for "Chrysler Theatre," 1966; comedy writer with Jerry Belson of episodes for "The Dick Van Dyke Show," 1962, "The Lucy Show," 1963, and "The Danny Thomas Show," 1964. Creator and executive producer of thirteen television series; writer and producer of

three screenplays with partner Jerry Belson; director of thirty television shows, a music video, five feature films, two commercials, and numerous pilots. *Military service:* U. S. Army, Special Services, 1956-58. *Member:* New York Dramatists Guild, Motion Picture Academy, Television Academy, Producer's Guild, Director's Guild, Screen Actors Guild, Writer's Guild, American Federation of Television and Radio Artists, Board of Governors of the Los Angeles Music Center, Musician's Union (Local 47), Sigma Delta Chi, Alpha Tau Omega.

■ Awards, Honors

Emmy Award from the National Academy of Television Arts and Sciences for the Best Episode of a Comedy, 1965, for "The Dick Van Dyke Show"; Nine other Emmy Awards and four Golden Globe Awards from the Hollywood Foreign Press Association, all for television series "Happy Days," "Laverne and Shirley," and "Mork and Mindy;" Arc of Excellence Award from the National Association of Retarded Citizens, 1978; Showman of the Year from the Publicist's Guild, 1979; Man of the Year from Hollywood Radio and Television Society's Broadcasting Awards, 1980, from the Los Angeles Free Clinic, 1982, and from the National Association of Television Program Executives, 1983; Meritorious Award from the California Governor's Committee for Employment of the Handicapped, 1980; "Star" on The Walk of Fame, Hollywood Blvd., 1983; Member of the Year from the Caucus for Producers, Writers and Directors, 1988; Best Soft Drink Commercial "Classic Coke" from *Advertising Age*, 1988; Award for the Best

Family Motion Picture (Drama) from the Youth in Film Awards, 1988, for "Beaches."

■ Writings

Television Series; Creator And Executive Producer:

(With J. Belson) "Hey Landlord," National Broadcasting Co. (NBC-TV), 1966-67.

(With J. Belson) "The Odd Couple," American Broadcasting Co. (ABC-TV), 1970-75.

"Me and the Chimp," CBS-TV, 1971-72.

"The Little People" (later named "The Brian Keith Show"), NBC-TV, 1972-74.

"Happy Days," ABC-TV, 1972-83.

"Barefoot in the Park," ABC-TV, 1975-76.

"Laverne and Shirley," ABC-TV, 1976-83.

"Blansky's Beauties," ABC-TV, 1977-78.

"Mork and Mindy," ABC-TV, 1978-82.

"Angie," NBC-TV, 1979-81.

"Who's Watching the Kids?," NBC-TV, 1980-81.

"Joannie Loves Chachi," ABC-TV, 1982-84.

"Nothing in Common" (based on film), NBC-TV, 1987-88.

Screenplays; Writer And Producer:

(With Jerry Belson) "How Sweet It Is!," National General, 1968.

(With J. Belson) "The Grasshopper," National General, 1970.

"Evil Roy Slade" (television movie), MCA-TV, 1971.

Stage Plays:

"Shelves," first produced in Chicago, Ill. at Pheasant Run Playhouse, February, 1976.

(Adapter) Lawrence Schwab, G. G. De Sylva, and Frank Mandel, *Good News* (libretto; words and music by Lew Brown, G. G. De Sylva, and Ray Henderson), Tams Witmark Music Library, 1978.

(With J. Belson) "The Roast" (two-act), first produced on Broadway at Winter Garden Theatre, May 8, 1980.

(With Lowell Ganz) "Wrong Turn at Lungfish," staged reading November, 1988.

Motion Picture Director:

(And executive producer) "Young Doctors in Love," Twentieth Century-Fox, 1982.

(Also writer with Neal Marshall) "The Flamingo Kid," ABC Motion Pictures, 1984.

"Nothing in Common," Tri-Star, 1986.

"Overboard," Metro-Goldwyn-Mayer/United Artists, 1987.

"Beaches," Touchstone, 1988.

■ Work In Progress

Director of "Three Thousand," a feature film for Touchstone.

■ Sidelights

"I was a mediocre journalist, a mediocre musician, a mediocre actor, a mediocre athlete. I had to find something I could do well."[1]

A surprising beginning for a man who, on the night of January 28, 1979, had created the three top-rated shows on network television. Garry Marshall had indeed found something he could do well...make people laugh. "I got a degree in journalism from Northwestern University but I wasn't very good at it. I wasn't a good student. Everybody seemed to be better than me. When I got out of school, I worked in the newspaper field but not very successfully. The reason was that I was too funny! So, I got into comedy writing.

"At that time, I wrote things for comedians. I would go to different night clubs and try to sell jokes. Some bought, some threw me out and a few took me under their wing. Phil Foster, in particular, was one of the people who helped me. He was the comedian who later became the father on 'Laverne and Shirley.'"[1]

The time was the early sixties and Marshall landed a job writing sketches for Jack Paar on "The Tonight Show." He wrote funny letters from imaginary kids from camp that Paar liked so much, he put Marshall on his writing staff. To Marshall, Paar quipped, "I like you, Garry, because you think like a four-year-old."[2] It was during his two-year stint with Paar that Marshall met Joey Bishop. One of the hottest comedians of his time, Bishop was a regular guest host. Recognizing talent when he saw it, Bishop eventually drafted Marshall for "The Joey Bishop Show," and in 1962 Garry Marshall found himself in Hollywood.

Teaming up with writer Jerry Belson, the two men proceeded to work on the hottest comedy shows of the decade, writing over one hundred episodes of shows like "The Lucy Show," "The Danny Thomas Show," and "The Dick Van Dyke Show," for which they won an Emmy Award for Best Episode of a Comedy. To this day, Marshall enjoys the collaborative process. "The big advantage to partnership at a typewriter is that you can truly combat

Henry Winkler (far left) and Ron Howard (far right) as they starred in the eleven-year television series "Happy Days."

loneliness, depression, rejection and all the other 'ections' a writer alone faces. As somebody once remarked, without a partner who are you gonna talk to in the elevator after your meeting with studio executives? A partner also eliminates your stupidest ideas faster. Otherwise the dumb ideas you come up with you might hang on to longer."[3]

In 1967, Marshall and Belson ventured into screenwriting. Their first effort was a motion picture entitled "How Sweet It Is," starring Debbie Reynolds, which the team also produced. That was followed by a film entitled "The Grasshopper," starring Jacqueline Bisset. While both films were well received by the film community, Marshall and Belson's careers as television writers were about to skyrocket. "I started doing pilots in the '60's'. I noticed that certain guys, like Sheldon Leonard ['The Danny Thomas Show'] and Quinn Martin ['The Fugitive']; whatever *they* did got on the air and in a good time slot, too. So I said to myself, 'How do *I* get to be one of those guys?' Well, I got to be one."[4]

Neil Simon's comedy, "The Odd Couple" was the toast of Broadway in the spring of 1965. The play, about the antics of two very different best friends trying to share an apartment and cope with divorce, features a hard-drinking sports writer, Oscar Madison and his fuss-budget roommate, Felix Unger. Marshall and Belson thought the play a perfect vehicle for television. Jack Klugman and Tony Randall were cast in the lead rolls. The series aired September 24, 1970 and ran successfully for five seasons. For the rest of the decade Marshall continued to create hit after hit.

"In the education of the American people I am Recess. I do Recess well. My shows are very positive. I still believe in love and having people love each other."[4]

"I do things that I like to see and that please me. Comedy is my tool, and how crazy the comedy or how serious the comedy or how emotional the comedy is up to me and the story. I think that my approach is not to do what everybody else is doing. In television I tried to do things that were counter

ABC's television series "The Odd Couple" starred Jack Klugman and Tony Randall.

The very popular television series "Laverne and Shirley" starred Penny Marshall (right) and Cindy Williams.

to what went on. I had done 'The Odd Couple,' a wonderful and very intelligent show. Prior to that, I had worked with Carl Reiner on 'The Dick Van Dyke Show.' But then I noticed that a lot of people were doing those types of shows, and there was an opening for another type of program. Nostalgia was becoming popular in those days, but all of it was serious. So I made a comedy nostalgia program called 'Happy Days.' There hadn't been one of those on since 'I Remember Mama.' Then I also saw there was a wave of shows featuring bright young women, all of whom had wonderful jobs, lovely clothes and looked like Mary Tyler Moore,...there were no blue collar girls on television at all. I also noticed that there was no physical comedy...since Lucy left, so I gave 'Laverne and Shirley' some of that stuff. With 'Mork and Mindy,' I found somebody who *had* to be on television because nobody had ever seen a man work like this—Robin Williams. Sometimes I built a show around a unique talent....I'm just trying to do what other people are *not* doing."[5]

Putting together a weekly situation comedy is not for the faint of heart. Monday morning, the script goes "to the table" with the actors. The following two days, the show is rehearsed in a rehearsal hall while the script is constantly being perfected. On Thursday, the company moves to the sound stage where the script is "blocked" for three cameras. Friday is show day in front of two "live" audiences. "Funny is funny. On television, in a nightclub, in the theater, movies, no matter where, funny is funny. And the key is the audience. You're funniest when you use the audience. I use the audience as a barometer. I listen to the 300 people, and I can *hear* whether they laugh or don't laugh; so I don't need subjective opinions about what's funny.

"The three-camera technique gives me the best chance to be funny, because I always have three cameras looking at *everything*. I don't have to pick the very best shot until later in the quietness of the editing room. Then I can listen to the audience, see where they laughed, and pick the funniest shot.

Pam Dawber and Robin Williams starred in the ABC television series "Mork and Mindy."

For me it works better than picking the shots electronically as you shoot.

"The...technique involves lots of rehearsal. We're often rewriting up to the very last moment. I have even rewritten lines in front of the audience. I welcome contributions from anybody in my shows, because comedy can come from any place. Many of my cameramen have given me funny lines. Gate guards have contributed. The more creative the atmosphere, the better."[6]

Marshall draws many of his stories from a strong memory of what it was like growing up in the Bronx. But it was not always an easy life. An asthmatic child, Marshall was plagued with allergies. Still, he looks back on his childhood with fondness. "I had a happy childhood. I was sick all the time, but I remember the happy times. If I get up in the morning and I'm not sick, I know it's going to be a heck of a day."[7]

"In the neighborhood where we grew up in—the Bronx—you only had a few choices. You were either an athlete or a gangster, or you were funny. We all grew up surrounded by the sense of laughter....I look at life with a bend so I always think I'll have comedy in my work."[5]

The "we" Marshall refers to are sisters, Ronnie Hallin, now a television producer, and Penny, whose career break came when her big brother cast her as Laverne De Fazio in the hit series "Laverne and Shirley." Penny has since become a motion picture director, her biggest hit being "Big," starring Tom Hanks. She cast Garry in a cameo role in her first film entitled "Jumpin' Jack Flash" a fifteen million dollar film starring Whoopi Goldberg. What did Garry think about the role reversal? "My first three pictures were six, nine and eleven million so already she's ahead of me but I'm delighted. I visited her on the set the first day and she seemed nervous. Nine weeks later when I came back to shoot my scene, she seemed perfectly relaxed and completely in charge....It was great being directed by my sister who always wanted to yell at her big brother anyway."[3]

Matt Dillon as he starred in the 1984 film "The Flamingo Kid."

Eventually, Marshall took a hiatus from his many years in television production. "I was in television too long. I had done it for twenty years...over 1,000 situation comedies—that was the only type of show that interested me in television—and I was no longer...scared."[8] "I think you have to be a little bit scared in order to do good work—fear keeps a person alert."

Convinced that television pigeonholes writers and knowing it's up to the writer to break free, Marshall began to direct motion pictures. His first time out, he played it safe directing a crazy comedy called "Young Doctors in Love." After that, he began to choose scripts that reflected his continued interest in the family. "I come from a pretty close family. I like to do stories about father/son, mother/daughter relationships."[1]

"The Flamingo Kid" is a coming-of-age story about eighteen-year-old, Brooklyn born, Jeffrey Wells (played by Matt Dillon). From a solid, working class family, Jeffrey takes a summer job at an elite club in Far Rockaway called the El Flamingo. Early

on, the boy's head is turned by the glamourous life of the club and especially by a high roller, super-salesman (played by Richard Crenna), who convinces Jeffrey that the way to "the top" is through the school of hard knocks. Jeffrey rebels against his father's beliefs, including long-standing plans for college, in lieu of the fast track and easy money. But as the summer wanes, Jeffrey sees that the supersalesman is really a fraud. Disillusioned but wiser, he reconciles with his father, realizing his values are not so old-fashioned after all. "The Flamingo Kid" is the type of coming-of-age story that is the hallmark of Garry Marshall's work.

From Richie Cunningham and "The Fonz" in "Happy Days" to Laverne De Fazio and Shirley Feeney in "Laverne and Shirley," to Jeffrey Wells in "The Flamingo Kid," Marshall writes about the dilemmas and ethical choices American teenagers face when trying to grow up: how they fit into their families and how they fit into their society. "I like to write about young people and how they grow up and what happens to them. I always feel that the three major influences on young people are their parents, their environment and their friends. So, I write about those three subjects a lot."[1]

Marshall's next film, "Nothing in Common," was a mature variation on the father/son theme. It is the story of successful, but free-spirited, David Basner (played by Tom Hanks), whose prolonged adolescence comes to an abrupt halt when his parents separate and his father, Max (played by Jackie Gleason), becomes chronically ill. "It is a story about a son having to take care of his father—I'm 55 and my father's now 86....For the last ten years I've been into that arena of taking care of one's parents as an adult. What I thought made 'Nothing in Common' particularly my kind of story was that David wasn't just an average Joe. He was a very funny person who has to get serious. To me that was interesting because it's not what people are used to. I think that threw a few people who saw the film. But most seemed to like that it showed a person could be serious and amusing in the same lifetime, which I think is real."[8]

"'The Flamingo Kid' was a teen story with adult ramifications. 'Nothing in Common' moves into somewhat meatier areas although the comedy is not far away. I'm in this field because I want to communicate. My best way to communicate is with comedy and drama in a mixture which, if I had to label it, I'd call emotional comedy. One personal gratification is I feel confident the drama in 'Nothing in Common' holds."[3]

In 1987, Marshall directed "Overboard," a wacky comedy starring Goldie Hawn and Kurt Russell. In this film, Hawn plays the spoiled, rich wife of Edward Herrmann. Suffering from amnesia after she hits her head when she tumbles from her yacht, she is saved by a local carpenter (played by Kurt Russell). Russell happens to be a single father who needs Hawn to fill in as "mom" to his four children whom he is about to lose to social services. Once again, the story involves a family, but the film is a light return to traditional comedy affectionately referred to as a "romp." And, it has as it's main topic Marshall's other favorite theme: the love story.

Marshall will certainly continue to direct and write comedies but will always be looking to do what the other guy ISN'T doing. He stresses, "I would like my films to be more offbeat than anything I did in TV."[8]

Barbara Hershey and Bette Midler as they appeared in the 1988 movie "Beaches."

Marshall in his role as the casino manager in the movie "Lost in America."

"Television can reach more people, but in film, you can use a little more poignant material. Television is also limited because of the censorship. Also, there are a lot of actors and actresses I want to work with who don't do television."[1]

One such film that fits these criteria was his project for 1988. Called "Beaches," it's the film adaptation of the popular novel by Iris Rainer Dart. It stars Bette Midler and Barbara Hershey. "It's a very strong story about female friendship. I've dealt with a lot of stories about male friendship but I haven't done female friendship since 'Laverne and Shirley.' This story delves into a very dramatic and realistic friendship between two women over a forty year period of time."[1]

In any event, whether shooting a dramatic film or a weekly "sit-com," Marshall is clearly a man who is happy with his work. "...I've done...over a thousand situation comedies. I can't look you in the eye and say that every one of those episodes was brilliant and perfect. Some *were* perfect. Some were good. Some were pretty good. Some were a little embarrassing—but every piece I've tried to make professional. I've never been ashamed of anything I've done. However, people often don't take comedy seriously. Woody Allen said that comedy isn't better than drama, but it's harder to do. He's absolutely right. Comedy *is* hard to do. Some people will always put you down for doing a certain kind of comedy. When the reviews of 'Nothing in Common' came out, a friend of mine said, 'You know, the reviews are so good that it's now safe to mention your *television* credits.'"[5]

Marshall is leading the life he always imagined, "I like to make people laugh. I didn't know how I would be doing it but I knew somewhere I would get a chance."[1]

Footnote Sources:

[1] Based on an interview by Deborah Jones for *Authors and Artists for Young Adults.*
[2] Maureen Orth and Martin Kasindorff, "Candy Store," *Newsweek*, March 7, 1977.
[3] Gary Ballard, "Happy Days Are 'Common' Now: TV/Film Champ Garry Marshall," *Drama-Logue*, August 7-13, 1986. Amended by G. Marshall.
[4] Dwight Whitney, "He Can Hiccough and Somebody Will Develop It into a Series," *TV Guide*, May 19, 1979.
[5] Michael Singer, "From the Director's Chair," *1987 5th Annual International Edition of Film Directors: A Complete Guide,* Lone Eagle Publishing, 1988.
[6] *Hollywood Reporter* (advertisement), Eastman Kodak Co., 1980.
[7] "Garry Marshall: Having Fun and Happy Endings," ABC Motion Pictures Press Department, press release for "Young Doctors In Love," 1982.
[8] Tom Hinckley, "Garry Marshall: Television's Man with the Midas Touch Turns to Film," *Cable Guide,* August, 1987.

■ **For More Information See**

Life, June 3, 1966.
Time, September 13, 1968, April 29, 1974, December 12, 1977, July 26, 1982.
New York Times, January 17, 1974, February 3, 1974, February 8, 1976, May 9, 1980, October 2, 1980 (p. D1ff).
Newsweek, March 29, 1976, March 7, 1977, July 26, 1982.
New West, January 31, 1977 (p. 62ff).
People Weekly, December 25, 1978-January 1, 1979 (p. 70).
New Leader, January 29, 1979.
Saturday Review, March 31, 1979.
Film Comment, July-August, 1979.
Los Angeles Times, September 4, 1979 (p. 8ff), December 13, 1981 (p. 44), December 27, 1984 (p. 1ff).
English Journal, November, 1979.
TV Guide, December 8, 1979 (p. 4ff).
New Yorker, May 19, 1980.
Los Angeles Herald-Examiner, August 28, 1980 (p. B1ff), December 29, 1984 (p. C1ff), April 1, 1987 (p. C1ff).
Contemporary Literary Criticism, Volume 17, Gale, 1981.
Joel Eisner and David Krinsky, *Television Comedy Series: An Episode Guide to 150 Sitcoms in Syndication,* McFarland, 1984.
Beverly Hills 213, August 20, 1986 (p. 6ff).
Character, February, 1988 (p. 1ff).

Scott O'Dell

B orn May 23, 1898, in Los Angeles, Calif; son of Bennett Mason (an official of the Union Pacific Railroad) and May Elizabeth (Gabriel) O'Dell. *Education:* Attended Occidental College, 1919, University of Wisconsin, 1920, Stanford University, 1920-21, and University of Rome, 1925. *Home:* Westchester County, N.Y. *Agent:* Harriet Wasserman, 137 East 36th St., New York, N.Y. 10016. *Office:* c/o Houghton Mifflin Co., 2 Park St., Boston, Mass. 02108.

■ Career

Formerly worked as a technical director for Paramount, and as a cameraman for Metro-Goldwyn-Mayer, a citrus rancher, taught a mail-order course in photoplay writing, book columnist for the *Los Angeles Mirror,* and book editor for the *Los Angeles Daily News,* 1947-55; full-time writer, 1934—. *Military service:* U.S. Air Force, 1942-43. *Member:* Authors Guild.

■ Awards, Honors

Rupert Hughes Award, 1960, John Newbery Medal from the American Library Association, Lewis Carroll Shelf Award, and Southern California Council on Literature for Children and Young People Notable Book Award, all 1961, Hans Christian Andersen Award of Merit from the International Board on Books for Young People, 1962, William Allen White Award, and German Juvenile International Award, both 1963, Nene Award from the Hawaii Library Association, 1964, and OMAR Award, 1985, all for *Island of the Blue Dolphins;* Newbery Honor Book, 1967, and German Juvenile International Award, 1968, both for *The King's Fifth;* Newbery Honor Book, 1968, for *The Black Pearl,* and 1971, for *Sing Down the Moon;* Hans Christian Andersen Medal, 1972, for his body of work.

Sing Down the Moon was selected one of Child Study Association of America's Children's Books of the Year, 1970, *The Treasure of Topo-el-Bampo,* 1972, *Child of Fire,* 1974, *The Hawk That Dare Not Hunt by Day,* 1975, and *Zia,* and *The 290,* both 1976; *Freedoms Foundation Award, 1973, for Sing Down the Moon; Child of Fire* was selected one of *New York Times* Outstanding Books, 1974; University of Southern Mississippi Medallion, 1976; Regina Medal from the Catholic Library Association, 1978, for his body of work; *Focal* Award from the Los Angeles Public Library, 1981, for excellence in creative work that enriches a child's understanding of California; Parents Choice Award for Literature from the Parents Choice Foundation, 1984, for *Alexandra,* and 1986, for *Streams to the River, River to the Sea;* Scott O'Dell Award for Historical Fiction, 1986, and one of Child Study Association of America's Children's Books of the Year, 1987, both for *Streams to the River, River to the Sea.*

■ Writings

Representative Photoplays Analyzed: Modern Authorship, Palmer Institute of Authorship, 1924.

Woman of Spain: A Story of Old California (novel), Houghton, 1934.

Hill of the Hawk (novel), Bobbs-Merill, 1947.

(With William Doyle) *Man Alone*, Bobbs-Merrill, 1953, published in England as *Lifer*, Longmans, 1954.

Country of the Sun, Southern California: An Informal History and Guide, Crowell, 1957.

The Sea Is Red: A Novel, Holt, 1958.

Island of the Blue Dolphins (ALA Notable Book), Houghton, 1960, large print edition, Isis, 1987.

The King's Fifth (*Horn Book* honor list; illustrated by Samuel Bryant), Houghton, 1966.

The Black Pearl (ALA Notable Book; *Horn Book* honor list; illustrated by Milton Johnson), Houghton, 1967.

(With Rhoda Kellogg) *The Psychology of Children's Art*, Communications Research Machines, 1967.

The Dark Canoe (illustrated by M. Johnson), Houghton, 1968.

Journey to Jericho (illustrated by Leonard Weisgard), Houghton, 1969.

Sing Down the Moon (ALA Notable Book; *Horn Book* honor list), Houghton, 1970.

The Treasure of Topo-el-Bampo, (illustrated by Lynd Ward), Houghton, 1972.

The Cruise of the Arctic Star (illustrated by S. Bryant), Houghton, 1973, large print edition, G. K. Hall, 1976.

Child of Fire (ALA Notable Book), Houghton, 1974.

The Hawk That Dare Not Hunt by Day, Houghton, 1975.

Zia (ALA Notable Book; illustrated by Ted Lewin), Houghton, 1976, British edition (illustrated by S. Reynolds), Oxford University Press, 1977.

The 290, Houghton, 1976.

Carlota, Houghton, 1977, British edition published as *The Daughter of Don Saturnino*, Oxford University Press, 1979.

Kathleen, Please Come Home, Houghton, 1978.

The Captive, Houghton, 1979.

Sarah Bishop, Houghton, 1980.

The Feathered Serpent, Houghton, 1981.

The Spanish Smile, Houghton, 1982. *The Castle in the Sea*, Houghton, 1983. *The Amethyst Ring*, Houghton, 1983.

Alexandra, Houghton, 1984.

The Road to Damietta, Houghton, 1985.

Streams to the River, River to the Sea: A Novel of Sacagawea, Houghton, 1986.

The Serpent Never Sleeps: A Novel of Jamestown and Pocahontas (illustrated by T. Lewin), Houghton, 1987.

Black Star, Bright Dawn, Houghton, 1988.

My Name Is Not Angelica, Houghton, 1989.

Contributor to periodicals, including *Mirror News* (Los Angeles), *Fortnight, Independent* (San Diego), and *Saturday Review*.

■ Adaptations

Motion Pictures:

"Island of the Blue Dolphins," Universal, 1964.

"The Black Pearl," Diamond Films, 1976.

Cassettes; Records; Filmstrips With Cassettes:

"Island of the Blue Dolphins" (cassette; filmstrip with cassette), Pied Piper Productions.

"Island of the Blue Dolphins: An Introduction" (filmstrip), Teaching Films, 1965.

"The Black Pearl" (record; cassette; filmstrip with cassette), Miller-Brody, 1974.

"Sing Down the Moon" (record; cassette; filmstrip with cassette), Miller-Brody, 1975.

"The King's Fifth" (record; cassette; filmstrip with cassette), Miller-Brody, 1976.

"Child of Fire" (cassette; record), Miller-Brody, 1976, (filmstrip with cassette), Random House, 1979.

"Zia" (cassette; record), Miller-Brody, 1977, (filmstrip with cassette), Random House, 1982.

Island of the Blue Dolphins, The Black Pearl, The Dark Canoe, and *The King's Fifth* are available in Braille. *Island of the Blue Dolphins, The King's Fifth, Child of Fire, The Cruise of the Arctic Star, Sing Down the Moon*, and *Zia* are available as talking books.

■ Work In Progress

Paradise Cove, a contemporary story about dolphins at a training center.

■ Sidelights

May 23, 1898. Born on Terminal Island, Los Angeles, California, to May Elizabeth Gabriel and Bennett Mason O'Dell, an official of the Union Pacific Railroad, O'Dell's great-grandmother was a first cousin of the Scottish novelist Sir Walter Scott (1771-1832). "Los Angeles was a frontier town when I was born there around the turn of the century. It had more horses than automobiles, more jack rabbits than people. The very first sound I remember was a wildcat scratching on the roof as I lay in bed.

"My father was a railroad man so we moved a lot, but never far. Wherever we went, it was into frontier country like Los Angeles. There was San Pedro, which is a part of Los Angeles. And Rattlesnake Island, across the bay from San Pedro, where we lived in a house on stilts and the waves came up and washed under us every day. And sailing ships went by.

"That is why, I suppose, the feel of the frontier and the sound of the sea are in my books."[1]

"[We also moved] to Claremont, just east of Los Angeles, to the foot of Mount Baldy—sagebrush country where descendants of the first Spanish settlers lived. And to Julian, an old gold-mining town southeast of Los Angeles on the Mexican border, in the heart of the Oriflamme Mountains, the ancestral home of the Diegueno Indians.

"That is why...many of the people I have written about are Indians, Spaniards and Mexicans."[2]

"I was four years old and I had awakened out of a long sleep. The room was dark. The sea made faint sounds among the eaves, like mice stirring. From far off came the sound of waves breaking upon the beach. Though I listened, I heard nothing else.

"Lying there in my small bed, in the deep night, it suddenly came to me that the house was deserted, that I was alone. Quickly I slid to the floor and groped along the hall to my mother's room. I felt the bed. It was empty.

"At that instant I heard from a distance the sound of music. By some strange alchemy of love and fear and memory, standing there in the empty room, music and my mother became one. I would find her where the music was. They would be together.

"I tried to open the front door, but it was locked and the back door was locked too. Then I noticed that the window above the kitchen sink was open. I found a chair and climbed upon it and thus reached the window....I grasped the window sill, squirmed outside, hung for a moment, fell sprawling on the sand, and picked myself up.

"Now the music was clear on the summer air. Against the sky I could see the glow of colored lights. I ran toward it, falling in the deep sand and getting up, running again, shirttails dragging at my ankles.

"I came to a boardwalk. The walk led to a pavilion, to the source of the glowing lights, where clusters of people moved about. But the music was still farther, beyond them; and I went toward it, feeling my way through a forest of legs and a sea of dresses, to a place where couples drifted about.

"There on a platform above them was the music and below the platform, the lights shining on her, was my mother. Her back was toward me but I knew well the golden hair. With my last breath I ran across the floor, unaware of the eyes that must have been turned upon me. I stretched out my arms and clutched her dress and though she was whirling, held on. As she turned and stared down at this apparition in a nightshirt, at her son, I am forced to say that she was not so glad to see me as I was to see her.

"The human heart, lonely and in need of love, is a vessel which needs replenishing."[3]

Dust jacket from O'Dell's first young adult novel.

"...A boy of eight," O'Dell recalled he was "towheaded and restless, who with other boys of his age went out on Saturday mornings in sun or rain in search of the world.

"This was a small world, but a world in microcosm. It was bounded by the deep water and wharves and mud flats of San Pedro Harbor. By the cliffs and reefs of Point Firmin and Portuguese Bend. By the hills of Palos Verdes, aflame with wild mustard in spring, lion-colored in summer.

"Many summer days we left the landlocked world and went to sea. How? Each of us on a separate log. The logs had been towed into the harbor in great rafts—from Oregon. They were twelve feet long or longer, rough with splinters and covered with tar. But to each of us young Magellans, they were proud canoes, dugouts fashioned by ax and fire. Graceful, fierce-prowed, the equal of any storm.

"We freed them from the deep-water slips where they waited for the saw mill. Astride, paddling with our hands, we set to sea, to the breakwater and beyond. We returned hours later, the watery world encompassed.

"Many mornings we went into the Palos Verdes Hills. There we turned over every likely rock, looking for small monsters. We thrust our hands down every squirrel and coyote hole in our path. Commonly we found an owl. This was the prize of all prizes. It was twice the size of your fist, soft-feathered, with great yellow eyes that blinked in the sudden sun.

"What did we do with this creature of the nocturnal air? We killed it, of course. We wrung its neck. We cut off its legs. For the exposed tendons of an owl's legs, when pulled in a certain way, made the tiny claws open and retract in a ghastly simulation of life.

"To this day, indeed to this very minute, I remember these depredations with horror."[3]

O'Dell was educated at Long Beach Polytechnic High School, then attended Occidental College in Los Angeles, University of Wisconsin, and Stanford University. "Grammar and high school fascinated me, too. But not college....By this time I had my heart set upon writing. However, most of the courses I was forced to take to graduate had little to do with learning to write. So I forgot graduation and took only the courses I wanted—psychology, philosophy, history and English.

"I therefore have a sense of comradeship with the students of today. I agree with those who say that they feel like prisoners marching in lockstep toward some unknown goal. I agree that classes are often too large, for I remember a Stanford class in Shakespeare which numbered seventy-six, seventy-five of whom were girls. What can you learn about Shakespeare in such surroundings, even if you're a girl?"[1]

"...I had never learned to study—I hadn't the patience, ability or motivation to remember a textbook."[4]

After college O'Dell moved on to Hollywood and taught a mail-order course in photoplay writing.

During 1924 and 1925, O'Dell published *Representative Photoplays Analyzed by Scott O'Dell* and worked as a technical director with Paramount Motion Picture Studio. He then attended the University of Rome while working with Metro-Goldwyn-Mayer. "...I was a cameraman on the second company of the original motion picture of 'Ben Hur,' carrying the first Technicolor camera, made by hand at M.I.T., around the Roman countryside."[1]

After returning to Hollywood O'Dell worked as a book editor for the *Los Angeles Daily News* and as a book columnist for the *Los Angeles Mirror.*

In 1934 he published his first novel, *Woman of Spain: A Story of Old California.* It was inspired by the stories he had heard in the Spanish settlements in the Pomona Valley while working in his father's orange grove near Claremont. With its variegated geography and history, California became a major source of inspiration for O'Dell. "...From the north where the Klamath winds seaward through blue forests south to the sand and rocks and mesquite of the Mexican border, live the Californians. Here among productive orange groves is Riverside, originally a Spanish grant, the town itself founded and flavored by English remittance men and retired Colonial officers. A few miles away on a desert Indian reservation are the pagan sun-worshippers of Palm Springs. A few miles in the other direction is Claremont, home of the eager, thoughtful, and reverent, lush with Eastern greenery planted by missionaries home from Africa and China and the far seas. Here is a town eight thousand feet up in the mountains where the leading citizens are an ex-barmaid from Newcastle and her husband, a feudist from Tennessee. In the Pacific cove is a colony of Portuguese fishermen. In this sunny valley Italians who raise grapes and make wine. And the men of the oil fields. The lumbermen in a hundred camps. The miners who tunnel the Sierras, the Mojave, the Santa Rosas.

Jacket painting by Ruth Sanderson for O'Dell's 1983 novel.

The Mexicans who live on the fringes of most towns and cities. Hollywood. San Pedro and its tuna fleets. And, of course, the cities of Los Angeles and San Francisco."[5]

In 1960 *Island of the Blue Dolphins*, his first novel for young adults, was published. "Places I have known, creatures I have loved are in *Island of the Blue Dolphins*. The islands—San Nicolas, Santa Cruz, San Miguel, Catalina, Anacapa, Todos Santos, San Martin, the Coronados—seen at dawn and at sunset, in all weathers over many years. Dolphin and otter playing. A mother gull pushing her grown brood from the nest, watching them plummet a hundred feet into the sea, then flying down to herd them onto their new home, a rock safe from the tide.

"And finally there is Carolina, the Tarascan girl of sixteen, who lived on the shores of Lake Patzcuaro in central Mexico. She was one of nine children, the oldest daughter of Pedro Flores who took care

of the small quinta my wife and I had rented for the summer.

"Carolina, when she first came to work for us, wore a long red skirt of closely woven wool. As a bride her mother had received the gift of sixty yards of this red cloth from her betrothed, a custom of the Tarascans. With it, by winding it around and around her waist, she made a skirt. At night she used it as a blanket for herself and her husband, and later for their children, against the fierce cold of the mountains. For each girl child she cut lengths of the cloth and this in turn became a skirt. The red skirt, the *falda roja* which Carolina wore, came to her in this fashion. She wore it proudly, as a shield against the world, in the way Karana [the heroine of *Island of the Blue Dolphins*] wore the skirt of cormorant feathers. The two girls are much alike."[3]

"*Island of the Blue Dolphins* began in anger, anger at the hunters who invade the mountains where I live and who slaughter everything that creeps or walks or flies. This anger also was directed at myself, at the young man of many years ago, who thoughtlessly committed the same crimes against nature. . . .

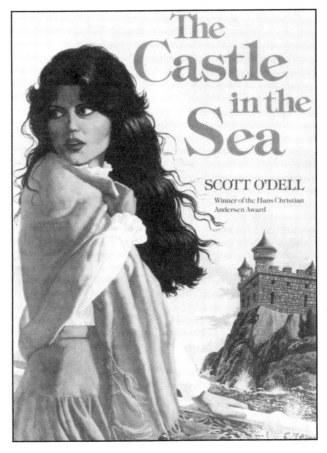

Dust jacket for the 1980 Houghton Mifflin edition.

"This horror, muted but nonetheless real, colours the latter part of the book and the latter part only, because my Indian girl began her life, as most children do, in the closed world of selfishness where everything—whether clothed in fur or feathers—was an object of indifferent cruelty.

"Through her I wished to say to the young and to all who wish to listen that we have a chance to come into a new relationship to the things around us. Once, in Defoe's day, we were cunning, manipulative children, living in a palace of nature. In her brief lifetime, she made the change from that world, where everything lived only to be exploited, into a humane and meaningful world. . . ."[6]

Island of the Blue Dolphins was adapted into a film by Universal in 1964.

In 1966, he published *The King's Fifth*, a tale of Conquistadors and Indians pitted against each other throughout much of Mexico and what is now the southwestern part of the United States during 1540-1541. Several Spaniards, infected by the lust for gold, set out with a Zuni girl as their guide and interpreter. Yet the treasure, once found, brings them nothing but grief. Finally, Esteban, the young narrator, is sentenced to three years for having thrown the gold into a sulphur pit without having given the king his fifth as required by law. "Certainly a lot [of research went into]. . .*The King's Fifth.* That was an overly ambitious book when I first started it. All the cities were allegorical cities. I woke up one morning and found that I was competing with Dante. So I quit that and started over."[7]

In 1967 *The King's Fifth* was a Newbery Honor Book, received the German Juvenile International Award, and Hawaii Library Association's Nene Award.

The Black Pearl, his third novel for young readers was based on a legend from Baja, California. It is the story of young Ramon, who finds the Pearl of Heaven in a lagoon believed to be the home of the great Devilfish. After the pearl has failed to buy divine protection from the Madonna for the fleet of Ramon's father, Ramon finally returns it to her as a gift of love. The book was a Newbery Honor Book and later adapted into a film.

1968. "Some years ago I wrote a story called *The Dark Canoe.* These three provocative words, as you remember, were spoken by Captain Ahab on board the whaler *Pequod* as he pursued through Pacific seas the monstrous White Whale, his implacable enemy, Moby Dick. . . .

"I liked Melville's *Moby Dick* when I first read it as a boy, for its story of a strange captain and crew and their adventurous fate. I liked it when I read it again as a young man, for the same reasons and for others as well—for one thing, the glimpse it gave me into the depths of the human heart. And later, reading it in maturity, these two readings of *Moby Dick* came to mind, but for the first time I began to see Melville's masterpiece for what it is—a fleshed-out symbol, a myth. It is a myth in the tradition of Pygmalion and Galatea, of stone-burdened Sisyphus, of Tantalus, of the ill-starred lovers Orpheus and Eurydice, in which man's feelings of terror at the mysteries of life—its lurking demonisms and its delights, man's most fervent hopes and secret desires—are given substance.

"Having read and thought about *Moby Dick* over many years, aware by returning to it from time to time with refreshed interest and new insights, which to me is the hallmark of a book's greatness, I was moved to write a story about Ahab's dark canoe.

"I was convinced, thinking of the story I wished to write, of the canoe's immortality. It lived in my mind. It therefore must live in the minds of others. And living, having floated Ishmael to safety, not yet finished with its appointed mission, where was it now? On what shores or ocean seas would I find it?

"I imagined it floating into Magdalena Bay in Baja California, still bearing the marks of the thirty life lines ending in thirty Turk's-head knots, put there by Ahab's carpenter.

"The plot of my story is conventional, but suspenseful enough, I hope, to hold a child's attention, to hold it long enough for the young reader to see and above all to feel what the story attempts to say.

"What I wished to say was both simple and many-leveled. It was this: The stories which have been written by great writers possess lives of their own. They live through the years and through the centuries. They are as substantial as mountains, more lasting than habitations. We know the odes of Sappho, for instance, but under what dust heap lies the place of her birth?"[8]

1969. Published *Journey to Jericho*, his first book for middle graders. "One of those summers my mother and I traveled across the country to visit an aunt and uncle who lived in a small coal-mining town in West Virginia. The miners with lamps on their caps, the blind mules that shoved the carts back and forth in the mine, the electric dolly that hauled the coal out of the mine and the small steam engine that pulled it away to the railroad tipple—all these things fascinated me. Remembering them and that long-ago summer, I wrote *Journey to Jericho*."[1]

1970-1972. Published *Sing Down the Moon*, a Newbery Honor Award book. "In 1961 I spent part of the summer in Navaho country, where the states of Arizona and New Mexico, Colorado and Utah meet. This story about Bright Morning and her flock of sheep is the result of those days among the Navahos. I think of it as a modest tribute not only to this Indian girl but also to the courage of the human spirit."[1]

"...The fact that this spirit happened to be in an Indian girl is really incidental. I'm not interested in the Navajos particularly—they're not my favorite tribe even. They were marauders—they rode in and took the crops of other Indians, after the harvest sometimes. But there was this thing that

Dust jacket from O'Dell's 1986 young adult novel.

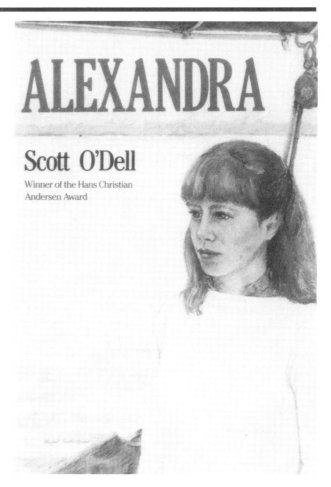

Hardcover jacket from the 1984 award-winning novel.

happened [in 1864] at the Canyon de Chelly. Carson and the government rounded up the Indians and drove them to Fort Sumner. The important thing was the story. If the story is a good story children will read it for the suspense, and you can use suspense to do things. In *Sing Down the Moon* I wanted to call children's attention to the fact that there are such things as endurance, as loyalty to your family, loyalty to the place where you live. Nowadays people are dispersed, can live anywhere they want to. That's the trouble here in California—we're just a bunch of uprooted people. You don't know your neighbor and he never speaks to you. But this Navajo girl—she did want to go back to where her family had lived and have a child and live in a cave on the side of the Canyon. Even though she knows her people were driven out, she still goes back and starts over again. I hope there's a lesson in this, an inspiration for children. It's very strong in me, this didactic, inspiration thing."[7]

The Treasure of Topo-el-Bampo published. Set during the late eighteenth century in Mexico's poorest mountain village near the country's richest silver mine, the story concerns two small donkeys who save the villagers from starvation when they return loaded with silver bars.

1973. Published *The Cruise of the Arctic Star*, which interweaves the author's experiences on a small-craft voyage from San Diego to Portland, episodes from California history, excerpts from books he loves, and information on marine ecology and seamanship.

1974. "...[*Child of Fire*] concerns five Chicano gangs and presents a problem that the ancestors of these boys met 400 years ago. Young Spaniards of the sixteenth-century, yearning for adventure, came to the Americas in search of gold. Their descendants, living in modern America, have the same desire for adventure, but no place to find it except in the world of drugs and pointless warfare. The Chicano, for all his proud heritage, is a prisoner of the *barrio*, a second-class citizen. *Child of Fire* deals with his problem, both realistically and symbolically and, I hope, with some understanding.

"...Though I don't think you'd find any evidence of it in my present writing, I have been influenced by [Joseph] Conrad. I was a great admirer of his for many years. What he did was more complex than I am able to handle....In *Child of Fire* I have a device which goes back to the Marlow situation in Conrad. I use a parole officer, in charge of fifty children, who tells the story of one particular boy. It has drawbacks of course, because you can only report what you have seen. I have a situation in which the boy leaves San Diego and goes on a tuna clipper to Ecuador, where there's a mutiny and where he's thrown in prison. In the end he escapes and gets back to San Diego. Well, he has to tell this story; there's no other way of getting it. It's not as dramatic as it would have been if the parole officer had gone with him, and so had been able to tell the story himself, like an omnipotent observer. But that was obviously impossible. So there are penalties."[7]

1975. Published *The Hawk That Dare Not Hunt by Day*. Set in England and western Europe in the first half of the sixteenth century, the novel tells about the tribulations of William Tyndale, the first Englishman to translate the Bible from Greek into the English vernacular. "I'm terribly interested in his story. He wanted every ploughboy to read the Bible as it came from the original Greek and Hebrew, not as it came from the Vulgate, and not as the priest read it in the pulpit. This is what Tyndale wanted to do, and this is what Tyndale

did—and he did it so beautifully that when the King James version came along they used 70 to 75 per cent of Tyndale in it. Today we speak Tyndale. It's extraordinary if you compare the passages he translated from the Greek with the same passages in the Latin. If you are really concerned with something it gets into the fabric of the story and is transmitted to the reader. That was D. H. Lawrence's feeling, and it's certainly one I share.

"I have only done things that I've been really enthusiastic about, stories that have stirred me. With Tyndale, and with this messianic quirk of mine, I feel that I am performing a mission; it may be a little grandiloquent to call it that, yet that is my feeling. Children speak the language, but they don't know where the hell it came from. They don't know whom to credit for it, and they certainly don't know Tyndale's story, how the man lived in attics and burrows and was pursued by spies all over Germany, Holland and Belgium, attempting to seize him and take him back to England. His Bible was smuggled into England. It had to be, because it was against the law to own it or read it. He very calmly gave up his life for this purpose. He was a hero."[7]

1976. *Zia*, a sequel to *Island of the Blue Dolphins* is set in 1853 at the Santa Barbara Mission in California. Fourteen-year-old Zia sets out on an adventurous journey to rescue her aunt, Karana, with whom she then spends a few happy weeks. Throughout the novel various episodes center around the mistreatment of Indians by Spaniards and Americans.

1979. Published *The Captive*, the first volume of a trilogy on Mayan, Aztec, and Incan civilizations. O'Dell had traveled to Central and South America. "I always visit a place I am going to write about. That gives me the true feeling of the locale, the weather, the land, the sky, the people who once lived there."[9]

1980. O'Dell now lives in Waccabuc, New York, with his second wife, Elizabeth Hall, an author of college textbooks and former editor-in-chief of *Human Nature* magazine. "There's a cave at the head of this lake. A small place where a young woman named Sarah Bishop lived during the Revolutionary War. I became interested in this girl. I began my research, but the only information was one short paragraph about her in a newspaper of the time when she died. I took that sparse information and created *Sarah Bishop*. I put fiction and fact together to create her. Sarah Bishop lives through me and my words."[9]

Celia Kaye starred in the 1965 Universal film "Island of the Blue Dolphins."

1981. Founded the annual Scott O'Dell Award for Historical Fiction, which carries a $5,000 prize. "This award is to encourage writers to write historical fiction, children to read historical fiction, and publishers to publish historical fiction.

"History has a very valid connection with what we are now. Many of my books are set in the past but the problems of isolation, moral decisions, greed, need for love and affection are problems of today as well. I am didactic; I do want to teach through books. Not heavy handedly but to provide a moral backdrop for readers to make their own decisions. After all, I come from a line of teachers and circuit riders going back two hundred years....

"Historical fiction has extreme value for children. Children have a strong feeling that they sprang full-grown from the forehead of Jove. Anything of the past is old hat. But no educated person, however, can live a complete life without a knowledge of where we come from. History has a direct bearing on children's lives."[9]

Published *The Feathered Serpent*, the second installment and *The Amethyst Ring*, the concluding volume in the trilogy on ancient America and its conquest by Spain.

1984. *Alexandra* is a contemporary novel set in Florida. It features a young woman who joins her grandfather's boat as a sponge diver. As before, O'Dell portrays a woman in an unconventional role. "I have been appalled by the status of women. Women have been treated as second-class citizens. I am diadactically in favor of the women's movement. The main character. . .is a typical young woman who does things men usually do. I am trying to show that women and men *do* have the same potential."[9]

1985. In *The Road to Damietta* sixteen-year-old Ricca tells the story of St. Francis of Assisi, whom she loves. The main historical event is the Fifth Crusade. "I can usually finish a book in six months or so, but I'm going to take a full year for St. Francis. I want to get it right, it's an important book. In it I'm going to make the strongest statement I can against war. It's simply dreadful the way the world is going. It's stupid!

"This book will deal with the futility of war, the immorality of war, and I'm going to make it as strong as I possibly can."[2]

"Writing is hard work. The only part of it I really enjoy is the research, which takes three or four months. . . .

"I write, when I do write, which is about half my time, from seven in the morning until noon, every day of the week. I use an electric typewriter, because when you turn it on it has a little purr that invites you to start writing instead of looking out the window. I sometimes use a pen and work very slowly. But I can write with anything and anywhere and have—in Spain and Italy, Germany and France and England and Mexico, in Rancho Santa Fe, a beautiful place in Southern California. . . .

"When I am not writing I like to read and to work in the sun. I like to garden, to plant trees of all kinds, to be on the sea, fishing some, watching the weather, the sea birds, the whales moving north and south with the seasons, the dolphins, and all the life of the changing waters."[1]

According to his publisher, Houghton Mifflin, O'Dell receives over 2,000 letters a year from readers. "There are, of course, a few letters that you would never miss. The letter, for example, from the girl in Minnesota who wrote, asking a dozen or more questions. To have answered them all would have taken two hours, which I didn't have. After a week or so, when she failed to hear from me, she wrote again. She said among other things: '. . .if I don't get a reply from you in five days I will send a letter to another author I know. Anyway, I like her books better than yours.'

"In their letters children ask dozens of questions. Some are personal, like 'How much money do you make?' but mostly they want to know how you work, how stories are put together, how long it takes to write a story, and what is the most important thing a writer should have."[1]

At 86, O'Dell reflected about old age: "I look over the lake and realize I'm living on borrowed time. I tell myself this is a wonderful place to live, and then I sometimes realize it may be the last time I'll see the seasons change; this may be my last winter. It's quite sobering.

"Also, at this age I seem to have nagging memories. I try to fight them, I try not to live in the past. I try not to dwell on them. It's a bottomless pit, living in the past. I'll remember things I did that I shouldn't have done, or things I should have done that I didn't do. I think of some of the relationships that would be very simple for me now, I'd understand them better. My father and I were not very close, for whatever reason. He would never confide in me, he was interested in me only superficially. And yet, if he were here today I believe we'd have a lot in common.

"It isn't self-pity that overcomes me. It's a sense of deep regret. It's not a depression, more of an aggravated melancholy. I get over it as fast as I can!

"Older people lose their rough spots. They've seen so many instances of petty quarrels. For example, I'm now more careful about what I say. I try to understand people better, and as a rule end up understanding them more than I want to."[2]

Footnote Sources:

[1] Scott O'Dell, publicity from Houghton.
[2] Allen Raymond, "A Visit with Scott O'Dell, Master Storyteller," *Early Years*, March, 1984.
[3] S. O'Dell, "Newbery Award Acceptance," *Horn Book*, August, 1961.
[4] Conrad Wesselhoeft, "*Blue Dolphins* Author Tells Why He Writes for Children," *New York Times*, April 15, 1984.
[5] S. O'Dell, "An Embarrassing Plenty," *Saturday Review*, October 30, 1943.
[6] S. O'Dell, *Psychology Today*, January, 1968.
[7] Justin Wintle and Emma Fisher, *The Pied Pipers: Interviews with the Influential Creators of Children's Literature*, Paddington Press, 1974.
[8] S. O'Dell, "Acceptance Speech: Hans Christian Andersen Award," *Horn Book*, October, 1972.
[9] Peter Roop, "Profile: Scott O'Dell," *Language Arts*, November, 1984.

■ For More Information See

New York Times Book Review, October, 1947 (p. 8), March 25, 1973 (p. 8), February 22, 1976 (p. 18), February 24, 1980 (p. 33), May 4, 1980 (p. 26), January 10, 1986 (p. 26).
Harry Warfel, *American Novelists of Today*, American Book, 1951.

Horn Book, April, 1960, December, 1974 (p. 695ff), June, 1976 (p. 291ff), April, 1977 (p. 160ff), April, 1982 (p. 137ff), June, 1983 (p. 315), February, 1984 (p. 94ff), September-October, 1986 (p. 599).

Chicago Sunday Tribune, May 8, 1960.

New York Herald Tribune Book Review, May 8, 1960.

San Francisco Chronicle, May 8, 1960.

Scott O'Dell, "Author's Note," *Island of the Blue Dolphins,* Houghton, 1960.

Library Journal, March 15, 1961 (p. 116ff).

Publishers Weekly, March 20, 1961 (p. 28ff), November 15, 1971 (p. 21), September 11, 1981 (p. 29).

American Library Assocation Bulletin, April, 1961 (p. 359).

Elementary English, October, 1961 (p. 373ff), April, 1975 (p. 442ff).

Wilson Library Bulletin, December, 1961 (p. 325).

Muriel Fuller, editor, *More Junior Authors,* H. W. Wilson, 1961.

John Rowe Townsend, *Written for Children: An Outline of English Language Children's Literature,* Lippincott, 1965.

Lee Kingman, editor, *Newbery and Caldecott Medal Books 1956-1965,* Horn Book, 1965.

Cornelia Meigs, editor, *A Critical History of Children's Literature,* Macmillan, 1969.

Constantine Georgiou, *Children and Their Literature,* Prentice-Hall, 1969.

J. R. Townsend, *A Sense of Story: Essays on Contemporary Writers for Children,* Lippincott, 1971.

Martha E. Ward and Dorothy A. Marquardt, *Authors of Books for Young People,* 2nd edition, Scarecrow, 1971.

Miriam Hoffman and Eva Samuels, *Authors and Illustrators of Children's Books,* Bowker, 1972.

American Libraries, June, 1973 (p. 356ff).

Author's Choice 2, Crowell, 1974.

"Meet the Newbery Author: Scott O'Dell" (filmstrip with record or cassette), Miller-Brody, 1974.

"Scott O'Dell" (videotape), Profiles in Literature, Temple University, 1976.

Children's Literature Review, Gale, Volume 1, 1976, Volume 16, 1989.

Catholic Library World, March, 1978 (p. 340ff).

D. L. Kirkpatrick, editor, *Twentieth-Century Children's Writers,* St. Martin's, 1978.

Washington Post Book World, March 9, 1980 (p. 7), January 9, 1983 (p. 11ff).

Jim Roginski, compiler, *Newbery and Caldecott Medalists and Honor Book Winners,* Libraries Unlimited, 1982.

Linda Kauffman Peterson and Marilyn Leathers Solt, *Newbery and Caldecott Medal and Honor Books, an Annotated Bibliography,* G. K. Hall, 1982.

Contemporary Authors, New Revision Series, Volume 12, Gale, 1984.

Contemporary Literary Criticism, Volume 30, Gale, 1984.

English Journal, April, 1984 (p. 69ff).

"A Visit with Scott O'Dell" (videotape), Houghton, 1986.

Dictionary of Literary Biography, Volume 52, Gale, 1986.

Collections:

De Grummond Collection at the University of Southern Mississippi.

Free Library of Philadelphia, Pennsylvania.

University of Oregon Library, Eugene.

Robert Newton Peck

B orn February 17, 1928, in Vermont; son of F. Haven (a farmer) and Lucile Peck; married Dorothy Houston (a librarian and painter), 1958; children: Christopher Haven, Anne Houston. *Education:* Rollins College, A.B., 1953; attended Cornell University. *Religion:* Protestant. *Home:* 500 Sweetwater Club Circle, Longwood, Fla. 32779.

■ Career

Author. Director of Rollins College Writers Conference, 1978—. *Military service:* U.S. Army, Infantry, 1945-47; served with 88th Division in Italy, Germany, and France.

■ Awards, Honors

Book World's Children's Spring Book Festival Award Honor Book, 1973, *Media & Methods* Award (paperback), and one of American Library Association's Best Books for Young Adults, both 1975, Colorado Children's Book Award from the University of Colorado, 1977, and one of New York Public Library's Books for the Teen Age, 1980, and 1981, all for *A Day No Pigs Would Die*; *Millie's Boy* was selected one of *New York Times*

Outstanding Books, 1973; *Millie's Boy* was selected one of Child Study Association of America's Children's Books of the Year, 1973, *Bee Tree and Other Stuff*, 1975, *Hamilton*, 1976, and *Soup on Ice*, 1987. *Hang for Treason* was selected one of New York Public Library's Books for the Teen Age, 1980, 1981, and 1982, and *Clunie*, 1980, and 1982; Mark Twain Award, 1981, for *Soup for President; Justice Lion* was selected a Notable Children's Trade Book in the Field of Social Studies by the National Council for Social Studies and the Children's Book Council, 1982, and *Spanish Hoof*, 1986; Michigan Young Readers Award from the Michigan Council of Teachers, 1984, for *Soup; Spanish Hoof* was exhibited at the Bologna International Children's Book Fair, 1985.

■ Writings

A Day No Pigs Would Die (ALA Notable Book), Knopf, 1972.
Millie's Boy, Knopf, 1973.
Soup (illustrated by Charles Gehm), Knopf, 1974.
Fawn, Little, Brown, 1975.
Wild Cat (illustrated by Hal Frenck), Holiday House, 1975.
Bee Tree and Other Stuff (poems; illustrated by Laura Lydecker), Walker, 1975.
Soup and Me (illustrated by Charles Lilly), Knopf, 1975.
Hamilton (illustrated by L. Lydecker), Little, Brown, 1976.
Hang for Treason, Doubleday, 1976.

Rabbits and Redcoats (illustrated by L. Lydecker), Walker, 1976.

King of Kazoo (musical; illustrated by William Bryan Park), Knopf, 1976.

Trig (illustrated by Pamela Johnson), Little, Brown, 1977.

Last Sunday (illustrated by Ben Stahl), Doubleday, 1977.

The King's Iron, Little, Brown, 1977.

Patooie (illustrated by Ted Lewin), Knopf, 1977.

Soup for President (illustrated by T. Lewin), Knopf, 1978.

Eagle Fur, Knopf, 1978.

Trig Sees Red (illustrated by P. Johnson), Little, Brown, 1978.

Basket Case, Doubleday, 1979.

Hub (illustrated by T. Lewin), Knopf, 1979.

Mr. Little (illustrated by B. Stahl), Doubleday, 1979.

Clunie, Knopf, 1979.

Soup's Drum (illustrated by Charles Robinson), Knopf, 1980.

Trig Goes Ape (illustrated by P. Johnson), Little, Brown, 1980.

Kirk's Law, Doubleday, 1981.

Justice Lion, Little, Brown, 1981.

Soup on Wheels (illustrated by C. Robinson), Knopf, 1981.

Banjo (illustrated by Andrew Glass), Knopf, 1982.

Trig or Treat (illustrated by P. Johnson), Little, Brown, 1982.

The Seminole Seed, Pineapple Press, 1983.

Soup in the Saddle (illustrated by C. Robinson), Knopf, 1983.

Dukes, Pineapple Press, 1984.

Soup's Goat (illustrated by C. Robinson), Knopf, 1984.

Spanish Hoof, Knopf, 1985.

Jo Silver, Pineapple Press, 1985.

Soup on Ice (illustrated by C. Robinson), Knopf, 1985.

Soup on Fire (illustrated by C. Robinson), Delacorte, 1987.

Soup's Uncle (illustrated by C. Robinson), Delacorte, 1988.

The Horse Hunters, Random House, 1988.

Hallapoosa, Walker, 1988.

Arly, Walker, 1989.

Soup's Hoop, Delacorte, 1990.

Nonfiction:

Path of Hunters: Animal Struggle in a Meadow (illustrated by Betty Fraser), Knopf, 1973.

Secrets of Successful Fiction, Writer's Digest, 1980.

Fiction Is Folks: How to Create Unforgettable Characters, Writer's Digest, 1983.

My Vermont, Peck Press, 1985.

My Vermont II, Peck Press, 1988.

■ **Adaptations**

"Soup" (teleplay), ABC-TV, 1978.

"Soup and Me" (Afterschool Special), ABC-TV, February 4, 1978.

"Soup for President" (Afterschool Special), November 18, 1978.

"A Day No Pigs Would Die" (cassette), Listening Library.

■ **Sidelights**

"I am tall, and awkward, and [a] stubborn Vermonter who wears mule-ear boots, a ten-gallon hat and what I like to think of as a country-boy grin.

"My favorite sport is curling; I play piano honky-tonk style; I'm a rotten dancer and I'm allergic to English walnuts. My speaking voice is about as melodic as a train wreck, but I do sing in a barbershop quartet."[1]

"Not surprising, as so many of my books feature a simple song or two which I've composed. I play self-taught ragtime piano, by ear, sometimes by fingers. To get raised as an uproader country boy means you've been treated to a spate of toe-tapping tunes.

"Music enters a child's *soul*, not his mind. It enters through an ear, not an eye. Even today, a sheet of music looks to me about as easy to savvy as a page in the Tokyo phonebook.

"Some of the most spiritual and rewarding moments of my fun-packed life occurred when I sang *lead* in three barbershop quartets. A lead singer has to snarl out the most authoritative part, and he's also usually the best looking. *Names* of barbershop quartets are always fun. We were the Humbugs, the Deep Throats, and the Broadjumpers.

"We were beer, cigars, outrageous macho jokes, and best of all, *buddies*...."[2]

"Socially, I'm about as sophisticated as a turnip...."[3]

"...I love our USA. I'm the corniest flag-waving patriot ever to skip along the pike. If you can't find scores of things, and folks, to admire in these United States, then perhaps loving is beyond your reach and grasp.

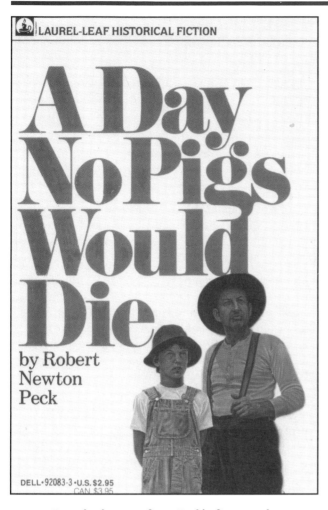

LAUREL-LEAF HISTORICAL FICTION

A Day No Pigs Would Die

by Robert Newton Peck

DELL•92083-3•U.S. $2.95
CAN $3.95

Paperback cover from Peck's first novel.

"My three morning rules are these: Up at 6:00, breakfast at 6:15, and at 6:30...back to bed. But come to think about it, my life has been mostly work. I was a mite too busy for hopes, prayers, or dreams. So here's my personal motto.

"Wish not for apples. Grow strong trees."[2]

Robert Newton Peck, son of F. Haven and Lucile Peck, was born in Vermont on February 17, 1928. As Peck's father was a farmer who earned his living butchering hogs, Peck's childhood memories of his encounters with nature figure prominently in his writing. "Farmers are the hardest-working people I know. Also the healthiest and happiest. Maybe there's a connection.

"Most of my wisdom (what little I have) was given to me by a mother, a father, an aunt and a grandmother...none of whom could read or write."[2]

"I have only to examine the ghosts of my boyhood, again to hear the scoldings and the wisdom, and my heart is moved by memory. My parents were Plain People, quiet farmer folk who led almost silent lives. However, when they spoke, we youngsters listened up proper. Perhaps because Papa and Mama spoke only when their thinking deserved words.

"Growing up on a farm, as I did, a kid doesn't really have to ask a bunch of dumb questions about Right or Wrong. Luckily, it's all there to see, to feel, and to tend.

"...Unnecessary chatter was considered frivolity. Still, I asked pesky questions, as kids do; and was told by Mama, Papa, Aunt Carrie, or my grandmother, to open my eyes and look.

"They promised I'd understand.

"Natural Law exists, and *acts*, so powerfully that it makes civil or canon law appear, by comparison, a tad flimsy. 'Obey!' our governments and churches warn, or you'll land in Hell or Sing Sing.

"...Nature's Law does not threaten. Instead, it *acts*.

"Furthermore, it acts unencumbered by human whim or will. It merely behaves, without morality. The strong seagull snatches a fish from the beak of a weaker gull. A tall oak will spread her branches upward, her roots below, taking sunlight and water and nourishment from lesser trees.

"Until a tempest topples her.

"My grandmother, when I was a tadpole, led me to a pine. Reaching upward, she pulled a normal clump of five needles in order to place it upon the five fingers of my small hand. Grandmother pointed to the tree, then to me, so I would forever know that we are brothers."[4]

Coming from an uneducated family, Peck was the first to learn to read and write. "...Miss Kelly...taught first, second, third, fourth, fifth, and sixth in a tumble-down, one-room, dirt-road school in rural Vermont.

"She believed in scholarship, manners, and soap.

"But more, she believed in *me*. In all of us, telling us that in America you don't have to be what you're born....My father...[did]...hard work, but he was a harder man. Like all hard men, he was kind, quiet, and gentle. I wanted to be like Papa, yet I wasn't sure I'd grow up only to kill hogs.

"'Robert,' said Miss Kelly, 'perhaps you'll surprise us all, and amount to something.'

"It was years later when somebody pointed to a large building and said, 'That's a library.'

"I didn't believe it, because in Miss Kelly's little one-room school, we all knew what a library was. Not a building. It was a *board!* A three-foot-long shelf in the corner, a plank, upon which sat our few precious worn-out books. According to custom, we washed our hands before touching them.

"So there we sat in her school, soldier straight, learning about people like Mark Twain and Calvin Coolidge, and Ty Cobb and Charles Lindbergh and Booker T. Washington.

"We were the sons and daughters of illiterate farmers, millworkers, and lumberjacks. Some of the folks, in town, called us uproaders. And we called *them* downhillers. But I knew they could do what I had me an itch to do.

"They could *read.*

"Sometimes, at home, a learned scholar would stop by, and he was always asked, following supper, to read to our family. There was only one book in our mountain home. It was black and large, yet we never referred to it as our Bible. It was known only as The Book.

"Then, after I'd fetched it, the clerk of the local feed store in town (if he happened to be our guest) would read to us. Mama's usual favorite was Isaiah, especially the part about swords into plowshares and spears into pruning hooks.

"We listened.

"The grown-up people nodded their heads, as if absorbing and agreeing with whatever verses were being read....

"At school...Miss Kelly read to us by the hour. She gave us *Tom Sawyer* and *The Wind in the Willows* and *Ivanhoe,* in an effort to lead us from the bondage of ignorance and poverty.

"She earned her thirteen dollars a week.

"I was the youngest of seven children, yet the first to attend any school. Papa and Mama had opposed my going. Yet when I finally introduced Papa to Miss Kelly, initially he said nothing. But he took off his hat.

"'Thank you,' Miss Kelly told my father, 'for giving me Robert. I shall try to be deserving of your trust.'

"'We hope he's got manners,' Papa told her with a straight face. 'And whatever he breaks, we'll pay for.'"[2]

"Every child hikes to a fork in the trail.

"Is it a wee eating fork, made of white plastic, and discarded by a littering picnicker? Oddly enough, no.

"As I see it, the fork is a choice between books or no books. I was lucky [that] Miss Kelly...was my...teacher....

"The most noble job in the world is being a teacher. A good one has to believe in himself, get kids to believe in him, then to believe in themselves.

"Miss Kelly once told us...that teachers are akin to farmers. Because a farmer gets up and goes to his garden; but she then added, she was more fortunate, as her garden came to her...."[5]

"She died at age ninety-seven. For me, this was difficult to believe, because when we were her pupils...[we] suspected that Miss Kelly was at least 144. I am most thankful that she lived to share in my success as a writer. I've dedicated more than one book to her, and she became almost as proud of me as I will ever be of her."[2]

"As I see it, an author turns his furrow and sows his seed somewhere between a farm and a school. A lot of my characters are teachers—all of whom are strong, fair, and respected....

"Perhaps my books shall, if worthy enough, become [Miss Kelly's] monument...."[5]

Peck's first successful story, *A Day No Pigs Would Die,* is a semi-autobiographical tale of his family and his childhood on the farm. "I wrote *A Day No Pigs Would Die* in twenty-one days. I had always wanted to write about my father but needed a way to bring the story-line into focus. I finally realized that 'the pig' was it; it allowed me to bring out his honor and decency and special kind of sophistication. He was so knowledgeable about relationships in the natural order and he accepted life for what it is—understanding its violence and its beauty. If I had to describe what PIGS mean to me I guess I think of it as the Bar Mitzvah of a gentile boy—and it also seems to be a little core of truth about living things."[1]

"You have only to read *A Day No Pigs Would Die* to know that my father's ghost will follow me forever. No, that's wrong. He will lead me. Haven Peck, like an honestly sweating Vermont plow, was worth following. His share still swims like quicksilver and knifes through a mud of trouble.

"My father...once told me this: 'It matters not what a man's religion is unless his dog and cat are the better for it.'

Charles Robinson's illustration for the softbound edition.

Paperback cover for the third book in the "Soup" series.

"As a writer, I believe that a professional way to show a character in a book is to allow the reader a look at, for example, a farmer tending his stock. It's my guess that a great deal of the success of my first novel, *A Day No Pigs Would Die*, stems from its intimate human-animal contact."[4]

"Basically, I am still a Vermont farmer.

"I can't con readers that bacon is made by duPont out of soybeans. Killing hogs is honest work. My father did it. So did I. One time, at a cocktail party, I watched people ram goose liver into their maws and then announce how opposed they all were to violence. My, how Papa would have darn near smiled."[5]

In 1958, Peck married a woman equally interested in books. "...I wed my favorite librarian. Dorrie (MLS, Columbia University). Who was my best man? Fred Rogers, better known as the famous 'Mister Rogers' on TV. He's a super guy and we disagree about everything. We will always be pals.

"Dorrie and I have two children.

"Christopher Haven Peck...and Ann Houston Peck....I hope they both grow up to have a tough gut and a gentle heart. Because I don't want to sire a world of macho men or feminist women, but rather a less strident society of ladies and gentlemen."[5]

1973. Peck's second book, *Path of Hunters: Animal Struggle in a Meadow*, published. "Respect for living creatures led to *Path of Hunters*, which examines the poetic yet brutal life and death struggle for survival among small animals in a meadow."[3]

"I'm sometimes frightened by a feeling that we're raising whole generations of kids who lack... awareness....They don't seem sensitive to the life all around them; their eyes don't seem to see what goes on within nature. Most of them seem to think that pork chops are made out of soybeans behind the counter at the supermarket. This feeling, more

Jacket for the 1975 novel.

than any other, led me to *Path of Hunters*. In examining the excitement of the life and death struggles for survival among small animals I hoped that some readers' eyes would be opened to the brutal truths of nature and all of its beauty."[1]

Peck has become known for the realism he employs when describing the often-brutal relationships between animals in the wild. Reviewer Edith C. Howley said of *Path of Hunters*, "Children accustomed to the charm of puppies and kittens and with the general concept of animals as furry, if not cuddly, friends going gently about their quaint business in the calm and peace of the country landscape will be jolted into another world if they read *Path of Hunters*. Here, in all its savage violence, is the bloodstained tapestry of life and death as the hunter in turn becomes the hunted.

"Birth, hunger and death are the main threads woven inexorably into that pattern called, euphemistically, the balance of nature. The writing is direct and compelling. The visit to the pet shop will never be quite the same again, and the awareness of the harsh reality beneath the quiet of the meadow will not easily be lost."[6]

A critic for the *Christian Science Monitor* said of *A Day No Pigs Would Die:* "In showing just how earthy farm life is and how stoic a farmer and his children must be Mr. Peck spares us nothing. Vivid animal mating scenes, butcherings, a cruel economy that forces a boy to help slaughter his beloved pig and his father to insist that he does—we get the lot."[7]

In response to the sometimes negative criticism of his realistic descriptions, Peck commented, "As a Vermont redneck author, I get tired of urbane reviewers....We farmers lead a physical life ....Yet we performed our work without hatred or vitriol...."[7]

Nature figures prominently in much of his work, and his concern for the animal kingdom is as pronounced as his belief in the necessity of working the land with your hands. "...*Work* is a solid thing to believe in. Vermonters usually do. Granite folk on granite land. Much like their statues in village squares, they are the granite sentries of liberty, standing free.

"Sure, I remember the guys I played on teams with, and drank beer with, and sang with...but I don't guess I remember them any more fondly than the men I *worked* alongside. Farmers, lumberjacks, old woodhooks at a paper mill, men I helped slaughter hogs, and fellow soldiers when I was a seventeen-year-old private overseas in the U.S. Army.

"These special people, so many of them unschooled, sit upon an honored throne in my heart.

"In later years, I worked as an advertising executive in New York City, with people whose hands were always clean. Yet sometimes, their mouths, deeds, and souls were so filthy. They frittered away their hours in bars and fancy restaurants, and frittered their money on an analyst's couch. Why? Because they somehow suspected that what they did for a living served no righful purpose. Their work built nothing. Fed no one."[2]

Peck's advice to future writers is this: "...Before you try to become a *novelist,* become a *naturalist.*

"Mother God has something to teach us all; and, like so many precious and holy things on our green and blue marble, Her lessons are entirely free. No tuition. No tepid textbooks, like the one you're now holding, written by the hand of some arrogant author who thinks *he* gave himself all of his gifts.

"Make a meadow your classroom. Go at night, because the darkness is Nature's dramatic stage.

Most animal life is nocturnal. Watch and learn; and cast aside the limp lessons given to you by fools like me.

"Why study Nature? To create characters who behave, in your pages, as real human beings, and only by the fervent study of stream and forest, and sky, will you discover exactly who you are. An analyst's couch won't point the way. Yet a child's arm, which points upward at a rainbow, will.

"Humankind looked into a starlit sky long before it saw a library reference room or a computer printout. Empty yourself of thought, to be filled by soul. And, as your neck begins to ache from stargazing, if you feel like it, cry...."[4]

1979. *Clunie*, story of a retarded girl, published. "...I dedicated the book to kids who can never read it, hoping that the kids who can will care."[5]

"It was a difficult book to write because I had to attempt to be not only a female but also a retarded teenage girl. I took several trips to a home for retarded children and observed them, day after day, as they tried to work or play or feed themselves.

"One particular young lady looked at me and smiled a chubby smile. Her shoe was untied. So I approached her very slowly, quietly, and then did a strange thing. Bending down, I untied my own shoe. I let her watch me as I retied it. Then I retied hers.

"That's all it took. She followed me everywhere I went as my shadow. And cried when I, out of necessity, went to the men's room.

"One day I brought a camera and took her picture.

"What she liked best was when I played the home's beat up piano. As I played, she sang. Not in words. Only noises. But whenever I'd stop playing to listen to her, she would stop. Then we would both laugh at each other. It became a game. It was one of the few areas in which this pathetic and wonderful girl manifested any intelligence.

"She talked but made no sense.

"I liked her, even though it would be hard to explain exactly why. It was somehow more than pity. Perhaps we all tend to warm to people who like us. She liked me. It was truly an honor, like when I won the Mark Twain Award. It was a genuine thrill.

"At night, after coming home from visiting her, I would lie awake and pretend that I was a retarded girl who had a very tall friend named Rob who played a piano for me.

"I did one other thing.

"Wearing a pair of heavy ski mittens, I tried to dress myself, eat, and play the piano. Not in front of her. These acts I performed in my own home, when alone. Our maid, who caught me at it, probably thought I was nuts. She was correct. Because, mittens and all, I was actually acting retarded.

"The female part was hardest. I tried wearing a long wig and brushed my false hair. It didn't help much.

"What helped was giving that special child a hug, a song, and a laugh. Merely allowing her simple and female thoughts to touch me as though I were not her special gentleman caller, but rather her sister, who cared. I decided that what I really wanted, and finally discovered, was the little girl inside me who wanted to please another child.

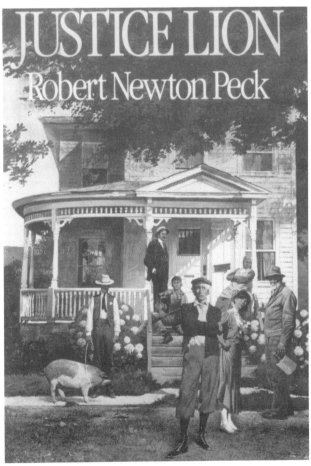

Dust jacket from the Little, Brown edition.

"To conclude, I believe that all humans are, inside, half male and half female. You are a product of a mother and a father, so it makes sense. God's plan.

"If you are a big strapper of a man, and you deeply love a woman, you can perhaps best show your love by being, in quiet and private moments, the *sister* that she always wished she had.

"Therefore, it is not surprising that both male and female characters, and characteristics, lie dormant inside you, waiting to be released upon your pages. This is my philosophy on the matter; and if you disagree, beware.

"I'll hit you with my purse."[4]

Critic Emily C. Farnsworth recommended the book with hopes that "...it might raise some consciousness about the sensitivities and needs of retarded teenagers...."[6]

The reviewer feels that Peck, however, may be resting on his laurels. "Characterization is really shallow....Clunie's oppressions are almost too bad to be true....The book is much too short for any real character development; thus, the conclusion loses much impact. This simply does not measure [up to] his previous works...."[6]

However, reviewer Patricia Lee Gauch said, "Robert Newton Peck has never been more the consummate storyteller than in [*Clunie*]...."[6]

1983. *Fiction Is Folks*, a writer's textbook composed for aspiring writers, published. "*Fiction Is Folks* will show you, chapter by chapter, how to flip over a rock and find folks for your fiction. How to recognize a character when you see him, or her, and then how to examine, calibrate, and hone a passel of personalities. After all, life is rife with people. They are your basic raw material.

"This is my second book on writing.

"My first, *Secrets of Successful Fiction*, was also published, in 1980, by *Writer's Digest*. Although that tiny text is chiefly a book on *style*, several of its chapters touch on characters and how they roll up their sleeves and work for you.

"It's true.

"My characters write my books.

"People, not authors, determine a plot. Because authors aren't *in* books. Characters are....

"Humor is the best tool of teaching. Too many textbooks are dull. Result? Teachers who use them can become dull. Since I like and respect teachers,

this book's purpose is to help profs, as well as emerging authors, discover the fun of writing.

"Education needs a face *lift*. A grin!

"Readers are people.

"Ergo, what interests people (and editors) most is other people, the ones that live in your pages.

"*Fiction Is Folks* is not only a guide to characterization for an emerging writer. It's also a text for teachers. My purpose is not to bore but rather to excite, to agitate, and to goose. Writing is fun. If you don't agree, then perhaps you're in the wrong business. Writing is work, for sure. You must make it your hobby, your dreams, and your secret love.

"Rapture in it.

"The easiest way for this to happen is when you, the author, fall in love with a character and share him or her with a neighbor. A gift to a reader. Forget the royalties. Because, you see, it isn't your greed that creates your novel.

"I am all my heroes.

"Most times, I get away with it. Yet, on occasion, my editor's eye will pop and his pencil itch, when he detects an obvious Peckian pronouncement. I expect this. When this occurs, an editor is merely performing his job, and well.

"These deletions, which willy-nilly always follow, don't always upset me. I'll fight to keep some of them in the story and even win a round or two.

"Again, I repeat: It's easier for an editor to delete than it is for him to add or to suggest additions for you to make. Therefore, I am not in the least shy about Pecking up my people. I dump more Peck into my characters than water into Jell-O.

"Why do I do this?

"The answer is pig simple. Because I've got so much of *me* to give. Like you, I am abrim with likes, dislikes, talents, cumbersome inabilities, joys, triumphs, and failures...so why should I even consider wasting such a storehouse?"[4]

"Compared to the work of so many talented authors, my novels aren't really so doggone great. Yet secretly, I truly believe that I am the best teacher of creative writing in the entire galaxy."[2]

"I didn't start out to write for any particular age group. If my books turn out to be right for teenagers, as well as adults and/or kids, it just happens that way. I can only write about what I know and I've never been shy about telling people what I know. As a matter of fact, when I told my

Illustration for the hardcover edition.

mother, who is eighty-two, that three of my books were about to be published by a very important publishing house, she thought for a minute, looked up at me and said, 'Son, you always did have a lot to say.'"[1]

Peck spends much of his time lecturing young adults at schools with hopes of having an impact on the teachers as well as the students. "My first hurdle, whenever I lecture (do a gig) at a college or university, is to open up minds. Not the minds of students, because theirs are already open. I try, and often fail, to open the minds of the *faculty*. They resent me, because I represent success in the off-campus world. Colleges persist in evaluating someone by what degree he holds, or what title. At lunch, bank presidents never ask me. On a campus, there are so many *doctors* I feel like I'm watching television's 'General Hospital.'

"Life is fun. It's a hoot and a holler. . . .

"I doubt I'll go to Heaven, that is, if I have a choice. So many of my closest buddies will probabl[y] go somewhere further south, where there's a red piano, a red poker table, and a red pool table with corner pockets that are eight inches wide. And I'll be there, filling inside straights with bourbon, and making old Hades a Heaven for the ladies."[2]

Footnote Sources:

1   "Reflections: A Profile of Robert Newton Peck," publicity from Random House.
2   *Something about the Author Autobiographical Series*, Volume 1, Gale, 1984.
3   Anne Commire, editor, *Something about the Author*, Volume 21, Gale, 1980.
4   Robert Newton Peck, *Fiction Is Folks*, Writer's Digest, 1983.
5   "From the Inside Out—The Author Speaks," publicity from Knopf.
6   *Contemporary Literary Criticism*, Volume 17, Gale, 1981.
7   *Contemporary Authors*, Volumes 81-84, Gale, 1979.

Cynthia Voigt

B orn February 25, 1942, in Boston, Mass.; daughter of Frederick C. (a corporate executive) and Elise (Keeney) Irving; married first husband September, 1964 (divorced, 1972); married Walter Voigt (a teacher), August 30, 1974; children: Jessica, Peter. *Education:* Smith College, B.A., 1963; graduate study at St. Michael's College (now College of Santa Fe). *Politics:* Independent. *Residence:* Annapolis, Md. *Office:* The Key School, 534 Carroll Dr., Annapolis, Md. 21403.

■ Career

J. Walter Thompson Advertising Agency, secretary, 1964; teacher of English at high school in Glen Burnie, Md., 1965-67; The Key School, Annapolis, Md., teacher of English, 1968-69, department chairman, 1971-79; part-time teacher and department chairman, 1981—; author of books for young readers, 1981—.

■ Awards, Honors

Homecoming was selected a Notable Children's Trade Book in the Field of Social Studies by the National Council for Social Studies and the Children's Book Council, and was an American Book Award nominee, both 1981; *Tell Me If the Lovers Are Losers* was selected one of American Library Assocation's Best Young Adult Books, 1982, and *A Solitary Blue*, 1983; Newbery Medal from the American Library Association, and Boston Globe-Horn Book Honor Book, both 1983, both for *Dicey's Song;* Edgar Allan Poe Award from the Mystery Writers of America for the Best Juvenile Mystery, 1984, for *The Callender Papers;* Newbery Honor Book, and *Boston Globe-Horn Book* Honor Book, both 1984, both for *A Solitary Blue; Come a Stranger* was selected one of Child Study Association of America's Children's Books of the Year, 1987.

■ Writings

Homecoming, Atheneum, 1981.
Tell Me If the Lovers Are Losers, Atheneum, 1982.
Dicey's Song (ALA Notable Book), Atheneum, 1982.
The Callender Papers, Atheneum, 1983.
A Solitary Blue (ALA Notable Book), Atheneum, 1983.
Building Blocks (Junior Literary Guild selection), Atheneum, 1984.
The Runner, Atheneum, 1985.
Jackaroo, Atheneum, 1985.
Izzy, Willy-Nilly, Atheneum, 1986.
Come a Stranger, Atheneum, 1986.
Stories about Rosie (Junior Literary Guild selection; illustrated by Dennis Kendrick), Atheneum, 1986.
Sons from Afar, Atheneum, 1987.

Tree by Leaf, Atheneum, 1988.
Seventeen against the Dealer, Atheneum, 1989.

■ Adaptations

"Dicey's Song" (cassette; filmstrip with cassette), Guidance Associates, 1986.

■ Sidelights

Since her first young-adult novel, *Homecoming*, appeared in 1981, Cynthia Voigt has had more than a dozen books published and has received the prestigious Newbery Medal for *Homecoming*'s sequel, *Dicey's Song*. She is recognized as an accomplished storyteller who creates well-developed characters, interesting plots, and authentic atmosphere. In her stories she examines such serious topics as child abandonment, verbal abuse, racism, and coping with amputation. "Writing is something I need to do to keep myself on an even keel. It's kept me quiet; it's kept me off the streets."[1]

Voigt's books are primarily set in the eastern part of the United States, a part of the country with which she is most familiar. She was born in Boston, Massachusetts in 1942, grew up in rural southern Connecticut, went to boarding school in Massachusetts, lived in Pennsylvania for a while, and is now living in Maryland. "I think what it comes down to is there are some parts of the world that just strike you as extremely lovely. If I were a sculptor, somehow I'd want to express this; if I were a painter (which I'd love to be), I'd want to paint them. What I want to do is wrap my words around them."[2]

She was reared in a family of two sisters, twin brothers, a father who was a corporate executive, and a mother. "Our family is not big by my mother's family standards. Most of my cousins come from families of eight or nine. I actually remember very little of my childhood, which makes me think it was quite happy. I suspect it might have been very close to perfect."[1]

"We lived in houses surrounded by spacious yards.

"Because my older sister was *thought* to be painfully shy, my parents decided to send us to nursery school together. I was a little young, but they felt I would be able to help her through. When it came time for the nursery school play, however, she was Miss Muffet, and I was the Spider. Later, when we got to dancing school—she was a Sweet Pea, and I was a Head of Cabbage.

"My grandmother lived in northern Connecticut, in a house three stories high; its corridors lined with bookcases. I remember reading *Nancy Drew*, *Cherry Ames*, *The Black Stallion*, and a Terhune book. One day, I pulled *The Secret Garden* off one of her shelves and read it. This was the first book I found entirely for myself, and I cherished it. There weren't any so-called 'young adult' books when I was growing up. If you were a good reader, once you hit fourth grade, things got a little thin. I started to read adult books, with my mother, making sure what I had chosen was not 'too adult.' I read Tolstoy, Shakespeare, Camus and many classics, except for *Moby Dick*, which I finally read in college. It knocked me out. I came to Dickens and Trollope later in life."[1]

When she was old enough, Voigt attended Dana Hall School in Wellesley, Massachusetts. "My mother and father had attended boarding schools and continued the tradition by sending their children as well. Dana Hall, a private girls' boarding school, gave us a great deal of intellectual as well as physical freedom, and I loved it. We could go downtown on our own, which in the fifties in a girls' boarding school was just this side of licentious. Knowing the school trusted us, I believe, helped us to grow up.

"I decided in the ninth grade that I wanted to become a writer. At first, I wrote mostly short stories and poetry. I didn't even know the word 'submission' then, let alone the subtler vagaries of publishing."[1]

She graduated from Dana Hall School "with distinction," president of her senior class and a member of the Cum Laude Society. The next four years were spent at Smith College in Northampton, Massachusetts. "I took creative writing courses in college but considered them real bombs. Clearly what I was submitting didn't catch anyone's eye. I never had a bad teacher like my character, Mr. Chappelle in *A Solitary Blue*. There were a few male teachers at Smith who resented teaching women, feeling themselves too good for the position. We had very little patience with that attitude. Mr. Chappelle grew primarily out of my own experience as a teacher. I've never seen anyone quite as extreme as my character, but writers only need to see the edges of a situation to be inspired to make it come alive."[1]

Following graduation, Voigt moved to New York City where she worked for the J. Walter Thompson Advertising Agency. "New York was the place to go after college. It seemed that it took an eternity

Dust jacket from Voigt's first novel.

to find a job, but in fact it took only two weeks. I could type, but didn't know shorthand. I have a great memory, however, and was able to take dictation. I worked for a wonderful woman in public relations, who at the time was putting together a centennial history. She had led a very interesting and exciting life. A vaudevillian, her best act was tap dancing while playing the xylophone blindfolded!

"I moved into a tiny apartment in Greenwich Village, spending half of my monthly earnings on rent. The lady next door owned killer German Shepherds and was in the habit of talking to herself and answering herself while her dogs leapt savagely against her windows. It was a fun year.

"I married in 1964 and moved with my first husband to Santa Fe, New Mexico. I was to work as a secretary to help support us while he was in school. But even with my New York experience it was difficult to find a job. I drifted into the Department of Education one day, and asked what I would have to do to qualify myself to teach

school. They learned that I'd attended Smith College, and signed me up for accrediting courses at a Christian Brothers college. Within six months I met the terms of certification. I vowed I would never teach when I left Smith, and yet, the minute I walked into a classroom, I loved it."[1]

She and her husband moved East where he finished school at St. John's in Annapolis, and Voigt found her home. Although the marriage was dissolved in 1972 after the birth of her daughter Jessica, Voigt's love for Annapolis, the Eastern Shore and Maryland never has. "I had been writing throughout college, but during most of my first marriage, I didn't write much at all. My *not* writing was in many ways a symptom of what was wrong in the marriage. I was living alone with my daughter, which is in a sense like living alone, because a small child is simply an extension of yourself. Like many women, as soon as I was separated, I found myself washing floors regularly, keeping the house nice, just to prove to myself that I was really okay! I also began writing again. To support us I worked as a tutor. I kept a regular schedule so that I could have an hour to write at the end of each day.

"I was by this time teaching in the public school system. After three years I took a job with The Key School in Annapolis. . . . They were so happy with my performance they allowed me to bring my baby daughter Jessica into the classroom with me for a year, after which, she went to day care.

"I was assigned to teach English in second, fifth and seventh grades. The second graders were a kick and a half. I assigned book reports to my fifth graders. I would go to the library and starting with the letter 'A' peruse books at the fifth, sixth, and seventh-grade age level. If a book looked interesting, I checked it out. I once went home with thirty books! It was then that I realized one could tell stories which had the shape of real books—novels—for kids the age of my students. I began to get ideas for young adult novels and juvenile books. That first year of teaching, and *reading* really paid off in spades. I felt I had suddenly discovered and was exploring a new country.

"My future mother-in-law, who was enrolled in a library science course in children's literature, recommended two books to me: *Harriet the Spy* and *Dorp Dead*. Though there are many books I bring into the classroom year after year—*Mrs. Frisbee, Book of Three, The Gammage Cup* and the short stories by Elaine Konigsburg—*Dorp Dead* has become my favorite teaching tool."[1]

In 1974 she married Walter Voigt, a teacher of Latin and Greek at The Key School in Maryland. "I was teaching full time, but was able to continue the writing I'd begun while I was living alone by sticking to my regime of one hour a day.

"I became pregnant and decided to teach part time. One of the things I wanted was more time to write. The summer I was pregnant I wrote the first draft of *The Callender Papers*. When my son, Peter, was an infant, I took him to school and taught with him in a 'Snuggli.' When he was a year old, I wrote *Tell Me If the Lovers Are Losers*, and the next year (he was in a playpen in the faculty lounge next to my classroom), I began *Homecoming*.

"One day while I was writing *Tell Me If the Lovers Are Losers*, I went to the market and saw a car full of kids left to wait alone in the parking lot. As the electric supermarket doors whooshed open, I asked myself 'What would happen if nobody ever came back for those kids?' I made some jottings in my notebook, and let them 'stew' for a year, the way most of my ideas do."[1]

Jacket illustration by Ronald Himler.

"...I'm the kind of mommy who never leaves her children alone in the car; for some reason I'm simply convinced that everyone else wants them as much as I do. I don't know why the thought struck me on that day, because you certainly see this frequently enough. That was where the story started. And certainly the story continued because kids are in one way much freer than adults. You know, if you're going to write about adults, that they generally have to go to work, which is usually fairly tedious and puts a frame to the narrative line. But kids have much more freedom to do things and have things happen. So not to have any adults around made the story possible to tell. And once I realized what I wanted to do, I knew I had to have the children abandoned."[3]

"When I sat down to write the story that grew from my question (and this is typical of my process) I made a list of character names. Then I tried them on to see if they fit. I knew Dicey was the main character, but was not sure precisely *who* she was. The more I wrote about her, the more real she became to me. I'd planned a book about half the size of *Homecoming*. But a few chapters into the novel, the grandmother became central and I began to see that there was a lot more going on than would fit in one book.

"I was writing chapter three of *Homecoming* and out of the darkness of the typewriter, Grandmother Tillerman leapt fully formed, like Athena. I could hear what she was saying, and began making notes. She was always very clear to me, and in some ways is a mirror image of her granddaughter, Dicey. I sometimes think that Dicey is the type of kid I would have liked to have been, and grandmother is the kind of old lady I would like to be.

"The idea of 'holding on, reaching out, and letting go' which runs through *Homecoming* was part of the rhythmic building of the book. I structured the novel around these three pieces of advice, and as each problem was solved, the next one would crop up. In the end, of course, there is no one right answer."[1]

Voigt wrestled with the plot of *Homecoming*, which was a series of dates and a map of red dots. In terms of plot, she admires the writing of Dick Francis. "The plumb line against which Voigt measures her own writing, however, is Shakespeare. "Measure yourself against Shakespeare. Most of us come out in the satisfactory category—which is not bad at all."[2]

Homecoming follows the four Tillerman children, led by thirteen-year-old Dicey, through the diffi-

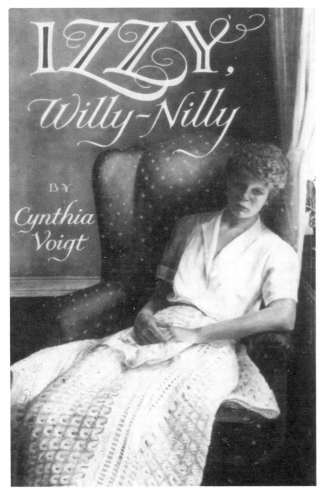

Jacket from the hardcover edition of the 1986 novel.

culties of finding a new home after their mother, overwhelmed by poverty, deserts them in a supermarket parking lot. It was published in 1981. "When I signed the contract for my first book, I looked at the time schedule with some surprise, realizing that in those same months I could produce two babies."[1]

Tell Me If the Lovers Are Losers, was published in 1982. The novel is set at an eastern college for young women and tells the story of three disparate roommates who come together in 1961 to play competitive volleyball that first semester. "Though *Tell Me If the Lovers Are Losers* is not what I would call autobiographical, it was in some ways inspired by my own experience at Smith. The book is not in any way factual; rather, it is *suggestive,* capturing the tone, the feeling of my years at college."[1]

Voigt returned to the Tillerman children in *Dicey's Song,* also published in 1982. She didn't expect the book to be published, "because it doesn't have any usual kind of plot. That was the fourth manuscript of mine that they had taken, but the other three all had what I understood to be definable plots. *Dicey's Song* is structured thematically rather than in terms of event. There's no tension over the mother's death except the inner tension. I was underestimating the publisher, even though I realized what a great risk they were taking in publishing *Homecoming.* While *Dicey's Song* was a book I loved, and was really glad I had written, it didn't seem to me that they would want to publish it. I think of *Dicey's Song* as the last section of *Homecoming;* rhythmically, and in terms of plot line, everything does connect. But in itself, it just simply doesn't have that plot line. You can't summarize it."[3]

"It never crossed my mind that a reader might have a problem reading *Dicey's Song,* without having read *Homecoming.* But after I had submitted the book, my editor, Gail Paris, asked me to write an introductory piece to give the reader some background. I was upset; I had written a killer first line and did not want to bury it with the introduction. However by this time I had learned to trust Gail, and so I wrote it. When I saw how the book was typeset, I realized that though I hadn't said a word, Atheneum knew as well as I did that the first line was important. Some readers have started from *A Solitary Blue* and worked their way back to *Homecoming* and it seems to work for them. I can't separate the three books."[1]

In 1983 *Dicey's Song* was selected one of American Library Association's Best Children's Books and won the Newbery Medal. "When I first heard that *Dicey's Song* had been awarded the Newbery Medal, I entered into a state of massive incoherence. I have not yet completely emerged from this state and suspect now I may never, but one of my first sensible thoughts during the time was: 'I did not know good news could pack such a wallop.' I didn't know good news could keep you awake into the night, distract you so effectively from all appointed tasks, make it difficult, when you confronted it head on, to breathe properly.

"...Forty-eight hours after the famous phone call, during which time the house had been reverberating with the words Newbery and Los Angeles, we went out for a family celebration dinner. [My son] Duffle leaned forward to announce to his grandmother the big news: 'We are going to Chicago, because Mommy won the Blueberry Award.' ...Duffle...keeps my feet on the ground."[4]

"For the Olympics there is training with a stop watch. A literary award, on the other hand, is chancy. You can't measure the achievement, for there is no sense of having earned it. With literary awards, it becomes a matter of with whom you stand, not where."[2]

"Writers need readers as they develop a new work. My husband is a wonderful reader, and my daughter has also become a very interested reader. She read the first three chapters of *Homecoming,* and by her reaction, I knew I had begun something worthwhile. Usually I write a rough draft then pull a fair copy off that when I'm sure the chapter will stand as is. I let my husband read each chapter in its rough form, and then Jessica reads the fair copy. I also let my editor read work in progress. Either I've become very fluid about letting people read my rough drafts, or my editor—lucky woman—has been taken into the family!"[1]

"...I have a long, rhapsodic speech about editors in me....The editor works upon, works over the manuscript, to enable it to be the best it can. An editor must be, more than anything else, dexterous, able to cover the territory between the publisher and the writer as well as the records of music, stories and song. They not only make available but also give space and forms to responses."[4]

In 1983 Voigt broke away from the Tillerman family to tell the story of Jean Wainwright's thirteenth summer in 1894. Robin McKinley, in a 1983 *Children's Book Review Service* article, called it "a highly enjoyable and stylishly written Gothic mystery....Voigt occasionally comes dangerously near to permitting Jean, the narrator, to be too stupid to be believed—always a risk in the atmospheric had-I-but-known type of mystery—but through her deft prose and Jean's real youth and innocence, she brings it off successfully."

For Voigt, it was a literary exercise. "I had read many gothics and decided to try *The Callender Papers* as an exercise in plotting, which I felt was a distinct weakness in my writing. I finished, but didn't submit the novel. Then one day Jessica, who was feeling bored, came to my study and picked up the manuscript. She read the book standing up—just as she read her beloved *Nancy Drew* books. 'Gee, I guess *The Callender Papers* works,' I thought to myself. Of course, the book went through major revisions before it was finally published."

"Every revision has been slightly different for me. *Homecoming* needed to come down in length by nearly two hundred pages. *The Callender Papers* was not well written in the first draft; all of my characters sounded exactly the same to me, and overall, the language needed polishing. So I went over the manuscript again and again. *Tell Me If the Lovers Are Losers* took thematic revision, because the ideas were not clearly worked out."[1]

Because *The Callendar Papers* was set in the late nineteenth century, both dialogue and narrative had to agree with the setting to make it plausible. This tone, according to Voigt, is not difficult to sustain. "Remember when you were taking tests, and they'd sit you down and forty-five minutes later you would have written a three- or four-page essay or answered a hundred questions? You just set your mind to the task and went over the hurdles. You put your mind in a certain gear for the SATs and a different one for an essay test or a paper-writing assignment. I seem to be able to set my inner ear that way. So once I had my attitude established, I had no difficulty at all in making that slightly stiff prose—and kind of liked it, as a matter of fact. And I read a lot of gothics anyway."[3]

"I need to focus on one book at a time. I don't submit ideas, I submit manuscripts. Because I revise a lot, even in the early stages of a book, I prefer not to submit until I'm certain what I have will work.

"I usually begin a book with a character, or, less often, an idea. Once I have the character and some notion of plot, the theme becomes apparent to me."[1]

"Some books grow out of others, like shoots out of a felled tree. *Dicey's Song* grew out of *Homecoming.* As I finished *Homecoming,* I knew what 'the next one' would be. *A Solitary Blue* grew out of *Dicey's Song* in that same fashion. As I wrote about Jeff in Dicey's story, where he had a certain purpose to serve, I found myself thinking about his particular story, what had happened to him, how he had come to be where he was, and who he was. That story wanted telling. I wanted to try telling it. This was so clear to me that when I said to my mother, 'You know what the next one will be' and she answered, 'Of course, about the story Gram tells the children'—well, I was completely surprised. I have no intention of telling the birthday party story; I have no idea how Bullet got out of going to that birthday party.

"But Jeff's story, I knew how that would go, what his life had been like, and why Dicey was so important to him. In writing the book, I ran into some interesting problems. One was the problem of how to cover so much time. Most of the things that happen to Jeff happen slowly, step by step. The book covers ten years of his life. This clearly

Michael Garland's jacket painting for the 1985 novel.

Voigt has found several of her characters mysterious and elusive. "It was difficult for me to cook up a reason why a woman would leave her children—something which happens in both *Homecoming* and *A Solitary Blue*. I don't think it is easy for women to leave their children, and that's one reason why I had to make the mother in *Homecoming* crazy. There seemed to me to be no other conceivable way that a woman would leave her children. Melody, Jeff's mother in *A Solitary Blue* was a very hard character to write. I was interested in capturing the kind of person who tends to be long on charm, but is absolutely false. Melody wants to take care of the entire world, a common human failing—it is so much easier to concern ourselves with other people's problems while our own personal world is neglected and goes to hell.

"No, it's not the same to write about a girl going through the sexual changes of puberty as it is to write about a boy going through them. But I feel quite comfortable with my male characters. I believe there are real differences between the sexes, but we are all human beings and so have a lot

constitutes a problem in writing—to reflect the long length of time without misrepresenting the rhythm of the story, to show the major events but keep clear their place in the whole context. Another interesting problem was to introduce the Tillermans from the outside, from somebody else's point of view, to think about them as subordinate characters whom my main character would meet, and have impressions of. I had to think of how my imaginary family would look through the eyes of my imaginary character. That problem was simply fun to work on because it is always fun (and often illuminating) to try to perceive through someone else's eyes.

"So I have now a felled tree with two shoots coming off of it, or a felled tree, a felled shoot, and a shoot off of it, and I am beginning to wonder seriously what the next one will be. I am sharpening my metaphorical ax. My daughter has told me what she thinks. 'You've got to write about Jeff and Dicey,' she said. This time I am not all surprised."[5]

Dust jacket of Voigt's second novel.

in common; it seems to me that shared *humanity* is crucial in storytelling.

"I don't shelter my characters from the world any more than I would keep them from going to the bathroom. The Depression and World War II were experiences that shaped and informed me while I was growing up, just as Vietnam has influenced kids growing up today."[1]

"In 1984 Voigt wrote an interesting time-travel story about a twelve-year-old boy who, living in 1974, finds himself in the bedroom of another boy of the Depression era who turns out to be his father. Elizabeth Sachs in a 1986 *Horn Book* review of *Building Blocks*, said that the "story suggests in a very subtle way that there are good reasons why parents are not all they could or should be. A child's compassion for parents is important."

Voigt is never quite sure how her readers will accept her books while she's writing them. "When I'm writing, I'm most concerned with trying to express what I'm thinking. I have the most willing suspension of disbelief east of the Alleghenies, so I really believe in what I'm writing. I'm trying to say in the best possible way whatever it is I have in mind to say. When I come to a scene, I know what I want it to do; and I know the ones I'm going to dicker around with for weeks before I'm through with them, even though I write a draft and copy it over and correct it. It takes me a long time to be satisfied with some of the scenes, and others just seem to come out the way they're supposed to. . . ."[3]

The Runner is the fourth Tillerman story, set a generation before *Dicey's Song*. The hero, Bullet (he named himself) is a seventeen-year-old runner who, because of his determination, always wins. Alice Digilio, a reviewer for the *Washington Post*, called Bullet ". . .a young tragic hero. Silent, unyielding, Bullet keeps to his principles and goes after his personal goals with no compromises—not with circumstances and certainly not with other people. His tragic flaw, if you will, is the classic one of hubris. He thinks he can remain above it all. Bullet, for whom honesty and doing one's best are the motivations for everything, desperately wants his friends to share the same aspirations. Yet he refuses to try and convince others to set those goals. When his friends fail to be as good as they can be, he wants 'not to care.'

"Those who have read the earlier Tillerman novels will also know what becomes of Bullet. Those who meet him here for the first time will not be surprised at his fate. Bullet is certainly a prickly character; if we met him in say, the high school lunch room, he might seem cold and aloof. We might even 'want not to care' about him. Voigt's accomplishment is to make us care about Bullet, and care deeply."[6]

Voigt's characters have tough problems to work through, but she respects young people too much to offer pat solutions. "One of the things that strikes me about a lot of textbooks and teachers is that they *don't* seem to respect the intelligence of the people to whom they're supposed to be addressing themselves. I don't know why I write for young people. I think of myself, as a matter of fact, as someone who writes for people who like to read. I don't want to label myself; that's what it is. And my books seem to have a fairly broad readership. Some people feel that, somehow or other, it's not as hard to write for children; it's not as ambitious. There's certainly not as much money in it, which is probably a great blessing. But I know perfectly well from the years of teaching that the boldest publishing, and a lot of the most consistently good editing work, is going on in children's books. And even before I'd thought of writing for that market, it struck me that that was where the reading I most consistently enjoyed was going on."[3]

Censorship for children is, according to Voigt, a matter of intelligent judgment. ". . .In a sense, children are safeguarded by whatever they're ignorant of. On the other hand, for example, I don't let my son watch the standard cartoons on television, because they are so unintelligent. I don't like regular doses of unintelligent material going into his head. You pick up patterns of thought and patterns of reacting to things—I don't mean behavior patterns; I just mean that if you watch nothing but sludge all day long, it's hard to keep the mind alive. The brain is sort of like a muscle; you have to exercise it. It'll jump through hoops if you make it. . . .Every year my students ask me what would happen to Shakespeare if there were no schools to teach him. In a sense, he probably would become a great deal like the masters of music, who are known only to a small audience. But for an actor, or just someone who loves the theater, there's nothing like him. I tell my students they're underprivileged, because your average illiterate Elizabethan could understand everything that was going on. That's enough to make them pause, which is all I ask them to do—to pause and look carefully at it.

"What kids should read is never clear to me. I do know that censorship is dangerous—as a mindset more than anything else—and I think that healthy attitudes towards all kinds of things are great gifts to give children, to undermine the salacious and the licentious and the vulgar. But what effect censorship has on that, I don't know. Sometimes kids have to rebel, and reading books that their parents don't want them to read is a good way to rebel. It's fairly harmless. It's cheap. I don't think it's a problem we should ignore; we should know what's going on, whatever we feel we can do about it, or want to do about it. I don't think we need to protect them from unpleasantness. Another teacher I work with says that the reason for talking about things like love and death and misery in a classroom is because the kids are going to have to face them, and if you've thought about something like that before you face it, then you have something to bring to what may otherwise be a situation that's impossible to handle. All kinds of moral decisions, I think, benefit from early safe thought, where it's not a crisis. It may or may not help you in choosing the right thing to do when the time comes, but at least you won't by lying to yourself."[3]

Sometimes, though, books are kept from children because adults just don't think they're capable of reading them. "...It is alarming, because a lot of people underestimate what kids can do. There's a degree-of-difficulty test where you count lines per sentence, syllables per sentence, and number of letters per word to determine the degree of reading difficulty. On that check, it's Aristotle who comes out at the fourth-grade level. I do a seat-of-the-pants judgment whenever I make up a book report list. It has to do with content and attitude as much as vocabulary and sentence structure."[3]

Although writing has made her famous, teaching still remains a favorite avocation. "My personal theory about teaching is that when you teach you mimic those who taught you well. I had several excellent teachers along the way and when I teach, I remember them and sometimes even hear myself echo them."[1]

"...At this point I have a wonderful schedule. I teach twelfth-grade English, and I teach one class a day. I've evolved a two-pronged approach to teaching writing. One prong is the traditional expository prose approach. But anybody in any of my classes has what we call the writing notebook. It's one of those black marble notebooks. They're supposed to bring it with them to class every day, and they take quizzes and essay tests in it, and write short essays in it. But they also do what I call bizarre writing assignments in it....The seniors came in and I gave them this question: if they could make immediately some change in humankind, what change would they make? Then I asked them what effects they hoped it would have. When they finished, I suggested they might want to consider what negative effect it might have that they hadn't previously foreseen. That was a five- or ten-minute writing assignment. Sometimes I ask them what colors Thursday is and why, or what they would change their name to.

"I can often see in this relaxed writing a kind of thinking or use of language that I haven't seen in the expository prose but that is useful to it. And it teaches them how to play with things and not to be frightened of an assignment. I've gone in with the title of a book that we haven't read yet and said, 'Write a plot summary.' And I'm happy when, instead of saying, 'But I haven't read the book,' they don't say anything and just start writing. They don't have to feel they know the answer, and they can just get in there and horse around, which is a good way to discover what you're thinking.

"The notebooks make wonderful reading. They usually make me laugh. And often the ones that are really stunning are from unexpected sources, which is good for me and for them. It shows that just because somebody isn't adept at spelling or sentence structure doesn't mean he hasn't got something incredibly interesting to say."[3]

When asked if there were more Tillerman books in her literary future, Voigt answered: "One of my judgments when I'm writing something is to look at it and ask, 'Is this working?' My feeling is almost as if the story was somehow there and I opened the door to find it. So I'm responsible to the story itself. There's something sort of passive in it. I do a lot of writing in alpha mode when I don't even know what time it is. *Dicey's Song* was almost entirely written in that way; it was effortless writing with very little revision. It was as if I was telling myself the story inside my head. About the Tillerman stories, I think I know what the last one's going to be. But I don't know how many come between. Bullet's story, which is what *The Runner* is, crossed my mind when I was writing *Homecoming* and put him in there. It had been in the back of my mind for that two- or three-year period. In the meantime I was writing two other Tillerman books, which had come naturally one out of the other. The ideas get in my head, and then there's a time when it's the right time to write them, I hope. And that's when I sit down to do them. So I do know what I want the last one to be. What I *don't* know is how many more there are in between."[3]

Her advice to young writers is to "Do it, not for awards, but for the pleasure of writing. And remember that publication is often a matter of chance. *Homecoming* was turned down by three of the five editors to whom I submitted the first three chapters."[1]

Besides writing and teaching, Voigt enjoys, "going out to dinner, shopping with my son or daughter, and in the summer, trips to our island in the Chesapeake Bay where we enjoy the beach, go crabbing, read together, wash dishes. I'd love to have a house in Maine someday. It's so beautiful and quiet, and there are so many stars in the sky. When I see something I like, I always want to try and write it—that makes it *mine*, you see. It's almost as good as buying property—I put something in a book, and I almost own it. I suppose I'll have to write a book about Maine, perhaps that will make the dream come true."[1]

Voigt also enjoys walking in cemeteries. "There are so many stories in the tombstones, and cemeteries are eternal places. I especially love the place where William Butler Yeats is buried, as well as the cemetery at the foot of Edinburgh Castle."[1]

Of all her pastimes, however, writing remains her favorite. "I write. . .because I want to write. I don't consider myself a good storyteller, and I have no burning stories to tell. I have no solutions to the problems of the world. I think there are solutions for individual people and individual circumstances. My writing is my way of saying, 'Have you looked at it this way?' I do it. I enjoy it.

"It's a razzle-dazzle kind of fun to have a story come out and do well. That's wonderful. But it's only when you're up there working when it's actually real: that's what the whole thing is rooted in, and that's the only thing that actually counts."[2]

Footnote Sources:

[1] Anne Commire, editor, *Something about the Author*, Volume 48, Gale, 1987.
[2] Dorothy Kauffman, "Profile: Cynthia Voigt," *Language Arts*, December, 1985.
[3] From an interview in *Contemporary Authors: New Revision Series*, Volume 18, Gale, 1986.
[4] Cynthia Voigt, "Newbery Medal Acceptance," *Horn Book*, August, 1983.
[5] C. Voigt, "On the Writing of *A Solitary Blue*," *Language Arts*, November-December, 1983.
[6] Alice Digilio, "What Makes Bullet Run?," *Washington Post Book World*, July 14, 1985.

■ For More Information See

New York Times Book Review, May 10, 1981 (p. 38), May 16, 1982 (p. 28), March 6, 1983, August 14, 1983 (p. 29), November 27, 1983 (p.34ff).

Washington Post Book World, May 8, 1983, November 6, 1983, June 10, 1984, May 11, 1986 (p. 17ff).

Christian Science Monitor, May 13, 1983 (p. B2), November 1, 1985 (p. B1).

School Library Journal, November, 1983 (p. 33ff).

People Weekly, December 19, 1983.

Children's Literature in Education, spring, 1985 (p. 45ff), Volume 19, number 2, 1988 (p. 67ff).

Times Literary Supplement, August 30, 1985.

Lee Kingman, editor, *Newbery and Caldecott Medal Books: 1976-1985*, Horn Book, 1986.

Francelia Butler and Richard Rotert, editors, *Triumphs of the Spirit in Children's Literature*, Library Professional Publication, 1986.

Children's Literature Review, Volume 13, Gale, 1987.

Alice Walker

Born February 9, 1944, in Eatonton, Ga.; daughter of Willie Lee (a sharecropper and dairy farmer) and Minnie Tallulah (a field worker and maid; maiden name, Grant) Walker; married Melvyn Rosenman Leventhal (a civil rights lawyer), March 17, 1967 (divorced, 1976); children: Rebecca Grant. *Education:* Attended Spelman College, 1961-63; Sarah Lawrence College, B.A., 1965. *Residence:* San Francisco, Calif. *Agent:* Wendy Weil, Wendy Weil Literary Agency, Inc., 747 Third Ave., New York, N.Y. 10017.

■ Career

Writer. Has been a voter registration worker in Georgia, a worker in a Head Start program in Mississippi, and on the staff of the New York City welfare department. Writer-in-residence and teacher of black studies at Jackson State College, 1968-69, and Tougaloo College, 1970-71; lecturer in literature, Wellesley College and University of Massachusetts—Boston, both 1972-73; distinguished writer in Afro-American studies department, University of California, Berkeley, spring, 1982; Fannie Hurst Professor of Literature, Brandeis University, Waltham, Mass., fall, 1982. Lecturer and reader of own poetry at universities and conferences. Past member of board of trustees of Sarah Lawrence College. Consultant on black history to Friends of the Children of Mississippi, 1967.

■ Awards, Honors

Bread Loaf Writer's Conference, scholar, 1966; first prize, *American Scholar* essay contest, 1967; Merrill Writing Fellowship, 1967; McDowell Colony Fellowship, 1967, 1977-78; National Endowment for the Arts Grant, 1969; Radcliffe Institute Fellowship, 1971-73; National Book Award nomination, and Lillian Smith Award from the Southern Regional Council, both 1973, both for *Revolutionary Petunias;* Richard and Hilda Rosenthal Foundation Award from the American Academy and Institute of Arts and Letters, 1974, for *In Love and Trouble;* Guggenheim Fellowship, 1977-78; National Book Critics Circle Award nomination, 1982, and Pulitzer Prize, and American Book Award, both 1983, all for *The Color Purple; In Search of Our Mother's Garden* was selected one of American Library Association's Best Books for Young Adults, 1984.

■ Writings

Poetry:

Once: Poems, Harcourt, 1968.
Five Poems, Broadside Press, 1972.
Revolutionary Petunias and Other Poems, Harcourt, 1973.
Goodnight, Willie Lee, I'll See You in the Morning, Dial, 1979.

Horses Make a Landscape Look More Beautiful, Harcourt, 1984.

Fiction; Novels, Except As Indicated:

The Third Life of Grange Copeland, Harcourt, 1970.
In Love and Trouble: Stories of Black Women (short stories), Harcourt, 1973.
Meridian, Harcourt, 1976.
You Can't Keep a Good Woman Down (short stories), Harcourt, 1981.
The Color Purple, Harcourt, 1982.
The Temple of My Familiar, Harcourt, 1989.

Other:

Langston Hughes: American Poet (juvenile biography; illustrated by Don Miller), Crowell, 1973.
(Editor) *I Love Myself When I'm Laughing...and Then Again When I Am Looking Mean and Impressive: A Zora Neale Hurston Reader,* Feminist Press, 1979.
(Contributor) Dexter Fisher, editor, *The Third Woman: Minority Women Writers of the United States,* Harcourt, 1980.
In Search of Our Mothers' Garden: Womanist Prose, Harcourt, 1983.
Living by the Word: Selected Writings 1973-1987, Harcourt, 1988.
To Hell with Dying (juvenile; illustrated by Catherine Deeter), Harcourt, 1988.

Work Represented In Anthologies:

Helen Haynes, editor, *Voices of the Revolution,* E. & J. Kaplan (Philadelphia), 1967.
Langston Hughes, editor, *The Best Short Stories by Negro Writers from 1899 to the Present: An Anthology,* Little, Brown, 1967.
Robert Hayden, David J. Burrows, and Frederick R. Lapides, compilers, *Afro-American Literature: An Introduction,* Harcourt, 1971.
Toni Cade Bambara, compiler, *Tales and Stories for Black Folks,* Zenith Books, 1971.
Woodie King, compiler, *Black Short Story Anthology,* New American Library, 1972.
Arnold Adoff, compiler, *The Poetry of Black America: An Anthology of the Twentieth Century,* Harper, 1973.
Lindsay Patterson, editor, *A Rock against the Wind: Black Love Poems,* Dodd, 1973.
Sonia Sanchez, editor, *We Would Be Sorcerers: Twenty-five Stories by Black Americans,* Bantam, 1973.

Mary Anne Ferguson, compiler, *Images of Women in Literature,* Houghton, 1973.
Margaret Foley, editor, *Best American Short Stories 1973,* Hart-Davis, 1973.
M. Foley, editor, *Best American Short Stories 1974,* Houghton, 1974.
Michael S. Harper and Robert B. Stepto, editors, *Chants of Saints: A Gathering of Afro-American Literature, Art and Scholarship,* University of Illinois Press, 1980.
Mary Helen Washington, editor, *Midnight Birds: Stories of Contemporary Black Women Authors,* Anchor Press, 1980.

Contributor to periodicals, including *Negro Digest, Denver Quarterly, Harper's, Ms., Black World,* and *Essence.* Contributing editor, *Southern Voices, Freedomways,* and *Ms.*

■ Adaptations

"The Color Purple" (motion picture), Warner Bros., 1985.

■ Work In Progress

A children's book, *Finding the Green Stone.*

■ Sidelights

Walker was born February 9, 1944 in Eatonton, Georgia, about seventy-five miles southeast of Atlanta. She was the youngest of eight children, five boys and three girls, all of whom lived in a three- or four-room house in the country.

Her father, Willie Lee Walker, was a sharecropper and dairy farmer, earning around three hundred dollars a year. "Though it is more difficult to write about my father than about my mother, since I spent less time with him and knew him less well, it is equally as liberating. Partly this is because writing about people helps us to understand them, and understanding them helps us to accept them as part of ourselves. Since I share so many of my father's characteristics, physical and otherwise, coming to terms with what he has meant to my life is crucial to a full acceptance and love of myself.

"I'm positive my father never understood why I wrote. I wonder sometimes if the appearance, in 1968, of my first book, *Once,* poems largely about my experiences in the civil Rights movement and in other countries, notably African and Eastern European, surprised him. It is frustrating that, because he is now dead, I will never know.

"In fact, what I regret most about my relationship with my father is that it did not improve until after his death. For a long time I felt so shut off from him that we were unable to talk. I hadn't the experience, as a younger woman, to ask the questions I would ask now. These days I feel we are on good terms, spiritually (my dreams of him are deeply loving and comforting ones), and that we both understand our relationship was a casualty of exhaustion and circumstances. My birth, the eighth child, unplanned, must have elicited more anxiety than joy. It hurts me to think that for both my parents, poor people, my arrival represented many more years of backbreaking and spiritcrushing toil."[1]

Her mother, Minnie Tallulah Grant, was a field worker and maid. "In the late 1920s my mother ran away from home to marry my father. Marriage, if not running away, was expected of seventeen-year-old girls. By the time she was twenty, she had two children and was pregnant with a third. Five children later, I was born. And this is how I came to know my mother: she seemed a large, soft, loving-eyed woman who was rarely impatient in our home. Her quick, violent temper was on view only a few times a year, when she battled with the white landlord who had the misfortune to suggest to her that her children did not need to go to school.

"She made all the clothes we wore, even my brothers' overalls. She made all the towels and sheets we used. She spent the summers canning vegetables and fruits. She spent the winter evenings making quilts enough to cover all our beds.

"During the 'working' day, she labored beside—not behind—my father in the fields. Her day began before sunup, and did not end until late at night. There was never a moment for her to sit down, undisturbed, to unravel her own private thoughts; never a time free from interruption—by work or the noisy inquiries of her many children. And yet, it is to my mother—and all our mothers who were not famous—that I went in search of the secret of what has fed that muzzled and often mutilated, but vibrant, creative spirit that the black woman has inherited, and that pops out in wild and unlikely places to this day."[1]

"...Through years of listening to my mother's stories of her life, I have absorbed not only the stories themselves, but something of the manner in which she spoke, something of the urgency that involves the knowledge that her stories—like her life—must be recorded. It is probably for this reason that so much of what I have written is about

Cover from the 1983 paperback edition.

characters whose counterparts in real life are so much older than I am.

"But the telling of these stories, which came from my mother's lips as naturally as breathing, was not the only way my mother showed herself as an artist. For stories, too, were subject to being distracted, to dying without conclusion. Dinners must be started, and cotton must be gathered before the big rains. The artist that was and is my mother showed itself to me only after many years. This is what I finally noticed:

"Like Mem, a character in The Third Life of Grange Copeland, my mother adorned with flowers whatever shabby house we were forced to live in. And not just your typical straggly country stand of zinnias, either. She planted ambitious gardens—and still does—with over fifty different varieties of plants that bloom profusely from early March until late November. Before she left home for the fields, she watered her flowers, chopped up the grass, and laid out new beds. When she returned from the fields she might divide clumps of bulbs, dig a cold pit, uproot and replant roses, or prune branches from her taller bushes or trees—until night came and it was too dark to see.

"Whatever she planted grew as if by magic, and her fame as a grower of flowers spread over three counties. Because of her creativity with her flowers, even my memories of poverty are seen through a screen of blooms—sunflowers, petunias, roses, forsythia, spirea, delphiniums, verbena...and on and on.

"And I remember people coming to my mother's yard to be given cuttings from her flowers; I hear again the praise showered on her because whatever rocky soil she landed on, she turned into a garden. A garden so brilliant with colors, so original in its design, so magnificent with life and creativity, that to this day people drive by our house in Georgia—perfect strangers and imperfect strangers—and ask to stand or walk among my mother's art.

"I notice that it is only when my mother is working in her flowers that she is radiant, almost to the point of being invisible—except as Creator: hand and eye. She is involved in work her soul must have. Ordering the universe in the image of her personal conception of Beauty.

"Her face, as she prepares the Art that is her gift, is a legacy of respect she leaves to me, for all that illuminates and cherishes life. She has handed down respect for the possibilities—and the will to grasp them."[2]

Growing up black in Georgia proved difficult. "...Eatonton, Georgia, is also the birthplace of Joel Chandler Harris, and visitors are sometimes astonished to see a large iron rabbit on the courthouse lawn. It is a town of two streets, and according to my parents its social climate had changed hardly at all since they were children. That being so, on hot Saturday afternoons of my childhood I gazed longingly through the window of the corner drugstore where white youngsters sat on stools in air-conditioned comfort and drank Cokes and nibbled ice-cream cones. Black people could come in and buy, but what they bought they couldn't eat inside. When the first motel was built in Eatonton in the late fifties the general understanding of place was so clear the owners didn't even bother to put up a 'Whites Only' sign.

"I was an exile in my own town, and grew to despise its white citizens almost as much as I loved the Georgia countryside where I fished and swam and walked through fields of black-eyed Susans, or

sat in contemplation beside the giant pine tree my father 'owned,' because when he was a boy and walking five miles to school during the winter he and his schoolmates had built a fire each morning in the base of the tree, and the tree still lived—although there was a blackened triangular hole in it large enough for me to fit inside. This was my father's tree, and from it I had a view of fields his people had worked (and briefly owned) for generations, and could walk—in the afternoon—to the house where my mother was born; a leaning, weather-beaten ruin, it was true, but as essential to her sense of existence as one assumes Nixon's birthplace in California is to him. Probably more so, since my mother has always been careful to stay on good terms with the earth she occupies. But I would have to leave all this. Take my memories and run north. For I would not be a maid, and could not be a 'girl,' or a frightened half-citizen, or any of the things my brothers and sisters had already refused to be."

"My father inherited nothing of material value from his father, and when I came of age in the early sixties I awoke to the bitter knowledge that in order just to continue to love the land of my birth, I was expected to leave it. For black people—including my parents—had learned a long time ago that to stay willingly in a beloved but brutal place is to risk losing the love and being forced to acknowledge only the brutality.

"It is a part of the black Southern sensibility that we treasure memories; for such a long time, that is all of our homeland those of us who at one time or another were forced away from it have been allowed to have.

"I watched my brothers, one by one, leave our home and leave the South. I watched my sisters do the same. This was not unusual; abandonment, except for memories, was the common thing, except for those who 'could not do any better,' or those whose strength or stubbornness was so colossal they took the risk that others could not bear."[2]

Among Walker's memories are those of a simple country life which included "almost nothing that came from a store. As late as my own childhood in the 1950s, we had only raisins and perhaps a single banana for each child at Christmas, oranges, a peppermint stick broken into many pieces, a sliver for each child; perhaps during the year, a half dozen apples, nuts, and a bunch of grapes. All extravagantly expensive and considered rare. You ate all of the apple; sometimes, even, the seeds.

Walker with daughter, Rebecca, to whom she dedicated *In Search of Our Mothers' Gardens*. (Photo credit: Sara Krulwich/*NYT* Pictures.)

Everyone had a vegetable garden; a garden as large as there was energy to work it. In these gardens people raised an abundance of food: corn, tomatoes, okra, peas and beans, squash, peppers, etc., which they ate in summer and canned for winter. There was no chemical fertilizer. No one could have afforded it, had it existed, and there was no need for it. From the cows and pigs and goats, horses, mules and fowl that people also raised, they were never without ample organic manure.

"I never heard of anyone having cancer until I was grown."[3]

In 1952 Walker's life changed irrevocably. "I am eight years old and a tomboy. I have a cowboy hat, cowboy boots, checkered shirt and pants, all red. My playmates are my brothers, two and four years older than I. Their colors are black and green, the only difference in the way we are dressed. On Saturday nights we all go to the picture show, even my mother; Westerns are her favorite kind of movie. Back home, 'on the ranch,' we pretend we are Tom Mix, Hopalong Cassidy, Lash LaRue (we've even named one of our dogs Lash LaRue); we chase each other for hours rustling cattle, being

outlaws, delivering damsels from distress. Then my parents decide to buy my brothers guns. These are not 'real' guns. They shoot 'BBs,' copper pellets my brothers say will kill birds. Because I am a girl, I do not get a gun. Instantly I am relegated to the position of Indian. Now there appears a great distance between us. They shoot and shoot at everything with their new guns. I try to keep up with my bow and arrows.

"One day while I am standing on top of our makeshift 'garage'—pieces of tin nailed across some poles—holding my bow and arrow and looking out toward the fields, I feel an incredible blow in my right eye. I look down just in time to see my brother lower his gun.

"Both brothers rush to my side. My eye stings, and I cover it with my hand. 'If you tell,' they say, 'we will get a whipping. You don't want that to happen, do you?' I do not. 'Here is a piece of wire,' says the older brother, picking it up from the roof; 'say you stepped on one end of it and the other flew up and hit you.' The pain is beginning to start. 'Yes,' I say. 'Yes, I will say that is what happened.' If I do not say this is what happened, I know my brothers will find ways to make me wish I had. But now I will say anything that gets me to my mother.

"Confronted by our parents we stick to the lie agreed upon. They place me on a bench on the porch and I close my left eye while they examine the right. There is a tree growing from underneath the porch that climbs past the railing to the roof. It is the last thing my right eye sees. I watch as its trunk, its branches, and then its leaves are blotted out by the rising blood.

"I am in shock. First there is intense fever, which my father tries to break using lily leaves bound around my head. Then there are chills: my mother tries to get me to eat soup. Eventually, I do not know how, my parents learn what has happened. A week after the 'accident' they take me to see a doctor. 'Why did you wait so long to come?' he asks, looking into my eye and shaking his head. 'Eyes are sympathetic,' he says. 'If one is blind, the other will likely become blind too.'

"This comment of the doctor's terrifies me. But it is really how I look that bothers me most. Where the BB pellet struck there is a glob of whitish scar tissue, a hideous cataract, on my eye. Now when I stare at people—a favorite pastime, up to now—they will stare back. Not at the 'cute' little girl, but at her scar. For six years I do not stare at anyone, because I do not raise my head."[2]

"I believe, though, that it was from this period—from my solitary, lonely position, the position of an outcast—that I began to really see people and things, to really notice relationships and to learn to be patient enough to care about how they turned out. I no longer felt like the little girl I was. I felt old, and because I felt I was unpleasant to look at, filled with shame. I retreated into solitude, and read stories and began to write poems."[4]

Solitude was hard to find. "Sometimes I thought I'd gotten into the family by mistake. I always seemed to need more peace and quiet than anybody else. That's very difficult when you're living with ten people in three or four rooms. So I found what privacy I had by walking in the fields. We had to get our water from a spring, so that was a time to be alone, too."[5]

1958. At the age of fourteen, Walker visited her brother Bill in Boston. "Understanding my feelings of shame and ugliness he and his wife take me to a local hospital, where the 'glob' is removed by a doctor named O. Henry. There is still a small bluish crater where the scar tissue was, but the ugly white stuff is gone. Almost immediately I become a

different person from the girl who does not raise her head. Or so I think. Now that I've raised my head I win the boyfriend of my dreams. Now that I've raised my head I have plenty of friends. Now that I've raised my head classwork comes from my lips as faultlessly as Easter speeches did, and I leave high school as valedictorian, most popular student, and *queen*, hardly believing my luck."[2]

But before her graduation came the Civil Rights Movement. "In 1960, my mother bought a television set, and each day after school I watched Hamilton Holmes and Charlayne Hunter as they struggled to integrate—fair-skinned as they were—the University of Georgia. And then, one day, there appeared the face of Dr. Martin Luther King, Jr. What a funny name, I thought. At the moment I first saw him, he was being handcuffed and shoved into a police truck. He had dared to claim his rights as a native son, and had been arrested. He displayed no fear, but seemed calm and serene, unaware of his own extraordinary courage. His whole body, like his conscience, was at peace.

"At the moment I saw his resistance I knew I would never be able to live in this country without resisting everything that sought to disinherit me, and I would never be forced away from the land of my birth without a fight."[1]

During her high school years, Walker was given several gifts by her mother, things she bought on time with her meagre earnings working as a domestic in the houses of others. The first was a sewing machine. "I even made my own prom dress, such as it was, something chartreuse net, I think. But the message about independence and self-sufficiency was clear."[5]

The second was a suitcase "as nice a one as anyone in Eatonton had ever had. That suitcase gave me permission to travel and part of the joy in going very far from home was the message of that suitcase. Just a year later I was in Russia and Eastern Europe."[5]

And—"Oh yes, she bought me a typewriter when I was in high school. How did my mama ever get that typewriter? She must have ordered it from Sears. A typewriter and a little typewriter table. She did all this on less than twenty dollars a week. If that wasn't saying, 'Go write your ass off,' I don't know what you need."[5]

1961. After graduation Walker won a scholarship for the handicapped to go to Spelman College in Atlanta, Georgia, the oldest college for black

"My major advice to young black artists would be that they shut themselves up somewhere away from all the debates about who they are and what color they are and just turn out paintings and poems and short stories and novels." —Alice Walker

women in the country. "I used to have a dream in which there was a bus coming down the road and the bus driver would get out where I was waiting with my bag. He would hold his hand out for the fare—and I would put an eye in it.

"Of course, that's really true. If I had not lost the sight of one eye permanently, I wouldn't have qualified for the half-scholarship that Georgia gives people who are 'handicapped.' It literally cost an eye to get out."[5]

Her neighbors raised the seventy-five dollars for her bus fare to Atlanta. "When I left my hometown in Georgia at seventeen and went off to college, it was virtually the end of my always tenuous relationship with my father. This brilliant man—great at mathematics, unbeatable at storytelling, but unschooled beyond the primary grades—found the manners of his suddenly middle-class (by virtue of being at a college) daughter a barrier to easy contact, if not actually frightening. I found it painful to expose my thoughts in language that to him obscured more than it revealed. This separa-

tion, which neither of us wanted, is what poverty engenders. It is what injustice means.

"My father stood outside the bus that day, his hat—an old gray fedora—in his hands; helpless as I left the only world he would ever know....So we never spoke of this parting, or of the pain in his beautiful eyes as the bus left him there by the side of that lonely Georgia highway, and I moved—blinded by tears of guilt and relief—ever farther and farther away; until, by the time of his death, all I understood, *truly*, of my father's life, was how few of its possibilities he had realized, how relatively little of its probable grandeur I had known."[2]

The ride itself was the beginning of a new life. "When I left home for college in Atlanta in 1961 I ventured to sit near the front of the bus. A white woman (may her fingernails now be dust!) complained to the driver and he ordered me to move. But even as I moved, in confusion and anger and tears, I knew he had not seen the last of me."[2]

While at Spelman, Walker became acquainted with the radical historians Staunton Lynd and Howard

Zinn. When Zinn, who was white, was fired by the black president of Spelman, Walker gave up a lucrative prize in protest. She also came to know the leaders of the Student Non-Violent Coordinating Committee (S.N.C.C.) and demonstrated with them, most notably in the March on Washington. "Our bus left Boston before dawn on the day of the March. We were a jolly, boisterous crowd who managed to shout the words to 'We Shall Overcome' without a trace of sadness or doubt. At least on the surface. Underneath our bravado there was anxiety: Would Washington be ready for us? Would there be violence? Would we *be* Overcome? Could *we* Overcome? At any rate, we felt confident enough to try.

"It was the summer of my sophomore year in college in Atlanta and I had come to Boston as I usually did to find a job that would allow me to support myself through another year of school. No one else among my Boston relatives went to the March, but all of them watched it eagerly on TV. When I returned that night they claimed to have seen someone exactly like me among those milling about just to the left of Martin Luther King, Jr. But of course I was not anywhere near him. The crowds would not allow it. I was instead, perched on the limb of a tree far from the Lincoln Memorial, and although I managed to see very little of the speakers, I could hear everything.

"Martin King was a man who truly had his tongue wrapped around the roots of Southern black religious consciousness, and when his resounding voice swelled and broke over the heads of the thousands of people assembled at the Lincoln Memorial I felt what a Southern person brought up in the church *always* feels when those cadences—not the words themselves, necessarily, but the rhythmic spirals of passionate emotion, followed by even more passionate pauses—roll off the tongue of a really first-rate preacher. I felt my soul rising from the sheer force of Martin King's eloquent goodness.

"And it is impossible to regret hearing that speech, because no black person I knew had ever encouraged anybody to 'Go back to Mississippi...,' and I knew if this challenge were taken up by the millions of blacks who normally left the South for better fortunes in the North, a change couldn't help but come.

"This may not seem like much to other Americans, who constantly move about the country with nothing but restlessness and greed to prod them, but to the Southern black person brought up expecting to be run away from home—because of lack of jobs, money, power, and respect—it was a notion that took root in willing soil. We would fight to stay where we were born and raised and destroy the forces that sought to disinherit us. We would proceed with the revolution from our own homes.

"I thought of my seven brothers and sisters who had already left the South and I wanted to know: Why did they have to leave home to find a better life?"[2]

After her sophomore year, she transferred to Sarah Lawrence, in Bronxville, New York, on a scholarship. "...At Sarah Lawrence I found all that I was looking for at the time—freedom to come and go, to read leisurely, to go my own way, dress my own way, conduct my personal life as I saw fit. It was here that I wrote my first published short story and my first book, here that I learned to feel what I thought had some meaning, here that I felt no teacher or administrator breathing down my neck."[2]

Before her senior year, she spent the summer of 1964 on a fellowship in Africa. "We're going to have to debunk the myth that Africa is a heaven for black people—especially black women. We've been the mule of the world there, and the mule of the world here."[5]

She returned to Sarah Lawrence pregnant. "I felt at the mercy of everything, including my own body, which I had learned to accept as a kind of casing, over what I considered my real self. As long as it functioned properly, I dressed it, pampered it, led it into acceptable arms, and forgot about it. But now it refused to function properly. I was so sick I could not even bear the smell of fresh air. And I had no money, and I was, essentially—as I had been since grade school—alone. I felt there was no way out, and I was not romantic enough to believe in maternal instincts alone as a means of survival; in any case, I did not seem to possess those instincts. But I knew no one who knew about the secret, scary thing abortion was. And so, when all my efforts at finding an abortionist failed, I planned to kill myself, or—as I thought of it then—to 'give myself a little rest.' I stopped going down the hill to meals because I vomited incessantly, even when nothing came up but yellow, bitter, bile. I lay on my bed in a cold sweat, my head spinning.

"On the last day for miracles, one of my friends telephoned to say someone had given her a telephone number. I called from the school, hoping for nothing, and made an appointment. I went to see the doctor and he put me to sleep. When I woke up, my friend was standing over me holding a red rose. She was a blonde, gray-eyed girl, who loved horses and tennis, and she said nothing as she handed me back my life."[2]

"That week I wrote without stopping (except to eat and go to the toilet) almost all of the poems in *Once*—with the exception of one or two, perhaps, and those I no longer remember.

"I wrote them all in a tiny blue notebook that I can no longer find—the African ones first, because the vitality and color and friendships in Africa rushed over me in dreams the first night I slept. I had not thought about Africa (except to talk about it) since I returned. All the sculptures and weavings I had given away, because they seemed to emit an odor that made me more nauseous than the smell of fresh air. Then I wrote the suicide poems, because I felt I understood the part played in suicide by circumstances and fatigue. I also began to understand how alone woman is, because of her body. Then I wrote the love poems (love real and love imagined), and tried to reconcile myself to all things human. 'Johann' is the most extreme example of this need to love even the most unfamiliar, the most fearful. For, actually, when I traveled in Germany I was in a constant state of terror, and no amount of flattery from handsome young German men could shake it. Then I wrote the poems of struggle in the South. The picketing, the marching, all the things that had been buried, because when I thought about them the pain was a paralysis of intellectual and moral confusion. The anger and humiliation I had suffered was always in conflict with the elation, the exaltation, the *joy* I felt when I could leave each vicious encounter or confrontation whole, and no—like the people before me— spewing obscenities, or throwing bricks. For, during those encounters, I had begun to comprehend what it meant to be lost.

"Each morning, the poems finished during the night were stuffed under Muriel Rukeyser's door—her classroom was an old gardener's cottage in the middle of the campus. Then I would hurry back to my room to write some more. I didn't care what she did with the poems. I only knew I wanted someone to read them as if they were new leaves sprouting from an old tree. The same energy that impelled me to write them carried them to her door."[4]

Rukeyser gave the poems to her agent at Harcourt, but they weren't published until 1968. Walker did, however, publish her first short story "To Hell with Dying" which later became a children's book.

"There was, in fact, in my rural, farming, middle-Georgia childhood, in the late forties and early fifties, an old guitar player called Mr. Sweet. If people had used his given name, he would have been called Mr. Little; obviously nobody agreed that this was accurate. Sweet was. The only distinct memory I have is of him playing his guitar while sitting in an ancient, homemade (by my grandfather) oak-bottomed chair in my grandmother's cozy kitchen while she baked biscuits and a smothered chicken. He called the guitar his 'box.' I must have been eight or nine at the time.

"He was an extremely soulful player and singer, and his position there by the warm stove in the good-smelling kitchen, 'picking his box' and singing his own blues, while we sat around him silent and entranced, seemed inevitable and right. Although this is the only memory I have of him, and it is hazy, I know that Mr. Sweet was a fixture, a rare and honored presence in our family, and we were taught to respect him—no matter that he drank, loved to gamble and shoot off his gun, and went 'crazy' several times a year. He was an artist.

Cover from a 1983 collection of prose.

He went deep into his own pain and brought out words and music that made us happy, made us feel empathy for anyone in trouble, made us think. We were taught to be thankful that anyone would assume this risk. That he was offered the platter of chicken and biscuits first (as if he were the preacher and even if he was tipsy) seemed only just.

"Mr. Sweet died in the sixties, while I was a student at Sarah Lawrence...in an environment so different from the one in which he and my parents lived, and in which I had been brought up, that it might have existed on another planet. There were only three or four other black people there, and no poor people at all as far as the eye could see. For reasons not perhaps unrelated to this discrepancy, I was thinking of dying myself at the very time I got the news of his death. But something of my memory of Mr. Sweet stopped me: I remembered the magnitude of his problems—problems I was just beginning to truly understand—as a black man and as an artist, growing up poor, forced to endure the racist terrorism of the American South. He was unlucky in love, and no prince as a parent. *Irregardless*, as the old people said, and Mr. Sweet himself liked to say, not only had he lived to a ripe old age (I doubt that killing himself ever entered his head, however, since I think alcoholism was, in his case, a slow method of suicide), but he had continued to share all his troubles and his insights with anyone who would listen, taking special care to craft them for the necessary effect. *He continued to sing.*

"This was obviously my legacy, as someone who also wanted to be an artist and who was not only black and poor, but a woman besides, if only I had the guts to accept it.

"...On the day of Mr. Sweet's burial I wrote 'To Hell with Dying.' If in my poverty I had no other freedom—not even to say good-bye to him in death—I still had the freedom to love him and the means to express it, if only to myself. I wrote the story with tears pouring down my cheeks. I was grief-stricken, I was crazed, I was fighting for my own life. I was twenty-one."[1]

1965-1966. Graduating from Sarah Lawrence, Walker "...went to work for the New York City Welfare Department to support my writing, living on the Lower East Side between Avenue A and Avenue B in a building that had no front door. I'm not at all nostalgic for the place. I remained with the Welfare Department for four months, writing at night, but I couldn't stand it."[6]

"In 1965 I went back to Georgia to work part of the summer in Liberty County, helping to canvass voters and in general looking at the South to see if it was worth claiming. I suppose I decided it *was* worth something, because later, in 1966, I received my first writing fellowship and made eager plans to leave the country for Senegal, West Africa—but I never went. Instead I caught a plane to Mississippi, where I knew no one personally and only one woman by reputation. That summer marked the beginning of a realization that I could never live happily in Africa—or anywhere else—until I could live freely in Mississippi."[2]

"...I went to Mississippi, to be in the heart of the civil-rights movement, helping people who had been thrown off the farms or taken off the welfare roles for registering to vote. While working there, I met the civil-rights lawyer I later married—we became an interracial couple."[6]

Walker and Melvyn Rosenman Leventhal lived together in New York City the following year, where she worked as an editor at *Ms.* magazine and he worked for the N.A.A.C.P. Legal Defense Fund.

Also during this year she had her first essay, "The Civil Rights Movement: What Good Was It?" published. "It was my first published essay and won the three-hundred-dollar first prize in the annual *American Scholar* essay contest. The money was almost magically reassuring to us in those days of disaffected parents, outraged friends, and one-item meals, and kept us in tulips, peonies, daisies, and lamb chops for several months."[2]

On March 17, 1967 she and Leventhal were married. "Mel and I had been living together perfectly happily for almost a year, but we could see that, given the history, we couldn't go off into the world and do political work unless we were married. We could challenge the laws against intermarriage at the same time—in addition to which, we really loved each other."

"He was also the first person who consistently supported me in my struggle to write. Whenever we moved, the first thing he did was to fix a place for me to work. He might be astonished and sometimes horrified at what came out, but he was always right there."[5]

"When I married my husband there was a law that said I could not. When we moved to Mississippi three years after the lynching of Cheney, Schwerner and Goodman, it was a punishable crime for a black person and a white person of opposite sex to inhabit the same house. But I felt then—as I do now—that in order to be able to live at all in America I must be unafraid to live anywhere in it, and I must be able to live in the fashion and with whom I choose. Otherwise, I'd just as soon leave."[4]

Walker won a National Endowment for the Arts Grant for her first novel, *The Third Life of Grange Copeland*, which was to be completed at the McDowell Colony in New Hampshire and published in 1970.

In September, she and her husband moved to Jackson, Mississippi, where Leventhal continued his civil rights work and Walker worked as a black history consultant to the Friends of the Children of Mississippi, a Head Start program. She began to collect folklore and folkways from rural black women as examples of their creativity. "It began, this study, shortly after my husband and I moved to Mississippi to live. By the time we had overcome our anxiety that we might be beaten up, mobbed, or bombed, I had worked up a strong interest in how to teach history to mature women; in this case, fifty- and sixty-year-olds who had an average of five years of grammar school. The approach I finally devised was to have them write their own autobiographies. Reading them, we were often able to piece their years together with political and social movements that they were then better able to understand.

"Nor were all these women simply waiting around for me to show up and ask them to write about themselves. Mrs. Winson Hudson, whose house was bombed more than once by the KKK, was already writing her autobiography when I was introduced to her. A remarkable woman, living in Harmony, Mississippi, a half-day's drive from anywhere of note, she is acutely aware of history, of change, and of her function as a revolutionary leader....Her defense against the Klan was a big German shepherd dog who barked loudly when he heard the bombers coming, and two shotguns which she and her husband never hesitated to use. She wanted other people to know what it meant to fight alone against intimidation and murder, so she began to write it all down.

"From Mrs. Hudson I learned a new respect for women and began to search out the works of others. Women who were generally abused when they lived and wrote, or were laughed at and belittled, or were simply forgotten as soon as critics found it feasible. I found that, indeed, the majority of black women who tried to express themselves by writing and who tried to make a living doing so,

died in obscurity and poverty, usually before their time."[2]

1968-1969. Became a writer-in-residence at Jackson State College, where she was introduced to the work of Zora Neale Hurston. Walker researched Hurston's life and later edited an anthology of her work, *I Love Myself When I'm Laughing...And Then Again When I Am Looking Mean and Impressive*, which was published in 1979. She was also putting the final touches on *The Third Life of Grange Copeland* and was about to give birth to a daughter. "Three days after I finished the novel, Rebecca was born. The pregnancy: The first three months I vomited. The middle three I felt fine and flew off to look at ruins in Mexico. The last three I was so big at 170 pounds I looked like someone else, which did not please me.

"What is true about giving birth is...that it is miraculous. It might even be the one genuine miracle in life (which is, by the way, the basic belief of many 'primitive' religions). The 'miracle' of nonbeing, death, certainly pales, I would think, beside it. So to speak.

"Another writer and I were discussing the difficulty of working immediately after the birth of our children. 'I wrote nothing for a year, that didn't sound as though a baby were screaming right through the middle of it.'"[2]

1972-1973. Walker moved with her daughter to Cambridge, Massachusetts to lecture at Wellesley and the University of Massachusetts in Boston. Leventhal remained in Mississippi. "Always a rather moody, periodically depressed person, after two years in Mississippi I became—as I had occasionally been as a young adult—suicidal. I also found motherhood onerous, a threat to my writing. The habits of a lifetime—of easy mobility, of wandering and daydreams—must be, if not abandoned, at least drastically rearranged. And all the while there the fear that my young husband would not return from one of his trips to visit his clients in the Mississippi backwoods.

"It was the last of our seven years in Mississippi that made me wish never to see it again. For in that year the threat of self-destruction plagued me as it never had before. I no longer feared for my husband's safety. In fact, such is American media curiosity, he had become a celebrity to the same extent that he had earlier been 'an outside agitator' and a pariah. Since the Jackson school-desegregation cases were his, our daughter and I could watch him at least once or twice a week being interviewed on TV. Nor did I fear any longer for my own safety with or without my husband's company. In the beginning, going to the movies was agony for us. For several years we were the only interracial, married, home-owning couple in Mississippi. Our presence at the ticket booth caused an angry silence. But even this had ceased to be true that last year. More than any other place in this country, the large cities, at least in Mississippi, learned how not to misbehave in public. And the young are everywhere interested in their own pleasures, and those pleasures, in Mississippi, have become less and less attached to the humiliation of other people.

"I believe that part of my depression came out of anguish that I was not more violent than I was. For years I fantasized sneaking into various oppressors' houses perhaps disguised as a maid and dropping unplugged hand grenades in their laps. Yet, though I considered these people, who attacked and murdered our children, called us chimpanzees from their judges' benches, and made life a daily ordeal for us, the Hitlers of our time, I did not act out the fantasy. No one else, black, has lived out this fantasy—though I believe this particular one and others like it are rampant among us.

"The burden of a nonviolent, pacifist philosophy in a violent, nonpacifist society caused me to feel, almost always, as if I had not done enough."[1]

During this time, her father died. "He was racked with every poor man's disease—diabetes, heart trouble. You know, his death was harder than I had thought at the time. We were so estranged that when I heard—I was in an airport somewhere—I didn't think I felt anything. It was years later that I really felt it. We had a wonderful reconciliation after he died. . . .I didn't cry when he died, but that summer I was in terrible shape. And I went to Georgia and I went to the cemetery and I laid down on top of his grave. I wanted to see what he could see, if he could look up. And I started to cry. And all of the knottedness that had been in our relationship dissolved. And we're fine now."[7]

Also in 1973, Walker published *Revolutionary Petunias and Other Poems*, which was nominated for the National Book Award. It won the Lillian Smith Award of the Southern Regional Council. She also completed *In Love and Trouble: Stories of Black Women*, and a children's biography, *Langston Hughes, American Poet*. "Some of the stories in *In Love and Trouble* came out of my mother's stories, for instance, 'Strong Horse Tea.' She often talked about how poor people, 'in the olden days,' had to make up home remedies for sick people. She

used to crack me up with the story about my brother who stuttered and how he was stuttering and stuttering and they couldn't figure out what to do about it. So finally someone told her to hit him in the mouth with a cow's melt. As far as I can figure out, it's something like the spleen. Anyway, it's something raw and wet and bloody, and you get a grip on it and just hit the stutterer in the mouth with it. That would make anyone stop stuttering or stop talking altogether. But anyway, she did that; she hit him in the mouth with the cow's melt and he stopped stuttering.

"Anyway, my mother would ramble on and tell about how she would make tea out of the cow's hoof when one of us felt ill. Years later when I was living in Mississippi, when I wrote most of those stories, her world was all around me."[8]

1974. Walker and Leventhal moved back to New York to live in Brooklyn. "Living in Brooklyn. . .is remarkably like living in Mississippi, in fact. My Civil Rights-lawyer husband was suing racist real-estate dealers in Jackson before we left. He is now filing identical suits in Brooklyn. And, again, what makes life bearable, even happy occasionally, is the proximity of our neighbors, a multi-ethnic conglomerate of peacemakers in the war-torn city of New York. I lapse into the usual brownstoner's paean to my neighbor's rose gardens, the way they sweep their sidewalks, the way, in Brooklyn, anything is an excuse to plant another tree. My wonder that the people on my street, who have long since become my friends (willing to look after my house or my child on a moment's notice), are so civil and generous and *clean* they are nobody's idea of what New Yorkers are like."[2]

Walker continued working as a contributing editor at *Ms.* and completed her second novel, *Meridian*, about the civil rights movement. She also published *Goodnight, Willie Lee, I'll See You in the Morning*, a collection of poems whose title came from her mother's last farewell to her father at his funeral.

1976. Walker and Leventhal were divorced, but shared custody of Rebecca.

1977-1978. Walker visited Cuba with other Afro-American artists selected by the editors of *Black Scholar* and the Cuba Institute of Friendship Among Peoples. She also won a Guggenheim Fellowship and began work on *The Color Purple*. "I don't always know where the germ of a story comes from, but with *The Color Purple* I knew right away. I was hiking through the woods with my sister, Ruth, talking about a lovers' triangle of

Whoopi Goldberg starred in the 1985 Warner Bros.' film, "The Color Purple."

which we both knew. She said: 'And you know, one day The Wife asked The Other Woman for a pair of her drawers.' Instantly the missing piece of the story I was mentally writing—about two women who felt married to the same man—fell into place. And for months—through illnesses, divorce, several moves, travel abroad, all kinds of heartaches and revelations—I carried my sister's comment delicately balanced in the center of the novel's construction I was building in my head."[2]

She explained that the characters in the book actually spoke to her. "The people in the book were willing to visit me, but only after I stopped interrupting with poetry readings and lectures and getting on some plane.

"If you're silent for a long time, people just arrive in your mind. It makes you believe the world was created in silence."[5]

She also felt that her characters needed to be in the country, so she decided to leave Brooklyn for California. "I realized I was a country person—I'm just not used to small spaces, so I moved to San Francisco. I also have a little cabin in Mendocino, where I've just planted a hundred trees."[6]

She was accompanied in her move by her companion, Robert Allen, then editor of *Black Scholar*. She took a third floor walk-up apartment in the section of San Francisco near Divisadero Street, and alternated her time between country and city. A retainer from *Ms.* enabled her to keep working on *The Color Purple.*

1981. Published *You Can't Keep a Good Woman Down*, another collection of short stories.

1982. *The Color Purple* was published. Nominated for the National Book Critics Circle Award and the American Book Award, it won the Pulitzer Prize. It raised many controversial issues, including race relations, sexism and lesbianism. It also received praise and blame for its use of the vernacular "Black Folk English" as Walker describes it. "When I finished writing *The Color Purple* I sent it first to a leading black women's magazine, believing they would recognize its value better than anyone. The magazine declined to run an excerpt from it, however, because according to an editor, 'Black people don't talk like that.' And I suppose in her mind they never did, and if they did, who cared? Yet Celie speaks in the voice and uses the language of my step-grandmother, Rachel, an old black woman I loved. Did she not exist; or, in my memories of her, must I give her the proper English of, say, Nancy Reagan?

"And I say, yes, she did exist, and I can prove it to you, using the only thing that she, a poor woman, left me to remember her by—the sound of her voice. Her unique pattern of speech. Celie is created out of language. In *The Color Purple* you see Celie because you 'see' her voice. To suppress her voice is to complete the murder of her. And this, to my mind, is an attack upon the ancestors, which is, in fact, war against ourselves.

"For Celie's speech pattern and Celie's words reveal not only an intelligence that transforms illiterate speech into something that is, at times, very beautiful, as well as effective in conveying her sense of her world, but also what has been done to her by a racist and sexist system, and her intelligent blossoming as a human being despite her oppression demonstrates why her oppressors persist even today in trying to keep her down. For if and when Celie rises to her rightful, earned place in society across the planet, the world will be a different place, I can tell you."[1]

In 1983 she was approached by Steven Spielberg to make a movie of *The Color Purple*. "In ancient times, people believed that you thought with your heart. They didn't really know about the brain. In more modern times, people say you think with your brain. Only there are a few of us who still actually think with our hearts, and after talking to Steven, I had a lot of confidence that he was one."[9]

"For me, part of selling a book to the movies in the first place was a curiosity about the process and the experience 'of making movies.' It's wonderful just to see how it's done from beside the camera. It's a very different world there, very different from the world that I live in, made up out of, well, writing, and political things and gardening and my family."[10]

Walker began by writing the screenplay herself. "I went up to the country and spent about three months working on it. But Steven had no idea how tired I was....I had told Robert and Rebecca that after the novel and the Pulitzer, I would be theirs, because I had put them through a lot; they were always being interrupted, intruded upon. And then there I was going up to the country again to work on the screenplay....Rebecca started having a lot of physical ailments that I understood to be signals that she really needed attention, really wanted me home even though she was her usual supportive and plucky self, trying to give me the space I needed. But I could tell....

"So I finished a draft and sent it down to Steven. I added things like descriptions of the houses, the rooms, the clothes, the shoes, the parasols—things you wouldn't necessarily get from the book that they could use in the real screenplay. And I gave it up."[9]

With Walker's approval, Spielberg chose the Dutch screenwriter, Menno Meyjes, to finish the screenplay, with Walker's approval. "Even though he's not American, he comes from a part of Holland that has its own folk speech that is looked down upon by people who speak standard Dutch...and he had a real feel for what folk speech is and how it's not substandard, just different. I didn't have the feeling that Menno was a stranger."[9]

Walker insisted that at least half of the off-screen staff be women, blacks, or people from the third world. She visited the set often and was instrumental in choosing Whoopi Goldberg to play Celie. "I had seen her perform by accident at a very small cabaret in San Francisco called the Valencia Rose. She was just magical. I felt that she was the right person to play Celie all along, and when she wrote and said she'd like to play Celie, I had already agreed with her. The producers also liked her a lot."[10]

1984. Walker published another book of poems, *Horses Make the Landscape More Beautiful*. At this point Walker and Allen had moved to an even smaller town in Mendocino, Navarro, with Walker still keeping her San Francisco apartment for reading, meditation and writing. Much of her time in Navarro is spent gardening and observing the landscape.

Walker and Allen decided to form their own company, called Wild Trees Press, with Allen as general manager. "Everyone was into growing this and that. We got to thinking it would be nice to have a little cottage industry of our own. So we decided to grow books."[11]

In December of 1985 the film "The Color Purple" was released and met with instant success and controversy. Although it was nominated for eleven Oscars, it won none. The Beverly Hills Chapter of the N.A.A.C.P. and the Coalition Against Black Exploitation denounced it as racist and demeaning to black males. The book, too, was being banned in certain high schools for its explicit sexual language. "I learned that a certain Mrs. Green had objected to having her daughter, Donna, read *The Color Purple*. In her opinion the book was too sexually explicit, presented a stereotyped view of blacks, and degraded black people by its 'exposure' of their folk language.

"Mrs. Green had not actually read the book, according to the papers; she'd 'flipped' through it, scanned at least five pages, photocopied those five, and passed them out to the members of the Oakland school board. One of its members, who also had not read the book, a black woman (Mrs. Green hails as white), readily agreed that the book should be banned from the school. She termed it 'garbage.'

"Well.

"...I felt I had written the book as a gift to the people. All of them. If they wanted it, let them fight to keep it, as I had had to fight to deliver it. I was tired and deserved my rest. I consulted the ancestors on my position, and they agreed with me (in language that would have upset Mrs. Green).

"I feel I know what Mrs. Green was objecting to. When I learned she'd copied and distributed to the school board five pages from the book, I knew which five pages they were. They are the first five pages of the book. The same five pages *my* mother objected to, because she found the language so offensive. They are the pages that describe brutal sexual violence done to a nearly illiterate black womanchild, who then proceeds to write down what has happened to her in her own language, from her own point of view.

"Celie's stepfather, the rapist, warns her not to tell anybody but God about having been raped. But Celie's community had already made sure she would not feel free even to use the words she knew. In her backward, turn-of-the-century community, the words 'penis' and 'vagina' did not exist. Indeed, so off limits was any thought of the penis that the closest anyone got to it in language was to call it 'the man's thing.' As for 'vagina'—well, this is how my grandmother taught her girls to bathe:

"'Wash down as far as possible, then wash up as far as possible, then wash possible.'

"Of course if I had written of Celie's rape from the point of view of the rapist or that of the voyeur, very few people—other than feminists—would have been offended. We have been brainwashed to identify with the person who receives pleasure, no matter how perverted; we are used to seeing rape from the rapist's point of view. I could have written that Celie enjoyed her abuse and done it in such pretty, distancing language that many readers would have accepted it as normal. But to do this would have been to betray Celie; not only her experience of rape, but the integrity of her life, her life itself. For it is language more than anything else that reveals and validates one's existence, and if the language we actually speak is denied us, then it is inevitable that the form we are permitted to assume historically will be one of caricature, reflecting someone else's literary or social fantasy."[1]

In February, 1987, Walker, her daughter Rebecca, and her companion Allen visited Bali to celebrate her forty-second birthday. In June she joined protests against the Concord Naval Weapons Station at Port Chicago, California, where she was arrested and released the same day. "A lot of things went through my mind as I was being handcuffed....Had my statements to the press truly reflected my feelings about weapons and war? I had been asked why I was risking arrest and I had said because I can't stand knowing that the money I pay in taxes and that my own family needs—not to mention all the other poor and sick people in this country and world—pays for weapons and the policy that maims, kills, frightens, and horribly abuses babies, children, women, men, and the old. I don't want to be a murderer, I said.

"And once, as I was being lifted into the jail van, someone yelled, 'What do you have to say now, as you go off to jail?' and I made a joke that was the truth: 'I'm following my tax dollars,' I said."[1]

"Books are by-products of our lives. Deliver me from writers who say the way they live doesn't matter. I'm not sure a bad person can write a good book. If art doesn't make us better, then what on earth is it for?"[5] Not long after publishing *The Color Purple*, Walker developed a monstrous case of writer's block, so she repainted her house in Mendocino. "My psyche was saying 'turquoise-and-coral.'"[12] In her turquoise-and-coral bedroom, Walker dreamed up the vision that led to *The Temple of My Familiar*, a 480-page novel traversing 500,000 years in Africa, Europe and America. In her first book, "I was rewriting history as I feel it was. Now I'm going back further in time."[12] The new novel's title refers to "the natural, untamed spirit roaming the cosmos, its temple."[12] *The Temple of My Familiar* was published in 1989.

Footnote Sources:

[1] A. Walker, *Living by the Word*, Harcourt, 1988.
[2] Alice Walker, *In Search of Our Mothers' Gardens*, Harcourt, 1984.
[3] A. Walker, "America Should Have Closed Down on the First Day a Black Woman Observed That Supermarket Collards Tasted Like Water," *Ms.*, January, 1985.
[4] John O'Brien, editor, *Interviews with Black Writers*, Liveright, 1973.

[5] Gloria Steinem, "Do You Know This Woman? She Knows You: A Profile of Alice Walker," *Ms.*, June, 1982.

[6] Herbert Mitgang, "Alice Walker Recalls the Civil Rights Battle," *New York Times Biographical Service*, April, 1983.

[7] David Bradley, "Telling the Black Woman's Story," *New York Times Magazine*, January 8, 1984.

[8] Claudia Tate, editor, *Black Women Writers at Work*, Continuum, 1983.

[9] Susan Dworkin, "The Strange and Wonderful Story of the Making of 'The Color Purple,'" *Ms.*, December, 1985.

[10] William Goldstein, "Alice Walker on the Set of 'The Color Purple,'" *Publishers Weekly*, September 6, 1985.

[11] Pat Rose, "Growing Books at Wild Trees Press," *Small Press*, volume 2, November-December, 1986.

[12] *Time*, January 9, 1989.

■ For More Information See

Negro Digest, September-October, 1968.

Black Scholar, January/February, 1970 (p. 17), April, 1976, March/April, 1981 (p. 21).

Library Journal, June 15, 1970, May 1, 1988 (p. 81).

Publishers Weekly, August 31, 1970 (p. 195), March 11, 1988 (p. 95).

New South, fall, 1970 (p. 23)

American Scholar, winter, 1970-71, summer, 1973.

New Leader, January 25, 1971 (p. 19).

Poetry, February, 1971 (p. 328), March, 1980.

New Yorker, February 27, 1971 (p. 104), June 7, 1976 (p. 135), December 30, 1985 (p. 68).

New York Times Magazine, August 26, 1973 (p. 9ff).

Black World, September, 1973, August, 1974 (p. 10), October, 1974 (p. 51).

Nation, November 12, 1973, September 4, 1982 (p. 181).

Washington Post Book World, November 18, 1973 (p. 1), October 30, 1979, December 30, 1979, May 31, 1981, July 25, 1982.

Freedomways, winter, 1973.

Ms. February, 1974 (p. 42), May, 1974 (p. 64), March, 1975 (p. 74), January, 1977 (p. 58, 71), April, 1977 (p. 46), July, 1977, July, 1978, August, 1979 (p. 47), January, 1984 (p. 48), January, 1985 (p. 53), March, 1985 (p. 51), August, 1985 (p. 34), December, 1985 (p. 71), July, 1986 (p. 29), September, 1986 (p. 62), November, 1986 (p. 32), June, 1988 (p. 52).

New Republic, September 14, 1974 (p. 21), December 21, 1974, January 27, 1986 (p. .24)

College Language Association Journal, December, 1975 (p. 238), September, 1979 (p. 71).

CLA Journal, December, 1975 (p. 238), September, 1979 (p. 71), March, 1981 (p.262).

William Peden, *The American Short Story: Continuity and Change, 1940-1975*, 2nd edition, revised and enlarged, Houghton, 1975.

Contemporary Literary Criticism, Gale, Volume V, 1976, Volume VI, 1976, Volume IX, 1978, Volume XIX, 1981.

Parnassus: Poetry in Review, spring-summer, 1976 (p. 202).

Atlantic, June, 1976.

Essence, July, 1976, July, 1982 (p. 114), May, 1985 (p. 93), July, 1985 (p. 74).

Commonweal, April 29, 1977, February 11, 1983 (p. 93).

Black American Literature Forum, spring, 1977 (p. 3), winter, 1984 (p. 162ff).

Ebony, August, 1977 (p. 135), November, 1984 (p. 59), February, 1986 (p. 146).

Times Literary Supplement, August 19, 1977, June 18, 1982 (p. 676).

Roseann P. Bell and others, editors, *Sturdy Black Bridges: Visions of Black Women in Literature*, Anchor Press, 1979.

Janet Sternburg, *The Writer on Her Work*, Norton, 1980 (p. 121).

Black Women Novelists, Greenwood Press, 1980 (p. 180).

Dexter Fisher, editor, *The Third Woman: Minority Women Writers of the United States*, Houghton, 1980.

Dictionary of Literary Biography, Volume VI: *American Novelists since World War II*, Gale, 1980.

Los Angeles Times, April 29, 1981.

Newsweek, June 21, 1982 (p. 62).

Chicago Tribune Book World, August 1, 1982.

Detroit Free Press, August 8, 1982.

California Living, August, 15, 1982 (p. 16).

Detroit News, September 15, 1982.

Ann Arbor News, October 3, 1982.

Washington Post, October 15, 1982.

Peter Bruck and Wolfgang Karrer, editors, *The Afro-American Novel since 1960*, B. R. Gruener, 1982.

New York Times, April 16, 1983 (p. 13), February 12, 1984, April 7, 1985 (p. 12), October 7, 1985 (p. C17), January 18, 1986 (p. 6), August 23, 1987 (p. 14).

New York Daily News, April 19, 1983, February 23, 1986 (p. 12), March 30, 1986 (p. 8).

Leslie Hanscom, "A Homage in 'Purple,'" *Newsday*, May 5, 1983.

People Weekly, December 26, 1983 (p. 85), January, 1984 (p. 85), September 6, 1985 (p. 46).

Simthsonian, January, 1984 (p. 133).

Mari Evans, editor, *Black Women Writers, 1950-1980*, Doubleday, 1984.

English Journal, January, 1985 (p. 48).

Esquire, August, 1985 (p. 106).

Black Enterprise, August, 1985 (p. 130).

New Statesman, October 4, 1985 (p. 29), July 11, 1986 (p. 27).

Time, December 23, 1985 (p. 78), February 3, 1986 (p. 61).

Current Biography Yearbook, 1984, H. W. Wilson, 1985.

Ruth Perry and Martine Watson Brownley, *Mothering the Mind: Twelve Studies of Writers and Their Silent Partners*, Holmes and Meier, 1985.

Mother Jones, January, 1986 (p. 27), December, 1986 (p. 43).

Jet, February 10, 1986 (p. 28), December 15, 1986 (p. 60).

Christian Science Monitor, March 24, 1986 (p. 1).

Cumulative Index

Author/Artist Index

The following index gives the number of the volume
in which an author/artist's biographical sketch appears.